GLOBALIZATION

Also by Jan Aart Scholte

INTERNATIONAL RELATIONS OF SOCIAL CHANGE
CONTESTING GLOBAL GOVERNANCE: Multilateral Economic
Institutions and Global Social Movements (*co-author*)

Globalization

A Critical Introduction

Jan Aart Scholte

GLOBALIZATION
© Jan Aart Scholte 2000

St. Martin's Press, Scholarly and Reference Division, 175 Fifth Avenue, New York, N.Y. 10010

First published in the United States of America in 2000

This book is printed on paper suitable for recycling and made from fully managed and sustained forest sources.

Printed in Great Britain

ISBN 0–312–23631–X clothbound
ISBN 0–312–23632–8 paperback

CIP information is available from the Library of Congress

Summary of Contents

Contents

PART III   POLICY ISSUES

9   Globalization and (In)Security

10   Globalization and (In)Justice

11   Globalization and (Un)Democracy

12   Humane Global Futures

List of Boxes

Preface

Not another book on globalization! No doubt many a prospective reader will at first despair that a further title has squeezed onto already overcrowded shelves. Has this hype-propelled bandwagon not already slaughtered too many trees?

In some respects critics have grounds to complain that recent years have seen too much written about globalization. Aspiring academics, consultants, journalists and politicians have all rushed to have their say on 'the big G'. Publishers have been only too happy to flog wares that sell. Some have even slipped the term 'globalization' into titles of works that actually say nothing on the subject.

Yet despite this feverish output of words, we arguably still have far to go in consolidating concepts, methods and evidence with which to identify and measure globalization. Likewise, the literature to date has produced few tightly focused full-length assessments of the causes and consequences of globalization. In these circumstances, ideas of globalization have readily become so diverse, so broad, so loose, so changeable – in a word, so elusive – that one can pronounce virtually anything on the subject.

This situation is worrying. More is at stake in the analysis of globalization than publishers' revenues and the careers of would-be gurus. A clear, precise, explicit and consistently used concept of globalization can reveal a great deal about continuity and change in contemporary social life. Such a notion can also provide a basis for careful, critical and creative assessments of efficiency, security, justice, democracy and ecological integrity in today's world. Globalization is too important to be handled casually and opportunistically.

With these concerns to the fore, my objectives in writing this book have been:

(a) to develop a specific and distinct concept of globalization. Most existing formulations are steeped in ambiguity and inconsistency, or merely use 'globalization' as a synonym for other, older terms;

(b) to offer a multidimensional understanding of globalization. Most existing examinations are more narrowly focused, for example, in political economy, cultural studies, law, or social ecology;

(c) to address – squarely and systematically – questions concerning causation and consequence. Existing studies of globalization tend to offer only rather scattered observations on causation and limited coverage of consequences;

(d) to nurture a historical perspective that places contemporary developments in a long-term context. Many existing accounts of globalization have a shortsighted 'presentist' character;

(e) to appreciate the intricate interplay of continuity and change in globalization. Far too often, debate has become mired in polarized exchanges between smug 'realists' who deny change and exuberant 'globalists' who deny continuity;

(f) to ground the argument in a breadth and depth of both quantitative and qualitative evidence. Past treatments of globalization frequently rely too heavily on incidental illustration and anecdote;

(g) to acknowledge the diversity of experiences of globalization. Much of the existing literature remains silent on issues of context, overlooking different impacts and appreciations of globalization in relation to, for example, age, class, country, gender, nationality, race, religion, sexual proclivity, urban/rural location, and so on;

(h) to explore, carefully and systematically, a range of normative questions, particularly in relation to security, equity and democracy. Much past work on globalization involves facile celebration or unmeasured critique;

(i) to reflect on the implications of the knowledge developed through (a)–(h) for political action. Most existing academic works on globalization go little beyond general exhortations, if they consider policy responses at all;

(j) to avoid oversimplification yet remain accessible and engaging for a general reader. Too much public discussion of globalization has become soundbite, while too much academic treatment of the subject has slipped into unnecessary jargon and disempowering obfuscation.

In sum, I have aimed in this book to provide definition, description, periodization, explanation, judgement and – on the basis of this under-standing – cautious prescription. I have tried to be explicit with theory and careful with evidence. The account is intended to be transdisciplinary and also sensitive to social and historical context. The argument is meant to retain focus, clarity, consistency and accessibility.

The book of course falls short of these aspirations at various points, but I hope that the pursuit of foolhardy ambitions has nevertheless yielded a provocative argument. The book will achieve its purpose if others are inspired to refine, extend, critique or overthrow the knowledge presented here. In the process readers will, I hope, take globalization that much more seriously: in further research, in policy, and in the choices of everyday life.

JAN AART SCHOLTE

Acknowledgements

This book has been single-authored only in the immediate sense that one person has tapped the computer keyboard. Responsibility for the end-result is of course mine, but I have had many helping hands along the way.

For inspiration, critical reaction, access to source materials, and opportunities to test ideas I thank Hans Antlöv, Libby Assassi, Barrie Axford, Jim Baker, Roberto Bräuning, Angus Cameron, Anton Carpinschi, David Cooperrider, Mick Dillon, Mike Edwards, David Elliott, Cate Eschle, Huw Evans, Lucy Ford, Zie Gariyo, Bruce Graham, Jo Marie Griesgraber, Jeff Harrod, Vivien Hart, Richard Higgott, Michael Hitchcock, Steve Hobden, Patrick Hutchinson, Naeem Inayatullah, Barry Jones, Steve Koblik, Kelley Lee, Rohit Lekhi, Norman Lewis, Lily Ling, Nigel Llewellyn, Andrew Linklater, Alexandros Loizides, John Maclean, Kamal Malhotra, André Miroir, David Myhre, Peter Newell, Michael Nicholson, Anna Pallikaras, Angelo Panebianco, Charlotte Patton, Ruth Pearson, Dan Petre, Thomas Risse, Ben Rosamond, Mohamed Salih, Julian Saurin, Nico Schrijver, Martin Shaw, Vilen Sikorsky, Caroline Soper, Thomas Stelling, Susan Strange, Estela Suárez Aguilar, Peter Taylor, Caroline Thomas, Christopher Thorne, Stein Tønnesson, Marijke Torfs, Thanh-Dam Truong, Diana Tussie and Marc Williams.

In addition to providing the above kinds of support, the following colleagues have given me much-appreciated feedback on earlier drafts of writing related to this book: Michael Barnett, Jan Wisseman Christie, Robert Cox, Ian Douglas, Andrew Gamble, Stephen Gill, Duco Hellema, Jef Huysmans, Mark Laffey, Marianne Marchand, James Mittelman, Robert O'Brien, W. Ofuatey-Kodjoe, Spike Peterson, Michael Schechter, Richard Simeon, Steve Smith, Jill Steans, Peter Waterman and Gillian Youngs. Steven Kennedy's enthusiasm, astute criticisms, constructive suggestions and seemingly endless patience have gone well beyond any editor's call.

I have also accumulated debts to a number of institutions that made possible participation in conferences and seminars at which I developed the ideas presented in this book: the Academic Council on the United Nations System; the British International Studies Association; Case Western University; the Cunliffe Centre for the Study of Constitutionalism at the University of Sussex; the Ditchley Foundation; the Global Economic Institutions Programme of the Economic and Social Research Council; the Institute of Social Studies; Michigan State University; Pomona College;

the School of European Studies at the University of Sussex; the United Nations University; and the University of Warwick.

Much of the early writing of this book was completed during generous research leave from the University of Sussex in 1996. Part of that sabbatical was productively spent at the Centre for International Studies at the London School of Economics. Secondment to the Centre for the Study of Globalisation and Regionalisation at the University of Warwick in 1999–2000 helped me to complete the book.

Ashgate Press has kindly permitted me to reprint in Chapter 6 of this book some materials from my contribution in Patrick Hanafin and Melissa Williams (eds), *Identity, Rights and Constitutional Transformation* (Scholte, 1999a). Various other points in the argument have also appeared in an earlier form elsewhere (Scholte 1996a, b; 1997a, b; 1999b, c; 2000a, b).

The end of the list is the top of the list. My deepest thanks go to Masha for, among many other things, keeping matters in perspective when I did not, and to Polly for insisting that it is more fun to play outside the study.

JAN AART SCHOLTE

List of Abbreviations

ABM	anti-ballistic missile
ADR	American Depository Receipt
AIDS	acquired immunodeficiency syndrome
APEC	Asia Pacific Economic Cooperation
ARPANET	Advanced Research Projects Agency Network
ASEAN	Association of South East Asian Nations
AT&T	American Telephone and Telegraph Company
ATM	automated teller machine/Asynchronous Transfer Mode
BIS	Bank for International Settlements
BJP	*Bharatiya Janata Party*
BP	British Petroleum
BSE	bovine spongiform encephalitis
CACM	Central American Common Market
CDF	Comprehensive Development Framework
CEDAW	Convention on the Elimination of All Forms of Discrimination Against Women
CEO	Chief Executive Officer
CERD	Committee on the Elimination of Racial Discrimination
CFC	chlorofluorocarbon
CHIPS	Clearing House Interbank Payment System
CITES	Convention on International Trade in Endangered Species of Wild Fauna and Flora
CNN	Cable News Network
DBS	direct broadcast satellite
ECU	European Currency Unit
EDS	Electronic Data Services
EPZ	export processing zone
ERM	(European) exchange-rate mechanism
ESAF	Enhanced Structural Adjustment Facility
EU	European Union
FAO	Food and Agriculture Organization
FDI	foreign direct investment
FLAG	Fibreoptic Link Around the Globe
FPZ	free production zones
FT	*Financial Times*
FTA	free trade area
G7	Group of Seven
GATT	General Agreement on Tariffs and Trade

GDI	gender-related development index
GDP	gross domestic product
GDR	Global Depository Receipt
GEF	Global Environment Facility
GNP	gross national product
GSP	Generalized System of Preferences
hinwi	high net worth individual
HIPC	Highly Indebted Poor Countries
HIV	human immunodeficiency virus
IAEA	International Atomic Energy Agency
IAIS	International Association of Insurance Supervisors
IASC	International Accounting Standards Committee
IB	International Baccalaureate
ICAO	International Civil Aviation Organization
ICFTU	International Confederation of Free Trade Unions
IFAC	International Federation of Accountants
ILGA	International Lesbian and Gay Association
ILO	International Labour Organization
IMF	International Monetary Fund
INTELSAT	International Telecommunications Satellite Organization
IOSCO	International Organization of Securities Commissions
IPR	intellectual property right
ISDN	Integrated Services Digital Network
ISMA	International Securities Market Association
ISO	International Organization for Standardization
IT	information technology
ITT	International Telephone & Telegraph Corporation
ITU	International Telecommunication Union
IUCN	International Union for the Conservation of Nature
IUF	International Union of Food, Agricultural, Hotel, Restaurant, Catering, Tobacco and Allied Workers' Associations
LIBOR	London Inter-Bank Offered Rate
LME	London Metal Exchange
M&A	merger(s) and acquisition(s)
MAI	Multilateral Agreement on Investment
MERCOSUR	*Mercado Común del Sur* (Southern Common Market)
MOSOP	Movement for the Survival of the Ogoni People
NAFTA	North American Free Trade Agreement
NATO	North Atlantic Treaty Organization
NGO	nongovernmental organization
NIC	newly industrializing country
NPT	Treaty on the Non-Proliferation of Nuclear Weapons

NYSE	New York Stock Exchange
OAU	Organization of African Unity
ODA	official development assistance
OECD	Organization for Economic Cooperation and Development
OPCW	Organization for the Prohibition of Chemical Weapons
OPEC	Organization of Petroleum Exporting Countries
OPM	*Organisasi Papua Merdeka*
OSCE	Organization for Security and Cooperation in Europe
PANA	Pan African News Agency
PC	personal computer
PRGF	Poverty Reduction and Growth Facility
RSS	*Rashtriya Swayamsevak Sangh*
S&P	Standard and Poor's
SADC	Southern African Development Community
SDR	Special Drawing Right
SEZ	special economic zone
START	Strategic Arms Reduction Talks
SWIFT	Society for Worldwide Interbank Financial Telecommunications
TOEFL	Teaching of English as a Foreign Language
TRIPS	Trade-Related Aspects of Intellectual Property Rights
UN	United Nations
UNCTAD	United Nations Conference on Trade and Development
UNDP	United Nations Development Programme
UNEP	United Nations Environment Programme
UNESCO	United Nations Educational, Scientific and Cultural Organization
UNHCR	United Nations High Commissioner for Refugees
UNICEF	United Nations Children's Fund
UNIFEM	United Nations Development Fund for Women
UNPO	Unrepresented Nations and Peoples Organization
VAT	value-added tax
VHP	*Vishwa Hindu Parishad*
WEF	World Economic Forum
WIN	World Insurance Network
WIPO	World Intellectual Property Organization
WRI	World Resources Institute
WSJ	*Wall Street Journal*
WSJ-E	*Wall Street Journal* (Europe edition)
WTO	World Trade Organization
WWF	World Wildlife Federation/World Wide Fund for Nature

Introduction

Framework of analysis
Change and continuity
Policy issues

What is globalization? When has globalization emerged and spread? Why has globalization occurred? How, if at all, has globalization generated social change? What benefits and harms have flowed from globalization? Insofar as globalization can have ill effects, how might they be avoided? These questions, which grip much contemporary political debate, form the core concerns of this book.

As its title indicates, the volume gives a *critical* introduction. It is critical of widespread loose use of the term 'globalization'. It is critical of many unnuanced claims that have been made about globalization. It is critical of many consequences of globalization to date. At the same time, the book tries to construct an account of globalization that is more clear, precise and (in policy as well as intellectual terms) helpful.

'Globalization' stands out for a large public, spread across the world, as one of the defining terms of contemporary society. The first Director-General of the World Trade Organization (WTO), Renato Ruggiero, is far from alone in having described globalization as a reality 'which overwhelms all others' (WTO, 1996b). Although such pronouncements may slip into hyperbole, it is clear that substantial parts of humanity have staked significant parts of their policies, their fortunes, their careers, their identities and their convictions on the premise that ours is an increasingly global world.

Yet, if asked to specify what they understand by 'globalization', most people reply with considerable vagueness, inconsistency and confusion. Moreover, much discussion of globalization is steeped in oversimplification, exaggeration and wishful thinking. In spite of a deluge of publications on the subject, our analyses of globalization tend to remain conceptually inexact, empirically thin, historically and culturally illiterate, normatively shallow and politically naïve. Although globalization is widely assumed to be crucially important, we generally have scant idea what, more precisely, it entails. As media magnate Ted Turner has put it, 'globalization is in fast-forward, and the world's ability to understand and react to it is in slow motion' (UNDP, 1999: 100).

1

This highly unsatisfactory situation – one that has often also character-ized my own thinking – has prompted me to write this book. I make no claim to have resolved any of the many and deep disputes surrounding globalization. Little consensus exists on the subject in respect of defini-tions, evidence, explanations, implications, value judgements and prescrip-tions. My contribution will sooner make knowledge of globalization more rather than less contentious. However, I hope that this introductory text helps readers to engage with – and advance – what are often muddled and deadlocked debates.

The argument develops in three main stages. The first phase (Part I: Chapters 1–4) establishes a framework of analysis. The second phase (Part II: Chapters 5–8) examines impacts on social structures. The third phase (Part III: Chapters 9–12) explores normative and policy issues. The rest of this introduction summarizes the argument that is developed through this three-part structure.

Framework of analysis

The four chapters in Part I elaborate, in turn: the key issues in debates surrounding globalization; a general definition of the development; a chronology of the trend; and an account of the causal dynamics involved in globalization. These chapters both specify the approach adopted in this book and compare that perspective with the main competing viewpoints taken elsewhere in the literature on globalization.

Chapter 1, entitled 'What Is Happening?', surveys the wide array of claims and counterclaims that have been made in connection with globalization. Regarding definition, for example, some people equate 'global' relations with 'international' relations, while others emphasize a difference between the two notions. In respect of scale, some analysts see globalization as a pervasive and overriding fact of contemporary society, while others dismiss globalization as a fantasy. Concerning chronology, some say that globalization is a recent development, while others date its beginnings far back in history. On the question of social change, some assessments affirm that globalization is transforming our lives, while others assert that old social structures persist intact. In normative terms, some evaluations champion globalization, while others denounce its consequences. With regard to policy, people have promoted competing neoliberal, reformist and radical courses of action. In short, the first chapter summarizes what is at issue in current debates about globalization.

Chapter 2, on 'What Is "Global" about Globalization?', explores the vexed issue of definition in more detail. Five general conceptions are distinguished: globalization as internationalization; globalization as liberalization; globalization as universalization; globalization as westernization; and globalization as deterritorialization. It is argued that the first four definitions are largely redundant. Only the last notion gives 'globalization' a new and distinctive meaning – and at the same time identifies an important contemporary historical development. In the remainder of the book, therefore, globalization refers in the first place to the advent and spread of what are alternately called 'global', 'supraterritorial', 'transworld' or 'transborder' social spaces. That said – as Chapter 2 also stresses – the contemporary rise of supraterritoriality has by no means brought an end to territorial geography: global and territorial spaces co-exist and interrelate in complex fashions.

Chapter 3 focuses on 'Globalization in History', addressing the hotly contested questions of chronology and periodization. Here it is argued that, if globalization is understood as the spread of supraterritoriality, then the trend has mainly unfolded in recent history. True, the concept of the spherical planet as a single place attracted certain imaginations half a millennium ago, and global relations began to take more material form (for example, with telegraphic communications) from the middle of the nineteenth century. However, as evidence presented in Chapter 3 indicates, the greatest expansion of transworld relations has transpired since the 1960s, and at the moment the trend shows little sign of stopping, let alone reversing.

Chapter 4 explores 'What Causes Globalization?' This issue is key, since our assessment of the consequences of, and workable policy responses to, globalization depends largely on our interpretation of the forces that have generated the trend. The rise of supraterritoriality has, it is suggested here, resulted mainly from a combination of: (a) the emergence of global consciousness, as a product of rationalist knowledge; (b) certain turns in the development of capitalism; (c) technological innovations, especially in communications and data processing; and (d) the construction of enabling regulatory frameworks, especially through states and suprastate institutions.

In sum, Part I of the book establishes that globalization is a distinctive and significant feature of recent world history. Moreover, the dynamics of globalization involve several of the core forces of modern social life: rationalist knowledge, capitalist production, automated technology, and bureaucratic governance. True, much talk of globalization is muddled, redundant, unsubstantiated and hyped. However, the concept can be constructed in such a way that it brings to light important circumstances of contemporary social relations that other vocabulary and analysis does not reveal.

Change and continuity

Drawing on the general framework of analysis developed in Part I, Part II assesses in what ways and to what extent globalization has affected the social order. Globalization is simultaneously an effect and a cause. Whereas Chapter 4 examines the social forces that have given rise to globalization (that is, globalization as outcome), Chapters 5–8 consider how this reconfiguration of social space has in turn affected other aspects of social structure (that is, globalization as causal force). In a word, has globalization while reorganizing geography also generated wider social transformations?

In Chapter 5, on the subject of 'Globalization and Production', the rise of supraterritoriality is found to have done little thus far to challenge the predominance of capitalism, that is, an economy centred on surplus accumulation. On the contrary, the growth of transworld spaces has encouraged several major extensions of capitalist activity, including information industries and consumerism. The spread of global relations has also brought some notable shifts in the ways that processes of surplus accumulation operate. Examples include offshore arrangements and transborder corporate alliances. However, globalization has not put the structure of capitalism itself under threat. If anything, the current situation is one of hypercapitalism.

Chapter 6, regarding 'Globalization and Governance', first puts paid to the frequently heard claim that the contemporary globalizing world is witnessing a general retreat or even a demise of the state. On the contrary, states have remained a key locus of regulation and have thus far shown no sign of dissolution in the foreseeable future. However, globalization has prompted changes in several significant features of the state, for instance, in terms of the constituencies that it serves and the policy tools that it uses. In addition, the spread of supraterritorial relations has encouraged increased regulatory initiative by a host of substate, suprastate and nonstate agencies. In this way large-scale globalization during contemporary history has opened an era of post-sovereign governance. That said, this multilayered and diffuse organization of regulation has retained the general underlying bureaucratic structure that previously characterized state-centric governance.

Chapter 7, on 'Globalization and Community', begins by arguing that, contrary to some assumptions, the nationality principle can survive in a time of spreading supraterritoriality. Indeed, so far the nation has shown every sign of keeping its status as a major framework of social solidarity. On the other hand, contemporary globalization has often helped to loosen the links between national projects and states, in particular by promoting a growth of substate and transstate nationalist movements (for example, among the Welsh and the Kurds). In addition, the expansion of transworld spaces has facilitated the development of various nonterritorial communities, for instance, connected to class, gender or religion. Furthermore, globalization has encouraged modest growth in cosmopolitan attachments and an increase in hybrid identities. Yet none of these developments has substantially contradicted the general underlying communitarian approach to building collective solidarity, whereby a community is consolidated through us–them opposition of an in-group against out-groups.

Chapter 8 completes this book's assessment of change and continuity in social structures by examining 'Globalization and Knowledge'. This discussion starts by noting that the rise of supraterritoriality has generally been consistent with rationalism as the previously predominant structure of knowledge. Indeed, in a number of ways global relations have entailed an extension of modern rationality: that is, secular, anthropocentric, techno-scientific thinking. At the same time, globalization has also encouraged some anti-rationalist reactions, in forms such as religious revivalism and postmodernism. In addition, the spread of transworld relations has promoted some shifts in ontologies, in methodologies, and in aesthetics.

In sum, Part II of the book suggests that contemporary globalization, as a major reconfiguration of social geography, has propelled several important shifts in primary social structures. The growth of supraterritorial spaces has encouraged the emergence of: (a) new forms of capitalist production; (b) multilayered and more diffuse governance; (c) greater pluralism in the construction of community; and (d) increased questioning of rationalist knowledge. That said, globalization has thus far shown few signs of bringing an end to the predominance of capitalism in production, bureaucratism in governance, communitarianism in community, and rationalism in knowledge. In a word, then, globalization has generated an intricate interplay of continuity and change in the social order. Yet on the whole globalization has to date yielded change within continuity rather than deeper transformations.

Policy issues

As Part III of the book indicates, these changes and continuities in social structures can have both positive and negative impacts on daily life. The normative evaluation of globalization undertaken in the third set of chapters highlights themes of human security, social equity and democracy. Some readers might expect issues of efficiency also to be highlighted as a principal policy concern. For example, neoclassical economists would tend to judge globalization largely in terms of the gains or losses that it brings to the productive deployment of scarce world resources. However, the perspective taken in this book regards efficiency and economic growth as always secondary to – and in the service of – security, justice and democracy. Productivity is therefore not treated as a primary normative question in its own right.

Chapter 9, on the subject of 'Globalization and (In)Security', investigates how the rise of supraterritoriality has affected conditions of safety and confidence. The discussion examines human security in a multifaceted fashion, covering peace, ecological integrity, subsistence, employment, identity, social cohesion and knowledge. The evidence is found to be mixed. In some respects globalization has promoted increased human security, for example, with disincentives to war, improved means of humanitarian relief, new job opportunities, and greater cultural pluralism. However, in other ways globalization has perpetuated or even deepened warfare, environmental degradation, poverty, unemployment, exploitation of workers, and social disintegration. Thus globalization does not automatically increase or decrease human security. The outcomes are positive or negative depending on the policies that we adopt toward the new geography.

Chapter 10 considers the hotly contested question of 'Globalization and (In)Justice'. Social justice is examined here in terms of the distribution of life chances between classes, countries, sexes, races, urban/rural populations and age groups. Again the evidence turns up mixed. On the bright side, globalization has in certain cases improved possibilities for young people, poor countries, women and other subordinated social circles to realize their potentials. More negatively, however, globalization has thus far sustained or increased various arbitrary hierarchies in contemporary society. For example, gaps in opportunities have tended to widen during the period of accelerated globalization on class lines as well as between the North (the so-called 'First World') and the South (the so-called 'Third World') and the East (the current and former state-socialist countries). Structural inequalities have also often grown in respect of gender, race, urban/rural divisions and generations. The resultant increases in social injustice can be attributed at least partly to the spread of supraterritorial relations. Again, however, these inequities have flowed from the policies that we have applied to globalization rather than from globalization per se.

Chapter 11 addresses the problem of 'Globalization and (Un)Democracy'. Here claims that the contemporary social order offers greater popular power are assessed against arguments that globalization has deepened democratic deficits. The growth of global politics has brought some promising developments in respect of democracy, for example, through new information and communications technologies and an expansion of civil society. However, on balance the evidence to date has favoured the critics. Thus far we have lacked mechanisms to ensure that post-sovereign governance is adequately participatory, consultative, transparent and publicly accountable. Bold intellectual and institutional innovations are needed to refashion democracy for a globalizing world.

Circumstances in each of these major areas of normative concern – security, equity and democracy – have developed mainly as a result of policy choices in respect of globalization; hence different policy approaches could produce happier outcomes. Under the title of 'Humane Global Futures', Chapter 12 considers various measures that might steer supraterritorial relations in more positive directions. A host of policy revisions could allow globalization to yield increased human security, social justice and democracy within the current generation. Implementation of these proposals faces many technical and political challenges, but with creativity and determination different courses of globalization could be developed.

In sum, Part III of the book advances an indictment of *neoliberal* globalization, not a condemnation of globalization as such. (The distinguishing features of neoliberalism are detailed in Chapter 1.) Insofar as globalization to date has often increased insecurity, inequity and democratic deficits, these trends have flowed from the policy frameworks that have dominated our (mis)management of supraterritorial spaces in the late twentieth century. Alternative, better approaches are available for the future. Globalization is very much what we make of it.

To recapitulate, this book aims to advance understandings of globalization that are clear, nuanced, alert to negative consequences, and sensitive to political possibilities of change. Such knowledge should help us to shape globalization to maximally positive effects. For convenient reference, the core points of the overall argument are reviewed in the Box overleaf. Readers will also find boxes elsewhere in the book that summarize the contents of the respective chapters.

Core theses on globalization

(1a)   'globalization' is a transformation of social geography marked by the growth of supraterritorial spaces

but

(1b)   globalization does not entail the end of territorial geography; territoriality and supraterritoriality coexist in complex interrelations

(2)   although globalization made earlier appearances, the trend has unfolded with unprecedented speeds and to unprecedented extents since the 1960s

(3)   globalization appears today to have acquired certain juggernaut-like qualities, but it need not retain its present momentum indefinitely and could in principle reverse (though the chances of such a contraction seem remote at present)

(4)   although globalization has touched almost every person and locale in today's world, the trend has spread unevenly, being most concentrated among propertied and professional classes, in the North, in towns, and among younger generations

(5)   globalization has had multifaceted causal dynamics, with the principal spurs having come from rationalist knowledge, capitalist production, various technological innovations and certain regulatory measures

(6a)   globalization has not displaced deeper social structures in relation to production (capitalism), governance (the state and bureaucratism more generally), community (the nation and communitarianism more generally) and knowledge (rationalism)

but

(6b)   globalization has prompted important changes to certain attributes of capital, the state, the nation and modern rationality

and

(6c)   globalization has encouraged the growth of additional loci of governance besides the state, the spread of additional forms of community besides the nation, and the development of additional types of knowledge besides modern rationality

→

(7a)   contemporary globalization has had some important positive consequences with respect to cultural regeneration, communications, decentralization of power, economic efficiency and the range of available products

     but

(7b)   neoliberal policies toward globalization have had many negative consequences in regard to increased ecological degradation, persistent poverty, worsened working conditions, various cultural violences, widened arbitrary inequalities and deepened democratic deficits

(8a)   globalization is not inherently good or bad; its outcomes are largely the result of human decisions that can be debated and changed

     and

(8b)   a host of alternative policies could avoid the ills associated with neoliberal globalization

     but

(8c)   the political challenges of achieving effective full-scale reform must not be underestimated

Part I
Framework of Analysis

Since everything about globalization is deeply contested, we can take nothing for granted. Each account of the trend has to make its starting points explicit and clear. A lengthy first part of this book must therefore carefully establish a general framework for analysing globalization.

To this end Chapter 1 sets the scene of debate with a survey of the many points of disagreement about globalization. Chapter 2 develops the definition of globalization that guides the analysis in this book. Chapter 3 elaborates a chronology of globalization that corresponds to this conception. Chapter 4 then presents an account of the forces that have caused globalization. With this framework of analysis we become equipped to consider the consequences of globalization in Parts II and III of the book.

Chapter 1

What is Happening?

Main points of this chapter
Where do we start?
Continuity or change?
Liberation or shackles?
What to do?
Conclusion

Main points of this chapter

- globalization is a thoroughly contested subject
- the arguments extend across issues of definition, measurement, chronology, explanation, normative judgement, and policy
- the level of debate can be considerably raised from the loose claims that have often prevailed to date

---

A boutique in Portland, Oregon sells 'Global Clothing'. To mark post-Soviet times, a billboard in Moscow points consumers to a 'Super Shop' called 'Global USA', located down the street from Lenin's tomb. In a slum district of Kampala, capital of one of the poorest countries in today's world, a rusted sign advertises 'Global Health Services'. In Suceava, a provincial town in the northeastern corner of Romania, the director of a regional agricultural production agency asks dubiously, 'What does globalization offer us?' In Bangkok, a deputy head of the national planning board of the Royal Thai Government enthuses, 'We must globalize and localize!' In Cuernavaca, the director of a consultancy firm called Global Thinkers tells of Internet links just established between 20 schools in Mexico and 20 counterparts in Azerbaijan. In Copenhagen, 111 heads of state and government assemble in a World Summit to discuss the implications of globalization for poverty, employment and social cohesion.

These snapshots relate just a few of the countless occasions – across continents, age groups, classes, races, sexes, and urban and rural settings – when the present author encountered 'global-ness' while writing this book. No doubt all readers can assemble their own collection of such incidents, if perhaps not as territorially scattered as the above examples. It is today pretty well impossible to avoid the issue of globalization. 'Global-speak' has become standard fare among journalists, politicians, managers, advertisers, bankers, entertainers, officials, computer experts, and researchers the world over. The vocabulary of 'globalization' has entered almost all major languages. (Swahili is a rare exception – for the time being at any rate.) Daily life now brings continual references to 'global' institutions, 'global' markets, 'global' finance, 'global' communications, 'global' migration, 'global' security, etc.

'Globalization' has also become a heavily loaded word. People have linked the notion to well-nigh every purported contemporary social change, including an emergent information age, a retreat of the state, the demise of traditional cultures, and the advent of a postmodern epoch. In normative terms, some people have associated 'globalization' with progress, prosperity and peace. For others, however, the word has conjured up deprivation, disaster and doom. No one is indifferent. Most of us are confused.

In these circumstances, research into globalization has understandably become a major growth industry. The number of entries for 'globalization' in the catalogue of the United States Library of Congress multiplied from 34 in 1994 to 693 in 1999 (Waters, 1995: 2; LoC, 1999). Universities and think tanks have spawned a slew of courses and projects concerning global issues. Indeed, some have argued that globalization necessitates the creation of a new paradigm of social and political enquiry (Shaw, 1994, 1999; Cerny, 1996). As a sign of these times, I started this book while attached to an International Relations faculty and completed it in a Centre for the Study of Globalisation and Regionalisation.

The present opening chapter reviews the many claims and counterclaims about 'globalization' that these burgeoning studies have propounded. The first section below notes the highly diverse starting points that people have taken when they examine globalization. In other words, these paragraphs foreshadow the issues addressed in detail in the rest of Part I. The second section surveys various affirmations and denials of social change that analysts have connected to globalization. These paragraphs thus introduce the questions treated more fully in Part II. The third section assembles multiple plaudits and denunciations of globalization, while the fourth section lays out the contrasting policy lines that can be followed in governing globalization. These sections thereby review the matters that are handled at length in Part III of the book.

Where do we start?

Many debates about globalization never get past disputes over starting premises. For one thing, people often hold radically different definitions of the term. As a result they talk past each other. In addition, people tend to make widely varying assessments of the scale of globalization. At one end of the spectrum certain observers claim that we already live in a fully globalized world. At the opposite pole sceptics deny that any globalization whatsoever has occurred. On the question of chronology, some accounts trace globalization back to ancient history, while others date its origins back only several decades. With such contrasting starting points, many globalization debates are foredoomed to be deadlocked.

What's in a word?

Disputes and confusion about globalization often begin around the issue of definition. Indeed, many people invoke notions of globalization without indicating explicitly what they mean by the term. For example, various commentators have described globalization as 'a stage of capitalism' or 'late modernity' without specifying the content of such jargon. Or we face unfocused remarks that globalization is 'a new way of thinking'. Circular definitions are not much help either. All too often we encounter statements like 'globalization is the present process of becoming global' (Archer, 1990: 1). 'Globalization' becomes a label to cover whatever strikes our fancy. Little wonder, then, that many sceptics have dismissed the emptiness of 'globaloney' and 'global babble'.

Yet such wholesale rejections are unfair. After all, most key notions in social analysis are frequently used loosely and vaguely. Where are the airtight concepts of 'class', 'culture', 'money', 'law', 'development', 'international', etc.? Moreover, some usages of 'globalization' are considerably more precise than the examples given in the previous paragraph.

All the same, confusion persists because the more specific conceptions are highly diverse. At least five broad definitions of 'globalization' can be distinguished. These conceptions are in some ways related and to some extent overlapping, but their emphases are substantially different.

One common notion has conceived of globalization in terms of *internationalization*. From this perspective, 'global' is simply another adjective to describe cross-border relations between countries, and 'globalization' designates a growth of international exchange and interdependence. In this vein Paul Hirst and Grahame Thompson have identified globalization in terms of 'large and growing flows of trade and capital investment between countries' (1996a: 48). Evidence of such 'globalization' is purportedly also to be found in enlarged movements between countries of people, messages and ideas.

A second usage has viewed globalization as *liberalization*. Here 'globalization' refers to a process of removing government-imposed restrictions on movements between countries in order to create an 'open', 'borderless' world economy. On these lines one analyst suggests that 'globalization has become a prominent catchword for describing the process of international economic integration' (Sander, 1996: 27). Evidence for such 'globalization' in recent decades can be found in the widespread reduction or even abolition of regulatory trade barriers, foreign-exchange restrictions, capital controls and (for citizens of certain states) visas.

A third conception has equated globalization with *universalization*. Indeed, when Oliver Reiser and B. Davies coined the verb 'globalize' in the 1940s, they took it to mean 'universalize' and foresaw 'a planetary synthesis of cultures' in a 'global humanism' (1944: 39, 201, 205, 219, 225). In this usage, 'global' means 'worldwide', and 'globalization' is the process of spreading various objects and experiences to people at all corners of the earth. We could in this sense have a 'globalization' of the Gregorian calendar, automobiles, Chinese restaurants, decolonization, cattle farming, and much more.

A fourth definition has equated globalization with *westernization* or *modernization*, especially in an 'Americanized' form (Spybey, 1996; Taylor, 2000). Following this idea, globalization is a dynamic whereby the social structures of modernity (capitalism, rationalism, industrialism, bureaucratism, etc.) are spread the world over, normally destroying pre-existent cultures and local self-determination in the process. 'Globalization' in this sense is sometimes described as an imperialism of McDonald's, Hollywood and CNN (Schiller, 1991). Martin Khor has on these lines declared that 'globalization is what we in the Third World have for several centuries called colonization' (Khor, 1995; see also Ling, 2000).

A fifth idea identifies globalization as *deterritorialization* (or, as I would prefer to characterize it, a spread of supraterritoriality). Following this interpretation, globalization entails a reconfiguration of geography, so that social space is no longer wholly mapped in terms of territorial places, territorial distances and territorial borders. On these lines, for example, David Held and Tony McGrew have defined globalization as 'a process (or set of processes) which embodies a transformation in the spatial organization of social relations and transactions' (Held *et al.*, 1999: 16).

Each of these five conceptions can generate an elaborate and in one or the other way revealing account of contemporary history. For reasons that are set out in Chapter 2, the present book builds primarily on the fifth type of definition. For now it is merely important to stress that, in spite of some overlap between these five notions of globalization, their respective focuses are significantly different. Thus, for example, people who identify globalization as internationalization and people who approach it as deterritorialization develop very different understandings of world affairs. Due to irreconcilable definitions, many globalization debates are stalemated from the outset.

Fact or fantasy?

Both when they agree and when they disagree on the general definition of globalization, people often hold widely differing assessments regarding the extent of the development. On the one hand, analysts that we might characterize as 'globalists' claim that contemporary social relations have become thoroughly globalized. Globalists have also tended to regard globalization as the single most important fact of contemporary history. In contrast, ultra-sceptics have dismissed any notion of globalization as myth. Between these extremes other analysts have treated globalization as a significant trend, but one that coexists with other developments and is far from complete. Such moderate assessments have often also stressed the uneven incidence of globalization between countries, classes and other social divides.

Globalist pronouncements on the ubiquity of globalization have tended to issue either from gung-ho supporters of the trend or from its implacable opponents. The promoters have included a number of consultants and champions of new technologies. For example, management gurus like Kenichi Ohmae and John Naisbitt have created best-sellers with their praises of a 'borderless world' (Ohmae, 1990; Naisbitt, 1994). Much of the business press has heralded 'the stateless corporation' that maximizes efficiency and profits (Holstein, 1990). Similarly, many Internet enthusiasts have repeatedly overstated the number of online connections and the scale of electronic commerce. Many advertisers, journalists, politicians and others prone to hyperbole have also celebrated our present as a thoroughly globalized world.

Globalists have also included some strong critics of globalization, particularly among radical grassroots activists and dissident academics. For instance, a number of alarmists have suggested that global corporations now rule the world (Barnet and Cavanagh, 1994; Brecher and Costello, 1994; Korten, 1995; Berger, 1998–9). On similar lines many of the same critics have denounced global governance agencies like the World Bank and the WTO for usurping power from states and local governments (George and Sabelli, 1994; Barker and Mander, n.d.). Meanwhile a number of religious revivalists and reactionary nationalists have decried a deluge of globalization that is allegedly erasing traditional cultures.

Whether they are supporters or critics of globalization, globalists have tended to treat the trend as holding foremost and overriding importance in contemporary history. For example, several writers have taken the current growth of global communications to be as significant as the spread of printing presses 500 years ago, the invention of writing 5,000 years ago, or the development of human speech 40,000 years ago (Ploman, 1984: 37; Gates, 1995: 8–9). For his part the President of Brazil, Fernando Henrique Cardoso, has affirmed that the implications of global consciousness are as great for our day as was the Copernican revelation, five centuries ago, that the earth revolved about the sun rather than vice versa (Cardoso, 1996).

At an opposite extreme to globalists, ultra-sceptics have denied the existence of any such thing as globalization. For these analysts, all globe-talk is empty jargon, fad, hype, myth and rhetoric. Claims concerning globalization are greatly exaggerated, if not utter fantasy. Doubters have dismissed talk of 'globalization' as new-fangled vocabulary for age-old conditions of world politics. In their eyes, contemporary history holds nothing novel or distinctive that could be called 'globalization'. Studies of this phantom subject are therefore a waste of time. Shut this book!

From the ultra-sceptics' standpoint, the so-called 'global' economy is mythical (Zysman, 1996). Purportedly 'global' companies are in fact deeply embedded in their respective home countries, and their actions are thoroughly enmeshed in the logic of interstate relations (Kapstein, 1991–2; Ruigrok and Van Tulder, 1995; Doremus *et al.*, 1998). Indeed, alleged 'globalization' has done and will do nothing to alter the basic fact of world politics, namely, the sovereign state (Krasner, 1994; Nicholson, 1999). So-called 'global' governance institutions have not exercised any power separately from their state members. Talk of 'global' civil society and 'global' culture is similarly nonsense.

Meanwhile moderates like the present author have fallen between the globalist and ultra-sceptical extremes. From such a perspective globalization is indeed a distinctive and important development in contemporary world history. However, its scale and consequences need to be carefully measured and qualified. Nor is globalization the only, or always the most significant, trend in today's society. Rather, it unfolds alongside – and is closely interlinked with – other major social forces, like shifts in structures of production, governance, community and knowledge.

In addition, moderate assessments of the scale of globalization have often emphasized the uneven spread of the trend. On such an account, some countries (like the USA) and regions (like Western Europe) have generally experienced more globalization than others (like Afghanistan or Sub-Saharan Africa). Likewise, urban centres have on the whole accumu-lated more global connections than rural areas. Global relations have also tended to fall unevenly across different classes and age groups. In a word, measurements of globalization are far more complex than both the globalists and the ultra-sceptics make out.

Old or new?

Along with definition and scale, another principal issue in debates about globalization concerns chronology. Is the spread of global relations new to contemporary history? Or did the trend start several generations, centuries or even millennia ago? Or is globalization a cyclical phenomenon that comes and goes from time to time? As might be expected, the chronology that we describe varies with the definition that we adopt.

For example, analysts who define globalization in terms of internationalization or liberalization often regard the process as a recurrent trend that has appeared at several previous junctures in the history of the modern states-system. In this vein Ian Clark has distinguished alternating phases of 'globalization' and 'fragmentation' in international history (Clark, 1997). A number of studies have emphasized that, in proportional terms, levels of cross-border trade, migration and investment were as high (if not higher) in the late nineteenth century as they were in the run-up to 2000 (cf. Zevin, 1992; Hirst and Thompson, 1996b; Wade, 1996). On the grounds of such evidence many commentators have declared that there is nothing new in contemporary globalization.

Other accounts also give globalization a long history, but view it in linear rather than cyclical terms. These authors generally hold that globalization started on a small scale anywhere from 100 to 500 years ago and reached unprecedented rates in recent decades. In this fashion, Roland Robertson has spoken of a 'germination phase' of globalization between the early fifteenth and the mid-eighteenth centuries and a 'take-off' period from the middle of the nineteenth century (1992: 58–9). For their part, the business analyst Michael Porter and the world-systems theorist Christopher Chase-Dunn have located the start of globalization in the late nineteenth century (Porter, 1986: 42; Chase-Dunn, 1989: 2).

Meanwhile, other arguments suggest that globalization has been entirely novel to present times. Global relations only dawned with the jet aeroplane and the computer. From such a perspective, current history is experiencing a 'first global revolution' and a sudden leap to 'new realities' (King and Scheider, 1991; Drucker, 1989).

By adopting a conception of globalization as the rise of supraterritoriality, the present book draws mostly from the second of the general chronological frameworks just summarized. Global connections have certain antecedents in earlier centuries, but they have figured as a pervasive, major aspect of social life mainly since the 1960s. Various indicators are presented in Chapter 3 to demonstrate these exponential recent increases. That said, exact measurement of supraterritorial relations remains difficult, inasmuch as most social data (trade and investment flows, political participation, recreational activities, etc.) are collected in relation to national and other territorial units. We lack sufficient *global* statistics.

Continuity or change?

Along with arguments over definition, scale and history, discussions of globalization tend in good part to be debates about social change. Many people share the intuition, articulated here by the sociologist Anthony Giddens, that 'the emergence of globalized orders means that the world we live "in" is different from that of previous ages' (1991: 225). Accepting Philadelphia's Liberty Medal in 1994, Prague's playwright-politician Václav Havel suggested that, whereas previously war provided the chief stimulus to social transformation, today forces of change emanate mainly from globalization. Countless contemporary social commentators have been tempted at one or the other moment to issue a similar sweeping pronouncement.

Yet what, more specifically, is the character of social change in the context of globalization? Indeed, has the process actually reshaped the primary structures of social relations? Is there anything veritably new in this 'new world order'? Or has globalization merely generated superficial shifts (that is, at the level of objects, institutions, perceptions, etc.) while leaving the underlying social order intact? With some simplification we can distinguish four general areas of debate about globalization and social change.

Production

A first set of claims posits that globalization has transformed the nature of economic activity. For example, conventional wisdom in business studies has it that global markets, global competition and global management have fundamentally reshaped the visions, organization and behaviour of firms (Porter, 1990; Pucik *et al.*, 1992; Bleeke and Ernst, 1993; Taylor and Weber, 1996; Bartlett and Ghoshal, 1998). Globalization is also widely associated with technological revolutions in transport, communications and data processing. These developments have changed what we produce and how we produce it. Many observers have in this light characterized the global economy as an informational, knowledge-based, post-industrial or service economy (Bell, 1973; Katz, 1988; Carnoy *et al.*, 1993; Castells, 1989, 1996–7; Bryson and Daniels, 1998). With a grand sweep, Alvin and Heidi Toffler affirm that human history has entered a 'third wave' of knowledge society after the 'first wave' of peasant life and the 'second wave' of industrial civilization (Toffler, 1980; Toffler and Toffler, 1994). Certain commentators have furthermore associated expanding global relations with a decline or even demise of capitalism. Thus some accounts have spoken of 'late capitalism' (intimating that this mode of production nears termination) or a 'post-capitalist society' (suggesting that we have already moved beyond capitalism) (Jameson, 1991; Drucker, 1993).

These affirmations of structural change in the economy have provoked equally strongly asserted counterclaims of continuity. For example, some analysts have insisted on the persistent centrality of manufacturing industry in a global economy (Cohen and Zysman, 1987). More generally, Marxists and other critics have highlighted the underlying continuity of capitalism in globalization (Magdoff, 1992; Chesnaid, 1994; Amin, 1996; Marshall, 1996; Went, 1996; Burbach *et al.*, 1997; McChesney *et al.*, 1998; Berger *et al.*, 1998–9). These arguments often note that the spread of global relations involves shifts (or, to invoke the jargon, a 'restructuring') in the ways that surplus accumulation occurs. For example, globalization may bring a new world division of labour, a rise of regionalism, greater concentration of production in giant corporations, more accumulation through consumerism and finance, and a move from so-called 'Fordist' to 'post-Fordist' regimes of labour management. (These points are covered in detail in Chapter 5.) However, such changes are underlain by continuity: globalization leaves capitalism as entrenched as ever, if not more so.

Governance

A second set of claims and counterclaims about the changes wrought by globalization relates to governance, especially the fate of the state. For example, various commentators say that contemporary globalization has deprived the state of sovereignty (Camilleri and Falk, 1992; Wriston, 1992; Sassen, 1997). More broadly, many analysts have linked the growth of global relations to 'the diminished nation-state', 'the decline of the nation-state' and 'the retreat of the state' (Cable, 1995; Schmidt, 1995; Strange, 1996). Other writers have gone still further to announce 'a crisis of the nation-state' and 'the extinction of nation-states' (Horsman and Marshall, 1994; Dunn, 1995; Ohmae, 1995; Khan, 1996; Bauman, 1998: ch 4).

Such assertions have triggered a host of rebuttals. For example, certain authors insist that globalization has done nothing to undermine sovereign statehood (Thomson and Krasner, 1989; Krasner, 1993). According to this view a state could, if it wished, extricate itself from global relations. Related arguments have affirmed that global flows (in communications, ecology, etc.) do not necessarily undermine the state and indeed may in some cases strengthen it (Mann, 1997). Likewise, these perspectives maintain that the state retains substantial capacities to govern global economic activities (Boyer and Drache, 1996; Hirst and Thompson, 1996b;

Weiss, 1998). Indeed, states (especially the major states) remain the prime regulatory force even in that purportedly most globalized of sectors, finance (Kapstein, 1994; Pauly, 1997; Helleiner, 1998, 1999).

A third general strand in debates about globalization and governance focuses less on questions of the viability of the state and more on shifts in the contours of regulatory authority. For these authors, globalization has taken world politics away from the state-centric, sovereignty-based model of governance (the so-called 'Westphalian system') that held sway prior to the late twentieth century (Rosenau and Czempiel, 1992; Rosenau, 1997; Scholte, 1997b; Herod *et al.*, 1998; Held *et al.*, 1999). Although national governments remain crucially important, governance has become more multilayered. Authority is increasingly diffused across substate (municipal and provincial) and suprastate (regional and transworld) agencies as well as state organs. At the same time, a 'new multilateralism' has arisen in which: (a) 'international organizations' have developed into 'global governance agencies' with a certain autonomy from states; and (b) global firms and global civil society actors have become instrumental in various regulatory processes (R. W. Cox, 1997; Cutler, 1999; Schechter, 1999a, b). In these circumstances sovereignty has acquired substantially different meanings and dynamics (Lapidoth, 1992; Spruyt, 1994; Gelber, 1997; Schrijver, 1997; Clark, 1999: ch 4). Indeed, perhaps these changes are so great that we should abandon rather than redefine the term 'sovereignty'. Meanwhile, although contemporary globalization has not threatened the existence of the state, the process has stimulated changes in its forms and functions (Jessop, 1994; Camilleri *et al.*, 1995; Panitch, 1996; Evans, 1997; Scholte, 1997a; Shaw, 1997). To take one example, Phil Cerny has described a 'competition state' that takes measures (in exchange-rate, fiscal, monetary, regulatory and trade policies) to attract and retain footloose global capital (1990: ch 8; 1997; also Bratton, 1996). For his part, Bob Jessop has discerned a shift under the pressures of global capital from a Keynesian welfare state to what he calls a 'Schumpeterian workfare state' that subordinates social policy to the demands of labour market flexibility and the constraints of international competition (1993: 9). In short, on these lines of argument states survive under globalization, but governance has become substantially different.

Culture

Another issue of globalization and social change that has provoked considerable controversy relates to culture. In academic circles, these debates have unfolded mainly in anthropological and sociological writings (Featherstone, 1990; King, 1991; Mlinar, 1992; Robertson, 1992; Friedman, 1994; Hannerz, 1996; Scott, 1997; Jameson and Miyoshi, 1998; Meyer and

Geschiere, 1998). However, the question has also been a matter of much popular speculation: does globalization make people more the same or more different?

On the one hand, many commentators (particularly those who conceive of globalization in terms of liberalization or westernization) have argued that the process brings a worldwide 'cultural synchronization' (Hamelink, 1983: 3; also Tomlinson, 1995). In the words of Theodore Levitt, an early champion of global markets, 'everywhere everything gets more and more like everything else as the world's preference structure is relentlessly homogenized' (1983: 93). For these analysts, globalization has harmonized and unified, often crushing traditional ways of life when they have deviated from the dominant pattern. As a result, diversity has had its day, and we approach a 'postnational age' (Guéhenno, 1995: 57; also Brown, 1995). Globalization introduces a single world culture centred on consumerism, mass media, Americana, and the English language. Depending on one's perspective, this homogenization entails either progressive cosmopolitanism or oppressive imperialism.

In contrast, other diagnoses have linked globalization with enduring or even increased cultural diversity (Appadurai, 1990; Hannerz, 1992: ch 7; Cable, 1994). For one thing, such accounts emphasize, global communications, markets, etc. are often adapted to fit diverse local contexts. Through so-called 'glocalization', global news reports, global products, global social movements and the like take different forms and make different impacts depending on local particularities (Robertson, 1995; K.R. Cox, 1997). Likewise, large-scale globalization has not kept countless people from continuing to embrace national differences (Smith, 1990a; Foster, 1991; Buell, 1994). Indeed, many groups have championed national, religious and other particularisms as a reaction to and defence against a universalizing 'McWorld' (Barber, 1996). For followers of Samuel Huntington, cultural politics under globalization is marked by a clash of civilizations: Confucian, Eastern Orthodox, Hindu, Islamic, Western, etc. (Huntington, 1996). Others argue that globalization has promoted fragmentation, with a growth of substate identity politics like ethno-nationalism and indigenous peoples' movements (Halperin and Scheffer, 1992; Wilmer, 1993; Connor, 1994). In addition, some accounts suggest that global relations have increased opportunities for the development of nonterritorial cultures and communities, for example, connected to class, gender, race, religion and sexuality. These various issues are elaborated in Chapter 7. The key point to stress for the moment is that while some analysts maintain that globalization leads to homogenization, others argue that it breeds heterogenization.

A further tendency in debates about globalization and culture has highlighted the creation of new patterns of meaning, identity and community. From this perspective, globalization has intensified intercultural relations, in the process encouraging countless new combinations and blurring distinctions between nations and between civilizations. Various authors have in this respect associated globalization with 'creolization' and 'hybridization' (Hannerz, 1987; Nederveen Pieterse, 1995). A number of political theorists have moreover suggested that these cultural developments create a need for alternative forms and ethics of community, away from the old communitarian habits of dualistic 'us–them' oppositions between neatly defined and separated groups (Blaney and Inayatullah, 1994; Shapiro, 1994; Scholte, 1996b, 1999c; Shapiro and Alker, 1996; Linklater, 1998).

Modernity and postmodernity

A final major point of debate concerning globalization and social change relates to questions of modernity and postmodernity (Robertson, 1992: ch 9; Featherstone, 1995). Researchers broadly concur that globalization has developed out of modern society. Giddens has put this thesis most strongly by declaring that 'modernity is inherently globalizing' (1990: 63, 177). To be sure, analysts disagree about the particular aspects of modernity that have generated globalization. For example, Marxists have treated modern capitalist production as the primary cause, whereas many liberals have regarded modern industrial technology as the chief stimulus. Others have put the spotlight on modern rationalist knowledge or the modern bureaucratic state. However, a general consensus prevails that globalization has in one way or another been a product of the modern social order.

Major disagreements have arisen, though, regarding the consequences of globalization for modernity. On the one hand, some sociologists have linked globalization with the development of 'high', 'advanced' or 'radical' modernity (Giddens, 1990, 1991; Spybey, 1996). The implication of these adjectives is that the spread of global relations has extended and deepened the hold of modern structures like rationalism, bureaucratism, capitalism and industrialism. In a variation on this theme, Ulrich Beck has associated globalization with a 'new' and 'reflexive' modernity, a 'modernization of modernization' that replaces industrial society with a risk society riven by insecurities (Beck, 1986, 1997). At the same time, Giddens and others have sometimes also spoken of 'late' modernity, as though to suggest that globalization is taking society to the verge of a postmodern era (Giddens, 1991).

Meanwhile other analysts argue that globalization has effected the dawn of postmodernity. Authors interpret the precise character of 'postmodernity' quite differently, though, and are often not very explicit about definitions. As a result, debates about postmodernity can readily become confused. For example, some writers take postmodernity to be broadly equivalent to a post-industrial society. In contrast, David Harvey has applied the label 'postmodernity' to global capitalism and associated cultural changes (Harvey, 1989). For his part, Martin Albrow has declared that 'the Global Age' lies beyond modernity, because globality supplants rationality and the nation-state as the primary bases of social organization (Albrow, 1996). Meanwhile other theorists who carry the label of 'postmodernism' have identified postmodernity as a global world of 'informationalized', 'mediatized', 'hyperreal', 'virtual', 'simulated' social experiences in which people lose a stable sense of identity and knowledge (Axford, 1995; Luke, 1995; Ó Tuathail, 1996: ch 7).

The preceding survey makes it plain that no easy answer is available to the question of globalization and social change. Do global relations reproduce capitalism or introduce post-capitalist modes of production? Do global politics perpetuate statism or create post-statist modes of governance? When it comes to culture, does globalization involve homogenization, heterogenization or hybridization? Does the globalizing world have a modern or a postmodern character? The present book makes no claims to provide definitive responses to these questions. However, the chapters in Part II attempt carefully weighed assessments of continuity and change in social structure.

Liberation or shackles?

Next to disputes over starting premises and questions of social change, a third cluster of globalization debates concerns normative issues. In a word, is globalization a good or a bad thing? Does it enhance or detract from the human condition? Does it produce a utopia or a hell? Does it take history to a peak of progress or a trough of despair?

On these matters, too, opinion is highly divided. On the one hand, many people have welcomed globalization as an emancipatory force. For enthusiasts, global relations increase efficiency, welfare, democracy, community and peace. Globalization is a 'win–win' scenario where everyone in an emergent 'world society' benefits. Against this rosy picture, many other people have rejected what has been variously described as 'global pillage', 'global *apartheid*' and 'the global trap' (Brecher and Costello, 1994; Alexander, 1996; Martin and Schumann, 1996). For critics, global relations undermine security, equity and democracy. The rest of this section considers normative debates about globalization in more detail under these three general headings.

Security

The first of these themes, security, encompasses various issues connected with human experiences of safety and confidence. Does globalization encourage protection or danger, stability or uncertainty, well-being or misery, social integration or alienation, calm or stress, hope or fear?

Security has various dimensions: bodily safety, ecological integrity, material welfare, cultural preservation, and more. Indeed, one effect of globalization debates has been to broaden the security agenda in world politics beyond the military affairs of states (Thomas and Wilkin, 1999). Yet major disagreement has reigned regarding the effects of globalization on each dimension of security.

The traditional focus of security has concerned peace and violence. Analysts who link globalization with a spread of free trade and democracy have often connected these developments with a decline in warfare. Observe, they emphasize, that armed conflict has disappeared between states in the more globalized parts of the world. By this account, globalization involves the growth of international cooperation and a one-world community. On broadly such lines, Hans-Henrik Holm and Georg Sørensen have in their assessment of globalization described an emergence of 'postmodern states' for whom warfare is unthinkable (1995: 204).

In the opposite corner, prophets of doom have forecast 'the coming anarchy' of 'global disorder' (Kaplan, 1994; Harvey, 1995). From this pessimistic perspective, globalization has bred intolerance and violence – as manifested in ultranationalism, racism, religious fundamentalism and terrorism. Civil wars have proliferated as globalization has weakened the state, especially in the East and the South. The technologies of globalization (computers, missiles, satellites, etc.) have produced a barbarism of techno-war and a voyeurism of media war. The pains of global economic restructuring, often pursued through policies sponsored by global institutions like the International Monetary Fund (IMF), have sparked urban riots (Walton and Seddon, 1994). At the same time global sex tourism, global trade in prostitutes, and the mail-order marriage business have increased the vulnerability of and violence towards women (Pettman, 1996; Skrobanek *et al.*, 1997; Kempadoo and Doezema, 1998). Globalization has also generated new types of illegality such as computer crime and money laundering, as well as transborder criminal networks such as the Sicily-based Cosa Nostra and the Colombia-based Cali cartel (Williams, 1994; Shelley, 1995; Mittelman and Johnston, 1999).

A second major security concern in globalization debates is ecological integrity. On this subject the optimists have stressed how much global conferences, global research programmes and global environmentalist groups have raised ecological awareness throughout the contemporary world (McCormick, 1989). The technologies of globalization can – in the case of digital computers, for example – vastly enhance environmental management. Global laws and institutions can provide indispensable frameworks of ecological protection and regeneration (Haas *et al.*, 1993; Young *et al.*, 1996). To take one outstanding example, global conventions and monitoring bodies have been 'healing the sky' from ozone depletion (Tanner, 1997).

For other observers, however, globalization entails an environmental catastrophe. Since the 1960s a spate of Cassandras have warned of 'the chasm ahead', 'the closing circle' and 'global collapse' (Peccei, 1969; Commoner, 1971; Meadows *et al.*, 1992). Many global ecological problems allegedly threaten human survival. Consider exhaustion of natural resources, excessive world population growth, nuclear holocaust, acid rain, ozone depletion, climate change, species extinction, HIV/AIDS, BSE ('mad cow disease') and genetically modified food crops. Meanwhile global trade has taken pollution to new heights, and global institutions like the World Bank have engineered ecologically unsustainable 'development' (Rich, 1994; Reed, 1996). Worries about global ecological despoliation have lain at the heart of Beck's previously mentioned 'risk society' (Beck, 1988).

Next to bodily security and ecological security, globalization is generally held also to have far-reaching implications for economic security. The enthusiasts have emphasized the gains in efficiency and economic growth that allegedly result when the world becomes a single open marketplace (Bergsten, 1996; Bryan and Farrell, 1996; Burtless *et al.*, 1998: ch 2). Moreover, global trade is said to enhance consumer satisfaction, distributing more products to more people at lower prices. With regard to employment, global investment creates jobs at host sites, and technological advances connected with globalization reduce the burdens of human labour in many industries. Globalization has also served as a primary engine of economic development, particularly in the so-called 'newly industrializing countries' (NICs). Meanwhile, when disasters strike, global communications and global organizations make possible humanitarian relief operations with a speed and on a scale never before available. In short, for its champions, globalization is a formula for unprecedented material prosperity across the world.

For the critics, however, globalization has calamitous consequences for economic security (Mander and Goldsmith, 1996). Global capitalism, warns William Greider, 'appears to be running out of control toward some sort of abyss' (1997: 12). The 'mad money' of 'casino capitalism' in global financial markets threatens even the largest of fortunes (Strange, 1986, 1998). Wild fluctuations in foreign exchange rates, stock prices and other financial values can destroy livelihoods in an instant. Global capital outflows have brought even major national economies like Mexico, Korea and Russia to their knees in a matter of days. In the South and the East, global finance has saddled countries large and small with crippling debts and other economic crises. Concurrently, the pressures of global competition have reduced aid flows to poor countries. 'Globalization' and 'development' are antithetical, say the critics (Raghavan *et al.*, 1996; McMichael, 1996a; Hoogvelt, 1997; Thomas and Wilkin, 1997). Meanwhile all over the world economic restructuring in the face of globalization has unravelled welfare provisions for vulnerable sectors of society (Cornia *et al.*, 1987–8; Ghai, 1991; Chossudovsky, 1997). Unemployment has burgeoned as countless companies relocate and 'downsize' in response to global competition. Full employment has become unrealizable. Some analysts have even foreseen a 'jobless future' and 'the end of work' (Aronowitz and DiFazio, 1994; Rifkin, 1995). As for people who remain in waged employment, they have been caught in a 'race to the bottom' of working conditions between 'lean and mean' global firms (Brecher and Costello, 1994; Tilly, 1995; Kapstein, 1996). In this 'world war' of 'savage capitalism' (Robinson, 1996a: 13, 27), governments and workforces will do anything to maintain the 'confidence' of global markets.

A more ideational concern in globalization debates relates to culture and knowledge: do global circumstances make people secure in their ways of being and understanding? On this subject the optimists have celebrated the cultural pluralism and innovation that global relations purportedly promote. In line with previously described claims about heterogenization and hybridization, these commentators have argued that globalization creates space for thousands of flowers to bloom. Furthermore, the enthusiasts maintain, global communications like jet tourism, electronic mass media and the Internet promote greater intercultural understanding and are laying the foundations for a veritable world community.

In contrast, other commentators have suggested that globalization undermines cultural and intellectual security. From their perspective, global relations involve cultural imperialism (cf. Tomlinson, 1991; Petras, 1993; Golding and Harris, 1997). This new world order imposes 'western' and especially 'American' meanings that both obliterate older traditions and restrict the development of new alternatives. The resultant loss of cultural resources is not only tragic in its own right, but also limits the capacities of humankind to respond creatively and effectively to political, ecological and economic challenges.

From another angle, some analysts have affirmed that intense blending of cultures through globalization unsettles any and all truth claims. Even the Enlightenment vision of human progress becomes a casualty. Science is dead, relativism reigns, intellectual security dissolves.

In sum, globalization has generated intense debates about human security. At one extreme, enthusiasts have linked globalization to an 'end of history' where peace, sustainability, prosperity and truth are assured (Fukuyama, 1992). At another extreme, alarmists have warned of the 'global turmoil' of a 'new world disorder' (Brzezinski, 1993). These issues are treated at greater length in Chapter 9. For the moment it suffices to note that globalization debates are littered with polarized claims and counterclaims about security.

Equity

Alongside security, social justice is a second major focal point of normative debates about globalization. Do people have equal opportunities to participate in global relations; or does globalization arbitrarily bypass, marginalize and silence much of the world's population? Do people fairly share the costs and the benefits of globalization; or does the process increase maldistribution in the world? Is globalization a force for social equity or exploitation?

Most comments in the justice debate have stressed the negative, namely, that globalization has allegedly sustained and indeed often deepened arbitrary social hierarchies. With respect to class, for example, many have claimed that globalization has increased the advantages of already privileged strata. Income gaps have grown in almost every country as wealthy circles have taken the lion's share of the material benefits from globalization. At the same time, many argue, global markets have undermined the Keynesian welfare state as a promoter of social justice (Teeple, 1995; Gray, 1998).

Critics have also frequently alleged that globalization has perpetuated if not heightened inequity in relations between countries (Hurrell and Woods, 1999). In these accounts, globalization is a post-colonial imperialism that has not only reinvigorated the exploitation of the South by the North, but also added former communist-ruled areas to the list of victims. For poor countries, globalization allegedly means perpetual financial and related economic crises, the immiserating effects of structural adjustment programmes imposed by the IMF and the World Bank, further subordination in world trade, ecological problems without economic benefits, and the cultural imperialism of global communications (Thomas and Wilkin, 1997). In the eyes of the pessimists, globalization has frustrated hopes and expectations that decolonization would give the South equal opportunity and self-determination in world affairs.

Meanwhile many feminists have linked globalization with gender injustices (Peterson and Runyan, 1999). For example, women are said to have had less access than men to global communications networks, global financial markets, global corporate management and global governance institutions. The global trade regime has allegedly had gender-differentiated effects that can disadvantage women (Joekes and Weston, 1994; Moon, 1995). Women have provided the bulk of low-paid and poorly protected labour in global service industries ('electronic sweat-shops') and the 'global factories' of export processing zones (Fuentes and Ehrenreich, 1983; Runyan, 1996). At the same time the pains of global economic restructuring (e.g. reduced public services) have fallen dispro-portionately on women (Vickers, 1991; Beneria and Feldman, 1992; Aslanbeigui *et al.*, 1994; Rajput and Swarup, 1994; Sparr, 1994; Marchand and Runyan, 2000).

Similarly, global relations have, by some claims, perpetuated and intensified racial injustices. Like women, people of colour have through a 'global *apartheid*' faced structural barriers to access new realms of communications, organization, finance and markets (Falk, 1993; Mazrui, 1994). Several critics have suggested – implicitly or explicitly – that global agencies like the IMF and the World Bank have harboured institutional racism (Budhoo, 1990: 7, 48–9; Rich, 1994: 246–9). Meanwhile declining economic security in the North as a result of globalization has purportedly encouraged a growth of racial intolerance in society at large. Racism has also been quite plain in immigration controls against people of colour in the so-called 'open' world economy (Alexander, 1996: 181–3, 253). More subtle subordination has occurred through the global mass media's usual portrayal of black people 'either as victims of disaster or as exotic extras' (Alexander, 1996: 252).

Other commentators have highlighted still further inequities of global-ization in respect of rural peoples (Flora, 1990; McMichael, 1996b). The countryside has allegedly benefited far less from global flows than towns, as globalization perpetuates an urban bias in development efforts. Mean-while the 'global agro-food system' is said to have promoted big industrial and finance capital in the countryside at the expense of smallholder livelihoods and food security (LeHeron, 1993; McMichael, 1993, 1994; Whatmore, 1994). In particular, the ongoing transformation of the world economy has purportedly accelerated a process of 'global depeasantiza-tion' whereby dispossessed rural populations have poured into sprawling urban slums (Araghi, 1995).

While many critics have regarded globalization as a catastrophe for social justice, others have made more positive diagnoses. For example, enthusiasts have argued that everyone is – or will be – better off in a global economy. Look, they say, at Chile, China, Hungary, Kuwait and Uganda. Many people may struggle during the transition to a globalized world, and some classes and countries may gain more, or sooner, than others. However, by following the right policies, in the long run substantial benefits will accrue to all. Already, the optimists affirm, global companies and industries have offered women more opportunities to enter paid employment, while global governance agencies and global social movements have helped to give gender equity issues a higher profile (Pietilä and Vickers, 1994; Stienstra, 1994). Global regimes have also done much to advance principles of racial equality and human rights more generally, including for children and disabled persons. Global economic institutions like the World Bank and global nongovernmental organizations like Oxfam are, say some, addressing problems of rural development more effectively than state programmes have ever done.

So does globalization favour the privileged and exploit the vulnerable? Or does globalization open new possibilities for a just world order? Chapter 10 assesses a range of available evidence.

Democracy

A third area in the spotlight of normative debates about globalization is democracy, that is, the possibility for all members of a polity equally and collectively to shape its destiny (Holden, 2000). What does 'becoming global' imply for actual and potential governance 'by the people'? Does globalization enhance or undermine popular participation and consultation in the formulation, implementation and evaluation of policy? Does globalization widen or restrict debate of public affairs? Does globalization make governance institutions more or less representative, transparent and publicly accountable?

Many commentators have celebrated globalization as an occasion of unprecedented democratization. Following the end of the Cold War liberal democracy has spread to more states than ever (Huntington, 1991; Shin, 1994; Diamond and Plattner, 1996). The military are out in Latin America and Asia. *Apartheid* is over in South Africa. The wall is down in Europe. Multiparty politics, 'free and fair' elections to representative institutions, and legal guarantees of civil rights have become the worldwide norm. Global governance institutions and global civil society have greatly promoted human rights and norms of so-called 'good governance'. The global mass media have encouraged democracy activists from China to Nigeria, Yugoslavia to Chile.

Many analysts have also championed (alleged) more general democratizing potentials of the technologies of globalization (Abramson *et al.*, 1988; Rheingold, 1993; Budge, 1996; Hill and Hughes, 1998). With particular exuberance, Walter Wriston has enthused that 'the information age is rapidly giving power to the people in parts of the world and in a way that only a few years ago seemed impossible' (1992: 170–1). Electronic communications have given citizens access to unprecedented amounts of information at unprecedented speeds. Telephone, e-mail, radio and television have allowed citizens to relay their views to governing authorities as never before. Electronic communications have also enabled civic activists across the planet to exchange views and coordinate strategies in global democratic campaigns for progressive social change (Frederick, 1993; Lee, 1996; Harcourt, 1999).

However, against this applause, sceptics have painted globalization as antithetical to democracy (Robinson, 1996a: 20–1; Gill, 1996). Various authors have associated this new world order with 'low-intensity democracy' and 'polyarchy' where a narrow élite holds control (Gills *et al.*, 1993; Robinson, 1996b). In apocalyptic terms, Claude Ake has described a 'deadly threat' of globalization that irreversibly shrinks democratic space and renders political participation irrelevant (1999: 179–80).

In particular, many critics have highlighted the purported inadequacy in a globalizing world of democracy through the state. Of course, some objectors have rejected the principle that the state can ever be a suitable vehicle for democratic governance. For these dissidents, formal democracy of the ballot box is a cruel veneer for structural injustice. What use, they ask, are referenda and multiparty elections organized by the state if these exercises do nothing to end class inequities, North–South gaps, gender hierarchies, and the subordination of minorities? For these critics, the modern state has never been democratic, and globalization has merely brought these intrinsic failings into sharper focus.

Other analysts have maintained that, while the state was an important agent of the popular will in an earlier era, forces of globalization have critically undermined the democratic capacities of national governments (Connolly, 1991; Held and McGrew, 1993; McGrew, 1997b). For example, say these commentators, states cannot tame the tyranny of global corporations (Korten, 1995). Global financial markets, too, have often constrained the possibilities for democratization (Armijo, 1999). In addition, states – particularly small states – cannot ensure democracy for their citizens in respect of global governance bodies like the International Atomic Energy Agency (IAEA) and the WTO. On this line of argument, *territorial* mechanisms like the state cannot – certainly by themselves – secure democratic governance of *supraterritorial* phenomena such as global communications and global ecological problems. Ironically, then, unprecedented numbers of states have adopted liberal democracy at the very moment when state-centric democracy has passed its historical sell-by date.

On notions of electronic democracy, sceptics have emphasized that only a minority of the world's population – and a highly unrepresentative minority at that – has had access to the Internet (Loader, 1998). As for home voting via interactive television, this practice would 'privatize politics and replace deliberative debate in public with the unconsidered instant expressions of private prejudices' (Barber, 1996: 270). Meanwhile new information and communications technologies supply authorities with unprecedented capacities for intrusive surveillance and the manipulation of public opinion.

Yet the critics have not been only negative. Many of them have also regarded globalization optimistically as an opportunity to reconstruct democracy. The resultant new frameworks might well give voice and respond to popular needs and wants better than state-centric mechanisms of old were ever able to do. For example, some commentators have welcomed globalization as a force that facilitates devolution and the principle of subsidiarity, whereby governing power is always located at the closest possible point to the citizen. Other reformers have stressed the need for a democratization of governance at the regional level, for instance, in relation to the European Union (EU). Meanwhile other analysts have advanced ideas of 'cosmopolitan democracy' through trans-world institutions (Held, 1995a, b; Archibugi *et al.*, 1998). A number of specific proposals have suggested the creation in the United Nations of a People's Assembly of grassroots representatives alongside the General Assembly of states. In other ways, too, promoters of innovation in democratic practice have endorsed the development of civil society as a 'multilateralism from below' that pursues the public good (Falk, 1992a, 1995; Smouts, 1999). Likewise, a number of political theorists have regarded globalization as a stimulus to develop new and more effective modes of citizenship (Steenbergen, 1994; Lacarrieu and Raggio, 1997; Castles and Davidson, 2000; Vandenberg, 2000). In short, for these authors democracy is historically contingent, and globalization by altering the contours of governance demands that democracy be refashioned today.

As with issues of security and equity, then, little agreement exists concerning the implications of globalization for democracy. For some globalization is a blessing for collective self-determination, while for others it is a bane. The relative merits of the various arguments are evaluated in Chapter 11.

What to do?

On top of disagreeing about starting premises, explanations and normative assessments, people have also taken radically different positions on the policy course to adopt *vis-à-vis* globalization. On the one hand, neoliberals have argued that globalization should be guided by market forces: public authorities should only facilitate and not interfere with these dynamics. In contrast, reformists have maintained that globalization should be deliberately steered with public policies, including suprastate as well as state measures. From a more radical position, traditionalists have sought to 'de-globalize' and return to a pre-global status quo ante. Meanwhile other radicals like global socialists and postmodernists have advocated a continuation of globalization, but in tandem with a revolutionary transformation away from other social structures like capitalism or rationalism.

Neoliberalism

As the name suggests, 'neo'-liberalism is a new line on an old story. It draws on several centuries of modern thought dating back to treatises by the likes of John Locke and Adam Smith. Neoliberalism builds on the convictions of classical liberalism that market forces will bring prosperity, liberty, democracy and peace to the whole of humankind. In particular, liberal trade theorists have argued since the seventeenth century that state borders should not form an artificial barrier (with tariffs and other officially imposed restrictions) to the efficient allocation of resources in the world economy.

Neoliberals have in recent decades revived classical liberal arguments against proactive state intervention to guide or restrict operations of the market, now in an economy that has become increasingly global. Indeed, neoliberals have argued that the state lacks the capacity to control globalization. Public agencies should therefore let global markets work their magic unhindered by official limitations. To be sure, governments and multilateral institutions are necessary to facilitate globalization on neoliberal lines. For example, official regimes usually play an indispensable role in harmonizing technical standards between countries. Moreover, when the population is reluctant, implementation of a neoliberal agenda depends on strong pressure from the state and/or suprastate agencies like the IMF (A. Gamble, 1994). However, in neoliberal eyes the public sector should not attempt to direct the course of market forces in the global realm.

For neoliberals, then, globalization should be approached with a large-scale retreat of official regulation. In particular, neoliberals have prescribed the abolition of most state-imposed limitations on movements between countries of money, goods, services and capital. (Logically, neoliberalism should also promote unrestricted cross-border movements of workers, though its proponents have rarely raised this point.) With respect to indicators of value, neoliberals have advocated the removal of state controls on prices, wages and foreign exchange rates. Neoliberals have furthermore argued for a major contraction of state ownership of productive assets, that is, thoroughgoing privatization. And neoliberals have urged reductions in state provision of welfare guarantees, looking instead to market arrangements and the voluntary sector to play a greater role in relation to pensions, health care and other social insurances. In short, neoliberals have rejected the statist strategies of economic management that prevailed (whether in a socialist, a fascist or a welfarist form) across the world between the 1930s and the 1970s. (For more on neoliberal policies, see Williamson, 1990; Gill, 1995.)

Neoliberalism has generally prevailed as the reigning policy framework in contemporary globalization. Indeed, as later chapters make clear, this approach has generously served powerful interests, particularly those related to dominant classes and countries in today's world. Most governments – including in particular those of the major states – have promoted neoliberal policies toward globalization, especially since the early 1980s. From the side of multilateral institutions, agencies such as the IMF, the WTO and the Organization for Economic Cooperation and Development (OECD) have continually linked globalization with liberalization. Champions of neoliberal globalization have also abounded in commercial circles, particularly in the financial markets and among managers of transborder firms. Business associations like the International Organization of Employers and the World Economic Forum (WEF) have likewise figured as bastions of neoliberalism. In the mass media, major business-oriented newspapers like the *Wall Street Journal* (*WSJ*) and the *Financial Times* (*FT*) have generally supported neoliberal policies. In academic quarters, mainstream economists have extolled the virtues of global free markets from positions at renowned and obscure universities alike. Other researchers have promoted neoliberal policies through influential think tanks such as the Institute for International Economics in Washington, DC (Bergsten, 1996).

Given this widespread hold on centres of power, neoliberalism has generally ranked as policy orthodoxy in respect of globalization. Indeed, in the late twentieth century neoliberal ideas gained widespread unquestioned acceptance as 'commonsense'. Enjoying the strongest backing in official, business and academic circles, neoliberal measures have usually been the easiest to implement. Other policy approaches (discussed below) have in good part involved reactions against neoliberal policies and their purported harmful consequences. Starting from much weaker political bases, however, these alternative policy lines have generally faced major difficulties when it comes to implementation.

Reformism

Reformism – or what could otherwise be called global social democracy – has presented the strongest challenge to neoliberal policies on globalization. This second general approach has drawn on traditions including Keynesian economics, the New Deal and the Great Society in the USA, and post-1945 West European welfarism. Reformists posit (with liberals) that capitalism can be a major force for social good; however, they argue (against liberals) that achievement of these positive results requires carefully designed and executed public policies. Indeed, say reformists, unconstrained capitalism tends to produce substantial personal, social and environmental harms. Like any market, global markets can 'fail' and require 'corrections' in the form of policy interventions by public agencies.

Reformists have proposed a wide variety of policies to promote the positive possibilities and counter the negative potentials of capitalism. For example, they have advocated controls on cross-border movements of resources when such constraints would reduce damaging market instabilities, social inequities and environmental costs. In addition, reformists have prescribed various official guarantees of minimum standards (including basic incomes, labour protections and environmental controls) to protect vulnerable circles from the ravages of unleashed capitalism. Other reformist policies have sought actively to promote opportunities for structurally vulnerable social groups like people of colour, underprivileged classes, and women. Furthermore, reformists have often argued for anti-trust measures and other official controls to limit corporate power.

Old-style reformism concentrated on state measures to steer capitalism in progressive directions; however, a statist strategy is often inadequate to manage global capitalism. Hence many contemporary reformists have stressed the need for global public policies in which suprastate institutions play a major part (Deacon, 1997; Reinicke, 1998; Kaul *et al.*, 1999). For example, a reformist programme might advocate enforceable global codes of conduct to govern global companies and mandatory global environmental regulations to promote global ecological integrity. Some reformists have also urged that bodies like the IMF or a new world central bank should devise mechanisms to establish greater stability and justice in global financial markets. In addition, say reformists, global institutions should pursue programmes to improve opportunities in the global economy for disadvantaged social circles.

The later 1990s saw reformist challenges to neoliberalism grow to some strength. For example, social democrats took the reins of state in Argentina, Brazil, Britain, the Czech Republic, Germany, South Africa and elsewhere. Organs of the United Nations system have also harboured many reformist voices. For example, the former UN Secretary-General, Boutros Boutros-Ghali, warned in the mid-1990s against 'globalization without control' (Boutros-Ghali, 1995b). The International Labour Organization (ILO) has promoted greater labour protection in global capitalism, while the United Nations Development Programme (UNDP) has popularized many global reform proposals through the *Human Development Report*, issued annually beginning in 1990. The World Bank, too, has under the presidency of James Wolfensohn since 1995 taken various reformist initiatives. Reformist approaches to globalization have also been pursued in various quarters of civil society. For example, the International Confederation of Free Trade Unions (ICFTU) has advocated 'international policies and institutions to manage the process of globalization in the service of the needs and aspirations of people' (ICFTU, 1998: 9). A number of nongovernmental organizations (NGOs) have similarly called for reform of multilateral economic agencies in order to address the negative consequences of neoliberal globalization. Various academics and journalists, too, have called for a renewal of social democracy, reconstructed to meet new global realities (Hutton, 1996; Martin and Schumann, 1996; Giddens, 1998). Given this broad – albeit generally still fairly shallow – rise of reformism, neoliberal approaches to globalization today no longer hold as powerful a position that as they did during the 1980s.

Radicalism

Other critiques of neoliberalism have gone further than reformism and attack the underlying structural bases of contemporary globalization. Social democrats have in principle accepted globalization and the main forces that have generated it to date, including capitalist production, modern technology and rationalist knowledge (discussed further in Chapter 4). In contrast, radicals have sought either to reverse globalization or to continue it on different structural grounds.

Those radicals who wish to unravel globalization and return to a preglobal status quo ante might be termed 'traditionalists'. For such critics, globalization has been destroying treasured aspects of pre-existent social orders, and 'de-globalization' is needed in order to recover economic health, ecological balance, cultural integrity and democracy (Mander and Goldsmith, 1996). In traditionalist eyes, globalization is intrinsically harmful. Being incorrigible, the trend must be stopped and indeed reversed.

Traditionalist calls for de-globalization have come in diverse forms, including economic nationalism, religious revivalism and radical environmentalism. In their different ways these rejections of globalization have each sought to regain a purportedly better pre-global past. Economic nationalists (a group that has included many old-style socialists) have put the emphasis on reestablishing self-determination of countries by delinking them from global economic networks (Raghavan *et al.*, 1996; Hewison, 1999). Religious revivalists among some Buddhists, Christians, Hindus,

Jews and Muslims have 'gone local' to retrieve the original beliefs and practices of their faith. (It is however important to stress that not all religious responses to globalization have taken a 'fundamentalist' line. See, for example, Muzaffar, 1993 for a modernist Islamic approach, Küng, 1990 for a self-styled 'postmodern' Christian perspective, and Sulak, 1999 for a modernist Buddhist view.) Meanwhile radical environmentalists have aimed to restore pre-modern respect of and harmony with nature through self-sufficient local communities. (In contrast, mainstream environmentalists have taken a reformist approach of advocating so-called 'sustainable development'.)

In contrast to the reactive orientation of traditionalism, other radical responses to globalization have taken a proactive stance. From such a perspective the answer is not to reverse globalization, but to continue it on different foundations. Proactive radicals charge that reformist strategies are inadequate, since they fail to address the deeper structural causes of the ills of contemporary globalization.

For example, global socialists regard capitalism as an incorrigible evil and have sought to build a post-capitalist globalization. These radicals have dismissed as outdated the traditional socialist strategy of overturning capitalism through a proletarian capture of the state. Instead, global socialists have promoted transworld movements of workers, women and other oppressed persons as the way to achieve a post-capitalist world that is free of social exploitation (Gills, 1997; Waterman, 1998).

From another proactive radical angle, some postmodernist critics of contemporary society have rejected the rationalist knowledge structure and exclusionary identity politics that have predominated in globalization to date. These postmodernists have seen in global politics welcome opportunities to develop greater pluralism in knowledge, identities and culture generally (Harvey, 1989; Albrow, 1996; Ó Tuathail, 1996; Shapiro and Alker, 1996). That said, many other postmodernist thinkers have not directly addressed the problem of globalization.

On the whole radical policies toward globalization have attracted much weaker followings than neoliberalism or reformism. True, radical reactions against globalization have erupted from time to time in highly visible grassroots protests. However, ultranationalist parties have rarely gained more than a handful of seats in general elections. Likewise, demonstrations such as the 1999 'Battle of Seattle' against the WTO have thus far remained relatively small and passing affairs. For its part, global socialism has tended to remain restricted to a fringe of political activists and radical academics. Even governments like those of China and Cuba that have continued to carry a socialist label have tended in practice to accommodate more than resist global capitalism. Similarly, as is elaborated in Chapter 8, postmodernist perspectives on contemporary society have also thus far stayed on the margins, gaining ground chiefly among dissident academics and in the arts in the OECD countries. In short, radical responses to globalization have taken no noteworthy lasting hold in official quarters (at state or suprastate level), in markets, or in most grassroots circles.

The above sketches of competing policy reponses to globalization are of course compressed and oversimplified. The purpose at this stage of the book is merely to indicate the diversity of available policy approaches. Further details are presented in later chapters.

Moreover, particularly in Chapter 12, it will be seen that the policy position taken in this book could be characterized as 'ambitious reform-ism'. Neoliberalism is rejected for exacting excessive and largely avoidable harms as it pursues market efficiency and economic growth. Major corrective public policies are urged in order to realize more of the positive potentials of globalization. Some inspiration is taken from socialist principles of radical redistribution and postmodernist ideas concerning new kinds of knowledge and identity politics. However, full-scale radical programmes for epochal social transformation are regarded as being at present intellectually underdeveloped and politically impracticable. The main thrust of the prescriptions for future globalization advanced in this book is therefore reformist: the proposals build on rather than reject currently prevailing social structures.

Conclusion

As this chapter has indicated – and as the summary in the Box below recapitulates – the only consensus about globalization is that it is contested. People have held widely differing views regarding definition, scale, chronology, impact and policy. Everyone – including each reader of this book – has to see their way through the debates to their own account of globalization.

Following this review of debates, what can we conclude about the present state of knowledge about globalization? Clearly a great deal has been said and written on the subject. Indeed, thanks to burgeoning research we are today much better placed than we were only a few years ago to make some sense of globalization.

Nevertheless, our understanding of the process remains quite limited in important respects. Moreover, the level of globalization debates is often disappointing. Much discussion is couched in soundbite. Many claims take extreme and overgeneralized forms. Political prejudice often weighs heavily, so that people pronounce too much and listen too little. Most accounts lack careful, precise and consistent conceptualization. Arguments tend to be empirically thin. Discussions usually emphasize one aspect

---

Globalization debates in summary

Starting premises
- competing definitions: internationalization or something different?
- varying measurements of scale: globalism or scepticism?
- contrasting chronologies: old or new?

Implications for social structure
- old capitalism, new capitalism or post-capitalism?
- persistent statism or post-sovereign governance?
- cultural homogeneity or heterogeneity?
- an extension of modernity or the dawn of postmodernity?

Impacts on the human condition
- increased or decreased security?
- more or less justice?
- greater or reduced democracy?

Policy responses
- neoliberal reliance on market forces?
- reformist reliance on public policies?
- radical reliance on social revolution?

(cultural, ecological, economic, historical, legal or political) rather than drawing these dimensions together. Finally, the protagonists in globalization debates are disproportionately urban, white, middle-class, Judaeo-Christian, English-speaking men resident in the North (especially the USA and the UK).

Perforce I can do little in my own writing (short of remaining silent) to counter the last of these shortcomings. However, I hope that this book makes some inroads on the other limitations. Current knowledge of globalization may be largely confused and contradictory, but that is no reason to abandon the topic as vacuous buzzword. On the contrary, when (as seen above) key issues of security, justice and democracy are so prominently in play, social responsibility demands that researchers give globalization serious attention.

The remaining chapters of this book return to the different contentious points surveyed in successive sections of this opening chapter. Chapters 2–4 elaborate starting premises. Chapters 5–8 examine implications for social structures. Chapters 9–11 explore impacts on the human condition. Chapter 12 considers policy options. In each case we try to see ourselves through the debates to a clear and sustainable position.

Chapter 2

What is 'Global' about Globalization?

Main points of this chapter
Rise of a buzzword
Redundant concepts of globalization
A distinctive concept of globalization
A survey of global activities
Farewell to methodological territorialism?
Globality and territoriality

Main points of this chapter

- a clear and specific definition of globalization is needed to develop sustainable explanations, precise evaluations, and effective policies
- the notion of 'supraterritoriality' (alternatively, 'transworld' or 'transborder' relations) gives 'global-ness' a distinctive meaning
- with such a definition, globalization describes a significant change in the organization of social space, that is, a move to a new geography
- the rise of supraterritoriality has not meant – either logically or in practice – the end of territoriality as a key aspect of social geography

---

Chapter 1 has painted a picture of considerable confusion about globalization. Debates on this subject are littered with all manner of definitions, chronologies, explanations and evaluations. Can anything in this mass of claims and counterclaims fit into a coherent story? That is the task of the remainder of this book.

A vital first step in that process is to define the core concept. What, indeed, is 'global' about globalization (Maclean, 1999)? What distinctive meaning, if any, can be associated with the notion of 'global-ness'? Unclarity, imprecision and inconsistency in respect of definitions have produced a lot of confusion and stalemate in knowledge about, and responses to, globalization. Today hundreds of millions of lips have spoken the word globalization; yet few of us have consistently employed a clear, specific and distinctive definition of the term.

For many people this ambiguity is untroubling. They accept that globalization is a vague concept and see little point in trying to define it exactly. On this relaxed approach, 'globalization' is a malleable, catchall term that can be invoked in whatever way the user finds convenient.

Such an attitude may suit the politician and the marketing agent, but it is unsatisfactory when it comes to serious social analysis and the policy recommendations that flow from it. Definitions fundamentally shape descriptions, explanations, evaluations, prescriptions and actions. In other words, they affect our entire understanding of a problem. If a core definition is slippery, then the knowledge built upon it is likely to be similarly loose and, in turn, the policies constructed on the basis of that knowledge can very well be misguided. Hence definition is more than an academic and lexicographical issue. Our concept of 'the global' has major political as well as intellectual implications.

Of course no definitions of globality (the condition of being global) and globalization (the process of becoming more global) can be completely unambiguous, objective, fixed and final. Every conception – including the one developed here – reflects a specific historical context, a given theoretical perspective, certain normative commitments and particular political interests. However, the impossibility of a definitive definition does not reduce the need for rigorous conceptualization. An explicit and consistently applied definition gives focus and internal coherence to an argument and the policies that flow from it. So we do need carefully to define 'globalization', albeit with a recognition that any definition is subject to criticism, reconsideration and revision.

The rest of this chapter develops one such working definition of globalization. First some context is provided below with a brief history of 'global' terminology. Thereafter five common conceptions of globalization (previously introduced in Chapter 1) are surveyed. Four of them are found to be redundant: namely, globalization as internationalization; globalization as liberalization; globalization as universalization; and globalization as westernization. These four definitions are viable in their own terms, but they do not offer new understanding or highlight new historical conditions. The rest of the chapter then elaborates a fifth notion that offers additional, distinctive and important insight into contemporary world politics: namely, globalization as the rise of supraterritoriality. This conception requires us fundamentally to rethink some of our assumptions about social relations, particularly in relation to space.

That said, as is stressed again at the end of the chapter, globalization as it is understood in this book refers to *relative* deterritorialization. Territory still matters in the contemporary globalizing world. Indeed, as later chapters make clear, globalization (as an increasing transcendance of territorial space) can also be linked to processes of *reterritorialization* such as localization and regionalization. In short, while the spread of supraterritoriality means that some aspects of social space are no longer reducible to territorial geography, it by no means follows that territoriality has become irrelevant.

Rise of a buzzword

'Global-speak' has become popular only quite recently. The word 'globe' began to refer to 'the planet' several centuries ago, once it was determined that the earth was round. However, in popular English parlance the adjective 'global' did not until the 1890s begin to designate 'the whole world' in addition to its earlier meaning of 'spherical' (OED, 1989: VI, 582). The terms 'globalize' and 'globalism' were coined in a treatise published 50 years later (Reiser and Davies, 1944: 212, 219). The noun 'globalization' first appeared in a dictionary (of American English) in 1961 (Webster, 1961: 965).

Before the last decades of the twentieth century, discussions of world affairs nearly always invoked the vocabulary of 'international' rather than 'global' relations. As recently as the mid-1980s, concepts of 'global governance', 'global markets', 'global ecology' and 'global gender issues' were virtually unknown. With isolated exceptions, words such as 'global', 'globality', 'globalization' and 'globalism' are absent from titles published before 1975.

Although an Americanism in the first instance, notions of globalization have quickly spread across dozens of other languages since the 1980s. For their part, *globalizzazione* in Italian, *globalización* in Spanish, *globalizaçao* in Portuguese, *глобализация* in Russian and *Globalisierung* in German closely mirror the English formulation. The French *mondialisation*, the Romanian *mondializare*, and the Dutch *mondialisering* have conveyed broadly the same idea in the form of 'worldization'. However, of late the terms *globalisation*, *globalizare*, and *globalisering* have tended to become more popular in these three languages. Outside the Indo-European languages we find the Chinese *Quanqiuhua*, the Finnish *globalisaatio*, the Indonesian *globalisasi*, the Korean *Gukje Hwa*, the Nepali *bishwavya-pikaran*, the Sinhalese *jatyanthareekaranaya*, the Tagalog *globalisasyon*, the Thai *lokanuvat*, the Timorese *luan bo'ot* and the Vietnamese *toan kou hoa*. All are new terms, or ascribe a new meaning to a pre-existent word.

When new vocabulary gains currency, it is often because it captures an important change that is taking place in the world. New terminology is needed to describe new conditions. For example, when Jeremy Bentham coined the word 'international' in the 1780s, it caught hold because it resonated of a growing trend of his day, namely, the rise of nation-states and cross-border transactions between them. People had not spoken of 'international relations' before this time, since social affairs had not previously been organized so deeply around national communities governed by territorial states.

The current spread of 'global talk' is also unlikely to be accidental. The popularity of this new terminology arguably reflects a widespread intuition that social relations have in contemporary times acquired an important new character. The challenge – indeed, the urgent need – is to move beyond the buzzword. When thinkers of the eighteenth century failed to clarify the emergent notion 'international', that concept became one of the weakest analytical lynchpins for many generations of modern social inquiry. As Peter Taylor has so rightly warned, 'we must ensure [that the term] globalization does not go down the same conceptually chaotic route as its 200-year old ancestor' (1995: 14).

Redundant concepts of globalization

So what distinctive idea can 'global-ness' convey? Approached in certain senses, 'globality' and 'globalization' open no substantial new insights that have not been available through pre-existent terminology. Sceptics have with good reason rejected such usages as soundbites. The following paragraphs find four of the five general notions of 'global' relations identified in Chapter 1 to be redundant in this way. The rest of the present chapter then develops the fifth conception – globality as supraterritoriality – which offers a qualitatively different understanding of social relations. This definition cannot be so readily dismissed as old hat and on the contrary tells us something new and important.

Probably the most common usage in everyday language has conceived of globalization as internationalization. As such, globalization refers to increases of interaction and interdependence between people in different countries. Considerable rises in cross-border exchanges have indeed occurred in recent decades, so it is understandable that the term globalization has come for many to mean internationalization.

However, interconnections between countries have also intensified at various earlier times during the 500-year history of the modern states-system. In particular, as already noted in Chapter 1, the late nineteenth century witnessed levels of cross-border migration, direct investment, finance and trade that, proportionately, are broadly comparable with those of the present. No vocabulary of 'globalization' was needed on previous occasions of internationalization, and the terminology of 'international relations' arguably remains quite sufficient to examine contemporary cross-border transactions and interlinkages. We should reserve the new word to designate something different.

A second definition – used especially by neoliberals as well as some of their more vociferous critics – has identified globalization as liberalization. In these cases a global world is one without regulatory barriers to transfers of resources between countries. In recent history we have indeed witnessed many reductions of statutory constraints on cross-border movements of goods, services, money and financial instruments. Hence, as with the first definition, it is understandable that people might associate globalization with liberalization.

Yet this second notion is also redundant. The long-established liberal discourse of 'free' trade is quite adequate to convey these ideas. 'Global-speak' was not needed in earlier times of widespread liberalization like the third quarter of the nineteenth century. There seems little need now to invent a new vocabulary for this old phenomenon. Again, let us look for a distinctive meaning of globalization.

A third common conception – globalization as universalization – also fails the test of providing new insight. True, more people and cultural phenomena than ever have in recent history spread to all habitable corners of the planet. However, moves toward universalization are hardly new to the contemporary world. For example, Clive Gamble writes of 'our global prehistory', arguing that the transcontinental spread of the human species – begun a million years ago – constitutes the initial instance of globalization (1994: ix, 8–9). Closer to our present, several world religions have for a thousand years and more extended across large expanses of the earth. Transoceanic trade has for centuries distributed various goods in 'global' (read world-scale) markets. Yet the pre-existent vocabulary of 'universality' and 'universalization' is quite adequate to describe these age-old conditions. In this regard, too, a new terminology of 'globalization' is unnecessary.

What of a fourth definition, that of globalization as westernization? This usage has arisen particularly in various arguments about post-colonial imperialism. Often in these cases globalization is associated with a process of homogenization, as all the world becomes western, modern and, more particularly, American. Such a conception is not surprising at a time when Madison Avenue and Hollywood have acquired such a planetary reach.

However, intercontinental westernization, too, has unfolded since long before the recent emergence of globe-talk. Concepts of 'modernization' or (for those who prefer an explicitly radical term) 'imperialism' are more than sufficient to convey ideas of westernization, Europeanization and Americanization. We do not need a new vocabulary of globalization to remake an old analysis. (Moreover, as is indicated in Chapter 7, the assumption that globalization undermines cultural diversity requires substantial qualification.)

The preceding remarks endorse the sceptics' position that talk of 'globalization' can be a social scientist's jargon, a journalist's catchphrase, a publisher's sales pitch, a politician's slogan, and a businessperson's fetish. Indeed, the four definitions outlined above between them cover most academic, official, corporate and popular discussion of things 'global'. Critics are right to assail the historical illiteracy that marks most claims of novelty associated with globality.

A distinctive concept of globalization

Yet can *all* talk of globality be dismissed as fad and hype? Are ideas of globalization *always* reducible to internationalization, liberalization, universalization or westernization? If new terminology spreads so far and attracts so much attention, might it not be more than a synonym for pre-existent vocabulary? Can we distinguish and specify such a distinctive concept of globalization?

Important new insight into relatively new conditions is in fact available from a fifth type of definition. This conceptualization identifies globalization as deterritorialization – or, as I would prefer, the growth of 'supraterritorial' relations between people. In this usage, 'globalization' refers to a far-reaching change in the nature of social space. The proliferation and spread of supraterritorial – or what we can alternatively term 'transworld' or 'transborder' – connections brings an end to what could be called 'territorialism', that is, a situation where social geography is entirely territorial. Although, as already stressed, territory still matters very much in our globalizing world, it no longer constitutes the whole of our geography.

A reconfiguration of social space has far-reaching significance. After all, space is one of the primary dimensions of social relations. Geography ranks on a par with culture, ecology, economy, politics and psychology as a core determinant of social life. The spatial contours of a society strongly influence the nature of production, governance, identity and community in that society – and vice versa. For example, differences between the lives of desert nomads, mountain villagers and island seafarers are largely attributable to contrasts in the places that they inhabit. The spatial and other primary aspects of social relations are deeply interconnected and mutually constitutive. If the character of society's map changes, then its culture, ecology, economics, politics and social psychology are likely to shift as well.

To be sure, we are referring here to questions of *macro* social space, that is, relating to the geographical setting of larger collective life: districts, countries, etc. Social space also has *micro* aspects that lie within a person's realm of direct sensory experience, such as the built environment. However, micro spaces are not of immediate concern to a discussion of globalization. (For more on different kinds of space and the relationship between space and society, see Lefebvre, 1974; Gregory and Urry, 1985; Massey, 1994.)

Each of the four other conceptions of globality discussed above is reconcilable with territorialist constructions of social space. In other words, these definitions presume that the map of society is solely and completely territorial. In territorial geography, relations between people are mapped on the earth's surface and measured on a three-dimensional grid of longitude, latitude and altitude. In a territorial framework, 'place' refers to a fixed location on such a map; 'distance' refers to the length of a track that connects points on this map; and 'border' refers to a line on this map which divides tracts on the earth's surface from each other. Territorialism implies that macro social space is wholly organized in terms of units such as districts, towns, provinces, countries and regions. In times of *statist* territorialism more particularly, countries have held pride of place above the other kinds of territorial realms.

Until recently, social geography across the world had a territorialist character. Indeed, even today many people use the terms 'geography' and 'territory' interchangeably, as if to exclude the possibility that space could be nonterritorial. Under conditions of territorialism, people identify their 'place' in the world primarily in relation to territorial locations. (In most cases this territorial reference point is fixed, though for nomadic groups the spot may shift.) In times of nationalism, the foremost territorial 'home' has usually been a country. Moreover, in a territorialist world the length of territorial distances between places and the presence or absence of territorial (especially state) borders between places tends heavily to influence the general frequency and significance of contacts that people at different sites might have with each other. Thus people normally have most of their interactions and affiliations with others who share the same territorial space: for example, the same village, the same county, the same country, or the same continent.

Yet current history has witnessed a proliferation of social connections that are at least partly – and often quite substantially – detached from a territorial logic of the kind just described. Take, for instance, telephone calls, electronic finance and the depletion of stratospheric ozone. Such phenomena cannot be situated at a fixed territorial location. They operate largely without regard of territorial distance. They substantially bypass territorial borders. Thus, technologically speaking, a telephone conversation can occur across an ocean as readily as across a street. Today money deposited with a major bank is mostly stored in 'placeless' cyberspace rather than in a vault. Ozone depletion exists everywhere on earth at the same time, and its relative distribution across different parts of the world shifts without regard to territorial distances or borders. The geography of these *global* conditions cannot be understood in terms of territoriality alone; they also reside in the world as a single place – that is, in a *transworld* space.

Understood in this sense, globality marks a distinct kind of space–time compression, and one that is mostly new to contemporary history. To be sure, the world has long been 'shrinking', as territorial distances have been covered in progressively shorter time intervals. Thus, whereas Marco Polo took years to complete his journey across Eurasia in the thirteenth century, by 1850 a sea voyage from South East Asia to North West Europe could be completed in 59 days. In the twentieth century, motorized ships and land vehicles took progressively less time again to link territorial locations. Nevertheless, such transport still requires measurable time spans to cross territorial distances, and these movements still face substantial controls at territorial frontiers. Although speed has markedly increased, proximity in these cases is still closely related to territorial distance and borders.

In the case of global transactions, in contrast, 'place' is not territorially fixed, territorial distance is covered in effectively no time, and territorial boundaries present no particular impediment. Satellite television, the US dollar, the women's movement, the anthropogenic greenhouse effect and many other contemporary conditions have a pronounced *supraterritorial* quality. Globality (as supraterritoriality) describes circumstances where territorial space is substantially transcended. Phenomena like Coca-Cola and faxes 'touch down' at territorial locations, but they are also global in the sense that they can extend anywhere in the world at the same time and can unite locations anywhere in effectively no time. The geography of, for instance, Visa credit cards and world service broadcasts has little to do with territorial distances, and these *transborder* flows – that is, relations that transcend territorial frontiers – largely escape controls at state boundaries. Likewise, where, using specific and fixed territorial coordinates, could we situate Special Drawing Rights (SDRs), the Rushdie affair, the magazine *Elle*, the debt of the Brazilian government, karaoke, the production of a Ford automobile, and the law firm Clifford Chance?

All such circumstances reside at least partly across the planet as one more or less seamless sphere. Global conditions like Internet connections can and do surface simultaneously at any point on earth that is equipped to host them. Global phenomena like a news flash can and do move almost instantaneously across any distance on the planet.

Place, distance and borders only retrieve vital significance in respect of global activities when the earth is contrasted to extraterrestrial domains. Thus, for example, the 'border' of the New York Stock Exchange lies at the communications satellites that orbit the earth and instantaneously transmit messages from investors the world over to Wall Street. Time again becomes a significant factor in respect of radio signals when they have to cover interplanetary and longer distances. However, within the domain of our planet, location, distance and borders place no insurmountable constraints on supraterritorial relations. In this sense they are suitably called 'global' phenomena.

Various researchers across a range of academic disciplines have discerned a rise of supraterritoriality in contemporary history without using that precise word. Already at mid-century, for example, the philosopher Martin Heidegger proclaimed the advent of 'distancelessness' and an 'abolition of every possibility of remoteness' (1950: 165–6). Forty years later the geographer David Harvey described 'processes that so revolutionize the objective qualities of space and time that we are forced to alter, sometimes in quite radical ways, how we represent the world to ourselves' (1989: 240). The sociologist Manuel Castells has distinguished a 'network society', in which a new 'space of flows' exists alongside the old 'space of places' (1989: 348; 1996–7). In the field of International Relations, John Ruggie has written of a 'nonterritorial region' in contemporary world affairs (1993: 172).

Hence globality in the sense of transworld simultaneity and instantaneity – in the sense of a single world space – refers to something distinctive that other vocabulary does not cover. Some readers may cringe at the apparent jargon of 'globality', 'supraterritoriality', 'transworld' connections and 'transborder' relations. Yet pre-existent words like 'international', 'supranational' and 'transnational' do not adequately capture the key *geographical* point at issue. New terminology is unavoidable.

As already intimated, the present analysis employs the four adjectives 'global', 'supraterritorial', 'transworld' and 'transborder' as synonyms. Partly this practice is a stylistic device that permits some variation of vocabulary. More importantly, however, different readers may find that one or the other of these words – or their use in combination – is more effective in denoting the distinctive type of social geography that is under discussion here.

The difference between globality and internationality needs in particular to be stressed. Whereas international relations are *inter*territorial relations, global relations are *supra*territorial relations. International relations are *cross*-border exchanges *over* distance, while global relations are *trans*-border exchanges *without* distance. Thus global economics is different from international economics, global politics is different from international politics, and so on. Internationality is embedded in territorial space; globality transcends that geography.

In addition, global (as *trans*border) relations are not the same as *open*-border transactions. True, contemporary liberalization has sometimes occurred in tandem with globalization. The recent large-scale removal of statutory restrictions on transactions between countries has both responded to and facilitated the rise of supraterritoriality. However, the two trends remain distinct. Liberalization is a question of regulation, whereas globalization (as relative deterritorialization) is a question of geography.

Global events are also distinct from universal circumstances. Universality means being spread worldwide, while globality implies qualities of transworld concurrence and coordination. True, universalization has sometimes transpired in tandem with globalization, both encouraging and being encouraged by the growth of supraterritoriality. However, the two trends remain distinct. Universality says something about territorial extent, whereas globality says something about space–time relations.

Likewise, global conditions are not by definition the same as western, European, American or modern conditions. To be sure (as is further seen in Chapter 4), modern social forces like rationalist knowledge, capitalist production and machine technology have done much to propel the rise of supraterritoriality. In addition, governments, firms and other actors based in Western Europe and the USA have ranked among the most enthusiastic promoters of globalization. However, globality and modernity are not equivalent. At most it might be argued that globalization marks an advanced phase of modernization, although, as noted earlier, some analyses associate globalization with a move to postmodernity.

To stress this key point once more: globalization as it is understood here is *not* the same thing as internationalization, liberalization, universalization or modernization. It is crucial to note that commentators who reject the novelty and transformative potential of 'globalization' have almost invariably conflated the term with one of the four redundant usages. To appreciate the arguments put forward in this book, the logic and the evidence must be assessed in the light of a fifth, different definition of globalization as the rise of supraterritoriality and, therefore, a relative deterritorialization of social life. I would ask sceptical readers please to suspend (at least temporarily) their preconceived definitions and to give the suggested alternative notion of globalization a hearing in the chapters that follow.

A survey of global activities

To clarify further the concept of globalization as the rise of supraterritoriality, it may be useful briefly to survey a range of transborder activities in contemporary social life. Such a review also reinforces the claim that globality has become a significant feature across contemporary society, though – to stress the key qualification again – it has not affected all the world's people in the same ways and to the same extent.

In terms of *communications*, for example, a wide range of supraterritorial connections have been forged through air corridors, electromagnetic waves and light pulses. Global communications enable persons anywhere on earth to have nearly immediate contact with each other, largely irrespective of the territorial distances and territorial borders that lie between them. For instance, jet aeroplanes accomplish overnight transworld deliveries of people, post, and other cargoes. Unpiloted missiles likewise can in little time carry shipments across any territorial distance and past any territorial border. (Indeed, one such weapon has been appropriately called 'Minuteman'.) In the area of telecommunications, the telegraph, telephone, facsimile, telex, videoconference and computer networks allow signs, text, images and sound to move instantaneously between people, regardless of their territorial position or the territorial distances and borders between them. Fibre-optic cables have vastly increased the volumes of material that can be sent via telecommunications. Electronic mass media such as radio and television broadcast messages everywhere on earth in effectively no time. In addition, certain newspapers, magazines, books, music recordings, films and videos are released simultaneously across the world.

A second group of global activities has appeared in respect of *markets*. A global market exists when a product is distributed and sold in a transworld space through a coordinated supraterritorial business strategy. In this way consumers dispersed across the world concurrently purchase the same good or service, often under a single brand name like Pepsi-Cola or Toyota. Already in the 1980s Howard Perlmutter of the Wharton Business School identified 136 industries where a global marketing strategy had supposedly become vital to commercial success (Main, 1989: 55). The enormous range of global commodities has come to include many raw materials, packaged foods, bottled beverages, cigarettes, designer clothes, household articles and appliances, pharmaceuticals, music recordings, audio-visual productions, printed publications, online information services, financial instruments, office equipment, armaments, transport vehicles, travel services and more. Citicorp has proclaimed itself to be 'your global bank' and Peter Stuyvesant has marketed itself as 'the global cigarette'. Transborder products have come to figure in the everyday lives of most of humanity, whether through actual purchases or through unfulfilled desires evoked by global advertising.

Some, though by far not all, global commodities are connected with a third type of supraterritorial activity, namely, transworld *production*. In so-called 'global factories', different stages of a production process are sited at several (perhaps widely scattered) locations. Thus, in principle, the research centre, design unit, procurement office, fabrication plant, finishing point, assembly line, quality control operations, data processing office, advertising bureau and after-sales service could each be situated in different provinces, countries and regions. Supraterritorial production involves intra-firm trade within a global company as well as, if not more than, international trade between countries. Through so-called 'global sourcing', a producer draws the necessary inputs from anywhere in the world. Differences in local costs of labour, regulation and taxation figure more importantly in these business calculations than the costs of transport across distance and borders between the various sites in the global production chain. Supraterritorial production has developed especially in the manufacture of textiles, clothing, motor vehicles, leather goods, sports articles, toys, optical products, consumer electronics, semiconductors, aeroplanes and construction equipment.

Global communications, global markets and global production have all promoted, and been facilitated by, a fourth area of global activity, namely, in relation to *money*. For one thing, the 'American' dollar, the 'Japanese' yen, the 'German' mark and other major 'national' currencies have undergone a significant degree of deterritorialization. They circulate globally, being used anywhere on earth at the same time and moving (electronically and via air transport) anywhere on earth in effectively no time. In addition, the SDR and the euro have emerged through the IMF and the EU, respectively, as suprastate monies with transworld use. Many bankcards can extract cash in local currency from the thousands of automated teller machines (ATMs) across the world that are connected to supraterritorial networks like Cirrus. Meanwhile digital money can be stored on certain smart cards (so-called 'electronic purses') in multiple currencies at once. Several credit cards like Visa, MasterCard and American Express can be used for payments at countless establishments in almost every country across the planet. In these various ways money has become considerably (though of course not completely) detached from territorial space.

Globalization has also transpired in many areas of *finance*. For instance, most foreign exchange transactions today take place through a round-the-world, round-the-clock market that connects the dealing rooms of London, New York, Tokyo, Zürich, Frankfurt, Hong Kong, Singapore, Paris and Sydney. In global banking, depositors place their savings in a global currency and/or at a global bank and/or at a global branch location such as a so-called 'offshore' financial centre. These practices contrast with territorial banking, in which clients deposit their savings in their national currency at a local or national bank within their country of residence. Meanwhile global bank loans occur when a lender (or a syndicate of lenders, perhaps across several countries) provides credit in a global currency. Thus, for example, a group of banks based in Austria, the Netherlands and the UK might issue a loan in US dollars to a borrower in the Dominican Republic. The level of interest on such a credit is generally not the prevailing national percentage, but a function of a supraterritorial benchmark like the London Inter-Bank Offered Rate (LIBOR). Similarly, global bonds (often called 'eurobonds' in the trade) involve a supraterritorial currency as well as borrowers, investors, a syndicate of managers, and a securities exchange that are spread across multiple countries. Global transactions also occur on similar lines in respect of medium-term notes and short-term credit instruments like treasury bills and commercial paper. In equity markets, meanwhile, global shares are company stocks that are listed simultaneously on several securities exchanges across the world. For their part derivatives can have a global character when, for example, the same futures contract is traded simultaneously on the Chicago, Singapore and London markets, as well as through electronic links between them. Many contemporary insurance policies, too, have global coverage in a global currency and/or are handled by global companies in global financial centres. In addition, many private and institutional investors maintain global portfolios. That is, they spread their funds across banks, stocks, bonds, money-market tools and derivatives contracts from around the world. Indeed, with global dealing, a broker can buy and sell financial instruments anywhere in the world instantaneously with a telephone call or the click of a mouse. It is clear, even without delving into the often obscure technical details of financial markets, that much of today's foreign exchange, banking, securities, derivatives and insurance business occurs with considerable delinkage from territorial space.

As one might expect, global communications, global markets, global production, global monies and global finance have given rise to many global *organizations*. Some of these supraterritorial institutions have regulatory functions and can suitably be called global governance agencies. For example, the activities of UN organs, the IMF, the World Bank, the WTO, the Bank for International Settlements (BIS) and other such bodies extend across the planet. These institutions formulate, implement and to some extent enforce a host of transworld norms, rules and procedures in wide-ranging areas including technical standards and (purportedly) universal human rights. Other global organizations pursue mainly commercial activities. They include tens of thousands of global companies, often imprecisely named 'multinational corporations'. In addition, businesses have developed various types of transborder coalitions (through joint ventures, subcontracting, franchises and so on) that are collectively called 'strategic alliances'. Finally, many civic associations today have a global organization. On the one hand, so-called 'global civil society' includes thousands of transborder agencies. These business lobbies, trade union confederations, religious bodies, NGOs and other nonofficial, noncommercial organizations have a transworld membership and maintain operations across many countries simultaneously. In addition, many localized civic groups organize globally with each other through transborder networks and coalitions.

Ecologically, a planetary life-support system has of course operated from the moment that life first appeared on earth, namely, in respect of the atmosphere and the hydrosphere. However, in contemporary history *social ecology* has also gained certain supraterritorial qualities. In other words, not only natural environmental developments, but also anthropogenic (i.e. human-induced) ecological changes have acquired a global dimension. For example, the anthropogenic greenhouse effect is allegedly producing planetary climate change, popularly known as 'global warming'. Neither the causes nor the effects of this trend can be territorially specified and restricted. Similarly, as noted earlier, stratospheric ozone depletion is effectively a placeless, distanceless, borderless anthropogenic condition. With respect to the biosphere, the contemporary world-as-a-single-place is experiencing major reductions both in the numbers of species of life and in the variety of genes that circulate within individual species. Like climate change and so-called 'ozone holes', the loss of biological diversity has a number of supraterritorial sources and consequences. Other ecological conditions with an at least partly global character include radioactive fallout, transborder migrations of sulphur dioxide and nitrogen oxide (so-called 'acid rain'), the depletion of tropical moist forests, desertification, changes in sea level, marine pollution, and possible future shortages of fresh water and arable soil. Although the severity of these various environmental problems can be debated, it is clear that none of them can be territorially contained.

Finally, globality is evident in social activity through global *consciousness*. That is, social space has a supraterritorial dimension in part because we often think globally. Thus, in addition to holding microcosmic conceptions of 'society' as a district or a country, many people now also hold macrocosmic notions, where the planet is regarded as a 'global village'. With globalization we conceive of the world not only as a patchwork of territorial realms, but also as a single place where territorial distance and borders are (at least in certain respects) irrelevant. We identify the planet as a principal source of our food supplies, our entertainments and our friends. Global consciousness also takes form as certain languages (e.g. English and Spanish), certain narratives (e.g. the *Dallas* television series), certain icons (e.g. the Teletubbies) and other symbols obtain transworld currency. Awareness of the world as a single place is furthermore evident in events like global sports competitions,

Global activities in summary

Communications
- air transport
- telecommunications
- electronic mass media
- global publications

Markets
- global products
- global sales strategies

Production
- global production chains
- global sourcing of inputs

Money
- global currencies
- bank cards connected to global ATM networks
- digital cash on electronic purses
- global credit cards

Finance
- global foreign-exchange markets
- global banking (both deposits and loans)
- global bonds ('eurobonds') and bond trading
- global shares and share dealing
- global derivatives markets
- global insurance business

Organizations
- global governance agencies
- global companies
- global corporate strategic alliances
- global civic associations

Social ecology
- global atmosphere (climate change, ozone depletion, radioactive fallout, acid rain)
- global biosphere (loss of biological diversity, deforestation)
- global hydrosphere (rising sea level, marine pollution, reduced fresh water)
- global geosphere (desertification, loss of arable soil)

Consciousness
- conceptions of the world as a single place
- global symbols
- global events
- global solidarities

global trade fairs, global tours by music superstars, and global conferences. In addition, global consciousness arises when people conceive of their social affiliations in nonterritorial terms, for example, with transborder solidarities based on class, gender, generation, race, religion and sexuality. In respect of thought patterns, Malcolm Waters has emphasized the point that 'the phenomenology of globalization is reflexive' as 'the inhabitants of the planet self-consciously orient themselves to the world as a whole' (1995: 63).

All of the many instances of globality just described (and summarized in the Box above) are discussed in greater detail later in this book, where these activities are also related to questions of deeper social structure. The present concise survey merely serves to demonstrate the widespread incidence of supraterritorial circumstances across much of contemporary social relations. Cumulatively, all of these global communications, markets, production processes, monies, finances, organizations, ecological developments and thoughts indicate that social space cannot today be understood in terms of territorial geography alone.

Farewell to methodological territorialism?

If contemporary social geography is not territorialist, then we need to adjust traditional approaches of social research. In other words, we must change the prevailing methodology, the established ways of conducting social inquiry. Methodological territorialism has had a pervasive and deep hold on the conventions of social research; thus globalization (when understood as the spread of supraterritoriality) implies a major reorientation of approach.

Methodological territorialism refers here to the practice of understanding the social world and conducting studies about it through the lens of territorial geography. Territorialist method means formulating concepts and questions, constructing hypotheses, gathering and interpreting empirical evidence, and drawing conclusions all in a territorial spatial framework. These habits are so engrained in prevailing methodology that most social researchers reproduce them unconsciously.

Methodological territorialism lies at the heart of mainstream conceptions of geography, economy, governance, community and society. Thus geographers have traditionally conceived of the world in terms of bordered territorial (especially country) units. Likewise, macroeconomists have normally studied production and distribution in relation to national (read territorial) and international (read interterritorial) activity. Students of politics have automatically treated governance as a territorial question (i.e. of local and national governments, with the latter sometimes meeting in so-called 'international' organizations). Similarly, anthropologists have usually conceived of culture and community with reference to territorial units (i.e. local and national peoples). Finally, territorialist habits have had most sociologists presume that 'society' by definition takes a territorial form: 'Chilean society', 'Iranian society', 'Hungarian society', etc.

Like any analytical device, methodological territorialism involves simplification. It offered a broadly viable intellectual shortcut in an earlier day of social inquiry. After all, the Westphalian states-system that arose in the seventeenth century and spread worldwide by the middle of the twentieth century was quintessentially territorial. Likewise, the mercantile and industrial activity that dominated capitalism during this period operated almost exclusively in territorial space. Similarly, the main forms of collective identities during these times (namely, ethnic groups and state-nations) had pronounced territorial referents. Nor did anthropogenic global ecological changes occur on any significant scale prior to the mid-twentieth century. Hence methodological territorialism reflected the social conditions of a particular epoch when bordered territorial units, separated by distance, formed far and away the overriding geographical framework for macro-level social organization.

However, territorialist analysis is not a timeless method. On the contrary, no scholarly research undertaken a thousand years ago made reference to bounded territorial spaces. After all, countries, states, nations and societies did not in that earlier epoch exist as clearly delineated territorial forms. Indeed, the world was not mapped as a sphere until the fourth century BC (by Dicaerchus in Sicily), and a grid to locate points on a map was not introduced until the second century AD (by Zhang Heng in China) (Douglas, 1996: 22). Maps showing the continents in anything like the territorial shape that we would recognize today were not drawn before the late fifteenth century. It took a further two hundred years before the first maps depicting bordered country units appeared (Campbell, 1987; Whitfield, 1994). Not until the high tide of colonialism in the late nineteenth and early twentieth centuries did a territorialist logic extend across all regions of human habitation on earth.

If methodological territorialism is a historical phenomenon, then it has an end as well as a beginning. There is no reason why, once installed, territorialist assumptions should last in perpetuity. The emergence of the states-system, the growth of mercantile and industrial capitalism, and the rise of national identities all understandably prompted the development of methodological territorialism several centuries ago. However, today widespread and accelerated globalization may stimulate another reconceptualization. If contemporary human circumstances have gained a substantial global dimension, then we need to develop an alternative, nonterritorialist cartography of social life.

To put the point starkly, how can territorialist thinking possibly be applied to today's world, given that it contains:

- nearly 1.5 billion (i.e. thousand million) commercial airline passengers per annum
- 17,000 strategic nuclear warheads for rapid delivery across any terrestrial distance
- nearly 900 million telephone lines
- 2 billion radio sets
- a billion television receivers
- 180 million Internet users
- thousands of global products
- several hundred million global credit cards
- yearly foreign-exchange turnover of $450 trillion (i.e. thousand billion)
- several trillion US dollars' worth of offshore bank deposits
- $60 trillion in annual transborder movements of securitized funds
- 44,500 transborder companies with collective annual sales of $7 trillion
- over 250 multilateral regulatory institutions
- 16,500 transborder civil society associations
- accelerated global warming
- enormous reductions in biological diversity

This list could be substantially lengthened, and most of the numbers currently show notable upward tendencies. None of the above circumstances existed to a remotely comparable extent in 1960 or at any earlier juncture in history. Of course, as statistics, each of the various indicators can be queried in one way or another. However, such a large accumulation of data surely suggests a significant trend away from territorialist social organization.

Indeed, it is arguably dangerous to give methodological territorialism further lease on life in the contemporary globalizing world. For one thing, territorialist assumptions about space are obviously unsuitable in respect of global ecological problems. Likewise, if significant parts of capitalism now operate with relative autonomy from territorial space, then old intellectual frameworks cannot adequately address the issues of distributive justice which have always accompanied processes of surplus accumulation. Similarly, a political theory that offers today's world only territorial constructions of community and democracy is obsolete. Evidence now abounds that contemporary globalization poses far-reaching challenges to ecological integrity, social equity, social cohesion and democracy. Hence the stakes in the call for the construction of a post-territorialist methodology are much more than academic.

Globality and territoriality

That said, we should not replace territorialism with a globalist methodology that neglects territorial spaces. The end of territorial*ism* owing to globalization has not meant the end of territoria*lity*. To say that social geography can no longer be understood in terms of territoriality *alone* is not to say that territoriality has become irrelevant. We inhabit a global*izing* rather than a fully global*ized* world. Indeed, the rise of supraterritoriality shows no sign of producing an end to territoriality.

The present book concentrates on the global aspects of contemporary history; however, many situations in social life at the start of the twenty-first century of course remain highly territorial. For example, many communication networks like road links, railways and shipping lanes are distinctly territorial. In addition, territorial borders continue to exert considerable influence on flows of merchandise trade, investment and migration (Helliwell, 1998). Lots of commodities (including countless foods, clothes, household items and entertainments) remain bound to particular territorial markets. Many production processes are still linked to specific places and limited to single countries. Territorially based commodities derived from agriculture and mining have persisted at the same time that supraterritorial commodities like information and communications have risen to prominence. Many currencies, credit cards and other money forms have restricted circulation within a given territorial space. Likewise, most people on earth today continue to hold their bank accounts locally or do no banking at all. Many local authorities, firms and civic groups maintain few if any direct links with global organizations. Much ecological degradation remains localized in terms of, for example, overgrazing, salination, or dumping of toxic wastes. In relation to social consciousness, Kidron and Segal have cautioned that 'some people see the world as their village' but 'most see their village as the world' (1995: 13). David Harvey has suggested that place-bound identities might actually have become *more* rather than less important in a world of diminishing territorial barriers (1993: 4).

The wording in this chapter has been deliberately formulated to indicate the continuing importance of territoriality next to spreading globality. For example, it has been explicitly said that globalization brings a *relative* rather than a complete deterritorialization of social life. Global relations have *substantially* rather than totally transcended territorial space. They are *partly* rather than wholly detached from territorial logics. Although territoriality places no *insurmountable* constraints on global circumstances, supraterritorial phenomena still have to engage at some level with territorial places, territorial governments and territorial identities. Much

more globalization – more than is in prospect for a long time to come –
would need to take place before territorial space became irrelevant.

Thus change (the proliferation of global connections) interrelates with
continuity (the persistence of territorial spaces). The challenge for social
research is to examine the intricate interplay of globality and territoriality.
Thus, for example, contemporary military strategy combines supraterritorial technologies like supersonic aircraft, missile rockets, radar and spy
satellites with territorial weaponry like tanks and artillery. Most telecommunications operators work under the approval of territorial states
and set their charges in relation to territorial units (that is, it costs such-
and-such to call Peru). Reception research has shown that local cultures
can produce highly divergent interpretations of a global mass media
production. Listeners and viewers bring a wide range of place-related
customs, needs, expectations and preferences to the global performance. A
number of global products have their source at fixed territorial locations,
such as the vineyards of Champagne or the diamond mines of South
Africa. On the sales end, global marketers often have to adjust article
design and advertising for a transworld product in ways that appeal to
local sensibilities. For example, McDonald's in India has a mutton-based
'Maharaja Mac' on its menu in place of the otherwise ubiquitous beef
burger. As already mentioned, local circumstances also deeply affect a
company's decision to situate part of its production process in one
province or country rather than another. In respect of global money, the
values and flows of supraterritorial currencies are influenced by decisions
taken by territorial states regarding money supply targets and interest
rates. Meanwhile even the most global of financial transactions are
conducted primarily at territorial places, especially the so-called 'global
cities' like London, New York, and Tokyo. As for global organizations,
their various branch offices have to pay at least some heed of locally
prevailing laws and customs. Moreover, many global firms have continued
to reflect, at least partly, a national style of business connected with their
country of origin. In the area of ecology, global problems have different
impacts at different territorial locales. To take but one obvious example,
the prospective rise in sea level on account of global warming has more
serious implications for coastal zones and small island states than elsewhere. Globality and territoriality can also intertwine in consciousness.
For instance, diasporas of Armenians, Chinese, Ghanaians, Irish and Sikhs
feel transworld unity and at the same time forge their solidarity around a
shared connection to a territorial homeland.

Finally, globalization is not antithetical to territoriality insofar as the
trend can be linked to many processes of *reterritorialization*. Such
developments occur when certain territorial units decline in significance
and other territorial configurations obtain increased importance. For

example, as is elaborated in Chapter 6, globalization has in various ways encouraged the concurrent contemporary trend of regionalization. In addition, the spread of supraterritorial circumstances has in many countries helped local authorities to gain greater autonomy *vis-à-vis* the national state. Furthermore, as is elaborated in Chapter 7, globalization has contributed to ethnic revivals which have encouraged the disintegration of pre-existent territorial states (like the former Czechoslovakia, Soviet Union and Yugoslavia) and their replacement with new ones.

The preceding paragraphs have highlighted the continuing relevance of territoriality in the contemporary globalizing world. At the same time, it is clear that territory acquires different kinds of significance when it intersects with global spaces. The move from three-dimensional geography (longitude, latitude and altitude) to four-dimensional space (these three plus globality) fundamentally changes the map of social relations. As later chapters indicate, this reconfiguration of geography has important implications for structures of production, governance, community and knowledge. We no longer inhabit a territorial*ist* world, and this change requires substantial shifts in the ways that we theorize and practise politics.

Chapter 3

Globalization in History

Main points of this chapter
The emergence of a global imagination: to the 18th century
Incipient globalization: 1850s–1950s
Full-scale globalization: 1960s–present
Conclusion

Main points of this chapter

- in terms of ideas of the planet as a single place, globality can be traced back many centuries
- material global relations began to develop from the middle of the nineteenth century
- the main, greatly accelerated rise of supraterritoriality has occurred since the 1960s

---

When did globalization start? How has it spread over time? Where will it go in the future? These are questions of globalization in history.

In its starkest form, the principal debate concerning the chronology and periodization of globalization is whether the development is old or new. At one extreme, proponents of an 'all-change' thesis do not look beyond the current generation and presume that globalization is entirely a recent historical turn. At another extreme, proponents of an 'all-continuity' argument highlight antecedents to contemporary developments – some-times running back many centuries – and assume that these earlier manifestations of globality had a level of prominence and intensity similar to that witnessed today. Both of these perspectives are flawed. The 'all-change' thesis suffers from historical myopia. The 'all-continuity' thesis suffers from insensitivity to proportion.

If we define globalization in terms of the spread of supraterritoriality, then its chronology has both longer term and contemporary dimensions. Some development of supraterritorial circumstances can be traced back several centuries, but large-scale, accelerated globalization has occurred chiefly during recent decades.

We can broadly distinguish three phases of globalization to date. First, global consciousness began to tease secular imaginations half a millennium ago. Second, supraterritoriality made its initial more substantial appearances from the middle of the nineteenth century and spread at a mostly gradual rate for the next hundred years. Third, global relations have mainly proliferated and attained their greatest significance since the 1960s.

Several footnotes are in order before we proceed to elaborate this three-part chronology. First – to give the obvious reminder – the historical survey presented in this chapter corresponds to a conception of globalization as the expansion of supraterritorial spaces. Were we to define globalization as internationalization, liberalization, universalization or westernization, then different chronologies and periodizations would apply.

Second, periodization is artificially neat. In practice sociohistorical developments cannot be divided into wholly discrete phases. Thus transitions between the three stages of globalization have not occurred clearly and completely at precise dates. Nevertheless, the historical shorthand of periodization gives us helpful general bearings.

Third, the periodization proposed here is not definitive. Alternative chronologies are available. For example, Roland Robertson has distinguished five phases of globalization between the early fifteenth and late twentieth centuries (1992: 58–9).

Fourth, although globalization to date has shown progressive acceleration, the trend is not inherently linear. In principle globalization could in a future fourth phase slow, stall or reverse. However, owing to the strong forces that currently propel globalization (as discussed in Chapter 4), most present signs point to considerable additional growth of supraterritoriality in the years to come.

Finally, a note must be added concerning the data that are presented below as evidence of the emergence and spread of global relations. Some of the statistics refer to *cross-border* activities: for example, international telephone calls, international civic associations and international bank loans. These figures underestimate the extent of globalization. After all, intranational telecommunications, intranational civic activities that address global problems, and intranational electronic finance also manifest supraterritorial qualities. However, because the concept of globality-as-supraterritoriality has not yet consolidated in social analysis, various global (as distinct from international) statistics are not available. Nevertheless, we can use some data on cross-border transactions to infer increases in supraterritorial relations.

The emergence of a global imagination: to the 18th century

Globalization has no origin, in the sense of a exact starting point. Rather, the trend had a long gestation period without a precise moment of conception. The technology to produce material supraterritorial social space did not begin to become available until the nineteenth century, for example, with the invention of the telegraph and the telephone. However, global consciousness had already entered some imaginations well before this time.

Ideas of the earth as a single place are latent in several of those knowledges that we call, perhaps tellingly, *world* religions. The first such faiths emerged during the fifth and sixth centuries BC with Zoroastrianism and Buddhism. More concretely, Jews have for centuries held a notion of supraterritorial community that unites their diaspora, wherever on earth it might extend. Meanwhile Christianity manifested globalist aspirations long before Isaac Watt published his hymn 'Jesus Shall Reign Where'er the Sun' in 1719. The Muslim faithful of the eighth and subsequent centuries were inspired by a vision of one world under Islam.

Intimations of secular global thinking can be traced back half a millennium. For example, in the fourteenth century several writers including Dubois, Dante and Marsilius of Padua made proposals for suprastate governance that would encompass at least all of Christendom (cf. Hinsley, 1963: ch 1). Notions of international law, which consolidated from the sixteenth century onwards, likewise held the premise that a single set of secular rules should apply across the whole 'civilized' world. Needless to say, the means (in terms of global communications and global organizations) were not available at this time to implement regulations that could be applied simultaneously and instantaneously anywhere on earth.

On the other hand, a few creative minds of the sixteenth century were already beginning to imagine the possibility of global communication. In literature, for instance, Shakespeare's Puck in *A Midsummer Night's Dream* thought to 'put a girdle round about the earth in forty minutes' (1595–6: 38). Meanwhile Mother Skipton of Yorkshire prophesied that 'around the world thought will fly, in the twinkling of an eye' (Young, 1991: 1). Ideas of globality also inspired several voyagers of the fifteenth and sixteenth centuries to attempt a circumnavigation of the earth, a feat first accomplished in 1522.

Incipient global consciousness was also evident in Enlightenment thought of the eighteenth century. Philosophers such as A. R. J. Turgot, Johann Gottfried Herder and the Marquis de Condorcet were concerned with the history of humanity as a whole and moreover discerned a trend toward a social unification of the world (Kilminster, 1997: 262–4). Turgot, for example, forecast that, 'finally commercial and political ties unite all parts of the globe' (1750: 41).

Other early global thinking emerged in the context of the development of capitalism. For example, during the eighteenth century a number of

London-based transatlantic traders considered themselves to be 'citizens of the world' (Hancock, 1995). Indeed, David Hume wrote, with reference to the rentier class of his day, 'These are men who have no connections with state, who enjoy their revenue in any part of the globe in which they choose to reside' (1741–2: 363).

However, capitalist transactions themselves remained thoroughly territorialized during this period. True, entrepreneurs sold coffee between and across continents as early as the thirteenth century, and transoceanic trade in tea, cocoa, cane sugar, precious metals, spices, tobacco and furs followed several hundred years later. However, this commerce involved only a few articles, traded in relatively small quantities, by a handful of companies, for a tiny minority of the world's population. Nor were these forerunners to global products distributed, priced and sold in the context of a tightly coordinated transworld marketing strategy.

Likewise, *international* money and finance of early capitalist development did not have qualities of simultaneous and instantaneous exchanges involving any place on earth. Between the thirteenth and fifteenth centuries, bankers in Italy made long-distance loans to England, Flanders and the Balkans. In the eighteenth century commercial houses in Amsterdam and Geneva lent money to governments across Europe as well as to the newly founded American federation (Cameron and Bovykin, 1991). Meanwhile two merchant banks, Hope & Co and Barings, operated on stock exchanges in several countries. However, these international financial dealings were quite rare. They were also bilateral: that is, conducted between financiers in one country and a client in a second country. Moreover, it took considerable time to transact the business over distance. For example, although the speed was remarkable for its day, it still took a number of days for financial panic to travel several hundred kilometres between London and Amsterdam in 1745 and between London and Paris in 1825 (Neal, 1985).

In sum, prior to the nineteenth century globality had little existence outside the mind. Supraterritorial communications, markets, production, monies, finance, organizations and social ecology were absent. Moreover, global consciousness touched few minds of this early period. Even for that small minority, globality was usually a passing rather than a central thought.

Incipient globalization: 1850s–1950s

The means to take globality beyond the imagination into more substantive social relations began to develop from the middle of the nineteenth century. The hundred years after 1850 saw the advent of the first global communications technologies, the consolidation of the first global markets, some elements of global finance, and a degree of globality in certain organizations. In extent, this globalization can in no way be compared with the accelerated rise of supraterritoriality that we have witnessed since the middle of the twentieth century. Moreover, transborder production chains and transworld ecological problems were wholly absent at this earlier time. Nevertheless, much groundwork for subsequent full-scale globalization was laid between the mid-nineteenth and mid-twentieth centuries.

Communications

Supraterritorial communications emerged during the phase of incipient globalization with the spread of distance-conquering telegraph lines from the 1850s, transborder telephone connections and radio communications from the 1890s, and intercontinental air transport from 1919.

The telegraph provided the first means of global communications. Submarine telegraph links became available in the early 1850s across several seas within Europe. A transatlantic cable came permanently into use from 1866. Five years later telegraph lines stretched continuously from Europe to as far as China, Japan and Australia, although the first transpacific cable did not become operational until 1903 (Ahvenainen, 1981). With these connections, information could cross the world in a few days rather than a month. The telegraph's significance for globalization was presciently articulated at mid-century by the novelist Nathaniel Hawthorne, who exclaimed through one of his characters that 'by means of electricity, the world of matter has become a great nerve, vibrating thousands of miles in a breathless point of time' (1851: 273).

The late nineteenth century also introduced distanceless voice communication by telephone. The first transborder telephone calls became possible with a line connecting London and Paris in 1891. Two-way telephone messages across the Atlantic Ocean were first achieved via radio waves in 1926. During the next five years radio telephony also came to link Buenos Aires with Madrid, Batavia (now Jakarta) with Amsterdam, and London with Cape Town, Sydney and Auckland. By 1933 an advertisement of the American Telephone and Telegraph Company (AT&T) could justifiably claim that 'the world is bound together by telephone' (Young, 1991).

As for radio, the first transborder wireless transmission came in 1899, across the English Channel. A transatlantic radio signal was successfully received for the first time in 1901. World services on the wireless developed from 1924. The first planetary radio event occurred in January 1930, when the speech of King George V opening the London Naval Conference was relayed simultaneously to 242 radio stations spread across six continents.

By the mid-1930s the world counted 57 million radio receivers, more than 1,100 radio stations, and 1,354 transborder radio programmes (Huth, 1937).

The early twentieth century also witnessed the advent of mechanized air transport. Air mail services began in 1918, and the first nonstop transatlantic flight was achieved in 1919. A team of pilots crossed the Eurasian landmass from Amsterdam to Batavia in just over four days in 1933. In 1942 a recently defeated candidate for the US presidency could experience what he called 'one world' by flying around the planet in 160 hours (Willkie, 1943).

However, Wendell Willkie had very small company with his jet lag in the 1940s. Before the 1960s global communications were, with the exception of radio, outside the experience of all but small circles of people. Early transworld telegraphy, telephony and air transport had relatively slow speeds, very low capacities, notoriously poor reliability and extremely high costs. For example, the price of a telephone call from London to New York in 1927 was almost a thousand times higher in real terms than the rate prevailing in 1996 (*FT*, 23 December 1996: 17). The fax machine exhibited at the World's Fair of 1939 required eighteen minutes to transmit a single sheet of paper (Gelernter, 1995).

Markets

The phase of incipient globalization also brought the start of some systematic transworld distribution, pricing, promotion and sale of certain commodities. For example, a prototypical global market in copper consolidated from the 1850s onwards, interlinking shipments from Australia, Chile, Cuba, England and the USA. The London Metal Exchange (LME), established in 1876, handled any deal in copper, tin, lead and zinc, wherever in the world the supplies originated and regardless of whether the cargoes ever landed on British soil (EIU, 1957). Global pricing dynamics also developed at this time in respect of grains and cotton, especially between the commodities exchanges at Buenos Aires, Cairo, Calcutta, Chicago, Liverpool, New York, Rio de Janeiro and Winnipeg (Baer and Saxon, 1949).

Global markets in brandname packaged goods also started to emerge in the late nineteenth century. For example, products such as Campbell Soup and Heinz foods became household articles across several countries from the mid-1880s. Coca-Cola was marketed in Britain, Canada, Cuba, Mexico and the USA within 20 years of the drink's introduction in 1886. Office equipment from Remington Typewriter, agricultural machinery from International Harvester, and appliances from Western Electric also began to be marketed between and across continents from the late nineteenth century. By the 1880s Singer covered three-quarters of the world market in sewing machines (Chandler, 1986: 415–16). With the expansion of colonial settlement and other transoceanic migration during this period, expatriates from Europe, Asia and North America took their demand for 'home' products with them to all corners of the earth. In 1899 J. Walter Thompson was the first advertising agency to open an office outside its country of origin, presaging the development of transborder commercial promotion campaigns (Mattelart, 1989: 3).

The range of global products continued to grow in the early twentieth century. Transborder marketing was started for Bayer aspirin, Gillette razors, National Cash Register and Otis Elevator. From the outset in 1908, Henry Ford regarded his best-selling automobile, the Model T, as a 'world car' (Spybey, 1996: 41). By 1929 Coca-Cola was bottled in 27 countries and sold in 78 lands. The supraterritorial character of the beverage was explicitly recognized during World War II, when it was promoted as 'the global high-sign' (Pendergrast, 1993). The basis for other well-known global products was laid with the arrival of Nescafé in 1938, the long-play phonograph in 1948, the Marlboro cowboy in 1954, and the first McDonald's restaurant in 1955.

Global markets in primary products also developed further in the first half of the twentieth century. While the LME and other commodity exchanges continued their operations, governments took the first initiatives (via multilateral commodity agreements) to establish transworld price controls on certain products, including sugar, coffee, rubber and tin. During the World War II, the Allies created a number of so-called Combined Boards for the global coordination of production and distribution of several dozen strategic raw materials and manufactures. After the war an International Emergency Food Council briefly operated a global programme to combat world hunger in 1946–7.

However, the globalization of markets prior to 1960 must not be overestimated. Products with simultaneous worldwide distribution and sale were few in number at this time. Moreover, even in these limited cases, marketing strategies lacked the tight transworld coordination that became possible in the late twentieth century with digital computers, advanced telecommunications and electronic mass media.

Money and finance

An incipient globalization of money and finance also occurred in the late nineteenth and early twentieth centuries. The sterling-based gold standard that prevailed from around 1870 to 1914 gave certain national currencies transworld circulation. The British pound was the prime global money of this day, but the Dutch guilder, the Japanese yen, the Mexican silver dollar and other denominations also figured in some trade and finance that were not directly connected to their 'home' jurisdictions. After the disruptions of World War I, a gold exchange standard was incompletely and temporarily restored in the 1920s. That said, foreign exchange trading during this phase of proto-globalization was minute compared to the levels of recent decades, and governments held small foreign exchange reserves.

Money became almost completely territorialized between the 1930s and the 1950s. True, a number of countries were at this time associated with the so-called sterling bloc or the dollar bloc. In addition, as colonies many other lands had their money closely linked to the currency of a distant metropole. However, these arrangements applied to rigidly bordered regional and imperial territories, not to global spaces.

Indeed, even under the two gold standards most money was shipped in paper and metal form over distance and across borders. Apart from limited sums of money wired by telegraph, currencies at this earlier time lacked the supraterritorial mobility made possible on a large scale later in the twentieth century by airborne shipments and transworld electronic fund transfers. Nor did the early spread of transborder relations involve distinct suprastate monies (like the SDR), traveller's cheques, global bank passes or global credit cards.

In finance, the gold standard and colonialism encouraged a number of commercial banks to develop overseas branch networks. On the eve of World War I, British-based institutions held between a quarter and a third of all bank deposits in countries including Argentina, Australia, Brazil and New Zealand (Jones, 1993: 40). The major banks of the day lent large sums across borders and suffered an international debt crisis in the 1870s when a world economic downturn stopped many repayments.

However, this *international* banking of the late nineteenth and early twentieth centuries was heavily constrained by territorial distance and borders. Very few people maintained bank accounts outside their country of residence. Offshore banking facilities did not appear (and then only on a small scale) until Luxembourg passed relevant legislation in 1929, followed by Guernsey in 1936, and Jersey and the Netherlands Antilles in 1940. Globally syndicated bank loans were also unknown at this time.

Something more akin to a global debt dynamic (that is, one that potentially encompasses places anywhere on earth and has near-instantaneous transworld effects) emerged after World War I. The German state owed enormous reparations to the Allies, who among themselves owed some $26.5 billion in war debt, much of it to the USA, which in turn made substantial loans to Germany in order to facilitate reparations payments. A string of multilateral conferences grappled with this complex web of financial obligations from 1920 until all war debts and reparations were cancelled in 1932.

In securities markets, meanwhile, the gold standard facilitated a proliferation of foreign bond issues in the late nineteenth century. For example, bonds issued in Europe funded much of the California Gold Rush as well as railway construction in the Americas, China and Russia. In total, the tsarist regime in Russia borrowed some $1.5 trillion in present-day US dollar values on the Paris bond market between 1880 and 1913.

In regard to stocks, listings of nonresident companies figured (as a proportion of total quotations) as significantly on the Amsterdam and London stock exchanges in the 1870s as they did in the 1980s (Neal, 1985: 226). On the other hand, no amount of discounting for inflation could take the £5 billion worth of externally listed shares in world finance of the late nineteenth century anywhere close to the figure of several trillion pounds today.

In any case, such securities transactions of the nineteenth century had a distinctly *international* character. That is, savers in one country invested in a second country using the currency of either the originating or the receiving country. The transactions involved no global money, no global syndicates of fund managers, no global pool of investors, and no global portfolios. Moreover, brokers lacked the technology for instantaneous transworld trading. Nor were electronic global clearing and settlement systems available.

In short, some money and finance obtained certain global features in the period 1870–1914. These characteristics resurfaced to a limited extent and temporarily during the 1920s. However, these monetary and financial transactions were on the whole more international than global. They occurred for the most part between country units and under major constraints of distance and borders.

Organizations

Incipient global communications, markets, money and finance encouraged – and were at the same time encouraged by – the formation of prototypical global organizations in the late nineteenth and early twentieth centuries. These institutions included a number of market actors, regulatory agencies and civil society bodies.

In terms of firms, the cross-border activities of certain banks, mining companies, agricultural businesses and manufacturers have already been mentioned. A few industrial concerns began not only to sell their goods across several countries in the nineteenth century, but also to establish subsidiaries to pursue production outside the base country. In the first such instance, the US-based gun maker Colt opened a factory in Britain in 1852 (Stopford and Strange, 1991: 13). Similarly, Siemens of Germany built a facility in Russia in 1855, and Kikkoman of Japan set up soy sauce manufacture in the USA in 1892 (Jones, 1996). By the early twentieth century several hundred firms operated across colonial empires or in several state jurisdictions at once. On the other hand, these companies did not pursue global production, in the sense that different stages of a process were sited at widely dispersed locations.

The late nineteenth century also witnessed the creation of the first regulatory agencies with a worldwide remit (Murphy, 1994). These bodies included the International Telegraph (now Telecommunication) Union (ITU), founded in 1865, and the General (now Universal) Postal Union, founded in 1874. Organizations for transworld monitoring of disease, weather and so on followed before the turn of the century. In the 1920s and 1930s the League of Nations developed an unprecedented breadth – if perhaps still relatively shallow depth – of transworld governance. The International Criminal Police Organization (Interpol) launched its transborder pursuit of lawbreakers in 1923. The formation of the BIS in 1930 introduced the first multilateral institution devoted specifically to monitoring transborder financial flows. The basis for still larger expansion of global governance was laid in the 1940s with the creation of the UN system, the Bretton Woods institutions (the IMF and the World Bank) and the General Agreement on Tariffs and Trade (GATT).

Parts of civil society, too, began to acquire incipient global features between the mid-nineteenth and mid-twentieth century. For example, a number of Christian missionary societies and several Islamic revival movements coordinated their respective proselytization efforts across several continents at this time. The World Zionist Congress was formed in 1897. Transatlantic peace movements held a sequence of meetings in the 1840s and again around the turn of the century. Frequent transborder consultations also transpired towards the end of the nineteenth century among campaigners for women's suffrage. The labour movement maintained its First International in 1864–72, a Second International in 1889–1914, and a Third International (the Comintern) in 1919–43. By 1914 unions had set up more than two dozen International Trade Secretariats to support workers in particular industries (Lorwin, 1953). Meanwhile business circles founded the International Chamber of Commerce in 1920. In the area of humanitarian relief the International Red Cross and Red Crescent Movement dates back to 1863, while the Save the Children Fund was started in 1919. In respect of environmentalism, the first transborder initiatives at wildlife conservation were taken around the turn of the century (McCormick, 1989).

However, all of these firms, regulatory agencies and civic associations had a pretty weak supraterritorial (as opposed to international) character. In general, they operated between countries rather than in the world as a single place. The territorially based members of the organization (that is, company affiliates, governments or branch associations) maintained a high degree of autonomy from any global head office. Indeed, the global communications infrastructure of the time was not adequate to conduct tightly coordinated transworld campaigns and policies. Moreover, these prototypical global organizations had heavily restricted mobility, with limited possibilities to relocate offices and facilities to other places in the world.

Consciousness

All of the above incipient material globalization helped to spread global thinking to more contexts and to wider circles of people from the mid-nineteenth century onwards. For example, notions of a global unit spread through popular culture with events such as world fairs, first staged in 1851, and the modern Olympic Games, first held in 1896. Mass circulation newspapers also began to bring information from around the planet within easy reach of literate people everywhere. In a forerunner to contemporary global tourism, the pioneering travel agent Thomas Cook led his first round-the-world excursion in 1872.

Meanwhile prototypical global organizations gave expression to, and in turn deepened, a sense of transborder community in various circles. Supraterritorial religious and labour solidarities have already been mentioned. In addition, the late nineteenth century witnessed several projects to foster transworld racial solidarity. For instance, white Anglo-Saxon imperial federalism gathered adherents across the British Empire in the 1870s and 1880s, while the first intercontinental Pan-African Congress was held in 1893. Meanwhile first-generation feminists of the late nineteenth and early twentieth centuries developed some transworld solidarity based on gender. In this vein the writer Virginia Woolf made her renowned declaration that: 'As a woman I want no country. As a woman my country is the whole world' (1938: 197).

Global thinking continued to surface during this period in other literary and academic circles as well. Karl Marx recognized an incipient supra-territorial dimension in capitalism, while early sociologists like Emile Durkheim and Leonard Hobhouse also made perceptive observations of emergent globality (Scholte, 1993b: 21). One or two researchers of the late nineteenth century also had premonitions of transborder ecological problems like acid rain and global warming (McCormick, 1989: 182; Myers, 1996: 1). In 1926 the Fabian Society in London saw fit to convene a series of lectures on 'The Shrinking World' (Toynbee, 1948: 97). A few years later José Ortega y Gasset declared that 'the content of existence for the average man of to-day includes the whole planet' (1930: 29).

That said, global consciousness was at this time not central to everyday life. Indeed, a UNESCO survey conducted in 1962 estimated that 70 per cent of the world's population was unaware of happenings beyond the village (Connor, 1994: 27). Package holidays – which spurred the rise of large-scale transborder tourism and the idea that vacations could be taken anywhere in the world – were not introduced until 1949. Relatively few people professed and acted on a strong sense of global class, gender, racial or religious solidarity. Territorial identities, especially those linked to state and nation, tended to sweep aside all other constructions of community.

In summary, during a second phase of globalization, between the mid-nineteenth and mid-twentieth centuries, supraterritoriality appeared in many more forms and with substantially greater intensity than in prior times. On the other hand, the extent and depth of this early globalization bears no comparison with developments since the 1960s. Moreover, many forms of globality did not exist at all before the mid-twentieth century, such as electronic transworld finance, transborder production chains,

---

Summary chronology of incipient globalization, 1850s–1950s

1851	first world's fair
1852	establishment of the first foreign manufacturing subsidiary
1863	start of the first transborder relief organization
1864	creation of the first transborder labour organization
1865	formation of the first global governance agency
1866	first permanent transoceanic telegraph cable
1870	emergence of the first transworld monetary regime
1872	first round-the-world tourist excursion
1891	first transborder telephone connection
1896	first global sports event
1899	first transborder radio transmission
1918	inauguration of air mail
1919	first nonstop transatlantic flight
1920	inauguration of the League of Nations
1926	first transatlantic telephone call
1929	creation of the first offshore banking arrangements
1930	formation of the Bank for International Settlements
1944	creation of the International Monetary Fund and the World Bank
1945	formation of the United Nations system
1947	signing of the General Agreement on Tariffs and Trade
1949	first package holiday
1954	advent of the Marlboro cowboy
1956	first transoceanic telephone cable

supraterritorial television broadcasts, computer networks and global youth culture. Hence, although globalization has a longer history, the antecedents to contemporary conditions must not be exaggerated.

Full-scale globalization: 1960s–present

If conceived as the growth of supraterritorial spaces, then globalization has unfolded mainly since the 1960s. Although transworld relations are not completely novel, the pace and scale of their expansion has become qualitatively greater during the last four decades of the twentieth century. These years have seen far and away the greatest increase in the number, variety, intensity, institutionalization, awareness and impact of supraterritorial phenomena.

Communications

One of the most striking contemporary accelerations of globalization has occurred in respect of electronic communications (cf. Cairncross, 1997; Mowlana, 1997). For one thing, the relevant infrastructure has vastly grown. Transoceanic cables became available for telephone as well as telegraph messages from 1956, when the first such link connected Scotland and Newfoundland. Direct dialling between countries was introduced between London and Paris in 1963, the same year that a 'hot line' was installed in the spirit of détente between the Kremlin and the White House. By 1990 transworld direct-dial telephony was available in over 200 countries.

Over the same period the introduction of satellites and fibre-optic cables has hugely increased the carrying capacities of the global communications infrastructure. AT&T launched the first telecommunications satellite in 1962. The International Telecommunications Satellite Organization (INTELSAT), founded in 1964, today links 19 orbitals with earth stations in over 200 countries (INTELSAT, 1999). In addition, other concerns between them operate some 150 further communications satellites (Demac, 1986). Several transoceanic and transcontinental fibre-optic cables have been laid since 1988. Whereas the submarine telephone cable laid in 1956 could carry a maximum of 60 calls simultaneously, the Fibreoptic Link Around the Globe (FLAG) laid in 1996–7 can transmit up to 600,000 conversations concurrently. As of 1999 the enterprise Global Crossing had plans to link 160 business centres across the world with a network of 1.2 million miles of fibre-optic cable (*FT*, 8 October 1999: XIII). Given the enormous capacities offered by satellites and fibre optics, transborder telephone traffic burgeoned from 33 billion minutes in 1990 to 70 billion minutes in 1998 (UNDP, 1999: 25).

Telephone connection points have likewise proliferated in the past half-century. The 1965 world total of 150 million fixed lines rose to 851 million by 1998. In addition, reduced costs and improved performance have since 1979 turned mobile telephones into a mass consumer good. The world count of these devices increased from less than a million in 1985 to 305 million in 1998, with projected further growth to nearly one billion by 2003 (*FT*, 8 October 1999: VIII). Moderately priced fax machines also came on the market in the mid-1980s and numbered nearly 30 million worldwide by the mid-1990s.

Fibre-optic cables have also created large supraterritorial spaces for computer networks. The first transoceanic computer link, using a telex connection, was achieved in 1963. Communication between dispersed computer networks occurred for the first time in 1969, in the so-called ARPANET between researchers at four US universities. Company-wide so-called 'intranets' have developed since the late 1980s to coordinate production and sales operations, wherever in the world the various bureaux and employees might be situated. The publicly accessible Internet, a transworld 'meganetwork' linking millions of individual computers, emerged in the 1980s and expanded hugely in the 1990s. The number of computer systems connected to the Internet (or 'hosts') grew from 200 in 1981 to 300,000 in 1990 and over 50,000,000 in 1999 (ISC, 1999). Estimates of current and projected Internet use vary widely; however, a fair guess calculates that 180 million people across the world were on-line by the late 1990s (*FT*, 8 October 1999: XX). Electronic correspondence (e-mail) through the Internet overcomes all barriers of territorial distance and borders. Since the early 1990s the Internet has also developed a graphical dimension, the so-called World Wide Web. The many thousands of 'sites' on the Web provide near-instantaneous access to all manner of information for readers anywhere on earth.

Like computer networks, supraterritorial communications via television are new to the time of accelerated globalization. Transoceanic television transmissions via satellite were first achieved in 1962. The first live satellite television broadcast occurred in respect of a concert by the Beatles in 1967. Since then, hundreds of millions of people have simultaneously watched other 'global events' such as championship sports, moon landings and war reports. The number of television receivers worldwide rose from 75 million in 1956 to 1,096 million in 1994 (Brown, 1990: 115; UNESCO, 1997: 6.5). Television density nearly doubled from 121 per 1,000 people worldwide in 1980 to 235 per 1,000 in 1995 (UNDP, 1999: 4). Television transmissions via direct broadcast satellite (DBS), first achieved in 1976, have taken the additional step of bypassing earth stations and beaming signals straight to individual dwellings via small parabolic dishes. One of the best-known DBS operations, Cable News Network (CNN), claimed in the mid-1990s that its transmissions from 17 satellites reached some 123 million reception points in around 140 countries (OECD, 1995: 105; *FT*, 9 December 1996: 19).

With respect to an older global mass medium, the world count of radio sets increased dramatically to some 2 billion in 1994, or 35 times the level of the 1930s (UNESCO, 1997: 6.4). The amount of transborder broadcasting by major government-sponsored radio stations doubled between 1960 and 1988, to a total of some 16,000 hours per week (UNESCO, 1989: 154). Incalculable additional amounts of globally relayed information are broadcast through local and national radio stations.

The growth of transworld air transport has also mainly transpired since the middle of the twentieth century. The decades since 1960 have brought massive increases in the numbers of aeroplanes, airports, routes and flights as well as in the speed, range and carrying capacities of the vehicles. The world total of air traffic between countries grew from 25 million passengers per annum in 1950 to over 400 million in 1996. The number of air travellers flying within as well as between countries on scheduled commercial flights reached nearly 1.5 billion per annum in 1997 (ICAO, 1998). Meanwhile transworld overnight air express deliveries have developed since the late 1960s through companies such as DHL, UPS and TNT.

Markets

Although some shops of the 1950s displayed several global products, the chief expansion of supraterritorial markets has occurred since the second half of the twentieth century. Today many supermarkets and department stores are *mainly* stocked with transborder articles. To give just a few of the thousands of examples, Twinings teas are now sold in 120 blends across over 90 countries. Kiwi shoe polish is marketed in 130 countries. Thames Television International productions are distributed in more than 90 countries. Interflora allows intimates to exchange bouquets in and between over 130 countries. By the late 1980s, *Reader's Digest* was issuing 28 million copies across 39 editions in 17 languages printed at 24 locations (Mattelart, 1989: 68). Selling its religious product, the Church of Jesus Christ of Latter Day Saints provides the Book of Mormon with translations into 86 languages for its ten million members across 159 countries.

Not only countless goods, but also some of their retail distributors have gone global since the 1970s (Treadgold, 1993). Well-known examples of such chains include Italy-based Benetton clothing shops, Japan-based 7-Eleven convenience stores and Sweden-based IKEA furniture warehouses. Alternatively, today's global consumer can – equipped with a sales catalogue, credit card, and telephone, television or Internet links – shop the world without leaving the house. Mail-order outlets and telesales units have undergone exponential growth, while electronic commerce on the World Wide Web is projected (perhaps overoptimistically) to expand from $2.6 billion in 1996 to over $300 billion in 2002 (Bacchetta *et al.*, 1998: 23; UNDP, 1999: 60). A few commodity exchanges (e.g. the New York Mercantile Exchange and the Sydney Futures Exchange) have established electronic links which enable instantaneous transworld trading between them.

Yet the contemporary accelerated globalization of markets has involved more than exponential growth in the *numbers* of products and outlets affected. Equally important has been the greater *intensity* of supraterritoriality in today's markets. Advances in transworld telephony, computer networks and air transport have allowed managers considerably to increase their supraterritorial coordination of distribution, promotion and sales activities. Local circumstances usually continue strongly to influence marketing decisions at the grassroots level, but in many companies the primary strategic framework has become global.

Production

As previously noted, transborder production processes and associated intra-firm trade did not exist in earlier phases of globalization. They first gained substantial proportions in the 1960s, when supraterritorial coordination developed especially in the production of semiconductors and consumer electronics. Subsequently the trend spread to the assembly phase in the manufacture of clothing, motor vehicles and appliances. More recently, many service industries have turned to global production, for example, by siting data processing operations in the Caribbean, India and Ireland.

As the preceding points indicate, global production has developed mainly, though not exclusively, through the location of the labour-intensive phases of a process at low-wage sites, particularly in the South. Indeed, many states with a large and relatively poorly skilled labour force have sought to lure global corporations to their jurisdictions with special tax and regulatory measures. These advantages have generally applied to designated special economic zones (SEZs), also known as export processing zones (EPZs) or free production zones (FPZs). Within these enclaves of so-called 'offshore' manufacture, global companies may enjoy subsidies, tax exemptions, the suspension of certain labour legislation, and so on.

Like the global production processes that flow through them, offshore zones are new to contemporary history. Although the first of these arrangements appeared in 1954 (in Ireland), host states have created most of these special areas since 1970. By the late 1980s there were around 260 EPZs in 67 countries, most prominently in Asia, the Caribbean and the *maquiladora* areas along the Mexican frontier with the USA (Lang and Hines, 1993: 82). The number multiplied further in the 1990s with, for example, several former communist-ruled countries joining the trend. Nearly 850 EPZs were in place worldwide at the turn of the millennium (UNDP, 1999: 86).

Money

As noted earlier, money was thoroughly territorialized in the mid-twentieth century. The Bretton Woods Agreements of 1944 provided for the creation of a dollar-centred gold standard, and this regime of fixed exchange rates became fully operational in 1959. Under the Bretton Woods arrangements the US dollar became a global currency, so much so that, by the early 1970s, the value of dollars circulating outside the USA exceeded the value of gold stocks held by the American central bank. In these circumstances the Nixon Administration halted dollar-gold convertibility in 1971.

However, in contrast to the return to monetary territorialism that followed earlier collapses of a gold standard in 1914 and the early 1930s, the demise of the Bretton Woods regime did nothing to halt the globalization of money. On the contrary, in the new situation of floating exchange rates the German mark, the Japanese yen, the Swiss franc and a dozen other national currencies joined the US dollar as global stores of value and means of exchange. In the 1990s trillions of dollars' worth of national denominations are used in innumerable transactions that never touch the 'home' soil. Meanwhile the aggregate value of official foreign exchange reserves in the world rose from $100 billion in 1970 to $1,579 billion in 1997 (Spero, 1990: 41; BIS, 1998b: 105).

At the same time other global monies appeared in the late twentieth century in the shape of suprastate currencies. The previously mentioned SDR was created in 1969 as a reserve denomination under the supervision of the IMF. Two releases of SDRs, one in 1970–2 and the other in 1979–81, added around $30 billion of this currency to the world money supply. In 1997 the Board of Governors of the IMF approved an as-yet unratified third disbursement. The most important regional suprastate money, the euro, entered into circulation in 1999. The euro had its forerunners in the European Unit of Account, devised in 1961 as a denomination for certain bonds, and the European Currency Unit (ECU), created in 1978 with wider uses. Both the ECU and the SDR have resided only in computer memories for accounting purposes, whereas the euro is meant soon to slip into pocketbooks for the transactions of everyday life.

Several other forms of supraterritorial money have also been new to the period of accelerated globalization: traveller's cheques, bank cards, credit cards and electronic purses. Certain bank passes allow the holder to extract money anywhere at anytime from ATMs, whose number increased to half a million worldwide in the mid-1990s. By that time MasterCard had come to be recognized at more than 12 million establishments in over 200 countries, while the American Express credit card was accepted at nearly 4 million locations in over 180 countries.

Through the developments just described, territorial currencies have lost the near-monopoly position that they held in respect of money in the middle of the twentieth century. Moreover, monetary globalization since the 1970s has far exceeded anything witnessed under the gold standards or before. For one thing, the amounts of money involved are far greater. In addition, the degree of deterritorialization of this money has much increased, particularly with the advent of electronic finance.

Finance

Unprecedented financial globalization has transpired in contemporary history with respect to foreign exchange dealings, banking, securities markets, derivatives business and the insurance industry. The volume of transactions on the world's wholesale foreign exchange markets rose fifteenfold in just two decades between 1979 and 1998, from $100 billion to $1.5 trillion per day (Martin, 1994: 260; UNDP, 1999: 25). Now more is traded in six hours on the world currency markets than the World Bank has lent in its entire history (Clark, 1999: 1). Meanwhile the retail sector has seen a worldwide proliferation of 'bureaux de change' where customers can walk off the street to buy and sell a score of currencies on demand. In the mid-1990s leading commercial banks established computerized global clearing arrangements that execute an immediate multilateral settlement of foreign exchange deals.

In banking, the second half of the twentieth century introduced the phenomenon of global deposits. In these accounts, savers use transworld bank networks to place their funds anywhere in the world. The world total of bank deposits owned by nonresidents rose from $20 billion in 1964 to $7.9 trillion in 1995 (IMF, 1993: 60–70; BIS, 1996: 7). Commercial banks in the world's main financial centres saw the share of their assets attributable to nonresident depositors rise from around 5 per cent in 1960 to around 40 per cent by 1990 (Porter, 1993: 54). In addition, several trillion US dollars' worth of bank deposits now lie in offshore finance centres, which have proliferated from the handful created before 1950 to several score of countries in the 1990s (Hampton, 1999). Among the larger centres, the Cayman Islands today host more than 500 offshore banks (alongside only six branches for local business), while over 200 are registered in Luxembourg and over 70 in Guernsey (Roberts, 1995).

With electronic communications the globalization of finance also allows monies to be transferred instantaneously between bank offices at whatever distance. Key conduits for these interbank movements are the computerized systems of CHIPS (the Clearing House Interbank Payment System) and SWIFT (the Society for Worldwide Interbank Financial Telecommunications). Begun in 1970, CHIPS typically processed $1.3 trillion per day in business payments as of 1999 (CHIPS, 2000). Started in 1977, SWIFT operations encompassed more than 6,800 financial institutions in 189 countries by 1999, carrying payments with an average daily value of more than $5 trillion (SWIFT, 2000).

Contemporary globalization has also affected the lending side of banking as never before. Credit was first created from global accounts in 1957, when Moscow Narodny Bank issued a loan of $800,000 in London. In other words, a bank based in one country made a loan in a second country using a globally circulating currency that originated in a third country. Supraterritorial lending by transborder syndicates of commercial banks began on a significant scale in the early 1970s and has expanded massively since. Aggregate outstanding balances on these loans rose from less than $200 billion in the early 1970s to almost $10,400 billion in 1990 (Martin, 1994: 260; BIS, 1998b: 144). Other supraterritorial lending has also taken place on a large scale since the 1960s through official multilateral financial agencies like the IMF, the World Bank Group, and the regional development banks for Africa, the Americas, Asia and Europe. The capital base of the IMF has risen tenfold since the 1960s, to almost $300 billion in 1999.

Global securities markets started in the 1960s with the advent of the eurobond market. The first eurobond issue came in July 1963, when the state highways authority in Italy issued bonds in London denominated in US dollars through managers in Belgium, Britain, Germany and the Netherlands. The annual volume of new borrowings of this kind grew to $5 billion in 1972, $43 billion in 1982, and $371 billion in 1995 (Kerr, 1984: 30–1, 51; OECD, 1996b). By the end of the 1980s only the secondary market for US domestic bonds remained larger than that for global bonds (Honeygold, 1989: 19).

In the equity markets, the quotations of US-based corporations Gillette and ITT on the London Stock Exchange were rare instances of extraterritorial share listings in 1950. Forty years later, externally based companies accounted for nearly half of the quotations on the Amsterdam and Frankfurt bourses, a third of those on the Zürich and Paris markets, and over a fifth of those on the London Stock Exchange (O'Brien, 1992: 45). A few global companies like Nestlé and Alcatel Alsthom have issued equities on as many as a dozen bourses across the world. The 1990s also saw the appearance of American Depository Receipts (ADRs) and Global Depository Receipts (GDRs). In these instruments, shares of companies based in Asia, Latin America and Eastern Europe are bundled into packages and traded at global financial centres.

Supraterritoriality has arisen not only in the shape of individual security instruments, but also in the ways that they are assembled in investment portfolios. Numerous investors (especially institutions such as pension funds, insurance companies and unit trusts) today operate global portfolios. Many of these investment companies have further deepened their supraterritorial character by registering offshore, particularly in Luxembourg, the Bahamas, Dublin and the Channel Islands.

Meanwhile electronic communications have enabled investors and dealers instantly to transmit and execute orders to buy and sell securities – in principle anywhere in the world. Moreover, since 1985 a number of stock exchanges have established transborder electronic links between them. Before 1980 transactions in bonds and equities between resident and nonresident investors were negligible. By 1997 the value of such exchanges was equivalent to 672 per cent of gross domestic product (GDP) in Italy, 253 per cent of GDP in Germany and 213 per cent of GDP in the USA (BIS, 1998b: 100).

Most payments connected with supraterritorial securities trading are effected through one of two computerized clearing houses: Euroclear, established in Brussels in 1968; and Cedel, operating since 1971 from Luxembourg. These giant electronic bookkeeping operations fulfil a role in global securities trading akin to that of SWIFT and CHIPS in supraterritorial banking. Between them, Euroclear and Cedel (now called Clearstream) had accumulated an annual turnover of nearly $60 trillion in 1999 (Euroclear, 2000).

Globalization has also burgeoned since the 1970s in regard to financial derivatives. This market started on the Chicago Mercantile Exchange in 1972 and has subsequently spread to several score of trading sites around the world. Global markets in futures, options and other types of derivatives contracts have developed in respect of foreign exchange rates, interest levels, bond and share prices, stock market indices and more. The total world annual turnover on organized derivatives exchanges alone (thus not counting the larger number of over-the-counter deals) stood at more than $350 trillion in 1997 (BIS, 1998b: 155–6). Like most major contemporary securities markets, the financial derivatives business is mainly electronic, using telephone lines and information display terminals that connect traders anywhere in the world. Moreover, several derivatives exchanges in different time zones (for example, London and Singapore, Chicago and Sydney) have established direct links to enable round-the-world, round-the-clock dealing in certain futures and options.

Still further supraterritoriality has spread in the insurance sector. All of the major insurance companies now operate across the major global financial centres. Meanwhile the six largest insurance brokers have developed a World Insurance Network (WIN) that allows them to transact business across the planet from their office computers.

In sum, then, finance has shifted very substantially out of the territorialist framework that defined most banking, securities, derivatives and insurance business before 1960. The amounts of money transacted are staggering: multiple trillions of US dollars' worth per day. Such figures dwarf the numbers associated with sales turnover in other global markets and investment in transborder production processes. It is understandable that many worries concerning 'globalization out of control' have centred on the financial sector.

Organizations

Not surprisingly, the previously described trends in communications, markets, production, money and finance have encouraged an unprecedented expansion of global organizations since the 1960s. This rise of supraterritoriality has occurred both in terms of the numbers of institutions that have a transborder network of offices and in terms of the degree of transworld mobility and coordination in their operations.

In the business sector, the count of firms that work simultaneously in several countries multiplied sixfold between the late 1960s and the mid-1990s. As of 1997 some 44,500 transborder companies between them maintained nearly 280,000 affiliates outside their base country. Total world stock of foreign direct investment (FDI) skyrocketed from $68 billion in 1960 to $3,200 billion in 1996 (UNCTAD, 1994: 131; 1997: 3, 7). Along with global organization through direct investment, companies have also formed thousands of transborder strategic alliances, particularly since the 1980s (cf. Gilroy, 1993). Organized crime syndicates like the Columbia-based Medellín cartel and the China-based Triads have added further to the volume of transworld 'business'. The current collective annual income of these mafias is estimated at $1.5 trillion (UNDP, 1999: 42; Mittelman and Johnston, 1999).

At the same time as proliferating in quantity, these corporate connections have also become more deeply global in quality. For one thing, as already noted in relation to global markets, transborder communications have permitted much more intensive supraterritorial coordination of contemporary business operations. In addition, FDI today has much greater transborder mobility, with companies more ready and able to relocate facilities within a global space. In one striking example, athletic suppliers Nike during a five-year period closed 20 factories and opened 35 others at new sites often thousands of miles away (Abegglen, 1994: 26).

Like the expansion of transborder firms, the greatest proliferation and growth of global civic bodies has also transpired since 1960. Of the 16,500 active transborder civic organizations counted by the Union of International Associations in 1998, less than 10 per cent were over 40 years old (UIA, 1998: 1764). In this light Lester Salamon has spoken of:

> a global 'associational revolution' that may prove to be as significant to the latter twentieth century as the rise of the nation-state was to the latter nineteenth.
>
> (1994: 109)

Countless further transborder associations (like many newsgroups on the Internet) have had a less formal and more transient character.

Global governance agencies have likewise grown at unprecedented rates in recent decades. The increase in the number of these organizations has been relatively modest, since many were created in the period of incipient globalization. That said, the UN system has acquired various additional agencies and programmes since the 1960s, and the OECD was established in 1962. Moreover, most transworld institutions have in recent decades experienced great expansion in their competences, membership, staff and budgets. As is elaborated in Chapter 6, transworld regulatory bodies have added wide-ranging and influential supraterritorial qualities to contemporary governance.

Social ecology

Anthropogenic global ecological change did not occur on any notable scale before the middle of the twentieth century. Prior to the early 1970s, no question of transborder environmental degradation held any sustained prominence on the political agenda. Since then, however, governments have signed over a hundred treaties on environmental issues. Scientists have undertaken several dozen major initiatives to study transborder ecological developments. Millions of citizens have joined environmental NGOs like the World Wide Fund for Nature (WWF) and Greenpeace.

Three global ecological problems have gained greatest attention in official circles and among the general public. One, the depletion of stratospheric ozone, accelerated from the 1960s and began to raise alarm in the 1980s. As of the mid-1990s, this shield of the earth's surface against biologically active ultraviolet radiation from outer space was thinning at a rate of 3 per cent per decade (GACGC, 1995: 1). The main assault on stratospheric ozone has come from chlorofluorocarbons (CFCs), widely used in industrial and consumer products since the 1950s.

A second widely discussed supraterritorial environmental issue – popularly known as 'global warming' – involves the anthropogenic increase in greenhouse gases and its consequences for the planetary climate. This human interference with the chemical composition of the atmosphere has come through the industrial production of greenhouse gases like carbon, methane, halocarbons and nitrous oxide. This activity dates back to the beginnings of industrialization in the middle of the eighteenth century, but most rises in the levels of greenhouse gases have occurred since the second half of the twentieth century. For example, carbon emissions from fossil fuel combustion grew from about 1.5 billion tons per annum in 1950 to an average of around 5.5 billion tons per annum in the 1980s (GACGC, 1995: 12; Porter and Brown, 1996: 6). The Intergovernmental Panel on Climate Change, formed in 1988, has concluded that the anthropogenic greenhouse effect has brought a rise in the mean surface temperature of the earth of between about 0.3°C and 0.6°C since the late nineteenth century (IPCC, 1995: 22). This global warming may have any number of consequences, including a rise in the average sea level, intensified soil erosion, altered patterns of disease and increased species extinction.

Loss of biological diversity is already large enough to constitute the third main instance of contemporary global ecological change. For example, it is estimated that three-quarters of crop varieties were lost in the course of the twentieth century (Porter and Brown, 1996: 12). Meanwhile whole packages of genes disappear when a species becomes extinct. Owing mainly to the exponential growth of human consumption of environmental assets over the past 150 years, the pace of extinction has increased between a 1,000 and 10,000 times (Wilson, 1988: 13). Different authorities have calculated that an average of anywhere between 20 and 200 species died out *each day* in the late twentieth century (Myers, 1993: 179; GACGC, 1995: 32). A middle-range estimate suggests that the rate of loss rose from around one species per annum at the turn of the century to six species per year in 1950 before skyrocketing to some 10,000 species annually in 1990 (Myers, 1985: 155). In spite of this exponential increase in extinctions, biodiversity is arguably still underappreciated as a global resource.

Other supraterritorial ecological problems mentioned briefly in Chapter 2 have also mainly emerged since the middle of the twentieth century. In respect of acid rain, for instance, annual world emissions of sulphur dioxide rose from some 70 million metric tons in 1950 to around 180 million metric tons in 1990 (Porter and Brown, 1996: 8). Transworld fallout from nuclear devices dates from the first detonations of atomic weapons in 1945 and spread to civilian facilities in 1986 with the explosion of the Chernobyl nuclear reactor. The depletion of tropical moist forests (or 'rainforests') has also mainly transpired since the second half of the twentieth century, thereby reducing one of the earth's principal sites of photosynthesis and major concentrations of biomass (crucial for the creation of new species). The worldwide construction of large dams in recent history has shifted ten trillion metric tons of water from the oceans to the continents and moved the earth's axis of rotation sixty centimetres from the North Pole towards western Canada (Myers, 1996: 1). Annual world consumption of fresh water quadrupled between the 1950s and the 1990s, while world per capita availability of fresh water declined by more than a third, raising fears of a developing global water shortage (Porter and Brown, 1996: 11). At the same time between a quarter and a third of the earth's land surface, home to 600–900 million people, is threatened to some degree with desertification (McCormick, 1989: 117; GACGC, 1995: 33).

The jury is still out on many questions concerning the precise character, causes, magnitude, rate and locational distribution of anthropogenic global environmental transformations, as well as the severity of their consequences for human and other life on earth. However, the substantial supraterritorial quality of these phenomena and their generally increased scale since the mid-twentieth century is indisputable.

Consciousness

Transworld ecological issues of the kind just described have provided one of the principal spurs to a continued growth of global consciousness as part of the accelerated spread of supraterritoriality since the 1960s. Exponential increases in global communications, global products, global money flows and global organizations, too, have made large proportions of humanity more aware of the world as a single place. Global consciousness perhaps gained its single greatest boost by the transworld publication in 1966 of pictures taken from outer space showing the earth as one location.

Whereas in earlier times only a narrow circle of intellectuals and businesspeople thought globally, and then usually only fleetingly, at the start of the twenty-first century globality is widely and deeply embedded in academic, commercial, official and popular thinking. Some 425 million holidays abroad were taken in 1990, and total receipts from travel between countries rose twentyfold from $19 billion in 1970 to $389 billion in 1996 (WTO, 1991: 11; UN, 1997: 184). Seasoned travellers boast a global collection of souvenirs. Meanwhile television daily takes even the most sedentary viewer across the planet in an instant. Every week brings a global news sensation, a global sports competition and a global conference of some prominence. In recognition of the growing importance of supraterritorial space, some statistics are now calculated on a global basis. For example, providers of financial data have devised several transborder share price indices, including the *FT/S&P Actuaries World Index*, started in 1987, and the *International Herald Tribune* World Stock Index, started in 1992.

Finally, accelerated globalization since the 1960s has also brought some growth in transworld solidarities. On the one hand, human disasters connected with disease, hunger, natural catastrophes and war have elicited global sympathies and assistance with a frequency and a scale not known in earlier times. In addition, as is discussed further in Chapter 7, a host of transborder communal bonds have deepened in contemporary history with respect to class, disability, gender, generation (especially youth culture), profession, religion, race and sexual orientation. People living under conditions of globalization have increasingly constructed significant aspects of their identity in supraterritorial terms.

Summary indicators of accelerated globalization in contemporary history

fixed telephone lines	from 150 million in 1965 to 851 million in 1998
mobile telephones	from 0 in 1978 to 305 million in 1998
Internet users	from 0 in 1985 to 180 million in 1998
radio sets	from 57 million in mid-1930s to 2,008 million in 1994
television receivers	from 75 million in 1956 to 1,096 million in 1994
international air travellers	from 25 million in 1950 to 400 million in 1996
receipts from international travel	from $19 billion in 1970 to $389 billion in 1996
EPZs	from 0 in 1953 to 850 in 1999
foreign exchange reserves	from $100 billion in 1970 to $1,579 billion in 1997
daily foreign exchange turnover	from $100 billion in 1979 to $1,500 billion in 1998
bank deposits by nonresidents	from $20 billion in 1964 to $7,900 billion in 1995
balances on transborder bank loans	from $200 billion early 1970s to $10,383 billion in 1997
issuance of global bonds	from 0 in 1962 to $371 billion in 1995
financial derivatives contracts	from 0 in 1971 to $70 trillion in 1998
world stock of FDI	from $66 billion in 1960 to $3,200 billion in 1996
transborder companies	from 7,000 in late 1960s to 44,508 in 1997
transborder civic associations	from 1,117 in 1956 to 16,586 in 1998
annual species extinction	from 6 in 1950 to 10,000 in 1990

Conclusion

Hence, when conceived as the rise of supraterritoriality, globalization is mainly new to contemporary history. Only since the 1960s has globality figured continually, comprehensively and centrally in the lives of a large proportion of humanity. Hundreds of millions of people now experience near-instantaneous written, auditory and/or visual contact with previously distant others several times per day.

The pace of globalization has on the whole progressively quickened with time. This does not mean that the development is linear and irreversible. For example, as noted earlier, money has over the past two centuries had alternating phases of territorialization and globalization. However, the forces behind the recent unprecedented spread of transworld relations are such that a return to the sort of territorialism that prevailed before 1960 seems unlikely in any short or medium term. Perhaps the expansion of supraterritoriality will not continue into the twenty-first century at the often breathtaking speed witnessed during the 1980s and 1990s. Yet most current signs point to further rather than less deterritorialization in the coming years. For the time being, to take a phrase from the *Wall Street Journal*, globalization 'is one buzzword that's here to stay' (26 September 1996: R2).

To be sure, as emphasized before, it is important not to exaggerate the extent of globalization. True, electronic mass media, transworld products and global ecological changes have touched almost all of humanity in recent history. However, world telephone density was in 1995 still limited to 12 sets per 100 head of population. At present less than three per cent of the world's population access the Internet. Transborder corporations directly employ only a tiny proportion of the world workforce, namely, 73 million persons as of 1992 (ILO, 1995: 45). A large majority of humanity alive today has never joined – let alone been actively involved in – a transborder civic association.

Clearly, then, globalization has not involved all people on earth to the same extent. For one thing, the large majority of global transactions has occurred between people in the North. Globalization has by no means bypassed countries of the East and the South, but telecommunications traffic, FDI, global financial flows and so on have been heavily concentrated in and between the OECD countries. In addition, the rise of supraterritoriality has touched urban centres (especially so-called 'global cities') more than rural areas. The trend has involved propertied and professional classes more than poorer and less literate circles. Women and people of colour have generally had less access to global spaces than men and white people. On various counts, then, contemporary globalization has often gone hand in hand with marginalization. This unevenness between countries and social groupings is elaborated later in the discussion of the inequities of contemporary globalization.

That said, accelerated globalization of recent decades has left almost no one and no locale completely untouched. This of course raises the question: affected in what way? This issue is addressed at length from Chapter 5 onwards. However, before examining the consequences of globalization we do well to consider the causes of the trend.

Chapter 4

What Causes Globalization?

Main points of this chapter

- globalization has unfolded as a structuration process, that is, it has involved an interrelation of structural forces and actor initiatives
- the main structural impulses to globalization have come from rationalist knowledge and capitalist production
- actor promotion of globalization has occurred chiefly through technological innovations and regulatory measures

---

Why has globalization (as the development and spread of supraterritoriality) attracted imaginations for half a millennium, taken more material form from the mid-nineteenth century, and moved into overdrive in the second half of the twentieth century? In the course of defining and describing globalization, preceding chapters have hinted at possible causes of the trend; however, the issue of explanation has not yet been explicitly and systematically addressed. That is the task of the present chapter.

Most accounts of globalization have given the issue of causation only passing attention or avoid it altogether. When this matter is addressed, the proffered explanation is usually asserted in general terms with but limited elaboration. Such loose treatment of a key question is clearly inadequate. Our responses to globalization should rest on a careful analysis of the forces that generate the trend. Policy initiatives in respect of supraterritorial relations are unlikely to produce the desired outcomes if those measures are not derived from an understanding of the dynamics of globalization. In order to prescribe and act more effectively, we need to diagnose well.

Globalization is susceptible to a variety of explanations. For example, some accounts have cited technological advances and dynamic entrepreneurship as the driving forces behind globalization. Others have highlighted the role of regulatory frameworks in first enabling and then steering globalization. For their part, Marxists have regarded capitalism as the engine of globalization, while other explanations have found the primary causes in the realm of knowledge structures and cultural politics.

As later sections of this chapter indicate, each of these perspectives provides some insight; however, each by itself gives an unduly limited understanding. A fuller account of globalization would combine elements from the different approaches. True, the resultant multifaceted explanation is rather messy. Many readers may prefer a more concise formula, where the dynamics of globalization are reduced to a single driving force. Yet excessive parsimony produces simplistic answers, and simplistic understanding may in turn generate flawed policies. In the case of globalization, as with other major historical trends, social relations involve complex interconnections that cannot be reduced to one sole primary cause like the state, technology, capitalism or cultural imperialism.

In the argument elaborated below, globalization is said to have transpired owing to:

1. the spread of rationalism as a dominant knowledge framework;
2. certain turns in capitalist development;
3. technological innovations in communications and data processing; and
4. the construction of enabling regulatory frameworks.

Certain further circumstances have also promoted the creation of global spaces. For example, nonterritorial bonds of collective identity and solidarity between women, ruling élites, youth and so on have facilitated the growth of many transworld networks. Moreover, other forces like the contemporary power of neoliberal discourse (described in Chapter 1) have shaped the particular course that globalization has taken at a particular time. However, the four abovenamed causes have constituted the principal necessary conditions for the rise of supraterritoriality.

None of these four main causes of globalization has held primacy over the others. The developments in rationalism, capitalism, technology and regulation have been inextricably interrelated. We cannot measure their causal impacts separately so as to conclude that, for example, rationalism has contributed 40 per cent of the cause of globalization, capitalism 30 per cent, technology 20 per cent, regulation 7 per cent and other factors 3 per cent. The explanation advanced here has a systemic character, where each of the primary forces is understood simultaneously to cause and be caused by the others. Thus all four conditions have been necessary to launch and subsequently to accelerate the rise of supraterritoriality. In this sense each of the four has had a causal significance of 100 per cent.

The structuration of globalization

Before elaborating on the four primary forces that have collectively propelled globalization, we need to address the broader agent-structure question. This age-old methodological debate concerns the degree to which sociohistorical developments (like the emergence and expansion of supraterritorial spaces) result from the intentions and choices of actors or from the power of social structures. (For more on this question see Scholte, 1993b: ch 7.) Clearly we need to devise our responses to globalization in the light of our assessment of the respective impacts on the trend of actor initiatives and structural forces.

To put matters simply, the agent-structure debate involves three general contending positions. One of these standpoints, methodological individualism, holds that social relations are wholly propelled by the aims and decisions of actors. Those agents might include official institutions, firms, civic organizations, small groups and individuals. From an individualist (or voluntarist) position, globalization has resulted from an accumulation of initiatives taken by persons and associations of their free will.

A second standpoint in the agent-structure debate, methodological structuralism, maintains that social history is wholly determined by deeply embedded organizing principles of social relations. Those configurations might include capitalism (as a production structure), patriarchy (as a gender structure), rationalism (as a knowledge structure), the states-system (as a governance structure), nationalism (as a community structure) and so on. From a structuralist (or determinist) position, globalization has resulted from structural forces over which actor intentions and decisions have no autonomous influence.

A third methodological standpoint – sometimes called the structuration postulate – rejects both the voluntarism of individualism and the determinism of structuralism. From this perspective, the course of social history results from mutually constituting agent choices and structural dispositions. Neither comes before the other: there is no chicken/actor without the egg/structure and vice versa. On the one hand, structural forces largely establish the range of options that are available to actors in a given historical context. Structures also generally encourage agents to take certain steps rather than others. At the same time, however, structures depend on an accumulation of actor decisions for their creation and subsequent perpetuation. Indeed, at moments of structural instability and flux, agents can have considerable influence in reshaping the social order. According to the structuration principle, then, globalization has transpired when structural conditions were ripe for it *and* when agents took the initiatives to make the possibilities actually happen.

The account of globalization developed in this book is a structuration argument. From this perspective the growth of supraterritoriality has been neither random (by individual whims) nor predetermined (by structural formulas). Rather, globalization has arisen through an interrelation of structural impulses and actor decisions. Structural forces connected with rationalism and capitalism began to create opportunities for globalization several hundred years ago. Various entrepreneurs, explorers, inventors, scholars and statespersons acted on these potentials and thereby opened the first transworld spaces. Crucial among these actor initiatives were a number of technological innovations and regulatory measures. These steps, together with further developments in rationalism and capitalism, by the middle of the twentieth century produced dynamics for a major spread of supraterritoriality. During the following decades, additional technological advances and enabling legislation made a rapid acceleration of globalization possible. Moreover, the *type* of regulatory framework adopted (in particular, its emphasis on liberalization) has substantially influenced the *kind* of globalization (mainly neoliberal) that we experienced in the late twentieth century.

Again, in this structuration argument neither the structural forces (rationalism and capitalism) nor the actor initiatives (technological innovations and regulatory decisions) have stood separately from, and causally prior to, the other in generating globalization. Rationalism and capitalism have established the structural conditions in which various technological and regulatory developments could promote globalization. Concurrently, actions taken in the areas of technology and regulation have sustained the structures of rationalism and capitalism in ways that furthered globalization. By now, at the start of the twenty-first century, globalization has accumulated sufficient momentum to become almost self-sustaining. Even so, actor initiatives continue to exert significant influence in shaping the specific directions (neoliberal or otherwise) that globalization can and does take.

The rest of this chapter examines in turn each of the four primary forces that have generated the emergence and subsequent expansion of supraterritorial spaces. These more detailed treatments are presented under separate headings below for the sake of analytical clarity. However, as already stressed, the four impulses have in practice been thoroughly interrelated; hence continual reference is made in the next sections to interconnections between rationalism, capitalism, technological innovation and regulation in the causation of globalization.

Rationalism

Several major social theories have highlighted the importance of knowledge structures in shaping social life. Thus, for example, the sociologist Max Weber understood modernity largely in terms of rationalist thinking. For his part, the philosopher Michel Foucault distinguished different sociohistorical contexts in terms of what he called the reigning *episteme* of each situation. Indeed, the way that people know their world has significant implications for the concrete circumstances of that world. Globalization has occurred in part because of certain powerful patterns of social consciousness.

This is not to take a methodologically idealist position that historical outcomes can be explained wholly and solely in terms of knowledge structures. On the contrary, the present account of globalization also gives due attention to material forces (that is, in terms of capitalism, technology and regulation). However, in the perspective adopted here knowledge frameworks have a significance that is not reducible to forces of production and governance. In short, the rise of supraterritoriality could not transpire in the absence of a mindset that would encourage such a development.

Rationalism is a general configuration of knowledge that has greatly promoted the spread of global thinking and, through it, the broader trend of globalization. This framework of knowledge has four main distinguishing features. For one thing, rationalism is secularist: it defines reality entirely in terms of the physical world, without reference to transcendent and divine forces. Second, rationalism is anthropocentric: it understands reality primarily in terms of human interests and activities (as opposed to, for example, ecological integrity). Third, rationalism has a 'scientist' character: it holds that phenomena can be understood in terms of single incontrovertible truths which are discoverable by rigorous application of objective research methods. Fourth, rationalism is instrumental: it assigns greatest value to insights that enable people to solve immediate problems.

When it reigns as a predominant social structure, rationalism tends to subordinate other kinds of knowledge. It elevates one way of 'making sense' over all others. Rationalists readily dismiss aesthetics, spirituality, emotion, and fantasy – or rather accept these and other 'irrationalities' only inasmuch as they complement and advance rational knowledge. 'Irrationality' is not seen to contain any primary truth in its own right.

Indeed, rationalism is something of a (secular) faith. Rationalists maintain that science enables humanity to discover the single, definitive, objective truths about phenomena. People can then apply this knowledge to harness natural and social forces for human betterment. Techno-scientific rationality thereby allows us to conquer disease, hunger, poverty, war, etc. and as a result to maximize the potentials of human life.

The effects of rationalist knowledge are manifested in all that we have regarded as 'reasonable' in modern society. For example, rationalism has prompted us to separate 'society' from 'nature' and to seek through scientific and technical means to subordinate natural forces for instrumental human purposes. Secular, anthropocentric, instrumental calculations have also provided a knowledge framework for capitalist production and the modern cult of efficiency. A rationalist mindset has likewise underlain the power of 'objective' secular law in modern social relations and the pervasiveness of bureaucracy in modern organizations (governments, firms, civic associations, schools, hospitals and so on). Rationalism has propelled the production of 'scientific' knowledge through universities and think tanks. Indeed, the rationalist knowledge structure is evident in the secular, largely anthropocentric, pseudo-scientific and substantially instrumental orientation of the present book.

Like any social structure, rationalism is a historical phenomenon. It has arisen at particular times and places under particular conditions. True, we can find instances of secular, anthropocentric, scientific, instrumental thinking in various ancient contexts. However, a rational*ist* social structure – i.e. one that systematically marginalizes other forms of knowing – is distinctive of modern history. Rationalism first consolidated in the so-called 'Enlightenment' that took hold in the North Atlantic area during the eighteenth century. Enlightenment thought removed the label of 'knowledge' from myth, faith and other 'traditional' ways of understanding. Subsequently rationalism has been carried, particularly through colonialism and informal imperialism, to all corners of the earth.

Rationalist thought has encouraged the rise of supraterritoriality in several general ways. For one thing, this structure of knowledge has laid an ideational basis for the other principal causes of globalization. The reliance of capitalist production on rationalist knowledge has already been noted. Likewise, the technologies that open supraterritorial spaces have developed in good part from scientific thinking and an anthropocentric, instrumentalist will to control nature. Meanwhile modern rationalist law and bureaucratic organization have formed a backdrop for the regulatory frameworks that have encouraged globalization.

In addition, certain impulses to create supraterritorial geography have come from the internal logic of rationalism itself. For example, the secularism of rationalism has encouraged people to construct 'the whole' of their existence in terms of our planet rather than, on traditional lines, in terms of the divine. Indeed, before the sixteenth century 'maps' of 'the world' often depicted relations between people and their god(s) as well as, or instead of, some terrestrial realm. For a secularist mindset, truth comes in the form of earthly – indeed, global – laws that escape the particularities of locality and prevail across whatever territorial distances and borders.

A number of significant impulses to globalization have therefore come from efforts to discover transworld truths. This quest has motivated both so-called 'explorers' of earlier times and world travellers of recent generations. Rationalism encourages a belief that people can gain comprehensive knowledge when they access and understand the terrestrial world as a whole. Globalization can be seen, in part, as the pursuit of this secularist holy grail.

Meanwhile the anthropocentrism of rationalism has directed our consciousness to the space occupied by humanity, namely, the earthly world. In an anthropocentric conception, the cosmos is seen not as the realm of the gods, nor as a biosphere of interdependent life forms, nor as the domain of a particular tribe. Rather, the rationalist lens focuses on the space of *homo sapiens*, that is, on the planet as a single place. This thought of the earth as the human home, too, has provided a crucial mental orientation for globalization.

The scientism and instrumentalism of rationalism have also been conducive to globalization. Scientific knowledge is nonterritorial: the truths revealed by 'objective' method are purportedly valid for anyone, anywhere, anytime. Such an orientation can feed expectations that certain products, regulations, technologies, art forms and the like can apply across the world at the same time. Meanwhile territorial geography (especially the hindrances of state borders) has frequently contradicted utilitarian notions of efficiency. For example, the instrumentalist logic of modern economic analysis has held that distance should be overcome and borders should fall in order to achieve the most productive world division of labour.

In a variety of ways, then, rationalist thinking has encouraged the growth of a global imagination and the various material supraterritorial activities (communications, markets, etc.) that global thinking promotes. For two hundred years, the Enlightenment mindset has in important respects opposed the principle of a territorial division of the earth. As Martin Albrow has succinctly put it, 'Reason knows no territorial limits' (1996: 32).

Capitalism

Although a rationalist mindset has been indispensable to the expansion of transworld spaces, developments in knowledge structures have not been sufficient by themselves to cause globalization. Material forces, too, have played a central role, *inter alia* in terms of structures of production. In particular, Marxist political economy has affirmed that capitalism is the driving force of globalization. Indeed, Karl Marx himself presciently anticipated the growth of supraterritorial domains when he wrote in *Grundrisse* that 'capital by its nature drives beyond every spatial barrier' to 'conquer the whole earth for its market' (1857–8: 524, 539).

As the above emphasis on relatively autonomous knowledge structures has indicated, the present argument rejects a materialist, economistic account that explains the development of supraterritorial relations entirely in terms of capitalism. However, impulses of surplus accumulation have figured centrally throughout the history of globalization. Moreover, it is hard to see how transworld connections could have emerged and proliferated in the absence of capitalism.

Capitalism is a structure of production where economic activity is oriented first and foremost to the accumulation of surplus. In other words, capitalist producers (who might be individuals, private firms, publicly owned enterprises or other collective actors) attempt to amass ever-greater resources in excess of their survival needs. Capitalist production contrasts with a subsistence economy (where no surpluses arise) and profligacy (where any surplus is immediately depleted through luxury consumption). Under capitalism surpluses are invested in further production, with the aim of acquiring additional surplus, which is then reinvested in still more production, in the hope of obtaining still more surplus, and so on. This perpetual quest to increase surplus value tends to bring more and more of an economy into a capitalist logic. Hence with time not only agriculture, mining, manufacturing, transport and finance, but also education, housing, social insurances, health and even genetic engineering can become contexts for accumulation.

A capitalist economy is thoroughly monetized. Marx in this light characterized money as 'the universal commodity' of capitalist social relations (1867: 89). Money greatly facilitates accumulation, for one thing since surpluses are most easily stored and moved in this fungible form. In addition, the manipulation of value by means of monetary calculations (including prices, wages, interest charges, dividends, taxes, currency revaluations, accounting formulas, etc.) offers abundant opportunities to transfer surplus, especially from the weak to the powerful.

Since all parties in a capitalist order are seeking to accumulate to one degree or another, this mode of production involves perpetual and pervasive contests over the distribution of surplus. Such competition occurs between firms, classes, races, sexes, countries and more. Some of the struggles are overt, for example, in wage disputes. Other conflicts remain latent, for instance, when many poor people in the South are unaware that much of their country's limited surplus value is being transferred to the North through the repayment of global debts. Countless experiences of this kind have shown historically that capitalism tends to breed exploitation and other inequities unless deliberate countervailing measures are implemented.

Surplus accumulation has transpired in one way or another for countless centuries, but capital*ism* is a comparatively recent phenomenon. When accumulation occurred in earlier times, it was temporary, limited, and involved only small circles of people. Not until the past several hundred years has capital accumulation reigned as the foremost and ubiquitous framework of production over a sustained period of time. From beginnings in Europe around the fifteenth century, capitalism spread to all continents by the twentieth century (albeit to different degrees). Today the structural power of capitalism is such that most of the world's population regard surplus accumulation as a 'natural' circumstance and can scarcely imagine, let alone pursue, an alternative mode of production.

Capitalism has spurred globalization in four principal ways. First, pushed by a capitalist logic, many firms have pursued global markets as a means to increase their sales volume. Expanded turnover at a given rate of profit obviously brings greater total accumulation. Moreover, higher production runs to supply global markets can bring significant economies of scale and thereby raise profit margins. Capitalist enterprises have therefore had major incentives to develop transworld distribution and sales networks and global communications infrastructures to support them.

Supraterritorial accounting has offered a second boon to accumulation. For example, managers can vary and alter prices in a coordinated fashion across a global sphere so that overall company profits are maximized. Indeed, higher profit margins at a mature market location can allow a firm to cover the temporary losses involved in establishing new sites at whatever other points on earth. A transworld pricing strategy can thereby yield greater total profits in the long run.

In addition, global accounting has given capitalists the possibility to concentrate profits at points of low taxation within a transworld space. In territorialist circumstances, surplus is bound within a particular state jurisdiction, and the capitalist is compelled to accept its tax regime. However, by moving into the cyberspace of electronic finance, capital can readily escape such obligations. Profits that have in practice been achieved, for example, in Italy can be made to appear on the balance sheet of a Luxembourg subsidiary with offshore taxation status. Likewise, 'hinwis' ('high net worth individuals') may significantly reduce their tax charges by registering their assets at offshore financial centres.

Third, global sourcing has provided important new ways to enhance accumulation, especially for big capital concentrated in megacorporations.

It clearly serves capitalist interests when firms can place their production facilities wherever the resources are optimal and the costs are lowest. Indeed, as we see in later chapters, the fear of seeing supraterritorial corporate assets go elsewhere can induce territorially bound workers and governments at host sites to temper demands regarding their share of surplus value.

In particular, global mobility has provided capitalists with an escape from the reduced rates of profit that accompanied corporatist arrangements in the OECD countries by the late 1960s (cf. Marglin, 1988). True, corporatist compromises between business, organized labour and government – epitomized in the Keynesian welfare state – secured capitalism by reducing overt class conflict at a time when socialism was gaining unprecedented strength across much of the world. However, this accommodation was bought at a price of progressive taxation, heavy social insurance charges and tight guarantees of wide-ranging workers' rights. In these ways corporatism reduced the room for accumulation by companies and investors. Globalization could allow business to retrieve an advantaged position, since capital thereby gained a supraterritorial mobility that labour and the state lacked. Transborder relocations – or merely the threat of such departures – has reconstructed the trilateral bargain heavily in favour of big capital. Workers and governments have been constrained to lower wages, corporate taxation, business regulation and various public expenditures on social security.

In broadly similar ways, globalization has offered capitalists a way to counter the strategies of socialism and economic statism that rose in much of the South during the mid-twentieth century. In the wake of large-scale decolonization, many states in Africa, Asia and Latin America asserted a will to control capitalist development within their jurisdictions. These governments expropriated many assets and often introduced centralized state planning of the national economy. Some voices in the South even called for reparations from the North as compensation for past capitalist exploitation. Globalization of production and finance has given big (mainly North-based) capital a means to counter these efforts at a major redistribution of world wealth. Indeed, today little remains of state socialism in either the South or the East.

Finally, as is further elaborated in Chapter 5, capitalism has spurred globalization insofar as the objects that circulate in supraterritorial space open up major additional opportunities for surplus accumulation. In other words, global communications and global financial flows have done more than enhance the possibilities for accumulation through primary production and traditional manufacturing. In addition, the finance, information and communications sectors have offered vast potentials for accumulation in their own right. Indeed, telephone systems, websites, foreign exchange dealing and the like have often generated very high profits. Thus the very process of creating supraterritorial spaces has been a boon to capitalism.

The preceding points should not be read to imply that every global capitalist venture has yielded the expected windfalls. On the contrary, 'going global' has hurt many corporations and investors who believed that this strategy offered a short, one-way street to superprofits. Global finance in particular has brought enormous volatility, including major losses for some. Nevertheless, hopes of enhanced accumulation have continued to stimulate globalization at a hugely accelerated rate, and (as is detailed in Chapter 5) many of those capitalist dreams have been substantially realized.

In sum, then, surplus accumulation has provided a number of powerful material impulses to the rise of supraterritoriality. That said, capitalism has by no means generated globalization by itself. For one thing, this production structure has depended on the concurrent existence of a rationalist knowledge structure that creates the secular, anthropocentric, instrumentalist mindset through which capitalism operates. In addition, various actors have had to supply the technological innovations and the regulatory frameworks that have made supraterritorial surplus accumulation possible. In short, as stressed earlier, the four primary causes of globalization have been co-dependent.

Technological innovation

In contrast to deeper, less immediately visible structural causes of globalization (rationalism and capitalism), technological developments that have enabled the rise of supraterritoriality are readily evident. Globalization patently could not have occurred in the absence of extensive innovations in respect of transport, communications and data processing. In addition, industrialization more generally has figured centrally in producing transworld environmental problems. Some authors have suggested that technological change has been the single driving force of globalization. (See Wriston, 1992 and, in more nuanced terms, Strange, 1990.)

As already emphasized, the present explanation of globalization rejects technological determinism. True, advances in communications and informatics have acquired a certain momentum of their own as, for example, the speed of digital processors and the capacities of cables have been continually increased. However, technological innovation has not been completely self-generating. It is necessary to consider also the deeper structural conditions (rationalism and capitalism) that have created a social order that has encouraged such developments. Moreover, these inventions could not have gained large-scale and ubiquitous application without regulatory frameworks that assured a substantial degree of technical standardization within and between countries. Hence an explanation of globalization that considers only technological forces is both superficial and incomplete.

That said, technology has clearly played a crucial role in creating transworld social spaces. The introduction of the telegraph in 1837, the telephone in 1876, the wireless in 1895, the aeroplane in 1903, the television in 1926, the liquid-fuelled rocket in 1927, the coaxial cable in the 1930s, and the digital computer in 1946 were all key events in the period of incipient globalization. In addition, the nineteenth-century creation of automated bottling, canning and refrigeration processes enabled certain consumer goods to become early global products. Meanwhile, the invention of CFCs in 1931 laid the basis for much subsequent global ozone depletion.

Further development of these technologies has done much to spur the acceleration of globalization after 1950. For example, the transistor radio, introduced in 1955, has offered greater portability and much improved reception. The capabilities of television have advanced with cable, satellite and digital technologies. The speed and capacity of aeroplanes have increased with the advent of commercial jets in the late 1950s, wide-body aircraft in 1969, and supersonic carriers in the early 1970s. Orbital satellites became available in 1958, followed by geostationary satellites (which hold a fixed position above the earth) in 1963. Intercontinental missiles arrived on the scene in 1957.

Continual advances in telecommunications technologies have also provided indispensable tools for global communications, global financial transactions, coordination of global production and marketing, and other global activities. For example, car, train, aeroplane and hand-held mobile telephones have all appeared alongside fixed-line connections. The late 1990s saw the introduction of satellite-based mobile telephone systems in which a handset can be reached instantly with a single telephone number at any location on earth. Other extensions of telephone technology in the period of accelerated globalization have included videophones and video-conferencing, voice mail, much-improved fax machines, and e-mail.

Meanwhile optical fibres have acquired ever-rising capacities since their invention in the late 1960s. The maximum load of a single strand of fibre-optic cable increased to 6,000 simultaneous voice conversations by the early 1980s and 600,000 concurrent telephone calls by the mid-1990s. The introduction since the 1980s of broadband technologies such as Integrated Services Digital Network (ISDN) and very high-speed Asynchronous Transfer Mode (ATM) has allowed fibre-optic cables to carry not only voice, but also large concentrations of digitized data, text, sound recordings, graphic material, and motion pictures.

Next to (and often interconnected with) air transport and electronic communications, digital information processing has been the other principal area of technological innovation that has spurred accelerated globalization in recent history. Global financial dealings and global administration in particular have depended on large-scale automated information management. Key events in this respect have included the introduction of commercial silicon microchips in 1971, personal computers (PCs) in 1981, and portable laptops shortly thereafter. Other developments have greatly increased the types, magnitudes, and speeds of data manipulation by computer. For example, producers of microprocessors have to date repeatedly confirmed 'Moore's Law'. First proposed in 1965 by one of the founders of Intel Corporation, this 'rule' holds that technological improvements generate a doubling of microchip capacity every eighteen months.

Already, then, technological innovations have provided much of the infrastructure for globalization. The future promises further advances that will increase the possibilities for supraterritorial relations many times over again. For example, digital radios that receive satellite transmissions will open new opportunities for low-cost, high-capacity transborder broadcasting. Emergent microcellular technology for mobile telephones will permit increased subscriber density and enlarged equipment capacities. Some of these pocket devices will transmit faxes and electronic mail as well as voice messages. Meanwhile future advances in fibre-optic cables will yield capacities running into the millions of telephone calls per hair-thin strand. Moore's Law looks set to survive well into the twenty-first century. In short, technological change has by no means run its course as an enabling force for the transcendance of territorial geography.

Regulation

Next to rationalism, capitalism and technological innovation, supportive regulatory frameworks have constituted the fourth principal force to spur globalization. Social relations are always marked by governance mechanisms of some kind, however loose and variable. There is no such thing as an unregulated social context, and no social change takes place in the absence of rules that stimulate, facilitate and confirm the transformations. In the case of globalization, too, various legal and institutional arrangements have played a key enabling role.

Much of this regulation has emanated from states. In addition, other rules and procedures conducive to globalization have developed through regional and transworld institutions created by states. Although many of these suprastate bodies have acquired a degree of autonomy from national governments, states continue to have considerable and often decisive inputs. Further support to globalization has come from various schemes of so-called 'self-regulation' by market-based institutions. This private-sector governance has required at least the acquiescence, if not the active encouragement, of states.

Hence, against the assumptions of many commentators, globalization and the state have been anything but antithetical. On the contrary, most supraterritorial relations would not have developed – or would have grown more slowly and ponderously – if state policies had not encouraged the process. Globalization and the state have thus been quite compatible and indeed co-dependent, though (as is elaborated in Chapter 6) the growth of transworld connections has in several important respects altered the character of the state.

Yet it is not the state as such that has been key to enabling globalization, but regulation. As indicated above, states alone have not been able to supply all of the legal and institutional bases for the rise of supraterritoriality. Various substate, suprastate and market bodies have also provided the necessary governance framework.

On no account are the preceding remarks meant to suggest that governance agencies have promoted globalization through the free will of policymakers. To say that the construction of supportive regulatory mechanisms has been indispensable to the expansion of global relations is not to say that the regulators have had an unconstrained choice of measures (with the implication that policymakers could have blocked most or all globalization if they had wished to do so). True, certain governments have taken particular steps to inhibit globalization, for example, by banning Internet software, by harassing civic associations with transworld links, or by restricting transborder capital flows. More-over, stronger states have clearly had more possibilities to influence the course of globalization than weaker states. Nevertheless, other forces – mainly those connected with rationalism, capitalism and technology – have put even regulators from the most powerful states under great pressure to facilitate the rise of supraterritoriality. Governments with strong reservations about globalization, too, have succumbed to at least a partial accommodation of the trend. Thus, for example, the King of Bhutan no longer outlaws television (as he previously tried to do), and Castro's Cuba has begun actively to lure global tourists. In short, the question has been less *whether* regulators would accommodate globalization and more *what kind* of regulatory frameworks they would erect to govern the trend. Contemporary policymakers cannot deny the growth of transworld relations, but they do have a variety of options on how to manage the speed and direction of the process.

One key way that regulation has promoted the spread of global relations is through standardization. Supraterritorial connections are obviously facilitated when the parties involved follow the same rules and routines. Much of this standardization has concerned the considerable (albeit sometimes far from complete) harmonization of the technologies that have underpinned globalization. For example, the hundreds of ITU recommendations governing technical standards in radio and telecommunications run to more than 10,000 pages in all. Meanwhile the International Organization for Standardization (ISO) has published over 10,000 standards covering pretty well all areas of technology (UIA, 1998: 1093). To give a more specific example, the growth of global markets was considerably aided with the development in the 1970s of standard models of 20- and 40-foot containers that fit ships, railway wagons and trucks worldwide.

Other standardization that facilitates globalization has occurred in respect of procedures and documentation. For instance, the EU has provided traders and governments in member countries with common customs forms. The Warsaw Convention of 1929 (amended in 1955) has prescribed a transworld format for airline tickets, while the International Civil Aviation Organization (ICAO) has overseen global rules for air navigation, *inter alia* to prevent collisions. Several private-sector associations like the International Accounting Standards Committee (IASC) and the International Federation of Accountants (IFAC) have since the 1970s developed global guidelines for corporate accounting and auditing. The International Organization of Securities Commissions (IOSCO), created in 1974, has discussed transworld standards for stock and bond markets, while the International Association of Insurance Supervisors (IAIS), formed in 1994, has done the same for the insurance business. Starting in 1996, the IMF has coordinated major initiatives to set global frameworks for the calculation and presentation of macroeconomic statistics.

Regulatory adjustments through state and suprastate agencies have also been crucial to the globalization of money. The gold standards of earlier times only operated as long as states upheld them. When key states withdrew from the arrangements in 1914, 1931 and 1971, the respective regimes collapsed. Similarly, the current framework of flexible exchange rates has depended on state policies to allow convertibility, together with overall regime supervision by the IMF. Indeed, most governments have in recent decades passed legislation to relax or abandon foreign exchange controls within their jurisdictions. By 1998 a total of 147 states had accepted Article VIII of the IMF, under which governments agree not to impose any restrictions on payments related to cross-border trade in goods and services.

Considerable further liberalization has transpired in respect of cross-border investment, thereby giving much additional stimulus to financial globalization. Starting with the USA in 1974 and the UK in 1979, dozens of states have removed restrictions on movements in and out of their jurisdictions of 'real' assets and portfolio capital (Helleiner, 1994; Kapstein, 1994). Proposals circulated in the late 1990s to amend the Articles of Agreement of the IMF so that member states would be required to annul controls on cross-border capital flows. Negotiations through the OECD in 1995–8 towards a Multilateral Agreement on Investment (MAI) pursued – unsuccessfully – a similar 'free flow' principle under which states would not discriminate between capital of foreign and domestic origin.

A host of other measures at state level have further encouraged the growth of supraterritorial finance. For example, numerous governments have amended legislation to allow nonresident ownership of bonds and equities on securities markets within the country in question. In addition, scores of states have since the 1980s established rules to permit entry into their jurisdictions of global banks and global securities firms. Moreover, the proliferation of offshore finance facilities has required governments to construct enabling statutory frameworks.

States have also removed many legal hindrances to cross-border trade in goods and services, thereby greatly facilitating the development of global markets and transborder production. It is clearly harder to create supra-territorial markets when tariffs, quotas, licensing procedures, technical standards, subsidies and other regulatory measures favour intra-state over cross-border transactions. Already some trade liberalization in the second half of the nineteenth century aided the early development of global products. Then high protectionism in the second quarter of the twentieth century discouraged further growth of transworld markets at that time. Thereafter eight rounds of multilateral negotiations between 1948 and 1994 under the GATT reduced average import duties on manufactures from over 40 per cent to only 3 per cent. The creation of the WTO in 1995 has brought a major effort also to liberalize cross-border trade in agriculture and various service sectors.

In addition, important spurs to transborder marketing and production have come during the past half-century with the creation at a regional level of various free trade areas (FTAs), customs unions and (in the case of the EU) a common market. FTAs are regional associations with zero-tariffs between member countries. They have appeared in – or are currently projected for – Central Europe, the cone of South America, North America, South Asia, South East Asia, Southern Africa, Western Europe and elsewhere. Especially in Europe, FTAs and customs unions (the latter have a common external tariff as well as an abolition of internal tariffs) have greatly encouraged transborder production as well as foreign direct investment more generally.

As previously indicated in Chapter 3, states and/or provincial governments have also promoted global production with the creation of hundreds of export processing zones. These sites of offshore manufacture are governed by especially business-friendly tax regimes, subsidy arrangements, investment codes, labour laws, environmental legislation, etc. Thus many companies have opted for transborder production partly because of the regulatory bait laid by states and/or substate authorities in EPZs.

More fundamentally important to the growth of global corporations has been the guarantee of property rights for supraterritorial capital. Legal backing of property claims has of course been integral to capitalist development for centuries, and the globalization of accumulation processes has constituted no exception. On the one hand, states have legislated to protect property rights for global capital within their respective jurisdictions. In addition, supraterritorial instruments to secure property claims on a transworld basis have appeared since the late nineteenth century in a score of conventions governing intellectual property rights (IPRs), including patents, trademarks, copyrights, industrial designs and so on. The World Intellectual Property Organization (WIPO) has seen the annual number of applications for global patents rise from under 3,000 in 1979 to over 54,000 in 1997 (UNDP, 1999: 67). The 1994 Agreement on Trade-Related Aspects of Intellectual Property Rights (TRIPS) strengthened guarantees of IPRs in global markets through the WTO. Meanwhile two treaties concluded at the end of 1996 extended copyright law to cyberspace.

Finally, regulation has enabled globalization with the legalization of transworld organizations. Thus, as noted earlier, states created the public multilateral organizations that have developed into today's transworld and regional governance agencies. In addition, governments have granted permission to global companies to invest within the various national jurisdictions and to global civic associations to operate within state domains.

In sum, then, regulation has promoted globalization in four main ways: technical and procedural standardization; liberalization of cross-border movements of money, investments, goods and services (but not labour); guarantees of property rights for global capital; and legalization of global organizations and activities. As stressed before, the construction of this legal infrastructure has not been the sole cause of globalization. On the contrary, other forces have placed policymakers under considerable pressure to enact these enabling measures. Nevertheless, supraterritoriality could not have spread in the absence of supportive regulatory frameworks.

Conclusion

The preceding explanation of globalization has highlighted causes connected with the rationalist structure of knowledge, the capitalist mode of production, technological innovation and regulation. These forces are summarized in the Box below. As emphasized throughout this chapter, these main prompters of globalization have been thoroughly interrelated. In other words, they constitute a single, multidimensional causal dynamic rather than separate factors.

Causal dynamics of globalization in summary

Rationalism
- secular conceptions of existence in terms of the earthly world
- anthropocentric focus on the planetary home of the human species
- scientific notions that 'objective' truths have transworld validity
- efficiency arguments against 'irrational' territorial divisions

Capitalism
- global markets to increase sales volume and achieve economies of scale
- global accounting of prices and tax liabilities to enhance profits
- global sourcing to minimize costs of production
- global commodities as additional channels of accumulation

Technological innovation
- air transport
- electronic communications
- digital information processing
- general industrialization as a primary source of global ecological change

Regulation
- technical and procedural standardization
- liberalization of cross-border movements of money, investments and trade
- guarantees of property rights for global capital
- legalization of global organizations and activities

In distinguishing a fourfold dynamic behind globalization, this discussion has not denied that further circumstances have also promoted the spread of transworld relations. For example, nonterritorial constructions of identity and community have encouraged countless people to acquire global consciousness, to pursue global communications and to form global associations on the basis of class, gender, profession, race, religion, sexual orientation and so on. However, identity politics and other secondary forces that we might mention (like neoliberal policies) have not been *necessary* conditions for globalization. Only the four primary causes have been indispensable for the process.

Of course, not every circumstance in the modern world system has favoured the rise of supraterritoriality. For example, territorial identities can work against globalization just as nonterritorial identities can promote the trend. In addition, as noted earlier, a number of states have taken measures to inhibit the growth of global flows. In respect of social structure, persistent nonrational knowledge and/or subsistence production have kept substantial circles of the world's population quite resistant to transworld relations. Meanwhile revolts against capitalism (like the Bolshevik Revolution) and rebellions against rationalism (like postmodernist thought) could involve opposition to the spread of supraterritoriality, although they have in practice generally not done so to date.

The existence of alternative and oppositional social forces reminds us that globalization has not been inevitable. No commentator of the fifteenth century could have forecast with certainty that social relations would acquire a major supraterritorial dimension five hundred years later. Even less could these ancestors have predicted that globalization would take the predominantly neoliberal course that we have witnessed in the 1980s and 1990s. The structural forces that have propelled globalization (rationalism and capitalism) were not preordained. They had to be created by an accumulation of actor initiatives over considerable time. To this day, agents remain necessary to reproduce those structures, albeit that opportunities effectively to reject rationalism and capitalism are at present severely constrained. Likewise, individual and group actors have made conscious decisions to supply the technological innovations and the regulatory frameworks that have underpinned globalization. By the same token, agents – that is, *we* – could in principle determine to undo or reshape the technologies and regimes that have given us supraterritorial social spaces. To repeat the key point: globalization has developed not according to a predetermined historical trajectory, but through structuration processes in which actors have had constrained but nevertheless significant choice.

That degree of initiative arguably becomes greater to the extent that we comprehend the dynamics of globalization. To understand the causes of globalization is therefore to be empowered. A workable explanation of globalization can point the way to effective measures to affect the rate and direction of the spread of supraterritoriality.

We have several options in this respect. First, if we want globalization to continue on its present mainly neoliberal course, then we should not question prevailing social structures of rationalism and capitalism, and we should promote a continuation, if not an extension, of current approaches to technological innovation and regulation. Second, if we want on traditionalist lines to undo globalization, then we must ask whether – and if so how – the forces of rationalism, capitalism, technological innovation and enabling regulation might be unravelled to return to a status quo ante. Third, if we determine that global spaces are for the time being here to stay, but wish on reformist lines to counter the adverse consequences of neoliberalism, then we broadly accept rationalist and capitalist structures and seek to manage technology and recraft regulation in ways that generate more desirable outcomes of globalization. Fourth, if on socialist or postmodernist lines we attribute the ills of contemporary globalization not just to neoliberal policies, but more fundamentally to underlying social structures, then we must ask whether – and if so how – current circumstances offer possibilities to transcend rationalism and/or capitalism.

As already noted in Chapter 1, and as is elaborated in Chapter 12, my position lies mainly in the reformist realm, while also drawing some inspiration from more radical critiques. However, before detailing possible policy responses to globalization it is advisable to determine the repercussions of supraterritorial relations to date. Hence, equipped with the definition, history and explanation of globalization developed in the preceding chapters, the next chapters of this book assess the consequences of the trend thus far. Then, at the end of the book, we consider what, if anything, we might do to improve the situation.

Part II
Change and Continuity

In Part I we have established that, when defined in terms of the rise of supraterritorial/transworld/transborder relations, globalization designates a far-reaching change, namely, a reconfiguration of social space. At the same time, the trend has also involved a significant continuity, insofar as territoriality has retained key importance in the new geography. Thus change and continuity have coexisted.

As seen in Chapter 4, globalization has emerged out of connections between the spatial dimension of social relations on the one hand and various economic, political and cultural conditions on the other. Since these aspects of social life are interrelated, globalization is a cause as well as an effect. In other words, it has not only *resulted from* other social forces, but has also simultaneously *impacted on* those circumstances. Part II of the book examines the consequences of globalization (a reconfiguration of space) for the wider social order.

Four broader aspects of social structure are considered in successive chapters. Chapter 5 explores the implications of contemporary globalization for production. Chapter 6 looks at repercussions for governance. Chapter 7 addresses effects on community. Chapter 8 assesses consequences for knowledge.

In each case the significance of globalization to date is found to have been change within continuity. Thus the rise of supraterritoriality has brought shifts within – but not a transcendence of – capitalism as the predominant structure of production. Likewise, contemporary globalization has yielded new forms – rather than an end – of bureaucratism as the strongest underlying framework of governance. Similarly, transworld networks have generated new collective solidarities, but still mainly on a pattern of communitarian identity politics. And globalization has on the whole encouraged shifts within rationalism, rather than a full-scale reconstruction of this predominant knowledge structure.

In sum, globalization has been a powerful force of social change, but the changes to date have not been epochal. The contemporary globalizing world remains capitalist, bureaucratic, communitarian and rationalist – and it has so far shown little sign of becoming anything different.

Chapter 5

Globalization and Production

Main points of this chapter
Expanded commodification
Altered organization
Conclusion

Main points of this chapter

- globalization has substantially strengthened the position of capitalism as the prevailing structure of production in contemporary history
- the growth of supraterritorial spaces has facilitated the extension of surplus accumulation to consumer, finance, information and communications sectors
- the expansion of transworld spaces has encouraged major shifts in the organization of capitalism, including the rise of offshore centres, transborder companies, corporate mergers and acquisitions, and oligopoly

---

We have seen in Chapter 4 that the capitalist mode of production has figured centrally in the causal dynamics of globalization. Now what, in turn, has the contemporary rapid growth of transworld spaces meant for the way that production is ordered? For example, has globalization brought no change to the prevailing capitalist framework? Or has the rise of supraterritoriality altered the forms of surplus accumulation? Or is globalization undoing capitalism and replacing it with a wholly different mode of production?

As mentioned in Chapter 1, a few authors have connected contemporary globalization with a retreat of capitalism. If capitalism is conceived as a structure of production dominated by processes of surplus accumulation, then it seems difficult to endorse such propositions. As noted in earlier chapters, globalization has involved huge expansions of supraterritorial money and finance, as well as the creation of thousands of transborder companies and strategic alliances, as well as the appearance of innumerable transworld products, as well as the emergence of major additional sectors of accumulation in the information and communications industries.

None of these developments points to a decline of capitalism, let alone its end. On the contrary, the trends sooner indicate that globalization has helped capitalism to become more widespread and entrenched than ever. If anything, we could connect globalization to 'hypercapitalism'.

This is by no means to affirm that the rise of supraterritoriality has left capitalism unaffected. Although the general structure of capitalism is as robust as ever, globalization has significantly altered the ways that accumulation occurs. These changes relate, on the one hand, to the scope of commodification and, on the other hand, to the organizational context of accumulation. In respect of commodification (this term is clarified below), globalization has spurred the growth of consumer capital, finance capital, and communication and information capital. As a result, more economic activity than ever has acquired a capitalist logic. In respect of organization, globalization has yielded much-enhanced accumulation through offshore centres and transborder companies. In addition, the growth of transworld spaces has encouraged an unprecedented wave of corporate mergers and acquisitions, which has contributed substantially to an increased concentration of capital. In short, although globalization has not transformed the primary structure of production – that is, taking us from capitalism to some post-capitalist circumstance – it has stimulated important changes within capitalism.

Expanded commodification

Following a Marxian understanding, 'commodities' are the objects through whose production and exchange surplus is created, extracted and amassed. Hence a resource becomes 'commodified' when it is incorporated into capitalist accumulation processes. For example, a forest might be commodified through exploitation by the timber industry, a song might be commodified through recording and sale by the music industry, and so on. One of the key features of capitalism therefore relates to the kinds of objects that function as commodities. Likewise, the range of resources that become commodified provides a broad indicator of the intensity of capitalism in a given social context.

The character of commodities (in the specific Marxian sense just described) has shifted throughout the history of capitalism. The following remarks perhaps present an overly neat periodization, but the general point holds that, over time, a continually widening spectrum of economic activity has turned capitalist. Early surplus accumulation involved chiefly commercial capital: that is, profit was acquired mainly through trade in agricultural and mining output as well as in certain luxury goods like furs and spices. From the late eighteenth century onwards, commercial capital was joined by industrial capital: that is, the range of commodities expanded to include manufactures from large-scale factory production. Subsequently, mainly from the late nineteenth century onwards, commercial and industrial capital were supplemented with finance capital: that is, financial instruments like stocks and bonds were also increasingly commodified. Trade in these 'articles' became a means of accumulation in its own right. In other words, the financial assets became to some degree divorced from 'real' assets.

Accelerated globalization since the 1960s has helped further to widen the scope of commodification in three general areas. First, consumerism – much of it related to global products – has extended the range of industrial capital. Whereas industrial capital previously concentrated on textiles, steel, chemicals, armaments and so on, it has since the twentieth century also encompassed a plethora of branded manufactures that are destined for immediate personal consumption. Second, the growth of supraterritoriality has greatly expanded the scope of finance capital. Global banking, global securities and global derivatives business have hugely increased both the volume and the variety of financial instruments that serve not so much as facilitators of other kinds of production, but as channels of accumulation in their own right. Third, globalization has encouraged a spread of commodification into new areas involving information and communications. As a result, items such as computer software and telephone calls have also become objects of accumulation.

Consumer capital

'Consumerism' describes behaviour where people frenetically acquire (and usually fairly quickly discard) a variety of goods that provide the user with some kind of instant but ephemeral gratification (cf. Featherstone, 1991; Sklair, 1995). This consumption centres on the satisfaction of transient desires, especially cravings for novelty, entertainment, fantasy, fashion and pleasure. Consumerism rejoices in excess – or indeed denies any such thing. 'Consumer capital' refers here to surplus accumulation that is realized in the context of this hedonistic consumption.

Although consumerism has antecedents prior to 1950, its main expansion has occurred since the second half of the twentieth century. Today consumer capitalism involves an enormous range of articles, including brand-name foods and beverages, designer clothing, (purported) health aids, motor cars, licit and illicit recreational drugs, tourism, audio-visual productions, and mass spectacles like lotteries and sporting fixtures. In all of these cases, the consumer purchases an instant (and usually transient) pleasurable experience. Indeed, many people have also taken consumerist expectations to settings such as education and health care where immediate gratification is often not available. Nevertheless, many contemporary universities and hospitals, too, have become obsessed with achieving 'customer satisfaction'.

Consumerism involves the generation as much as the satisfaction of desire. Consumers must be induced to purchase articles and experiences that they would otherwise consider unnecessary. In this regard design, packaging and display have become major preoccupations in contemporary markets. A careful branding strategy can turn the mundane into the exceptional.

To this end advertising has over the past century, and especially during recent decades, become a crucial adjunct to much capitalist enterprise. World expenditure on product promotion burgeoned from $7.4 billion in 1950 to $312.3 billion in 1993 (Clairmonte and Cavanagh, 1988: 155; Kanter, 1995: 75). Advertising through the electronic mass media alone rose in the second half of the 1990s from $270 to $358 billion per annum (*FT*, 16 December 1996: 15).

A core ritual of consumerism is 'shopping'. Over the past half-century this exercise has become routine activity for hundreds of millions of people. With seeming inexorability, shop-opening hours have increased in most corners of the world, sometimes against objections from traditional religious quarters. Indeed, for many residents of the contemporary world, Descartes could with only minimal exaggeration be repackaged to read: *'je shoppe donc je suis'*. Department stores and glittering arcades appear as temples, demanding at least a weekly visit, or more by the especially devout.

Another quintessentially consumerist activity is tourism. This voyeurism towards 'unique' and 'exotic' places has burgeoned since the 1960s. Annual transborder tourist arrivals rose to 456 million by 1990 and are expected to double again, to 937 million per annum, by 2010 (Knowles, 1994; *FT*, 7 January 1997: VII). In contrast to *travellers* of earlier generations, *tourists* purchase a packaged and branded product with largely prearranged and staged experiences of the would-be extraordinary. By 1998 travel and tourism attracted around $750 billion in world investment, generated over $3.5 trillion in annual expenditure (11.6 per cent of world GDP), and involved some 230 million jobs (10 per cent of the world's waged workforce (WTTC, 1998).

Consumerism has pervaded all corners of the contemporary world, though it has tended to affect city dwellers, middle classes and youth relatively more than other social circles. On the whole, consumerism has been more concentrated in the North than the South and the East. However, by the 1990s it had also become prominent in large urban centres of East and South East Asia, Eastern Europe and Latin America. Even a postage stamp issued in 1992 by purportedly 'communist' Vietnam unabashedly depicted a clearly marked Suzuki motorcycle draped in the insignia of Pepsi-Cola. After 1991 the government of India's New Economic Policy opened the country to consumerist icons like Pizza Hut and Kellogg's. Meanwhile Coca-Cola, expelled from India in 1977, returned in the 1990s on a larger scale than ever.

Consumerism has been intimately connected to globalization in three general ways. First, most of the principal consumerist articles have been transworld products. Goods like Sony, Lego, Armani and Michael Jackson have thrived on 'global branding'. Shopping malls – and airport duty-free zones foremost among them – are in large part celebrations of supraterritorial offerings. Transborder production has also furthered consumerism insofar as much of the output of global factories has consisted of packaged brand-name articles.

Second, many objects of consumerist desire have emerged directly from the technologies of globalization. Needless to say, mass tourism could not have developed on so large a scale without air travel. Meanwhile global communications technologies like electronic mass media have ranked among the chief suppliers of consumerist fad and fantasy, for example, with television programmes and countdowns of pop music hits. More recently, cable television and online communications have opened new, distanceless ways of shopping.

Third, global contexts have played a pivotal role in generating the hedonistic desires on which consumerism thrives. Advertising has largely operated through supraterritorial mass media: radio, television, transworld magazines, etc. A global event such as the Olympic Games has become as much a 'Gathering of the Brands' as a 'Gathering of the Nations' (*FT*, 22 July 1996: 21). On other occasions, globality has itself served as a marketing ploy, for example, when an advertisement for Coca-Cola stresses how people all over the world crave the drink.

The preceding remarks are not meant to imply that globalization has been a prerequisite for, let alone a sole cause of, the spread of consumerism. However, transworld products and global communications have in the event greatly facilitated this expansion and intensification of commodification. Globalization has made consumerism a far stronger force for the twenty-first century than it would otherwise have been.

Moreover, consumerism has provided a boon for surplus accumulation. On the one hand, branding and packaging have allowed suppliers heavily to mark up prices, thereby generating higher rates of profit. In addition, the ephemerality of consumerist fashions and pleasures has ensured that most of the products in question have a relatively short use life. Thus, when their incomes allow it, consumers quickly return to market for a new video, pack of cigarettes, automobile, paperback novel, holiday, music recording, etc.

Thanks both to marked-up prices (yielding higher returns) and to relatively short product lives (generating a higher frequency of purchase), consumerism has figured centrally in the survival and growth of contemporary industrial capitalism. Indeed, leading lights of consumerism have ranked prominently among the world's largest companies. The 1996 list of the top 100 corporations by market capitalization (that is, total share value) contained over twenty suppliers of consumerist articles. Their number included Coca-Cola, Philip Morris, Nestlé, Walt Disney, McDonald's, Gillette, 7-Eleven, Sony, and five automobile manufacturers (*WSJ*, 26 September 1996: R27).

Finance capital

Finance is 'commodified' when dealings in foreign exchange, securities, derivatives and the like are employed not only to further capitalist production in other sectors (agriculture, manufacture, etc.), but also as a means of accumulation in their own right. For instance, foreign exchange might be bought and resold in the hope of realizing profit as well as – or indeed instead of – enabling cross-border commerce. Likewise, investors may trade securities to gain profit from shifts in the prices of stocks and bonds rather than from payments of dividends and coupons. Financial derivatives, too, have since the 1980s often become only loosely connected to tangible resources. The derivatives then turn into objects of investment in themselves as much as (if not more than) tools of risk management. In all of the cases just mentioned, financial instruments come to have only partial – and perhaps only negligible – relation to other objects of value. The trade in financial instruments becomes a fairly self-contained circuit of accumulation.

The large-scale globalization of finance in current history has greatly stimulated the commodification of financial instruments. Some commodification of financial instruments developed in the nineteenth century, but the trend has become hugely more significant within contemporary capitalism. Since the 1970s the variety of financial instruments, the number of financial markets in the world, the magnitude of investments in financial instruments, and the volumes of trading have all skyrocketed well beyond any previous level. Much of this enormous expansion of financial activity has come through electronic, supraterritorial transactions.

Many indicators point towards an increased commodification of financial instruments. For example, the proportion of foreign exchange dealings that relate to transactions in 'real' goods fell from 90 per cent in the early 1970s to less than 5 per cent in the early 1990s (Tober, 1993: 105; Eatwell, 1995). In the 1970s the value of transworld movements of portfolio capital was roughly equal to that of direct investment, but by the 1990s these financial transfers had become three times as large as FDI (*FT*, 30 September 1994: XII). Although the following two figures are not directly comparable, it remains striking that the annual turnover on world financial markets in the mid-1990s topped $1,000 trillion, while world GDP was still well below $30 trillion. In other words, the value of around *ten days* of transactions on world financial markets approximated the value of *annual* world production of goods and services. Such figures imply that financial dealings have developed a logic that goes well beyond the so-called 'real' economy.

The contemporary proliferation of types of financial instruments also suggests a deeper commodification of finance. In the bond and money markets, for example, the traditional straight bond has been joined by floating-rate bonds, bonds with equity warrants, zero-coupon bonds, commercial paper, repurchase agreements, asset-backed securities and so on. Similarly, new forms of financial derivatives have appeared constantly in recent years. By the mid-1990s Euroclear handled about 90,000 different kinds of securities, with projected further increases to over half a million (*FT*, 19 June 1997: 20). Many of today's retail banks have become financial supermarkets, offering a dizzying array of saving and borrowing instruments as well as various brokerage services. Contemporary finance capitalism has also involved new kinds of institutional investors, including unit trusts (called mutual funds in North America), pension funds and insurance companies. For example, the total invested in US-based mutual funds topped $1 trillion in 1990, $2 trillion in 1993, and $3 trillion in 1996 (*FT*, 27 March 1996: 29).

Concurrently, financial trading centres have multiplied throughout the world. Recent years have seen new stock exchanges open in 70 countries across Africa, Asia, Eastern Europe and the former Soviet Union (Harris, 1998–9: 23). Securities exchanges have appeared in places such as Malawi and Myanmar where such an institution would have seemed very unlikely only a decade before. Most derivatives exchanges have also been created since the early 1980s, in cities such as Budapest, Kuala Lumpur and Sao Paôlo as well as major financial centres in the OECD countries.

Meanwhile turnover in the financial sector has burgeoned at market sites old and new. As mentioned in Chapter 3, foreign exchange dealing by the mid-1990s reached well over a trillion dollars per day. The level of secondary trading in bonds likewise has risen to many trillions of dollars' worth per annum. The average value of dealing on the world's five most active stock exchanges (Hong Kong, London, New York, Singapore and Tokyo) totalled more than $1 trillion daily in 1995 (*FT*, 28 March 1996: II). Average turnover on the New York Stock Exchange grew more than tenfold in the last quarter of the twentieth century. Whereas 30 million shares traded was a record day for the NYSE in the mid-1970s, in the mid-1990s this figure regularly topped 450 million shares. Derivatives dealings have skyrocketed to the point that the value of outstanding over-the-counter contracts reached $70 trillion in June 1998 (BIS, 1998a).

Increased turnover in financial markets has on the whole brought increased accumulation. For instance, foreign exchange business has since the 1970s provided banks with a major source of revenue. In one especially large 'killing', forex traders made £3 billion from the Bank of England's attempts in 1992 to stabilize sterling within the EU's exchange rate mechanism. George Soros alone acquired $1 billion betting against the pound on this occasion. Wild swings in the Brazilian real, the Indonesian rupiah, the Korean won, the Russian rouble and the Thai baht gave currency speculators field days in the late 1990s.

More generally, too, bank dealings – and those of transworld banking corporations prominently among them – have been a principal conduit of surplus accumulation during the period of accelerated globalization. True, banks have faced a number of crises. For example, looming defaults on massive commercial loans to the South suppressed profits across much of global banking in the mid-1980s. Likewise, property bubbles have burst in several countries at considerable cost to the banking sector. Nevertheless, on the whole profits for global banks have remained high and secure. Banks constituted the single largest group (18 in number) among the 100 largest world companies by market capitalization in the mid-1990s. They also accounted for 78 of the largest 500 corporations (FT500, 1997: 6–7).

Steep rises in stock market indexes through the 1980s and 1990s have likewise indicated a large growth in stores of surplus as a result of the heightened commodification of financial instruments. With the exception of Tokyo, all of the principal world stock exchanges have seen average share prices increase several times during this period. In London, for instance, the FTSE-100 Index rose from a level of 1,000 at its launch in 1984 to more than 6,000 in 1998. In New York the venerable Dow Jones Industrial Index not only finally broke the 1,000 level in early 1980s, but proceeded to exceed the 10,000 mark in 1999. In all, world stock market capitalization almost tripled in a decade: from $6.5 trillion in 1986 to $17.8 trillion in 1995 (IFC, 1996: 17).

Figures for profits from trade in financial derivatives are not generally publicized. However, the eagerness with which traders and institutions have developed this business implies that it has provided handsome returns. In any case large sums must have flowed into the coffers in order that the firms involved could pay dealers and managers their often astronomical salaries.

In sum, then, finance capital has generated many windfall profits in the present time of transworld trading. A large proportion of contemporary market transactions have been undertaken in a spirit of short-term speculation rather than for long-term investment. As a result, global finance capital has often been hugely volatile, placing participants on permanent alert and subjecting them to recurrent panics. The increased commodification of finance has created 'casino capitalism' and 'mad money' (Strange, 1986, 1998).

Like any casino, global finance has yielded major losses as well as big wins. For example, next to his gains George Soros has also lost $800 million on one day in 1987 and $600 million on another in 1994. World bond markets crashed in February 1994. A lone dealer in government bonds, Toshihide Iguchi of Daiwa Bank, accumulated losses of $1.1 billion until he was exposed in 1995. In equity markets, meanwhile, the Dow Jones Index has on several occasions since 1987 plummeted over 300 points in a single trading day. Long after the bubble burst on the Tokyo Stock Exchange, the Nikkei 225 Index has yet to come anywhere close to the level of 37,000 that it reached in 1989.

Securities exchanges in the so-called 'emerging markets' have tended to be even more volatile. For example, the devaluation crisis of the Mexican peso in December 1994 triggered massive sell-offs throughout Latin American stock markets in the first half of 1995. Likewise, a large-scale withdrawal of global capital from the Bangkok market in mid-1997 provoked similar investor stampedes across much of East and South East Asia. Further such crises afflicted Russia in August 1998 and Brazil in January 1999.

Global derivatives markets, too, have produced a succession of spectacular losses. In 1994 a trading subsidiary of MetallGesellschaft lost an estimated $1 billion on oil derivatives. At the end of the same year Orange County, California went bankrupt after losing almost $1.7 billion in the derivatives market. The rogue trader Nick Leeson brought down the venerable house of Barings with losses of $1.3 billion in February 1995. In another spectacular case, a copper futures dealer at Sumitomo Corporation, Yasuo Hamanaka, built up losses of $2.6 billion in the decade to June 1996. A hedge fund specializing in equity derivatives, Long Term Capital Management, was saved from collapse in September 1998 with a $3.6 billion rescue package. True, these figures become less astounding when they are considered as a proportion of overall amounts of contract trading. Nevertheless, such scenarios have reinforced fears that the speed and volume of transactions through transworld electronic channels could produce a domino effect in the derivatives market, whereby the bankruptcy of one participant could generate a systemic collapse.

Thus far, however, the global financial casino has found stability in its instability. On the whole it has yielded investors many more gains than losses, and the structure of capitalism has emerged as the clear overall winner. With little exaggeration it can be concluded that the contemporary growth of global financial markets has given surplus accumulation one of its greatest boosts in history.

Communication and information capital

In addition to consumer and finance capital, globalization has also created conditions for major growth in communication and information capital. Like financial instruments, data, messages, ideas and images circulate with particular ease in supraterritorial space by means of electronic networks. Telecommunications, digital data processing and mass media have become primary sites of surplus accumulation in recent decades.

As noted in Chapter 1, other commentators have discussed the growth of these new industries with concepts like 'post-industrial society', 'the information society', 'the information age', 'the services economy', 'the knowledge revolution', and so on. Yet these accounts have tended to downplay or ignore the capitalist character of the contemporary production of information and communications. 'Post-industrial society' (if one can speak of such a thing) is even more steeped in capitalism than was its 'industrial' predecessor. In this light references to 'the mode of information', 'reflexive accumulation' and 'cybernetic capitalism' better capture the nature of these developments (Poster, 1990; Robins and Webster, 1988).

Contemporary production of information and communications has extended the reach of commodification in four major respects: hardware, software, servicing and content. Hardware refers to the operating equipment through which information and communications are processed. The production of telephones, computers, satellites, television sets and the like has entailed a major expansion of factory-centred industrial capital in the second half of the twentieth century. Companies, governments, universities and households have spent huge sums to enhance their data processing capacities. World sales of PCs topped 80 million units in 1996, while receipts from the provision of semiconductors reached $50 billion in 1989 and $155 billion in 1995 (*FT*, 9 January 1996: 21; 26 September 1996: 5). Annual world revenues from telecommunications equipment have also well exceeded $100 billion. In many countries, investment in information and communications infrastructure has come to exceed investment in agriculture and 'smokestack industries' (cf. Sweezy and Magdoff, 1985). One oft-quoted analyst has estimated that a third of investment in the North since the 1960s has gone into equipment to handle data and information (Drucker, 1993: 75). Reflecting this shift, the share of office and telecommunications equipment in cross-border trade grew from 5 per cent in the early 1980s to 12 per cent in 1995, when it surpassed the value of agricultural exports (*FT*, 28 March 1996: 3). Such trends look likely to continue. For example, plans were announced in one year alone (1995) to build about 50 new plants for the manufacture of microchips, each factory costing about a billion US dollars.

Much surplus accumulation in contemporary history has also been pursued through the production of software, that is, the thousands of digital programmes that process information and communications through the hardware. Software producers have included corporate giants such as Microsoft and Cisco Systems, but also hundreds of smaller suppliers. Programmes to effect Internet communications alone generated sales of $2 billion per annum in the mid-1990s (*FT*, 9 April 1996: 15).

Servicing of the hardware and software just described has also grown to become a large and profitable industry. Computer technology in particular has required major support. In this field specialized companies like Electronic Data Services (EDS) and Integris have deployed tens of thousands of employees across the world and generated multiple billions of dollars in annual revenue.

Finally, information and communications industries have widened the scope of capitalism with large-scale commodification of the content that passes through electronic processing systems. In other words, the conveyance of data, ideas, messages and images through supraterritorial space has become a highly profitable business. Telephone calls, databases, mailing lists, connections to the Internet, television broadcasts, news services, market surveys, and the like have presented enormous new opportunities for accumulation. Telephone companies, online service providers, cable and satellite television suppliers, polling agencies and so on all levy subscriptions and/or other user charges. DBS services alone are expected to generate revenues of $16 billion in 2002 (*FT*, 14 April 1997: 21). In this way information and communications have become important to capitalism not only as facilitators of other processes of accumulation, but also as major objects of accumulation themselves (cf. Mosco, 1988). Indeed, some critics fear that information which is not amenable to commercial exploitation will become increasingly scarce.

Globalization has clearly lain at the heart of this commodification of information and communications. For one thing, the technologies in question are largely those of supraterritorial communications. In addition, transworld organizations have generated much of the increased demand for commodified information and communications. The operations of global companies, global associations and global governance bodies have been thoroughly dependent on telecommunications networks and computerized data transfers. Meanwhile publishers, broadcasters, film-makers and online service providers have flourished with transworld customer bases.

By and large the contemporary increased commodification of information has been a boon for accumulation. A study by the American Federation of Information Processing Societies estimated that revenues of the computer sector in the USA quadrupled in real terms during the 1980s (Schiller and Schiller, 1988: 149). Shares in information technology (IT) firms have also ranked among the high earners on equity markets since the 1980s. IT stock launches and mergers and acquisitions between IT companies have provided investment banks with some of their most lucrative business. Hardware providers like Intel, IBM, and Hewlett Packard have shot up the ranks to join the world's largest corporations. True, semiconductor earnings slumped in the mid-1990s, repeating the cycle of boom and bust that marked the industry in the 1970s and 1980s. The PC gold rush likewise receded in the mid-1990s, as even former market leaders Apple Macintosh and Olivetti struggled. Nevertheless, overall the computer sector has blessed capitalism, and high profits on software have placed industry leaders like Marc Andreessen, Michael Dell and Bill Gates among the world's wealthiest individuals.

Telecommunications, too, have generated great accumulation in contemporary history. In terms of market capitalization the value of this sector across the world quadrupled between 1986 and 1995, to over $600 billion (*FT*, 12 February 1996: 24). Annual turnover on telecoms equipment and services exceeded $600 billion in 1996 and could top $1,200 billion in the year 2000 (*WSJ-E*, 17 February 1997: 2). Both fixed-line and mobile telephone providers have enjoyed large profits in the 1990s. Lucrative capitalist potential helps to explain the flood of – and urgency behind – privatizations of telephone services around the world since the mid-1980s. Sixty-one telecoms privatizations occurred between 1990 and 1996, and several dozen more sell-offs followed in the late 1990s (EST, 1997: 5). In only one country anywhere in the world, Uruguay, has the privatization of the service been explicitly rejected. Concurrently, the WTO has given considerable priority to liberalizing the telecoms sector in cross-border commerce. As one commentator has summarized, 'deregulation and technological change are transforming the phone industry from a sleepy utility business into a high-growth competitive free-for-all' (Kuhn, 1995: 48). For example, over 80 new telecommunications companies were established in the Asia-Pacific region between 1990 and 1997 (EST, 1997: 6).

Other large-scale accumulation has occurred in the context of globalization through mass media corporations. Sales of the world's 50 largest multimedia businesses reached $110 billion in 1993, while the value of cross-border trade in printed materials, music, visual arts, cinema and associated equipment nearly tripled from $67 billion in 1980 to $200 billion in 1991 (UNDP, 1999: 33). Global media empires such as Time Warner,

Disney/ABC, Sony/CBS, Pearson Group and Reed Elsevier have figured prominently on the contemporary capitalist landscape (Herman and McChesney, 1997). Media tycoons like Rupert Murdoch and Silvio Berlusconi have ranked among the most colourful entrepreneurs in contemporary capitalism. True, flamboyance has not always enhanced the bottom line. For example, Time Warner failed to report a profit for many years after the 1989 merger (*FT*, 17 July 1996: 28). Nevertheless, capitalist ambitions have continued to fuel the growth of the media sector, whose value in Europe more than doubled during the first half of the 1990s (*FT*, 17 June 1996: 26). Indeed, in the mid-1990s broadcast media and publishing were the two most profitable industries in Europe (FT500, 1997: 17). In the USA, almost a fifth of the 400 richest persons as of 1989 obtained their wealth from the mass media (Petras, 1993: 141).

Spurred largely by globalization, then, information and communications industries have moved to the core of capitalism for the twenty-first century. Expecting that this trend will proceed further, global investment bankers like Merrill Lynch and Salomon Brothers have greatly expanded their telecommunications, media and IT divisions. In the light of such developments, Peter Drucker has conceded that his purported 'post-capitalist society' may in fact be a world economy dominated by information capitalism (1993: 166–7).

Summary

Taking the above remarks concerning commodification in sum, globalization has played an important role in redistributing the relative weights of accumulation away from 'merchandise' (commercial and industrial capital) toward 'intangibles' (finance, information and communications capital). In this way the 'real' economy has acquired a different 'reality'.

This is certainly not to claim that primary and industrial commodities have become insignificant in contemporary capitalism. However, they no longer dominate accumulation processes as they once did. The share of agriculture and manufacturing in measured world output dropped from 38.8 per cent in 1960 to 25.8 per cent in 1990 (ILO, 1995: 27). Among the world's largest 100 firms by market capitalization in 1995, a full three-fifths concentrated on consumer, finance and/or information industries. Chemicals and oil companies still carry weight, but other sectors that were prominent in the territorialized world of the late nineteenth century (e.g. mining, iron and steel, and railways) barely figure in the top corporate ranks today (FT500, 1996: 2).

It would seem telling in this light that, in general, countries where production continues to focus predominantly on extractive activities and heavy industry have become relatively poorer in the contemporary globalizing world. This is one reason for the greatly widened North–South gap since 1960. Likewise, the collapse of state socialism might be attributed in part to the failure of central planning adequately to generate consumer, finance, and information and communications sectors. The Soviet bloc could make a running in the early and mid-twentieth century, when industrial capital was dominant, but the regimes failed to meet the challenges of restructured capitalism in the globalizing late twentieth century.

Altered organization

Apart from shifts in respect of commodification, the other general area where globalization has brought changes to capitalism is the organizational setting of accumulation. Two developments in this regard – the growth of offshore centres and transborder companies – have been mentioned earlier while discussing the definition, history and causation of globalization. At the present juncture, however, our concern is to assess the consequences of these developments for surplus accumulation. In addition, two further trends in respect of capitalist organization are newly introduced below, namely, increased merger and acquisition activity and a greater concentration of capital in many sectors. Like the expansion of commodification, these organizational shifts have on the whole enhanced the possibilities of surplus accumulation. In these respects, too, globalization has thus far proved to be a bonanza for capitalism.

Offshore centres

As intimated in previous chapters, the offshore phenomenon has provided a major fillip to capitalist accumulation. Offshore centres generally offer nil or minimal rates of corporate, personal, capital gains, profit, inheritance and withholding taxes (Doggart, 1993; Hampton, 1999). These sites also entice capital with low costs, limited regulation, and statutory guarantees of confidentiality. Euphemisms affirm that offshore arrangements provide 'tax efficiency' and 'discretion'. To put the matter more explicitly, offshore arrangements have created enormous opportunities for accumulation.

As indicated earlier, states have created offshore zones both for global production processes and for global financial activities. Many of these sites, like the Bahamas or Bahrain, are islands that literally stand 'offshore'. Yet in countries like Bangladesh and Romania, EPZs are located 'onshore' in or near coastal areas. Meanwhile certain so-called 'offshore' centres such as Liechtenstein and Luxembourg are in fact landlocked. In this respect the term 'offshore' is somewhat of a misnomer.

It should be noted as well that offshore arrangements have not been a preserve of small states alone. Several major states have also passed the relevant legislation. For example, in the 1980s both Britain and China launched special economic zones for manufacturing. Offshore financial facilities were introduced in New York in 1981, in Tokyo in 1986, and in Bangkok in 1993.

Since so much of the relevant data (particularly in relation to offshore finance) is not publicly available, it is difficult to calculate with much precision the repercussions of these arrangements for contemporary capitalism. However, it would not seem far-fetched to suggest that off-shore legislation has in recent decades channelled more than a trillion extra dollars' worth of accumulation to private individuals and corporations.

The offshore phenomenon has arguably also benefited accumulation for companies and wealthy persons in indirect ways. For example, many governments have arguably lowered upper tax bands and loosened restrictive regulations on economic activity partly in order to discourage capital flight offshore. In addition, many trade unions have probably moderated their demands in respect of wages and other working conditions for fear of otherwise encouraging enterprises to relocate plants in EPZs (and other low-wage areas).

Transborder companies

As noted in earlier chapters, thousands of firms have in the context of globalization given their organization a substantial supraterritorial dimension, either by establishing affiliates in two or more countries or by forging strategic alliances with enterprises based in other countries. Some of these global company networks are huge. For example, as of the mid-1990s the Unilever corporation encompassed more than 500 subsidiaries in over 90 countries, and the mass media conglomerate Bertelsmann covered more than 600 affiliates in 53 countries. In the realm of strategic alliances, the WorldPartners Association, formed in 1993, has linked 19 telecommunications carriers in operations across over 35 countries. The advertising firms FCB and Publicis have since 1988 developed collaboration between their several hundred offices in over 70 countries.

Global companies have acquired a very prominent place in contemporary capitalism. For example, the collective annual sales of the 50 largest unitary global enterprises rose from $540 billion in 1975 to $2,100 billion in 1990, equivalent to around 10 per cent of recorded world product (Carnoy *et al.*, 1993: 49). Yearly sales by the foreign affiliates of all transborder companies increased from $2.4 trillion in 1982 to $6.4 trillion in 1994, equivalent to about a quarter of world product (UNCTAD, 1997: 17). By 1990 the largest 350 transworld companies between them conducted almost 40 per cent of the world's cross-border trade, and the largest 500 companies collectively accounted for over half (Lang and Hines, 1993: 34; Rugman and Verbeke, 1990: 1).

Although 'going global' has not opened a capitalist paradise to all firms, on the whole the fruits of transborder mobility and coordination have figured very positively in company profit margins. Global corporations have often sited their production and markets at the commercially most advantageous locations, wherever in the world those places might be. Moreover, even when plant and equipment remain fixed at certain locations, transborder companies have (as mentioned in Chapter 4) also increased their earnings through global accounting formulas. With transfer pricing, for instance, a firm can set prices on its intra-firm cross-border trade at such levels that profits flow to the balance sheets of those subsidiaries that are sited in states with the most advantageous tax, auditing or other regulatory conditions. Sometimes, then, the tricks of global accounting have been as important to accumulation as supraterritorial production and marketing.

A number of rough indicators suggest that transborder organization has served the purpose of surplus accumulation very well. For instance, the annual profits of the largest transworld enterprises have exceeded the GDPs of many low- and medium-income countries. Other studies have shown that, among US-based firms at least, the larger transborder corporations have tended to generate higher returns than intra-state firms, particularly since 1980. Some analysts have in this regard discerned a two-tiered stock market, with a clear contrast between global and national companies (Kuhn, 1995: 46, 48). By no means is it clear that, as some Marxists have suggested, the contemporary proliferation and growth of supraterritorial companies has been *necessary* to the survival of capitalism. Nevertheless, globalization of the firm has certainly – for the time being at least – yielded plentiful capitalist returns.

Transworld strategic alliances, too, have generally had positive implications for accumulation. True, some of these initiatives have yielded disappointing results. Indeed, certain studies have suggested that over 40 per cent of parties to strategic alliances have not regarded their partnerships as successful (Gilroy, 1993: 137). Yet even on this pessimistic assessment more than half of strategic alliances have borne fruit. Moreover, the proportion of profitable strategic alliances is likely to grow as firms acquire more experience with this still relatively novel mode of organization. Already many strategic alliances have allowed companies to pool resources, achieve economies of scale, share risk and shape markets to their joint advantage. For example, cross-licensing agreements between transborder pharmaceutical companies have generated very high profits in that sector (Gilroy, 1993: 152). Indeed, in some cases 'strategic alliance' appears to be a euphemism for 'cartel'.

Mergers and acquisitions

In a third general organizational trend of contemporary capitalism that is substantially connected with globalization, many companies have gone beyond strategic alliances to full-scale fusion through mergers and acquisitions (M&A). In the words of one investment banker, 'As companies go global, more acquisitions result' (*Fortune*, 1995: 40). Indeed, with 'conquests' by 'corporate raiders' and many 'hostile takeovers', M&A activity has acquired a vocabulary of (supraterritorial) warfare once reserved for (territorial) states.

The 1980s and 1990s saw successive flurries of M&A activity. The world total of these transactions more than doubled from 11,300 in 1990 to 24,600 in 1997 (UNDP, 1999: 32). The aggregate value of these deals rose to unprecedented levels of $1.1 trillion in 1996, $1.5 trillion in 1997 and nearly $2.1 trillion in 1998 (*WSJ-E*, 2 January 1998: R9; *FT*, 29 January 1999: I). Fusions across state borders numbered 2,141 with a total value of $67.3 billion in 1993, 2,553 with an aggregate value of $110.3 billion in 1994, and nearly 6,000 with a total value of $229.4 billion in 1995 (Went, 1996: 13; *FT*, 29 January 1996: 22).

The rise of supraterritoriality has not constituted the sole force behind 'merger mania' and 'takeover fever'; however, the growth of a global economy has spurred the trend in several respects. For example, transborder M&A has given many companies a means of quick entry into a target country. Rather than needing to build up an affiliate from scratch, the global company can purchase a going concern and in the process also dispense with a competitor. Governments have been loath to hinder such acquisitions, partly for fear of alienating supraterritorial capital that might otherwise locate in another jurisdiction.

Globalization has also encouraged much M&A activity within countries. Many 'domestic' fusions have had the specific aim to create a larger national firm that can hold its own in globalizing capitalism. In short, corporate combination has been a strategy for company survival in the face of global competition. On these occasions, too, governments have been reluctant to hamper M&A, for fear of prompting relocation and/or of undermining the position of 'their' firms in global markets.

The rise of supraterritoriality has also stimulated burgeoning M&A activity insofar as the deals have been especially prevalent in areas of production that lie at the heart of globalization. True, some fusions have transpired in older industries such as paper and utilities. However, 'global sectors' like consumer goods, finance, information and communications have dominated the flourishing M&A business of recent years.

In consumer industries, for example, corporate acquisitions have made major global players still larger in cases like Nestlé, Philip Morris, RJR Nabisco and Unilever. The pharmaceuticals sector witnessed some $80 billion of M&A business in the mid-1990s, including 16 deals of $1 billion or more (*FT*, 7 March 1996: 21). Several principal transworld hotel chains (Hilton, Sheraton, etc.) have also expanded by the M&A route. In addition, a number of aircraft manufacturers have merged with an eye to global positioning. In this spirit Lockheed acquired Martin Marietta in 1994, while Boeing merged with McDonnell Douglas in 1997.

In finance, various mergers between commercial banks have created veritable global giants like Tokyo-Mitsubishi Bank, Chase Manhattan (incorporating Chemical Bank) and HSBC (incorporating Midland Bank). Multiple other bank mergers and takeovers have occurred within and between EU countries in anticipation of their economic and monetary union. Most Canada-based banks have been involved in mergers, largely so that these institutions might hold their own in global financial markets.

A number of global banks have since the 1980s also taken over global securities houses, thereby ending the traditional separation of commercial and investment banks. Prime examples of these combinations include Crédit Suisse First Boston, Deutsche Morgan Grenfell and ING Barings. In addition, numerous banks have acquired insurance companies (or vice versa) to become so-called 'bancassurance' combinations. In the largest such transaction to date, Travelers Group took over Citicorp in 1998 in a deal worth $73 billion. Among themselves, too, insurance firms have undergone dozens of fusions largely in order to enhance their global market position.

As for the information and communications sectors, IT enterprises experienced 2,913 mergers and acquisitions in 1995 alone (*FT*, 29 January 1996: 22). Dozens of major telecommunications companies have likewise undertaken mergers and acquisitions to create veritable transborder carriers. For instance, Telefónica de España, newly privatized and the largest transborder company based in Spain, has bought into businesses in 18 countries. Various global media firms have also fused since the late 1980s, including Sony with CBS and Time Life with Warner Brothers (with further expansions in 1996 to acquire Turner Broadcasting and in 2000 to merge with America Online).

True, the 1990s also witnessed some important demergers, especially in respect of multi-business conglomerates. For example, IBM disaggregated into 14 smaller and potentially mutually competitive companies in 1991. Sandoz hived off its industrial chemicals division as a new company in

1995, before fusing with Ciba-Geigy in 1996 to form the pharmaceuticals giant Novartis. AT&T, Hanson, ICI and ITT have also embarked on demerger initiatives.

However, the list of breakups is relatively short next to the concurrent plethora of mergers and acquisitions. Moreover, 'spinning off' appears to have been a temporary fashion, mainly circulating in the boardrooms of UK- and US-based companies, along with a few other firms headquartered in France and Germany. The overall trend in present times of accelerated globalization has pointed decidedly towards increased combinations.

Mergers and acquisitions are not by themselves guarantees of profitability in globalizing markets, of course. Indeed, many fusions have failed in terms of subsequent share price performance, earnings growth, turnover of top executives, new product development, etc. The costs of major takeovers are also astronomical (although they bring high earnings to the investment banks that coordinate them). Nevertheless, even if the returns have sometimes fallen below expectations, the tendency to fuse companies in response to global market opportunities and competition has shown little sign of abating.

Concentration

Thanks largely to expanded M&A activity, globalizing capitalism has brought substantially increased concentration to many areas of production. Often the fusions have involved not a bolt-on acquisition of a small firm by a sector leader, but a 'mega-merger' of giants that radically transforms the competitive balance in a market. As a result, global capital has, on the whole, meant bigger and more centralized capital.

A handful of big firms now dominate many sectors. For example, in the mid-1990s the largest five companies in the respective areas of production accounted for 70 per cent of world markets in consumer durables, 60 per cent of air travel, over half of aircraft manufacture, over half of electronics and electrical equipment, over 40 per cent of global media, a third of chemicals, and some 30 per cent of world insurance sales (Harvey, 1995: 194). In 1998 the ten biggest firms in the respective world markets controlled almost 70 per cent of computer sales, 85 per cent of pesticides, and 86 per cent of telecommunications (UNDP, 1999: 67). Likewise, ten companies have come to control two-thirds of the world semiconductor industry (Lang and Hines, 1993: 35–6). Meanwhile business in the issuance and secondary trading of debt instruments has become more and more concentrated in a small group of investment houses (ISMA, 1995: 10). By 1998, just three firms between them handled over 75 per cent of the value of worldwide M&A deals (*FT*, 29 January 1999: 1). In cross-border trade, as of the early 1990s, five companies accounted for 77 per cent of cereal shipments, and four companies covered 87 per cent of tobacco shipments. Meanwhile the top three companies in their respective sectors effected 80 per cent of banana trade, 83 per cent of cocoa trade, and 85 per cent of tea trade (Madden, 1992: 46). Global chains owned almost a third of the world's hotel rooms in 1993, up from a quarter in 1989 (*FT*, 31 January 1997: 15). A few companies such as Associated Press, Reuters and Agence France Presse have dominated global news provision. Visa, MasterCard and American Express between them process 95 per cent of the world's credit card business (*FT*, 12 June 1996: 1). As of 1995, the big five of the music industry controlled more than two-thirds of the $40 billion world market in recordings (*FT*, 2 September 1996: 21; 27 September 1996: X). The Big Five of accountancy firms dominate across six continents.

In these circumstances, the largest 100 global companies have controlled anything up to half of total world FDI. The top 300 transborder firms have held 70 per cent of FDI and anywhere between a quarter and a third of all corporate assets (Dunning, 1993: 15; Harvey, 1995: 189). The 15 largest global companies have each reached annual sales whose value exceeds the GDP of over 120 countries (Went, 1996: 18)

To be sure, some developments have gone against the prevailing trend towards concentration. Indeed, new technologies and new methods of management have encouraged a growth of small firms in some sectors, including computer software, Internet service providers and biotechnology. That said, these small companies have often conducted most of their transactions with large global concerns. To that extent their autonomy has been severely restricted.

Overall, then, four decades of accelerated globalization have yielded conditions of considerable oligopoly in the world economy. Indeed, many corporate leaders have assumed that only the largest companies in a sector can profit in a global market. The much-discussed 'pressures of global competition' have made governments and citizens more ready to allow 'their' corporate flag carriers to acquire an oligopolistic position. Meanwhile no transworld anti-trust or competition agencies have emerged to monitor and if necessary to check this concentration, a point to which we return in Chapter 12.

Conclusion

The analysis in this chapter (summarized in the Box below) suggests that capitalism has been not only a primary cause, but also a chief consequence of globalization. Indeed, the growth of supraterritorial spaces has to date widened the range of surplus accumulation and deepened its hold in the world economy. Alternative modes of production have arguably never been as weak. In this light theses concerning 'late capitalism' and 'post-capitalism' seem decidedly misplaced.

Contemporary globalizing capitalism in summary

Expanded commodification
- consumerism
- exponential expansion of finance capital
- emergence of information and communications capital

Reorganization
- creation of profit-enhancing offshore arrangements
- proliferation of transborder corporate networks
- large waves of company mergers and acquisitions
- rise of global oligopolies

True, the reinvigoration of capitalism through the rise of supraterritoriality has been accompanied by considerable volatility and periodic crises. As the OECD has observed, globalization has entailed:

> a turbulent process of birth and death of firms, the rise and fall of whole sectors of activity and the reallocation of production within as well as between regions and countries.
>
> (*FT*, 30 September 1994: I)

However, these developments do little to suggest a terminal decline of capitalism as a structure of production. Surplus accumulation has continued robustly, however unstable the environment may have been for many individuals, firms and governments.

Hence for the time being we should concentrate not on risks that globalization might pose to the survival of capitalism, but on the harms that globalizing processes of surplus accumulation can do, particularly to vulnerable social circles. The contemporary growth of transworld capitalism can in this respect be linked: to substantially increased gaps of material welfare within and between countries; to heightened ecological degradation; to weakened social cohesion; and to reduced democratic controls on economic policy. These matters are elaborated in Part III.

Chapter 6

Globalization and Governance

Main points of this chapter
The reconstructed state
Multilayered public governance
Privatized governance
Conclusion

Main points of this chapter

- globalization has figured centrally in the emergence of post-sovereign governance
- states have remained crucial to governance, but globalization has spurred several shifts in their main attributes
- the rise of supraterritoriality has promoted moves toward multilayered governance, where regulatory competences are more dispersed across substate, state and suprastate agencies
- the growth of transworld spaces has encouraged some privatization of governance (that is, increased regulatory activity through nonofficial channels)
- post-sovereign governance has retained the deeply bureaucratic character that also previously marked statist governance

---

In Chapter 4 we saw that regulatory arrangements have constituted a primary determinant of both the onset and the subsequent speed and direction of globalization. Now we consider the converse effects that the rise of supraterritoriality has had on governance. How, if at all, has globalization changed the institutions that execute regulatory functions and/or the ways that they operate?

The most frequently discussed – and most vigorously disputed – question in respect of globalization and governance concerns the role of the state. As noted in Chapter 1, many commentators have linked globalization to a retreat or even demise of the state. Indeed, at first blush it does seem sensible to presume that the proliferation of *supraterritorial* relations would pose a challenge to the *territorial* state.

However, the death notices have been recklessly premature. As stressed in Chapter 2, the spread of transworld spaces has not meant the end of territorial spaces, and on this basis we could expect territorially based governance agencies like the state to survive quite well in a globalizing world. Indeed, as indicated in Chapter 4, states have played a key role in promoting the rise of supraterritoriality. Moreover, they remain prominent players in the contemporary governance of global flows and show every sign of retaining that significance in the twenty-first century. We therefore do well to abandon all assumptions that globality and the state are inherently contradictory.

This is not to say that globalization has left the state and governance more generally unchanged. In one broad sense, developments with respect to the state are comparable to those that have unfolded in regard to capitalism: in both cases, the core circumstance remains entrenched while some of its major features have altered. In respect of the state, globalization has prompted five general changes, namely: (1) the end of sovereignty; (2) reorientation to serve supraterritorial as well as territorial interests; (3) downward pressures on public-sector welfare guarantees; (4) redefinition of the use of warfare; and (5) increased reliance on multilateral regulatory arrangements. These five shifts in the character of the state are elaborated in the first section below.

Yet developments surrounding governance have also shown an important difference when compared to the situation regarding production. Whereas the contemporary large-scale growth of supraterritorial spaces has enhanced capitalism's position as the dominant structure of production, the same trend has caused the state to lose some predominance as a site of governance. This decline in relative primacy has transpired in two main ways. First, public-sector governance has become more multilayered. The rise of supraterritoriality has promoted shifts of many regulatory competences 'downwards' to substate authorities (at local and provincial levels) and 'upwards' to suprastate governance bodies (at regional and transworld levels). Second, globalization has encouraged a growth of regulatory activities through nonofficial bodies. As a result, governance has gained significant inputs from civic associations and firms. These two trends are detailed, respectively, in the second and third sections of this chapter.

These important changes noted, at a deeper structural level contemporary globalization has also yielded a key continuity in governance, namely that of bureaucratism. Neither the diffusion of public-sector authority nor the growth of private-sector regulation has displaced bureaucracy as the underlying principle of modern administration. Under a structure of bureaucratism, governance is mainly conducted through large-scale, relatively permanent, formally organized, impersonally managed and hierarchically ordered decision-taking procedures. The post-sovereign state, substate bodies, suprastate organs and nonstate regulatory agencies have all in the great majority of cases reproduced rather than challenged the general bureaucratic framework of administration. If anything, bureaucratism is more pervasive and stronger than ever in the present-day globalizing world.

In sum, then, large-scale accelerated globalization of contemporary history has produced change and continuity in governance. The rise of supraterritoriality has encouraged changes in the character of the state without undermining the state itself. Globalization has prompted a proliferation of sites of governance without undermining bureaucracy as the underlying framework of administration. Hence we can link the rise of supraterritoriality to the demise of the Westphalian international system (named after the treaty of 1648 that formalized the modern concept of sovereign statehood), but this post-sovereign condition has not been one of post-bureaucratic governance.

The reconstructed state

Whatever new world order might be emerging in the course of contemporary accelerated globalization, the state has remained a major part of it. Even in countries where ultra-neoliberal governments have ostensibly been committed to shrinking the public sector, states have often increased their payroll, budget and scope of regulation. The Bretton Woods institutions, too, have (perhaps belatedly) recognized the importance of the state for an effectively functioning global market (Dhonte and Kapur, 1997; World Bank, 1997b). True, many states have contracted in relation to privatizations, whose total value has run into hundreds of billions of dollars worldwide since the mid-1980s. Neoliberal states have also transferred some social security arrangements to the market. However, state expansion in other areas has generally more than compensated for such shrinkage.

Some of this enlargement of states has related quite closely to the spread of supraterritoriality. For instance, technologies of globalization have given states surveillance tools and military equipment of unprecedented sophistication and destructive potential, including computerized data banks, spy satellites and long-range missiles. In addition, the growth of global flows has encouraged some states to pursue greater environmental and consumer protection, to enact new data protection legislation, and so on.

To be sure, certain states have come under particular strain in the contemporary world. For instance, the 1990s witnessed some major implosions of government. Somalia presented perhaps the most striking example. Furthermore, recent decades have seen the division of several states, including Ethiopia, Yugoslavia, ex-Czechoslovakia and the former Soviet Union. Yet such developments have hardly signalled the end of the state. In most cases of threatened collapse, states have staged recoveries: Belgium, Lebanon, Uganda, etc. As for fragmentations, fusions and other recompositions of states, such events have been the stuff of world politics for centuries.

Rather than contracting or eliminating the state, the spread of supra-territoriality has tended to create a different kind of state. As many a political theorist has stressed, the state has never in its history been fixed. It is perpetually 'in motion, evolving, adapting, incorporating . . . always in some condition of transition' (Jarvis and Paolini, 1995: 5–6). In relation to globalization, reconfiguration of the state has, most significantly, involved a demise of sovereignty (that is, in the Westphalian understanding of that principle). In addition, the growth of transworld spaces can be linked to important changes in the constituencies and policy instruments of states.

Before addressing these developments in more detail, it is important to stress that states have had differential capacities to respond to globalization. Clearly, for example, the Japanese state has generally been able to exert far more influence in global spaces than the Bolivian state (cf. Adams *et al.*, 1999). Nevertheless, all states have in one way or another confronted the end of sovereignty and the broad policy adjustments described below.

The end of sovereignty

Prior to recent decades of accelerated globalization, governance in world – and at that time more distinctly *international* – politics was constructed mainly around the principle of sovereign statehood. By traditional conceptions, sovereignty entails a claim by the state to supreme, comprehensive, unqualified and exclusive rule over its territorial jurisdiction. With *supreme* rule, the sovereign state answers to no higher authority; it always has the final say in respect of its territorial realm and its cross-border relations with other countries. With *comprehensive* rule, the sovereign state governs all aspects of social life: money supply, language, military affairs, sexual behaviour, formal education, etc. With *unqualified* rule, sovereign states respect a norm of nonintervention in one another's territorial jurisdictions. With *exclusive* rule, the sovereign state does not share authority over its realm with any other party.

True, even in Westphalian times practice sometimes fell short of this definition of sovereignty. For example, most states at one time or another undertook military invasions and covert interventions into foreign jurisdictions. Westphalian states also never enjoyed full control of cross-border movements of money (Helleiner, 1999). In addition, colonial administrations often exercised only limited control over peripheral districts of their claimed territory. Meanwhile weaker states often lacked the resources to make good their legal pretensions to sovereignty.

Nevertheless, sovereignty remained hypothetically realizable in the territorialist world of old. A state could, by strengthening its means, graduate from mere legal sovereignty to positive sovereignty. Major states could substantially make good their claims to supreme, comprehensive, unqualified and exclusive territorial governance. Moreover, the principle of sovereignty enjoyed largely unquestioned acceptance in these earlier times. Religious universalists, liberal cosmopolitans and Marxist internationalists who rejected the norm constituted a small minority and were generally dismissed as utopians.

In the face of unprecedented globalization since the 1960s, states can no longer be sovereign in the traditional sense of the word. For both physical and ideational reasons, a state cannot in contemporary globalizing circumstances exercise ultimate, comprehensive, absolute and singular rule over a country and its foreign relations. State sovereignty depends on territorialism, where all events occur at fixed locations: either within territorial jurisdictions; or at designated points across tightly patrolled borders. The end of territorialism has therefore brought the end of sovereignty. Indeed, most new, post-colonial states (established in the time of accelerating globalization) have never been able to assert sovereignty except in name.

Many material conditions in the current globalizing world have transcended the territorialist geography that sovereignty presupposes. Computerized data transmissions, radio broadcasts, satellite remote sensing and telephone calls do not halt at customs posts. Moreover, such communications occur: (a) at speeds that make it difficult for state surveillance to detect them in advance; and (b) in quantities that a state, even with greatly enhanced capabilities, cannot comprehensively track. Electronic mass media have also detracted from a state's dominion over language construction and education. Nor can a state exercise complete authority over transborder associations or global companies. In addition, as detailed below, many regulations now come to the state from suprastate bodies and global law rather than being formulated by that state itself. Likewise, governments intervene in, rather than control, global trade. With the development of global currencies, credit cards and the like, even the most powerful state has lost sovereign authority over the money supply and exchange rates. Nor can a state successfully assert supreme and exclusive rule over the global financial flows that pass through its jurisdiction (or do they?). Transworld ecological conditions such as ozone depletion and biodiversity loss have similarly contradicted the material preconditions of sovereignty.

In short, even where contemporary states are legally entitled to do so, they have been quite unable singularly and fully to control the global spaces which affect their jurisdictions. To be sure, states can influence supraterritorial activities – sometimes quite substantially. However, even the best-endowed state has not had the means to assert *sovereign* control over transborder relations. Global circumstances cannot be fixed in a territorial space over which a state might aim to exercise absolute authority. Indeed, on many occasions transworld relations influence circumstances in a country without ever directly touching its soil.

At the same time as overturning the material preconditions for sovereignty, globalization has also loosened crucial affective underpinnings of sovereignty (in ways that are detailed in Chapter 7). On the one hand, the new geography has advanced various nonterritorial identities and communities. Transborder loyalties on lines such as class, gender, profession, race, religion and sexual orientation have diluted, rivalled and sometimes even overridden feelings of national solidarity that have in the past lent so much legitimacy to state sovereignty. At the same time, contemporary globalization has also often reinvigorated more localized solidarities. When faced with the vastness and seeming intangibility of globality, many people have turned away from the state to their local 'home' in order to nurture their possibilities of community and self-determination (Strassoldo, 1992). In addition, citizens and governors alike have in general become increasingly ready to give values such as economic growth, human rights and ecological integrity – none of which is strictly bound to territory – a higher priority than sovereign statehood.

On a range of counts, then, contemporary large-scale globalization has contradicted and subverted sovereign statehood. In this light, various authors have observed that the world has moved into 'the twilight of sovereignty' or 'beyond sovereignty' (Wriston, 1992; Soroos, 1986). These commentators have noted that 'sovereignty is no longer sacrosanct' or even that sovereignty 'has lost much of its relevance' (Chopra and Weiss, 1992; Lapidoth, 1992: 345). When certain theorists have argued that sovereignty is today as strong as ever (e.g. Krasner, 1993), closer inspection usually reveals that they are conflating 'sovereignty' with state power in general, rather than focusing (following traditional usage) on the specific attribute of supreme and exclusive rule over a territorial jurisdiction.

To be sure, the *concept* of sovereignty has remained very much alive in contemporary political discourse. The *idea* continues to have important impacts insofar as people believe that sovereignty persists or ought to be retrieved. Government leaders in many countries have regularly spoken of 'defending sovereignty' even if – in the traditional understanding of the term – it has no longer been in place to defend. Meanwhile, many citizens have clung to the illusion of sovereignty because they associate the principle with their cultural identity and broader security.

However, persistent rhetoric of sovereignty is quite different from continued viability of sovereignty. Under contemporary conditions of globalization, no amount of institution building would allow a state to achieve absolute, comprehensive, supreme and unilateral control of the global flows that affect its realm. At the same time, sovereignty has become discredited as the primary norm of world politics in substantial and influential circles of environmentalists, feminists, human rights advocates, investors, managers, religious revivalists, youth and so on.

A number of theorists have urged that, rather than assert the end of sovereignty, we should rethink the notion in order to make it relevant to the contemporary globalizing world (Williams, 1996; Clark, 1999: ch 4). These analysts rightly emphasize that key concepts are social constructs that evolve in response to changing historical contexts. Some commentators have spoken in this regard of emergent 'partial' or 'shrunken' sovereignty, as states surrender their prerogatives in certain areas. Or observers have introduced ideas of 'limited' and 'qualified' sovereignty, as states acquire numerous multilateral legal commitments. Or analysts have coined notions of 'pooled' and 'shared' sovereignty, in respect of various instances like the EU where regulation is undertaken jointly among states. Other theorists have, with Harry Gelber, reconceptualized sovereignty to mean a state's 'capacity to manage', thereby removing notions of unilateral, supreme and unconditional rule (Gelber, 1997: xi).

However, sovereignty has in its various historical formulations always retained a sense of singular, absolute, supreme governance. Whether people were in the past referring to divine sovereignty, monarchical sovereignty or national sovereignty, the concept was never about shrunken, limited or shared authority. Phrases such as 'partial sovereignty', 'qualified sovereignty' and 'pooled sovereignty' are – by all traditional definitions of sovereignty – contradictions in terms. Meanwhile, the idea of 'capacity to manage' tends to conflate sovereignty with state power in general, when historically 'sovereignty' has designated a particular kind of state power. In short, these various contemporary reconceptions of sovereignty so radically change the meaning of the term that it becomes confusing to retain the same word. It is therefore time to develop a new vocabulary of post-sovereign governance (cf. Czempiel and Rosenau, 1989).

Turns toward supraterritorial constituencies

As well as becoming post-sovereign, states have also changed in current times of globalization with regard to the constituencies that they serve. The sovereign state of old generally represented so-called 'domestic' or 'national' interests. It sought to advance the pursuits of its citizens in the wider world and to defend them against harmful so-called 'external' or 'foreign' intrusions. To be sure, sovereign states often favoured the interests of certain sectors of their resident populace more than others, for example, particular classes, religious denominations or ethnic groups. However, such privileged constituencies almost always lay within the given state's territory and among its citizens.

Under the influence of contemporary globalization, a state has become less consistent in holding a territorial line of defence of its 'inside' against its 'outside'. States no longer always clearly promote 'domestic' interests against those of 'foreigners'. Instead, post-sovereign states have tended to become arenas of collaboration and competition between a complex array of territorial and supraterritorial interests.

As an illustration of this trend, ministries from various states now often engage in transgovernmental cooperation with each other. Thus, for example, health departments might collaborate in regard to the management of an epidemic. Sometimes these transgovernmental activities have increased inter-ministerial divisions within states. For instance, in the United Nations Environment Programme (UNEP) environment ministers from around the world have regularly complained about economics ministers. Likewise, finance ministries and central banks have often found more commonality of views among themselves and with the multilateral financial institutions than with other departments in their respective states. In each of these and other cases supraterritorial concerns and connections have undermined the cohesiveness of the state.

Another kind of scenario that has broken the traditional pattern of defending 'the national interest' has seen some contemporary states promoting the cause of one or the other global social movement. For example, the Iranian state after 1979 gave extensive support to Islamicists across the world. Other states have from time to time carried the banner for global environmentalism or for a human rights issue. For instance, in June 1995 the German, Danish and Swedish states joined transworld protests by environmentalists against Royal Dutch/Shell's proposal to sink the Brent Spar oil platform. In addition, many governments in the South have taken heed of the priorities of transborder foundations and NGOs when designing and executing development policies.

Most strikingly to date, however, post-sovereign states have often served the interests of global capital in addition to (and on occasion instead of) national-territorial capital. (Needless to say, global capital includes not only 'foreign'-based enterprises, but also 'home'-based concerns with transborder operations.) Much contemporary state policy has thereby addressed the demands of global companies, transworld financial markets, supraterritorial mass media and telecommunications, and so on. As noted before, many governments have feared that, if they do not provide sufficiently appealing taxation and regulation environments, footloose global capital will desert them. In 1995 alone, 65 states liberalized their rules governing foreign direct investment (UNDP, 1999: 29). Likewise, many governments have offered subsidies and reduced corporate tax rates in scarcely disguised interstate tax competition for mobile business (Tanzi, 1996). Robert Cox has in this light described contemporary states as 'transmission belts from the global to the national economic spheres' (1993b: 260).

Cox exaggerates insofar as this metaphor could imply that the post-sovereign state has lost all sight of its 'internal', territorial constituency. In practice, the state has often been a site of struggle between territorial and supraterritorial capital. For example, even the radically neoliberal Thatcher Government prevaricated in the face of Nestlé's 1988 takeover of a 'British' institution, Rowntree Mackintosh. Especially in the more industrialized parts of the world, various states have responded to contemporary globalization with intensified trade protectionism in respect of certain 'domestic' businesses. Likewise, in the name of guarding 'national' interests, immigration controls have rarely been as tight as they are at the start of the twenty-first century, aided in particular by the intensified surveillance that can be conducted using new information technologies.

In short, it is not that globalization has brought an end to territorial constituencies, but that the clientele of governments has become partly global as well. *Raison d'état* has become more than *raison de la nation*. The state's attempts to serve both territorial and global interests can breed ambiguous policy, particularly when the two constituencies conflict.

Retreats from state welfarism

The growth of supraterritorial capitalist constituencies also appears to have put significant downward pressures on state provisions of social security in the contemporary globalizing world. Although data have yet to be fully assembled and systematically analysed, much evidence points to links between globalization (especially under the prevailing neoliberal ideology) and the oft-proclaimed 'decline of the welfare state' (cf. Esping-Andersen, 1994, 1996; Teeple, 1995; Bowles and Wagman, 1997).

The history of states during the first three-quarters of the twentieth century was in good part a story of growing cradle-to-the-grave public-sector guarantees of nutrition, health care, housing, education, minimum income and other welfare needs. At the same time, regimes of progressive taxation were introduced to effect a substantial redistribution of wealth in many countries. A number of circumstances generated this expansion of state-led social security programmes, including the spread of universal suffrage, pressure from organized labour, the Bolshevik challenge, and promises made by governing élites to suffering masses during the world wars and decolonization struggles.

The growing power of global capital contributed significantly to reversals of these trends during the last decades of the twentieth century. At a time when the finances of many social security systems were coming under strain in any case, the added pressure from transborder capital for decreased taxes and labour costs has further encouraged many governments to cut back social provisions in the name of 'global competitiveness'. Such reductions have been a cornerstone of many 'adjustment' packages in the South, 'reform' programmes in the North, and 'transition' policies in the former Soviet bloc.

No state has been able completely to buck this trend. When François Mitterand attempted as President of France in the early 1980s to resurrect policies of nationalization and Keynesian demand stimulation, capital outflows and censure from global economic institutions forced him to abandon the course. Even governments in Scandinavia, after largely resisting demands to retrench during the 1980s, felt compelled to scale down their public welfare mechanisms in the 1990s (Geyer *et al.*, 1999). True, states have reduced welfare entitlements at different rates and to different extents. In this regard the Scandinavian experiences and the Dutch 'polder model' of (fairly) socially sensitive restructuring have contrasted with more severe cuts in New Zealand and the USA. However, no state has escaped the downward pressures of neoliberal globalization on government guarantees of material welfare.

Certain parts of the welfare state have usually faced greater constraints than others. Governments have generally implemented the greatest cuts in respect of sunk costs such as unemployment benefits, provisions for the elderly, and untied official development assistance. Other rollbacks have often affected minimum wage levels, redistributive taxation, food subsidies, publicly provided infrastructure, and credit subsidies. In comparison, education and training budgets have tended to be less affected, particularly insofar as such spending is believed to enhance a country's position in global markets. That said, many economic restructuring programmes of the 1990s have come to incorporate so-called 'social safety nets' with the aim of reducing the worst pains for the poor and disadvantaged.

Yet almost no government anywhere today dares openly to pursue a programme of radical progressive redistribution of wealth. Various would-be socialists have, as statespersons facing global capitalism, tempered or reversed programmes of redistribution. This roll call has included Cardoso in Brazil, Murayama in Japan, Kok in the Netherlands, Kwasniewski in Poland, Mbeki in South Africa, Museveni in Uganda, and more. Meanwhile many other governments have unabashedly embraced neoliberal logic, arguing that growing inequalities of wealth and income are unavoidable side effects of increased efficiency and viable public finances.

Yet it would be mistaken to conclude that globalization and publicly provided social security are inherently in tension. Downward pressures arose in the late twentieth century as states addressed social welfare individually and in the context of interstate competition to attract global capital. However, other policy courses are available, including as yet little explored possibilities of global arrangements to underpin social security.

Altered patterns of warfare

Another by-product of contemporary widespread globalization has involved changes in the ways that states deploy armed force. Preparation for and engagement in armed struggle was a major spur to the rise of the modern state and subsequently remained one of its chief preoccupations. However, the means and purposes of warfare have continually shifted over time. The spread of supraterritoriality has arguably encouraged several further such changes in the contemporary world.

For one thing, the expansion of supraterritorial interests has generally reduced incentives for interstate war, particularly in those countries and social circles where globalization has proceeded the furthest. Interstate combat would generally advance little purpose for – and sooner positively harm – the global circulation of capital, transborder communities of religious, racial and class solidarity, the management of global environmental degradation, and so on. Perhaps a deeper insight lies behind the flippant observation that no two countries with McDonald's outlets have ever entered into armed conflict with each other (*Daily Telegraph*, 21 December 1996).

Yet contemporary accelerated globalization has by no means created post-military states. On the contrary, globalization has arguably encouraged an increased *inward* application of armed violence by the state. All but three of the 61 major armed conflicts recorded between 1989 and 1998 were civil wars (UNDP, 1999: 5). On various occasions contemporary police operations have aimed to secure the position of global companies, the implemention of structural adjustment programmes, or the privileges of an exploitative local élite that holds greater stakes in global markets than in its purported 'homeland'. Many other times states have unleashed armed force to repress subnational ethnic movements or religious resurgence, both of which have, for reasons elaborated in Chapter 7, often been fed by globalization. In these respects, too, the post-sovereign state has not abjured militarization so much as deployed armed force differently. These points are discussed further, with reference to human security, in Chapter 9.

Multilateralism

A fifth distinctive feature of post-sovereign states has been their greater proclivity to enter into multilateral governance arrangements, to the point that various researchers in the field of International Relations have spoken of the development of multilateral*ism*. In contrast to earlier generations, states under conditions of contemporary globalization have been less inclined to take unilateral initiatives in world affairs. Foreign policy has since the 1960s come very often to involve interstate arrangements, including regional integration schemes, the expanded UN system, Group of Seven (G7) consultations, and so on. These collective measures have frequently applied to 'internal affairs' as well as interstate relations. Thus multilateral policies have arisen in response to civil strife, labour policies, technology standards, industrial subsidies, local environmental protection schemes, and much more. Through multilateralism, as through so much else, globalization has dissolved the distinctions between 'domestic' and 'foreign' affairs that marked the Westphalian system.

The growth of multilateralism is mainly discussed in the next section under the headings of regionalization and transworld governance. However, multilateral arrangements are an interstate as well as suprastate phenomenon. In other words, 'suprastate' does not mean 'nonstate'. Although multilateral regimes have acquired a certain life of their own, beyond that of the participating states, they have remained integrally a matter of states, too.

The preceding discussion has indicated that contemporary globalization shows no sign of erasing the state. On the contrary, states remain one of the principal agencies through which the consequences of growing supraterritoriality can be addressed. However, the state in present times of globalization is not the same state of the territorialist Westphalian era.

Multilayered public governance

In the post-sovereign condition that has arisen with contemporary accelerated globalization, states are players in a complex public sector that also includes multiple substate and suprastate authorities. On the one hand, the expansion of supraterritoriality has encouraged a proliferation of direct transborder connections between local and provincial governments. At the same time, globalization has promoted a major growth of regional and transworld governance mechanisms. As a result of this multiplication of substate and suprastate arrangements alongside regulation through states, contemporary governance has become considerably more decentralized and fragmented. In this respect Hedley Bull was prescient to speculate in the mid-1970s about an emergent 'new mediævalism' in world politics with several different but also overlapping and interrelated layers of public authority (1977: 254–5, 264–76).

Globalization has furthered this dispersion of the public sector in three principal ways. First, as already discussed, the rapid contemporary growth of supraterritorial spaces has made sovereign statehood impracticable. Other institutions have moved in to fill the many resultant gaps in effective governance. Second, globalization has introduced a number of problems (transborder communications, global environmental change, etc.) in which substate and suprastate agencies may hold a comparative advantage over states, or at least a complementary role. Third, the growth of global communications, global organization, global finance and global consciousness has provided substate and suprastate authorities with infrastructures and mindsets to sustain their operations, including many activities that bypass states.

Indeed, the various substate and suprastate institutions have acquired a relative autonomy from states. In other words, these bodies now often take their own initiatives and are not wholly subordinated to states. Weaker states in particular are liable to influence by public governance agencies at other levels. However, the autonomy of local, provincial, regional and transworld bodies remains limited insofar as these institutions continue to interact with and be shaped by states. In short, largely on account of globalization, the public sector has become increasingly multifaceted, with no 'level' holding systematic primacy over the others, in the way that the state did in the former age of sovereignty.

Substate transborder governance

The delegation of various areas of public policy from the state to substate authorities is hardly new to the present time of accelerated globalization. However, the widespread contemporary trend of devolution from central to provincial, municipal and district levels is striking. The move has not spread universally, but it has surfaced in scores of countries across the world, often with the explicit urgings and the financial sponsorship of suprastate agencies like the EU or the multilateral development banks.

Furthermore, in a notable departure from state-centred practices of the Westphalian system, many substate governments have in recent decades developed direct transborder contacts with each other (Duchacek *et al.*, 1988; Hocking, 1993). These connections often have not directly involved central governments. Indeed, the policies pursued in this transstate diplomacy have sometimes run contrary to those prevailing at state level.

Considerable transborder governance of this kind has developed between municipalities. The trend is hardly surprising insofar as supraterritorial telecommunications webs, air corridors, capital flows and the like have connected so-called 'global cities' such as Los Angeles, Moscow, Paris and Singapore as much to one another as to their respective hinterlands. Yet in small and medium-sized towns, too, local governments have taken transborder policy initiatives on matters such as development cooperation, control of crime, and the promotion of human rights.

Formal regular transborder contacts between town councils began on a small scale in the early twentieth century through the International Union of Local Authorities, founded in 1913. The practice of twinning towns began in the 1950s. However, global links between municipal governments have mainly intensified since the late twentieth century, encouraged among other things by the Habitat programme of the UN. The various networks of cities include the World Association of Major Metropolises, launched in 1985, and regional organizations of urban authorities set up across Arab countries (1967), Africa (1975), Asia (1989), Europe (1990) and Latin America (1995). In regard to global ecological issues more specifically, the International Council for Local Environmental Initiatives, established in 1990, by the end of the decade connected 337 municipal authorities in 57 countries 'to achieve and monitor tangible improvements in global environmental conditions' (ICLEI, 1999; UIA, 1998: 951).

Other transborder governance through substate institutions has developed at the level of provinces and federal states. In China, for example, the governments of Guangdong, Xinjiang, Shandong and Yunnan Provinces have acquired sufficient autonomy in foreign policy from Beijing that some commentators have even wondered whether the country can stay united in the longer term (Goodman and Segal, 1994; Segal, 1994). In Russia, Tatarstan has similarly asserted its independence from the Kremlin in dealing with global capital. Meanwhile, in competition between the constituent states of India to attract transborder capital, Andhra Pradesh negotiated its own structural adjustment loan with the World Bank in 1997, separately from the central government in New Delhi. In northeastern Brazil, tax competition for capital contributed in the 1990s to a deterioration of public education in the state of Algoas and to a rebellion of underpaid police in the state of Ceara (Grunberg, 1998: 596). In the USA, 41 federal states maintained a total of 151 offices in other countries by 1992. Two decades earlier only 4 of the 50 states had had permanent representatives stationed abroad (Fry, 1995). In Europe, a Committee of the Regions established under the 1992 Maastricht Treaty has formalized direct consultation between suprastate institutions of the EU and substate tiers of government in the member-states. The many other instances of transborder substate collaboration in Europe include the so-called 'Four Motors' network, in operation since 1988 between Baden-Württemberg, Catalonia, Lombardy and Rhône-Alpes.

To repeat a key qualification, this growth of substate initiatives in world politics has *not* signalled the end of states as significant sites of regulation. Transstate activities of local and provincial governments illustrate the impracticability of sovereignty, but not any imminent demise of states. The European Commission's Director of Science and Technology almost certainly exaggerated upon declaring in 1994 that:

> in just a few decades, nation-states . . . will no longer be so relevant. Instead, rich regions built around cities such as Osaka, San Francisco and the four motors of Europe will acquire effective power.
>
> (Quoted in Runyan, 1996: 242)

Moreover, although substate authorities have gained greater autonomy from the state in the context of accelerated globalization, they have not necessarily gained greater policy initiative overall. After all, like states, municipal and provincial governments have faced pressures to accommodate global companies, global financial markets and global civic associations as well as (or more than) their local constituents. In addition, substate agencies have in contemporary history had to contend not only with the state, but also with new centres of suprastate governance that hold regional and transworld remits.

Regionalization

Recent times of accelerated globalization have witnessed a proliferation of multilateral regional regulatory schemes. No less than 109 regional agreements were reported to the GATT between 1948 and 1994, with the largest numbers coming in the 1970s and the 1990s (*The Economist*, 1995: 27–8). To be sure, some regional initiatives have not developed beyond paper agreements. However, others have promoted substantial growth of transstate laws and institutions, transborder production and markets, and suprastate identities.

Regionalization has transpired across the world. The most far-reaching instances have occurred in Western Europe, where 50 years of progressive widening and deepening of regional integration has culminated in the European Union of the 1990s. Other major regional governance projects have appeared in Central America (1960), East Africa (1967–77, relaunched in 1991), South East Asia (1968), the Caribbean (1973), West Africa (1975 and 1994), Southern Africa (1980 and 1993), the Persian Gulf (1981), Central Asia (1984), South Asia (1985), Central Europe (1989), the Black Sea area (1993), North America (1994) and the cone of South America (1995).

In the light of this trend, some commentators have speculated that governance in the twenty-first century could involve a new multilateralism of regions in place of the old multilateralism of states (Hettne *et al.*, 1999). Already 23 states of Africa and South America have since 1986 formed a Zone of Peace and Cooperation of the South Atlantic. Asia Pacific Economic Cooperation (APEC) has been pursued since 1989. The EU and the Association of South East Asian Nations (ASEAN) have held joint summit meetings in 1996 and 1998. Other proposals have suggested that coordination among the EU, the North American Free Trade Area (NAFTA) and East Asia could supplant and extend the present activities of the Group of Seven. To date, however, interregional relations have remained modest in scale.

Like substate agencies with transborder relations, a number of regional institutions have acquired a degree of autonomy from states. True, states have instigated regional projects and remain prominent participants in regionalization. However, in some ways states have also been constrained to 'go regional', for example, in order adequately to respond to global capital and transborder ecological problems. Moreover, regional governance has in a number of cases developed to a point that the regimes have acquired authority over member states as well as vice versa. The EU in particular has gone beyond an interstate arrangement, having its own Commission, Parliament, Court of Justice and Central Bank, together with some 20,000 regulatory measures generated by the 1990s.

Regionalization can at first blush seem to contradict globalization. After all, regions are territorial units, and regionalization entails a reconfiguration of territorial borders. In several other respects, however, regionalization and globalization have been complementary and interconnected. For one thing, technologies of supraterritorial transportation and communication have made possible tight coordination of activities on large regional scales. In addition, regional common markets have provided convenience and economies of scale for the distribution and sale of global products. Meanwhile, regional customs unions have facilitated the development of transborder production processes. Furthermore, regional governance arrangements have often proved to be an effective mechanism for the administration of global norms, for instance, in areas such as human rights and technical standardization. Moreover, the growth of transborder consciousness has prepared people intellectually for the construction of suprastate regional frameworks. Indeed, various observers have suggested that regional integration serves as an intermediate stage towards full-scale globality, that regional initiatives are stepping stones rather than stumbling blocks for globalization (Tober, 1993: 101; Hettne, 1994).

On the other hand, in some respects regionalization can also relate negatively to globalization. Regionalism can be a reaction against globalism, serving as a macronationalist, neoprotectionist defence against the turbulence of globalizing capitalism, the imposition of global cultures, and so on. Some EU controls on external trade and ever-tightening restrictions on immigration into the region well illustrate this reactive dynamic.

To be sure, globalization has not been the only force propelling the proliferation and growth of suprastate regional projects in contemporary history. Local, national and region-specific circumstances have also determined where regionalization has taken place, in what forms, at what speeds, and so on. However, regional schemes would not have appeared in such numbers – and developed as far as they have – in the absence of a concurrent large-scale growth of supraterritorial relations.

Transworld governance

Of course suprastate governance involves more than regional arrangements. Agencies like the UN organs, the Bretton Woods institutions, the WTO, the BIS and the OECD have regulatory roles that extend across regions. As noted in Chapter 3, the greatest growth of transworld governance institutions and associated legal instruments has occurred in recent decades. Indeed, as described in Chapter 4, these organizations have established many regulatory frameworks that have facilitated accelerated globalization in contemporary history.

Transworld governance has several distinctly global attributes. For one thing, many of the rules constructed through global governance agencies apply to the planet as a single place, irrespective of distances and borders. Moreover, the organizations execute their mandates using transworld communications networks. The agencies are also supraterritorial bureaucracies in the sense that their staff and funds are drawn from all corners of the world. Several of the institutions furthermore have developed their own 'diplomatic service'. For example, UNDP had some 150 Country Offices by the late 1990s, while the IMF and the World Bank each maintained resident missions in over 70 countries.

Several transworld governance institutions have acquired quite far-reaching competences. For example, as mentioned in Chapter 4, the World Trade Organization has obtained a far wider remit than any previous global trade regime. Moreover, under the 1994 Marrakesh Agreement that created the WTO, member-states have committed themselves (with no reservations allowed) to alter their statutes and procedures to conform with suprastate trade law. The WTO Trade Policy Review Body conducts periodic surveillance of member governments' commercial measures. Alleged violations of WTO rules are considered by panels of experts whose decisions are binding unless every state party to the global trade regime (including the initial complainant) votes to overturn the advice. More broadly, too, the consensus principle that prevailed in GATT operations has given way to a majority vote principle in its successor.

Formally, of course, states have had the 'sovereign choice' whether or not to join the WTO. However, the forces of globalizing markets, coupled with prevailing neoliberal discourse, have heavily constrained this supposed 'free will'. Indeed, to date no state has outright rejected the Marrakesh Agreement. On the contrary, a queue of states has waited to enter the WTO ever since its establishment. (For more on the WTO, see Hoekman and Kostecki, 1995; Jackson, 1998.)

Other considerable growth in public transworld economic governance has occurred through the International Monetary Fund. During its first 30 years the IMF held a modest brief to manage the Bretton Woods regime of fixed exchange rates. However, since the 1970s the Fund has intervened more intensely with its client governments. For one thing, the 'second-generation' IMF has undertaken comprehensive and detailed surveillance of economic performance: of individual member-states (annually); of the world economy as a whole (biannually); and since 1998 of certain regions as well. In addition, the IMF has performed major training and technical assistance services, largely in order to provide poorly equipped states with staff and tools that can better handle the policy challenges of globalization. Furthermore, the Fund has gone beyond its traditional stabilization measures (which effect short-term corrections of the balance of payments) to sponsor wide-ranging economic restructuring programmes in over 80 countries. Finally, the IMF has since the 1980s played a pivotal role in responding to crises in global finance. To the extent that the Fund has acted as a lender of last resort in such situations and has addressed questions concerning the supervision of global capital markets, it has moved towards becoming something of a suprastate central bank. (For more on the development of the IMF, see Denters, 1996; James, 1996.) Meanwhile the BIS has since 1974 developed some general principles for the oversight of global commercial banking, for example, on matters including capital adequacy ratios as well as payment and settlement systems.

The much-expanded activities of the Organization for Economic Co-operation and Development further illustrate the contemporary growth of transworld economic governance. In the 30 years after 1970 the number of OECD instruments (that is, decisions, recommendations, agreements, etc.) multiplied more than tenfold. These measures have especially addressed environmental issues, taxation, and transborder corporations, though they have also extended across a full spectrum of economic and social policies. Like the WTO and the IMF, the OECD has acquired a significant role in policy surveillance. At regular intervals (usually every 18 months) the organization releases an authoritative assessment of the macroeconomic conditions of each of its 29 member-states, including suggestions for policy adjustments. (For more on the OECD see Sullivan, 1997; Ougaard, 1999.)

The acceleration of global ecological degradation has also prompted a significant expansion of transworld governance in recent history. Some 200 multilateral environmental agreements have come into force, including conventions in respect of supraterritorial problems such as transboundary air pollution (1979), depletion of stratospheric ozone (1985), climate change (1992) and loss of biological diversity (1992). Since the 1970s most of the principal transworld regulatory agencies have created special organs and programmes to address ecological issues. The many initiatives of this kind include the OECD Environment Committee (1970), the World Bank Environment Department (1987), the UN Commission on Sustainable Development (1993), and the WTO Committee on Trade and Environment (1995).

Elsewhere, transworld governance has grown as an instrument of conflict management. In this vein the United Nations has undertaken multiple peacekeeping operations since 1956 and several humanitarian interventions in the 1990s. Even the usually sovereignty-obsessed government of China has endorsed the concept of UN peacekeeping and has since 1989 moreover participated in some of these activities (Kim, 1994: 49–53). In a further unprecedented initiative of suprastate conflict management, the UN provided assistance and supervision in some 90 national elections between 1990 and 1994 (Findlay, 1995: 49).

Finally, the period of accelerated globalization has also witnessed unprecedented growth of suprastate regimes in respect of human rights. Several global conventions on human rights (for example, concerning torture, racial discrimination and the protection of children) have acquired supervisory committees made up of experts who act in their personal capacity rather than as representatives of states. Meanwhile the UN Commission on Human Rights has since 1970 undertaken over 60 official examinations of country situations. Hardly any government now invokes (as Myanmar did in 1996) the 'domestic jurisdiction' clause of the United Nations Charter to deny entry to a UN human rights mission. The statute for a permanent International Criminal Court was completed in 1998 with 120 states in favour and just 7 opposed. If a sufficient number of states ratify the treaty, this tribunal will investigate and bring to justice individuals charged with genocide, war crimes and crimes against humanity (CICC, 1999). In the area of workers' rights, meanwhile, the ILO has come to monitor a transworld code encompassing (as of 1994) 174 Conventions and 181 Recommendations (Cunniah, 1995).

The rapid growth of transworld regulation described above has not heralded a demise of the state, let alone the rise of a sovereign world government. However, the trend has demonstrated – once again – the end of sovereign statehood. Although states have created transworld governance institutions, they have done so under substantial constraints of globalization. Nor have states fully controlled the actions and further development of transworld authorities once they are established.

Whatever the precise relationship with states, however, transworld regulatory agencies have clearly become a significant part of contemporary governance. Of course, this global governance has had many limitations in respect of neglected issues, double standards, limited enforcement, frequent poor coordination between institutions, pervasive understaffing, widespread underfunding and fragile legitimacy in the eyes of many if not most citizens. To give but one indicator, the 1996 operating budgets for three major global economic institutions ran to only $1,375 million for the World Bank, $471 million for the IMF, and just $93 million for the WTO (World Bank, 1996: 155; IMF, 1996: 217; WTO, 1996a: 153). Yet these substantial shortcomings do not negate the crucial point that post-sovereign governance involves notable transworld regulation.

In sum, then, given all of the above developments in substate and suprastate regimes, globalization has fostered a dispersal of regulatory competences. The post-sovereign state has increasingly shared tasks of governance with relatively autonomous local, provincial, regional and transworld agencies. In the resulting multilayered public sector, governance has tended to lack a clear centre of command and control of the sort that the sovereign state once provided.

Privatized governance

The decentralized character of post-sovereign governance becomes still more pronounced when we consider the contemporary growth of regulatory activity outside the public sector. Accelerated globalization since the 1960s has encouraged substantially increased participation in governance by civic organizations and firms. In some cases nonofficial bodies have even constructed and implemented regulations wholly outside of public channels. Such privatization of governance has involved business associations, NGOs, foundations, think tanks and even criminal syndicates (cf. Cutler *et al.*, 1999; Ronit and Schneider, 1999; Higgott *et al.*, 2000).

Contemporary accelerated globalization has contributed to the growth of nonofficial regulation in broadly the same fashions that it has promoted a dispersion of public-sector authority. Thus, by undercutting sovereignty and stimulating general flux in governance arrangements, the spread of supraterritoriality has increased the scope for private-sector agencies to become involved in regulatory activities. In addition, certain aspects of globalization like transborder finance and supraterritorial ecological degradation have proved to be especially amenable to regulatory initiatives by nonofficial organizations. Furthermore, like substate and suprastate institutions, private-sector bodies have used global networks to conduct governance, including in ways that bypass states.

The following paragraphs elaborate on several elements of private-sector initiative in contemporary governance under the influence of globalization. Particular attention is given to the role of nonofficial actors in: (a) implementing official policies; (b) participating in official policy-making processes; and (c) formulating regulations outside official circles.

Nonofficial implementation of official policy

As executors of policies formulated in official quarters, nongovernmental associations have been servants of the public sector. 'Contracting out' is quite new as a form of governance. At mid-century it was unthinkable that private agencies would implement public policy. However, globalization has (as seen above) loosened the grip of the state on governance, and neoliberal thinking has encouraged official bodies to tender a number of tasks to the private sector, especially in the provision of social services.

Significant marketization of state welfare programmes has transpired in North America, Western Europe and elsewhere (Salamon, 1993; 6 and Vidal, 1994). In regard to official development assistance (ODA), donor states have since the mid-1980s increasingly transferred aid not to governments of the South, but to NGOs. The share of ODA from OECD countries channelled though NGOs rose from 4.5 per cent in 1989 to 14 per cent in 1993 (Ghils, 1992: 422; Windsperger, 1997: 7). Likewise the World Bank has since the 1970s turned increasingly to civic groups to help fulfil its mandate. The rate of NGO involvement rose from 6 per cent of World Bank projects in the period 1973–88 to over 30 per cent of projects each year in the 1990s (O'Brien *et al.*, 2000).

NGOs have also figured prominently in humanitarian relief operations. The mid-1990s annual budgets of the giants in this field included $586 million for CARE International, $419 million for World Vision International, $350 million each for Oxfam and Save the Children, and $252 million for *Médecins sans frontières* (Smillie, 1999: 17–18). By comparison, the operating budget for the UN High Commissioner for Refugees has run at around $1 billion per annum. Not surprisingly, in view of these resource constraints, UNHCR in 1998 maintained connections with more than 500 NGOs as 'Partners in Action' (UNHCR, 1999).

In other situations, too, public-sector authorities have become quite dependent on support from civic associations for policy implementation (Weiss, 1998: Part III). For instance, NGOs have on various occasions provided important links for suprastate bodies like the UN to local communities, particularly in countries where the central state is weak.

Joint action between suprastate governance agencies and civic organizations has also at times furthered the implementation of a given policy against a resistant state. For example, such global-local collaborations were arguably important in the eventual success of the campaign against *apartheid* in South Africa.

To be sure, nonofficial actors have sometimes also frustrated the execution of public policies. For example, opposition from civic groups has forced modification, delay or cancellation of a number of World Bank projects (Nelson, 1995; Fox and Brown, 1998). However, the important point to make at the present juncture is that many private agents (especially NGOs) have become integrated into public policy implementation.

Nonofficial participation in official policymaking

Contemporary governance has also involved an unprecedented degree of direct participation in policymaking by civic associations. Across a wide spectrum of issues, official agencies and civic bodies have regularized information exchange, established joint working groups and so forth.

In some instances, nonofficial organizations have accepted invitations from states like Australia, Canada, Italy and the Netherlands to occupy places on government delegations, say, to UN-sponsored global conferences. Indeed, NGO staff members (as opposed to government officials) have represented several small island states in multilateral negotiations on climate change. Some businesspeople have donned government badges to participate in WTO talks. In China and parts of Africa the relationship between civic groups and the state has sometimes been so close that the associations in question have been dubbed GONGOs (that is, government-organized NGOs).

Suprastate agencies, too, have taken initiatives to incorporate civic associations into policymaking. For example, certain environmental organizations have held observer status in the body that oversees implementation of the 1987 Montreal Protocol on Substances that Deplete the Ozone Layer. The Codex Alimentarius Commission (a Rome-based suprastate agency on world food standards) and the International Organization for Standardization have regularly consulted global companies in the process of setting norms. Similarly, around 500 firms currently sit on one or the other committee of the International Telecommunication Union (*FT*, 8 October 1999: XLIX). For each country, the UN Committee on the Rights of the Child has almost always received an alternative report from civic groups alongside – and often challenging – the official submission from the government concerned.

By 1990 most of the major United Nations organs had established a special division for liaison with NGOs (UN, 1990; Weiss and Gordenker, 1996). The Marrakesh Agreement establishing the WTO likewise provided for 'appropriate arrangements for consultation and cooperation with nongovernmental organizations' (Article V). Numerous civic associations have opened bureaux near the headquarters of suprastate governance organizations. For instance, the ICFTU, the Institute of International Finance and Oxfam all have offices down the street from the IMF. UNESCO has even offered certain transborder associations office space within its headquarters building as well as financial support towards administrative costs (Hoggart, 1996: 102). Several commentators have proposed that a 'People's Assembly' and/or a 'Chamber of Companies' should be created in the UN alongside the General Assembly of states (Smouts, 1994). Meanwhile NGO Forums have exercised notable influence on the declarations and programmes of action at the various UN-sponsored global issue conferences of the 1990s. Such impact was especially apparent during the population meeting at Cairo in 1994, when interventions from the NGO Forum were instrumental in preserving commitments to family planning.

With activities such as those just surveyed, a new politics has emerged over the past several decades whereby many civic groups channel an important part of their efforts to shape official policy through suprastate agencies as well as (or even instead of) through governments. Such leapfrogging of the state has been noteworthy in campaigns to advance environmental regeneration, the autonomy of indigenous peoples, the position of women, opportunities for the disabled, and world peace. A good illustrative example is the Movement for the Survival of the Ogoni People (MOSOP), created in 1990. To further its struggle against Royal Dutch/Shell and the Nigerian state, MOSOP has used the support of transborder environmental, religious and human rights organizations, the backing of global retailers The Body Shop, and a sympathetic hearing in the global mass media (Boele, 1995). In short, it is possible in contemporary politics for grassroots groups to advance their causes through coalitions with NGOs, global governance agencies and even global companies. (See further Smith *et al.*, 1997; Keck and Sikkink, 1998.)

Nonofficial formulation of regulatory instruments

Adopting a role akin to legislators, a number of transborder associations have in the contemporary globalizing world taken the lead in the creation of authoritative rules. To illustrate this trend, the following paragraphs first consider two particularly active private-sector policymakers (namely, the Ford Foundation and the World Economic Forum) and then examine two areas of governance where nonofficial agencies have taken notable initiatives (namely, finance and environmental protection).

The Ford Foundation – whose board of directors includes no person from official circles – was established in 1936 to fund local social programmes in the state of Michigan. By the 1990s more than a third of total programme disbursements ($517 million in fiscal year 1998) were made outside the USA (Ford, 1999). Most of these monies have gone to nonofficial recipients rather than to governments, and Ford has insisted that its grants to NGOs should not be subject to scrutiny or approval by state authorities. Since the 1960s the Foundation has played a major role in, among other things, educating development economists, promoting the so-called Green Revolution in agriculture, sponsoring population control programmes, and linking environment and development policies. It has also fostered the growth of civil society associations and supported campaigns for national autonomy in Namibia, South Africa and the West Bank.

The World Economic Forum has assembled some 900 transborder companies under the motto of 'entrepreneurship in the global public interest' (WEF, 1999). Since its inauguration in 1971, the WEF has organized hundreds of country, regional and world meetings of business executives and government officials, including most prominently its annual jamborees in Davos, Switzerland. The Forum was instrumental in launching the Uruguay Round of world trade negotiations (1986–94) and has helped to forge links between local and global capital in China, India, Latin America and Russia as well as in post-*apartheid* South Africa. The WEF has also addressed interstate conflicts with conciliation attempts in such intractable affairs as the Arab–Israeli and Greco–Turkish disputes (WEF, 1994: 13–16).

In terms of governance in particular sectors, none has been more shaped by nonofficial initiatives than global finance. For instance, bond-rating agencies like Moody's Investors Service and Standard & Poor's have exercised considerable if subtle regulatory authority in respect of financial management (Sinclair, 1994; Friedman, 1999). As of 1996, these two organizations rated the creditworthiness not only of companies, but also of 65 and 57 states, respectively. Meanwhile the so-called London Club of 182 commercial banks has taken a prominent role since 1978 in handling problems concerning the repayment of transborder debts held in the South and the East. In the bond and equity sectors, bodies like the International Federation of Stock Exchanges, the International Primary Market Association, the International Securities Market Association and the International Council of Securities Associations have complemented the more official organization, IOSCO, in constituting something of a transworld securities and exchange commission. Nonofficial bodies like the Group of Thirty (composed of economists and businesspeople) and the Derivatives Policy Group (drawn from major investment banks) have taken a lead in developing rules for derivatives markets (G30, 1993; DPC, 1995). In transborder accountancy, the Big Five global firms (more than official agencies) have acted as the primary watchdogs for financial irregularities in global companies. Moreover, as noted in Chapter 4, the nonofficial International Accounting Standards Committee and International Federation of Accountants have respectively developed the main global accountancy and auditing norms currently in use.

Business associations have in the 1990s also taken several initiatives in respect of environmental standards. For example, the World Business Council for Sustainable Development, established in 1995 with a fusion of two groups formed earlier in the decade, has grown into a coalition of 125 global companies promising 'eco-efficient leadership' (WBCSD, 1999). On a sector basis, 60 insurance companies have adopted a Statement of Environmental Commitment by the Insurance Industry. For its part, a group of chemicals manufacturers has formulated a 'Responsible Care Programme'.

Many other nonofficial initiatives in environmental regulation have developed without direct commercial motivations. For example, the Ford, Packard and Rockefeller Foundations have given major backing to conservation programmes. In 1980 the World Conservation Union (IUCN) and the WWF collaborated with UNEP to launch a World Conservation Strategy that developed guidelines for states. On a similar pattern the World Resources Institute (WRI) formulated the Tropical Forestry Action Plan in 1985 jointly with the UN Food and Agriculture Organization (FAO) and UNDP. The International Council of Scientific Unions played an important advisory role to the World Meteorological Organization and UNEP in setting up the Intergovernmental Panel on Climate Change in 1988. The Secretariat for the Convention on International Trade in Endangered Species of Wild Fauna and Flora (CITES) has worked in close cooperation with the IUCN and the WWF. The IUCN, WRI and UNEP have jointly organized the Biodiversity Conservation Strategy Programme.

As policy implementers, policy advisers and policy formulators, then, private agents have gained a significant role in governance of the contemporary globalizing world. Many commentators have welcomed this development. For them, 'new ways of business', 'the valiant efforts of NGOs' and 'emancipatory new social movements' provide a progressive way forward to more effective and just regulation. On the other hand, sceptics have worried that the proven strengths of public-sector mechanisms may be lost and that private-sector regulatory activities can readily escape democratic controls. However, whatever assessment one holds of the trend, contemporary governance has clearly broadened beyond official agencies and instruments.

Conclusion

To recapitulate this chapter, contemporary large-scale globalization has produced a blend of continuity and change in the broad contours of governance, summarized in the Box below. A key continuity is the persistence of the state. A key change is the end of sovereignty. The state survives, but it has lost its previous claims to supreme, comprehensive, absolute and exclusive rule. The resultant post-sovereign state is a major part – but only a part – of a wider, multilayered complex of regulation in which private as well as public agencies play key roles.

In addition, as signalled at the start of this chapter, the growth of global spaces has not to date reduced the power of bureaucracy as a deeper structure of governance in modern society. Whether the administration of rules is executed through states or other agencies, regulation in the contemporary globalizing world has chiefly occurred in a bureaucratic mode. In other words, governance has continued to involve organizations that are: large (i.e. involving a substantial number of persons); permanent (i.e. long-running, with established procedures); formal (i.e. officially and explicitly constituted, with specifically defined positions and departments); impersonal (i.e. run primarily on technical grounds); and hierarchical (i.e. with rank-ordered offices under central supervision). Supraterritorial relations have proved as amenable to bureaucratized administration as the previous territorialist geography.

Globalization and governance in summary

Reconstructed statehood
- loss of sovereignty (in Westphalian terms of supreme and exclusive rule)
- service of both supraterritorial and territorial constituents
- retreat from direct state provision of comprehensive social welfare needs
- shifts in the instruments and targets of warfare
- increased participation in and reliance on multilateral arrangements

Multilayered public governance
- widespread devolution of competences from state to substate governments
- increased transborder collaboration between substate authorities
- proliferation and growth of multilateral regional regimes
- expanded role of transworld institutions and global laws

Privatized governance
- increased use of nonofficial agencies to implement public policies
- expanded involvement of civic associations in official policy formulation
- considerable construction of regulations by nonofficial bodies

True, certain organization theorists have discerned shifts from conventional bureaucracy toward decentralized, horizontal networks in contemporary decision-taking processes (Cooperrider and Dutton, 1999). For example, such a trend has been evident in some computer software companies and various transborder women's associations. However, it is easy to overstate the incidence of these changes and the degree to which they have departed from (as opposed to modifying) bureaucratic principles. Indeed, global governance agencies, global corporations and global civic associations have tended to be as bureaucratic as organizations come.

On current trends, then, globalization is not dissolving the state and bureaucratism in general any more than it is unravelling capitalism. Contemporary changes in governance are far more subtle and complex. If the trends described in this chapter pose a threat, then it is not to the state and bureaucracy, but to democracy. We explore the democratic deficits that have developed from contemporary globalization in Chapter 11.

Chapter 7

Globalization and Community

Main points of this chapter
Nations . . . and more nations
Nonterritorial communities
Cosmopolitanism
Hybridization
Conclusion

Main points of this chapter

- contemporary globalization has not fundamentally undermined the position of nationhood as a primary framework of collective solidarity, but it has helped to loosen some links between nations and states
- the growth of supraterritorial spaces has facilitated the development of various nonterritorial communities *inter alia* on class, gender, racial and religious lines
- the spread of transworld relations has encouraged some rise in cosmopolitan bonds
- expanded intercultural contacts in the context of globalization have increased hybridity in many personal identities

---

Following the economic and political emphases of the previous two chapters, we now examine some cultural consequences of globalization with a focus on community. Questions of collective affiliation, communal solidarity and societal cohesion lie at the heart of social life as much as – and in close connection with – questions of production and governance. Like structures of economy and regulation, frameworks of collective identity are historical constructions. Thus the question arises: what changes, if any, has the growth of supraterritorial spaces prompted in the prevailing patterns of community?

In the middle of the twentieth century, prior to accelerated and large-scale globalization, nationhood ranked as the predominant structure of community in world politics. The theologian Reinhold Niebuhr could at this time understandably declare that the nation was 'the most absolute of all human associations' (1932: 83). Other expressions of collective identity (like women's solidarity, labour unity and religious association) were usually firmly subordinated to the national framework. Hence these secondary affiliations were generally organized along national lines and could normally be expected to rally to 'the national interest'. In this light the political scientist Rupert Emerson in 1960 dubbed the nation 'the terminal community' that invariably prevailed 'when the chips are down' (1960: 95–6).

In the 1990s, after several decades of widespread globalization, certain commentators have proclaimed an impending 'end of the national project' (Brown, 1995). At first blush such a forecast might seem logical. After all, national communities have traditionally based their solidarity in good part on a population's shared devotion to a specific territorial homeland. A deterritorialization of social space might therefore bring a denationalization of community in its train.

However, as stressed before, the spread of supraterritoriality has involved only *relative* deterritorialization. Hence territorially constructed solidarities could in principle continue to thrive in a globalizing world. In practice, too, nations have remained buoyant and show little sign of disappearing. Ben Anderson has observed in this respect that 'the end of the era of nationalism . . . is not remotely in sight' (1991: 3).

Yet the survival of nations should not be taken to imply that the growth of transworld relations has had no repercussions on patterns of social solidarity. On the contrary, four important general shifts can be highlighted. These points are summarized in the next paragraphs and then elaborated successively in the body of the chapter.

First, much as globalization has brought reorientions in capitalism and the activities of states, so the trend has also encouraged some shifts in the forms that nations take. In particular, the growth of transworld spaces has tended to loosen the traditional connection between the state and the nation. Thus, along with the conventional state-nation (that is, a national community that links to a state jurisdiction), the contemporary world stage has also become cluttered with a host of ethno-nations, region-nations and transworld nations.

Second, globalization has also encouraged a rise of non-national frameworks of collective identity. In particular, as mentioned in passing earlier, global relations have promoted the growth of a number of nonterritorial solidarities. Such bonds have grown on lines *inter alia* of age, class, gender, race, religion and sexual orientation.

Third, the accelerated spread of supraterritoriality since the 1960s has promoted some increase in cosmopolitan attachments to a universal human community. However, the scale of this last trend must not be exaggerated. Globalization has to date shown little sign of supplanting particularistic group affiliations with a single world solidarity.

Fourth, globalization has contributed to a growth of hybrid identities and overlapping communities in contemporary world politics. The other three trends just described have often converged on single individuals. The resultant hybridization compels a person to negotiate several national and/ or nonterritorial affiliations within the self. Moreover, in a world where communities are usually constructed through reciprocal exclusion, people with hybrid identities (an increasing proportion of the population) tend to be lost souls.

This matter of exclusion points to a key continuity that has accompanied these four shifts in respect of community in the contemporary globalizing world. The rise of supraterritoriality has thus far brought no significant departure from the previously dominant dynamics of community construction. According to this deeper logic – which we might call communitarianism – social solidarity is established through 'us–them' oppositions. Under contemporary globalization, as in earlier modern history, large-scale communities have consolidated primarily through 'othering', where 'we' are separated from 'them', and the 'inside' is opposed to the 'outside'. Thus, for example, national solidarity has continued to thrive by 'othering' the foreigner. The cohesion of religious communities has persisted largely through opposition to nonbelievers. Similar dynamics have worked through white/black, male/female, proprietor/proletarian and other binary separations. Hence, much as capitalism has constituted an underlying continuity in regard to production, and bureaucratism has persisted at a deeper level in respect of governance, so communitarianism has entailed an underlying continuity in relation to community under contemporary globalization.

Nations . . . and more nations

What makes a nation? This is hardly the place to resolve a long-running, complicated and often heated debate. However, for the purpose of the present discussion a national community may be distinguished by four general features.

First, a nation encompasses a large population. Its size is such that each member has face-to-face contacts with only a minor proportion of the total national community. Nations are thereby distinguished from 'traditional' communities, which usually consist of relatively small populations with relatively close relations among most members.

Second, a nation is distinguished as a form of community by attachment to a specific territorial homeland. Each nation roots itself in a particular country, even if (as in the case of diasporas) the majority of the community resides outside that territory. In some cases, of course, two or more national projects have laid claim to the same tract of land. As a result, long and bitter conflicts have developed over, for example, Kashmir, Northern Ireland and Palestine.

Third, a nation defines itself through an emphasis of cultural attributes that set it apart from other people. These purportedly unique features may relate to language, customs, sensibilities, art forms, religion, race or more. Nations generally connect these marks of distinction to a shared heritage in the past and/or a common destiny in the future.

Fourth, on communitarian lines, nations are mutually constitutive. They do not arise autonomously, but through *inter-national* relations. Thus a nation identifies its distinctive features largely by drawing contrasts with 'foreigners'. In addition, nations have usually forged and sustained themselves in good part through acts of collective defence against 'external' intrusions such as military attacks or colonial domination. At the same time, nations have tended to consolidate in part by asserting privileges (like citizenship and welfare entitlements) for 'insiders' that are denied to 'outsiders'. On each of these counts, nationality and internationality have been two sides of the same coin.

Although nationalists usually affirm that their communities are primordial and natural associations, nations in the sense described above did not consolidate anywhere on earth until well into the nineteenth century. Only then did a fully-fledged national solidarity emerge: deeply rooted in consciousness; spread across all provinces, classes and religions in a population; and central to political organization and aspirations. Even the population of France, often depicted as the birthplace of the national idea, was not comprehensively 'nationalized' until the late nineteenth century (Weber, 1977).

If national communities are a historical and indeed comparatively recent phenomena, does globalization – by expanding supraterritorial spaces and emphasizing awareness of the world as a single place – herald the end of the national era? In certain ways, globalization has unsettled and indeed challenged the position of the nation as the predominant framework of community in world politics. For one thing, as is elaborated later in this chapter, the spread of supraterritoriality has aided the growth of both nonterritorial solidarities and cosmopolitan bonds. Given this increased plurality of communities, appeals to an overriding national interest today generally fall on unsteadier ground than they did in the first half of the twentieth century.

In addition, globalization has disrupted several aspects of social structure that have in the past encouraged the development of nations. For example, nationalism has historically thrived in the context of territorially bound commercial and industrial capitalism. However, as indicated in Chapter 5, globalization has shifted the balance of accumulation to include commodities that are much less tied to territorial geography. Moreover, territorial states have historically promoted most major national projects. States sponsored the language, symbols, education systems, infrastructure and wars that were crucial to the creation of nations. Yet trends described in Chapter 6 (the end of state sovereignty, the growth of supraterritorial constituencies of the state, the decline of interstate warfare) have weakened several of the dynamics that previously bolstered state-nations.

At the level of day-to-day events, too, globalization has made the question of national distinctiveness still more problematic than it has always to some extent been. Transworld relations have greatly intensified the interpenetration of languages, customs, artefacts and other purported hallmarks of 'unique' national character. As a result, it has often become more difficult clearly and precisely to distinguish nations from one another.

Yet, at the same time, many of the circumstances that encouraged the growth of national communities have persisted in spite of accelerated globalization. As stressed before, older territorially bound commerce and industry have not ceased to exist with the rise of global capitalism. Similarly, states have shown no sign of declining to irrelevance. Meanwhile entrenched national languages, national festivals, national infrastructures, national historiography and so forth are hardly likely to disappear in the short or even medium term. The discourse of nationality has remained prominent in global governance agencies such as the United *Nations* and the *International* Monetary Fund. Many a transborder women's organizer, global company manager and religious revivalist has retained at least a secondary national self-definition along with their nonterritorial identity.

Moreover, globality has in some ways positively reinforced national cohesion. For instance, the price structure of telecommunications has generally been set so that 'domestic' calls within the nation cost much less than 'international' calls over a similar distance. (That said, such cost differentials have substantially declined in recent years.) In addition, electronic mass media can be harnessed in the service of a national project, as wartime propaganda illustrated throughout the twentieth century. Nationalist pride has put much impetus behind the entry of flag-carrying companies into global capitalism. Korean corporate conglomerates, the *chaebols*, present a clear example in this regard. Several global spectacles like the Olympic Games and various World Cups have also thrived on nationalist sentiment.

Indeed, closer contact with the 'foreigner' through global networks has in some cases heightened rather than reduced awareness of, dedication to, and determination to preserve national distinctiveness. True, as suggested above, the growth of transworld spaces can in some ways blur national differences. On the other hand, closer inter-national encounters in global markets, global media and the like can also sharpen perceptions of national identity. Many a global tourist is only too glad to get back 'home'!

Moreover, by removing the protection previously afforded by territorial distance and borders, globalization has sometimes prompted nationalists to take reactive measures. Invoking a traditionalist discourse of the sort described in Chapter 1, many people have feared that global capital destroys national jobs, that global communications threaten national culture, that global governance undermines national self-determination, that global ecology endangers national health. These fears have provoked many a defensive move to preserve national communities. For example, recent years have seen a resurgence of calls for trade protectionism and widespread tightening of immigration controls. Many parts of Europe have experienced a revival of xenophobic nationalism, witnessed *inter alia* in the electoral advances of the Freedom Party in Austria, the National Front in France, the Progress Party in Norway, and the Greater Romania Party. In Australia the One Nation party briefly flourished in the late 1990s. Meanwhile one White House aspirant, Pat Buchanan, has urged 'cultural war' and the construction of an impenetrable 2,000-mile steel fence along the US border with Mexico, allegedly to protect the American worker from the ills of globalization. Thus the spread of supraterritoriality has in some quarters provoked great determination to retain national identities. In these circles, the more that distance and borders have disintegrated, the more that national differences have seemed precious.

In sum, then, the relationship between globalization and national communities has shown several contrary tendencies. In some ways trans-world relations have contradicted the nationality principle, but in other ways they have reinforced it. However, as noted before, nations in contemporary globalizing times have not been identical to those of earlier generations. In particular, the state-nation framework has become less dominant as a specific kind of nation. Globalization has encouraged a diversification of types of nations: state-nations, ethno-nations, region-nations and transworld nations.

State-nations

Before elaborating on the various nonstate forms of nation, it is well briefly to note that, as implied in the preceding paragraphs, the state-nation has in many respects proved to be quite resilient under contemporary conditions of accelerated globalization. For instance, the spread of supraterritoriality has apparently done nothing to reduce the urgency with which the Bonn/Berlin government sponsored German national reunification after 1989. Likewise, most of the new post-communist states in Eastern Europe and Central Asia (Croatia, Kazakstan,

Slovakia, etc.) have enthusiastically sought to forge a national community that matches their territorial jurisdiction. In the South, too, large-scale globalization has not deterred most newly decolonized states from pursuing strategies of nation-building (albeit with mixed records of success).

Moreover, state-nations old and new have often actively reaffirmed their cultural distinctiveness in the face of intensified globalization. For example, governments in France, Iceland, the Philippines and Russia have taken measures to counter the encroachments of global English. Meanwhile the Thatcher government in the UK reformed the national curriculum with a specific goal of giving greater emphasis to British history. Steps in recent decades to create the European Union have also often reinvigorated state-national sentiments. In Denmark, for instance, an electorate fearful of compromising its national identity initially rejected the Maastricht Treaty in spite of urgings to vote '*ja*' from both government and opposition parties, trade unions, and almost the whole of the print and electronic media.

Some governments have actually taken steps to reduce global flows in an effort to preserve state-national communities. For example, authorities in China, Malaysia, Saudi Arabia and elsewhere have at one time or another outlawed 'foreign' satellite broadcasts into their respective countries. Other regimes have adopted different technical standards in the hope of repelling this 'invasion' (Webster, 1984: 1172). In the 1970s and 1980s, states of the South led an (unsuccessful) drive for a New World Information and Communications Order that aimed among other things to enhance national control over mass communications and to give greater national character to the communicated material. In Hanoi the government passed rules in 1995 to enhance the 'Vietnamese' nature of advertising. The next year police dismantled various billboards promoting 'foreign' goods in a campaign of 'protection against poisonous cultural items' (*FT*, 2 February 1996: 14).

In other cases governments and nationalist movements have sought to harness forces of globalization in the service of a state-nation project. For example, state-sponsored airlines (now largely privatized) have in the past stimulated considerable national pride in many countries. Meanwhile state-owned and state-regulated mass media have often promoted national consciousness through their news and entertainment programmes. The Rede Globo network in Brazil and the Televisa group in Mexico have helped considerably to advance national identity via television in those two countries. The governments of India and Indonesia have used satellite broadcasting to the same end (Ploman, 1984: 102–3, 121). States have furthermore often sponsored national pavilions at world fairs and national teams in global sports competitions. The African National Congress and the Palestine Liberation Organization have used global governance agencies to good effect in their efforts to gain a state for their respective national projects.

All of this said, however, globalization has in other important respects weakened state-nations. For one thing, as elaborated below, the trend has promoted the growth of alternative frameworks of community. In addition, the rise of supraterritoriality has compromised the state's previous capacity to monopolize the construction of nations. For example, under prevailing neoliberal policies, the globalization of capital has made it next to impossible for states to expropriate enterprises in the purported 'national interest'. Through privatization and globalization, fewer communications networks (crucial to the formation of common cultures) are owned and operated by the state. With the growth of transworld relations, money has come to involve much more than state-sponsored national currency. In short, the post-sovereign state is unable to control many of the circumstances that spawn collective solidarities.

Some of the alternative communities that have developed in this situation are also nations, but these national associations do not correspond to an existing state. Between the mid-nineteenth and mid-twentieth centuries the state (as a structure of governance) and the nation (as a structure of community) were so tightly interwoven that people could presume that the two were inherently paired together. Indeed, to this day we often conflate the terms 'state' and 'nation', as well as 'citizenship' and 'nationality', even though the words refer to quite distinct things. Yet the distinguishing features of a nation – namely, large population, attachment to a territorial homeland, emphasis of cultural distinctiveness, and international reciprocal identification – today apply to many communities that are not connected to a sponsoring state.

Ethno-nations

Many nonstate communities in the contemporary globalizing world have taken the form of ethno-nations. These collectivities have often been designated as 'tribes', 'minorities', 'ethnic groups' and 'indigenous peoples'. Most ethno-nations have lain within a single state jurisdiction. However, groups like the Kurds in the Middle East and the Tutsis in Central Africa have resided across several states. Some of these 'mininationalisms' have sought secession from an existing state in order to create their own nation-state. Other ethno-nationalist movements have aimed at greater self-determination within an established state.

Ethnic and indigenous peoples' campaigns have proliferated and grown across the world in recent decades (cf. Halperin and Scheffer, 1992;

Wilmer, 1993). One source has counted, as of 1990, over 800 ethno-nationalist movements in a world of less than 200 states (Falk, 1992a: 202). Some of these strivings for autonomy arose as early as the end of the nineteenth century, for example, in the cases of the Basques, the Catalans, and the Scots (Smith, 1995: 52). However, most of the campaigns have developed more recently. True, ethno-nationalists have usually affirmed that their community is rooted in a premodern primordial identity. Many such claims are dubious. In any case, most nonstate ethnic movements have not produced full-scale cultural and political strivings to forge a national community until contemporary history.

Ethno-nationalist campaigns have booked a number of successes in the past thirty years, including the segmentation of several states. In some instances (such as the former Czechoslovakia, Soviet Union and Yugoslavia) the division has gained recognition in international law. In other cases (such as Cyprus, Somalia and Sudan) *de facto* splits have developed. Ethno-nationalist politics have also stimulated major constitutional reforms in Spain (1978), Lebanon (1990) and Belgium (1993). Other ethnically inspired constitutional proposals were rejected by the Canadian electorate in 1992 and the Québecois in 1995. Meanwhile the rights of aboriginal peoples have gained greater statutory protection in the Americas, Australia, New Zealand and Scandinavia.

However, the rise of ethno-nations has on many other occasions encountered significant (and all too often violent) resistance. Indeed, states in contemporary history have more frequently turned their military machines inwards against minority populations than outwards against other states. Ethnic conflicts lay at the heart of 18 of the 23 wars being fought in 1994 and 8 of the 13 then-ongoing UN peacekeeping operations (Gurr, 1994: 350).

Yet, striking though contemporary ethno-nationalism may be, it has in important respects not marked a transformation of underlying structures of community. 'Tribes', 'ethnic groups', 'indigenous peoples' and 'minorities' only redraw the map of nations: they do not contradict the nationality principle as such. Like state-nations, ethno-nations involve sizeable populaces. With the exception of nomadic peoples, ethno-nations are devoted to a fixed territorial place. Like state-nations, ethno-nations identify themselves by highlighting their cultural uniqueness. Following another well-known pattern, ethno-nations establish their identity and community through processes of inter-national 'othering': some of it defensive and some of it exclusionary. In short, ethnic movements have not challenged the principle of nationhood. Rather, they have reproduced it in new forms. Most significantly, widespread ethno-nationalism in today's world has often loosened the connection between nation and state, a development that in turn has promoted cultural pluralism.

Globalization has encouraged the growth of ethno-nations in three general ways. First, to draw again on a major previous point, globalization has reduced the relative power of the state. The eclipse of sovereignty has reduced the state's capacity to shape a nation that matches its jurisdiction. Ethnic movements have thereby had more room to grow. Moreover, in some countries, particularly in the South, ethno-nationalism has partly entailed a reaction against the state's service of supraterritorial constituents (global companies, global financial markets, global governance agencies, etc.) to the neglect of 'domestic' interests. Ethno-nations have then emerged as a form of community that promises to fulfil local needs better than the state-nation. Such a dynamic has apparently unfolded among, for example, the Moros, the Québecois and the Scots in their relations with the Philippine, Canadian and British states, respectively.

Second, ethno-national movements (especially indigenous peoples' campaigns) have sometimes exploited transworld relations to advance their causes. Representatives of different aboriginal groups have met together in global gatherings since the mid-1970s. On a more regular basis, too, air, telephone and computer networks have allowed, for example, the Navajo in America to aid the Saami in Scandinavia and the Cree in Canada to assist the Miskito in Central America. The Unrepresented Nations and Peoples Organization (UNPO) has since its creation in 1991 furthered the causes of more than 50 member communities (UNPO, 1995). In official circles, meanwhile, United Nations bodies have promoted the recent codification of indigenous peoples' rights in suprastate law. The UN also declared 1993 to be the International Year of the World's Indigenous People. Concurrently, publicity via the global mass media has helped to generate worldwide support for aboriginal movements like the Zapatistas of Chiapas State in Mexico and the Free Papua Organization (*Organisasi Papua Merdeka*, OPM) in Indonesia.

Third, globalization has encouraged the growth of ethnic movements in a reactive sense. Thus, much as the rise of supraterritoriality has reinvigorated the defensive dynamic of some state-nations, so it has also sometimes fuelled self-protective tendencies in ethno-nationalism. For example, global tourism has intensified native Hawaiian sensibilities. Global deforestation has spurred indigenous activism in Amazonia. The activation of the NAFTA agreement at the beginning of 1994 provided the immediate trigger for the Zapatista rebellion. In these and other cases, ethno-nationalism has held out a promise of cultural preservation and political autonomy at a more local level, against apparent homogenizing tendencies and 'external' rule in globalization.

To be sure, globalization has not been the only force behind the contemporary upsurge in ethno-nationalist movements. Circumstances connected with particular countries and localities have also determined when, and in what form, ethno-nationalist strivings have emerged. Indeed, globalization seems to have played little role in some of these campaigns, such as the long-running struggles of various hill peoples in South Asia. On the whole, however, the rise of supraterritoriality has figured significantly in making ethno-nationalism a major force of cultural politics in contemporary history.

Region-nations

Whereas the ethno-nationalist campaigns just described have sought to build a national community 'below' the state, regional projects have developed ideas of nationhood 'above' the state. These 'macronationalisms' have included the Pan-African, Pan-Arab, Pan-Asian, Pan-European and Pan-Turkish movements. For the most part such strivings have not challenged established states. Indeed, they have usually enjoyed collective state sponsorship through, for example, the Organization of African Unity, the League of Arab States, the Council of Europe and the European Union.

Proponents of region-nations have usually linked these putative communities to a common heritage that stretches far into the past. Shared experiences like the slave trade, Islam, Christendom or the Ottoman Empire are said to provide deep historical roots for present-day solidarity. The categories 'African', 'Arab', 'Asian' and 'European' became deeply institutionalized under colonialism of the late nineteenth and early twentieth centuries. Yet cultural-political strivings for community linked to a suprastate region are mainly a recent phenomenon. Some modest manifestations of Pan-Africanism appeared as early as the 1890s, and various associations to promote European unity emerged between the two world wars. However, the principal rise of macro-nations on a regional scale has occurred since the second half of the twentieth century, concurrently with accelerated globalization.

On the whole, region-nations have so far made more limited advances than ethno-national communities. For example, the Pan-Asian movement stalled after several conferences in the 1940s. (However, the last years of the twentieth century saw some determined assertions of 'Asian values' in economic development, especially with respect to human rights.) Perpetual quarrels among Arab governments have severely hampered the development of that regional community. Notions of an African identity have enjoyed widespread popular currency across that continent. Since 1983 a Pan African News Agency (PANA) has attempted to assert an autonomous regional voice in global journalism. However, on the whole Africanist sentiments have to date produced little in the way of sustained and focused campaigns for a deeper and more institutionalized regional community.

Pan-Turkism grew following the disintegration of the Soviet Union, but has thus far not developed beyond a vague aspiration. Meanwhile most other regional integration schemes (for example, in Central America, South Asia and elsewhere) have been commercial projects without an accompanying drive to deepen cultural bonds across the populations of the participating countries.

By comparison, European regional organizations have done the most to promote cultural unity alongside a common market. European symbols and experiences now abound in daily life around this region. Article 8 of the Maastricht Treaty even created the institution of EU citizenship. The idea of a European collective solidarity has gained considerable hold among some élites and younger generations in the EU. However, commitment to a regional community remains pretty shallow in the hearts and minds of many would-be Europeans.

These limitations noted, region-nations have still figured more prominently in contemporary world culture than in earlier times. Globalization has not been the sole impulse for this rise, but it has certainly encouraged the trend. The connections between the two developments have followed broadly the same lines that were previously mentioned in regard to ethno-nations. Namely, globalization has: (a) ended state sovereignty and thereby enhanced opportunities for the growth of transstate communities like region-nations; (b) supplied important means of communication and organization for building regional communities; and (c) provoked nationalist reactions, in this case on a regional level. The spurs that globalization has given to regional governance (discussed in Chapter 6) have also indirectly furthered the growth of regional communities.

Like ethno-nations, regional solidarities have proved to be nations in an alternative guise rather than a qualitatively different form of community. The various 'pan' movements have all shown the four broad distinguishing features of nationhood: that is, large population; attachment to a specific territory; stress on cultural uniqueness; and inside-outside differentiation. Hence in respect of regional solidarities, too, globalization has brought changes *in* rather than changes *of* the predominant framework of community in modern world politics.

Transworld nations

In addition to state-nations, ethno-nations and region-nations, the nationality principle has persisted in the contemporary globalizing world in the form of nations that have settled across several continents. Joel Kotkin has called these diasporas 'global tribes' (Kotkin, 1992). Prominent examples include the Armenians, Chinese, Indians, Irish, Jews, Palestinians and Sikhs. On a smaller scale, national ties have also sustained transworld communities of Ghanaian traders, Filipina domestic servants, Chilean exiles and others.

In earlier times, too, many immigrants continued for several generations to embrace the national culture of their previous homeland. Often they would live in distinct districts of the towns and countryside, segregating themselves from the population at large. Yet territorial distance and borders also separated these immigrant communities from their national roots. Hence their bonds with the homeland often lay mainly in the imagination rather than in regular concrete interactions. In these circumstances the cultures of, for example, Africans, African-Americans and Afro-Caribbeans substantially diverged. Likewise, the Ashkenazy (European), Falasha (Ethiopian) and Sephardic (Middle Eastern) Jews developed significantly different cultures during their isolation from one another.

In contrast, contemporary large-scale globalization has greatly enhanced the capacities of transworld nations to sustain substantial contacts (cf. Anderson, 1992). Supraterritorial communications such as direct-dial telephony and satellite television have permitted close interchanges within a global nation. For instance, television reports in the early 1990s reconnected the 250,000 ethnic Koreans living in Uzbekistan with 'compatriots' in East Asia who had all but forgotten them. Meanwhile listservs like Vietnet (linking the Vietnamese diaspora worldwide) can help to sustain collective identities among immigrants with a common national origin (My Vuong, 1999). Supraterritorial organizations have given some transworld nations an institutional basis. For instance, the World Union of Free Romanians, created in 1984, has linked members in two dozen countries. Supraterritorial finance has made it easier for families and other circles within a global nation to give each other pecuniary support. For example, funding from expatriates in Britain, Canada and the USA has supported Sikhist activism in the Punjab. Meanwhile supraterritorial markets have brought 'home' goods within easy reach of expatriates worldwide, enabling them more easily to sustain their national cuisine, national dress, etc.

In recognition of the global mobility of significant sectors of their populations, some states have recently increased the scope for dual citizenship. In cases like Turkey and the USA the change has been enacted with legal directives. In many other instances officials have turned a blind eye to statutory offences of holding more than one passport. On the other hand, with the decline of the Commonwealth project, the British state has narrowed the possibilities of dual citizenship *vis-à-vis* former colonial populations.

In sum, the preceding discussion indicates that globalization has gone hand in hand with various processes of nationalization: some of them connected to a state jurisdiction and others not. Although globality and nationality have been contradictory in some ways, they have been complementary in others. Globalization has weakened some national communities, but strengthened others. On no account has the rise of supraterritoriality spelled the end of national solidarity.

Nonterritorial communities

Although globalization has not dissolved the nationality principle, this transformation of geography has ended the near-monopoly that this notion held on structures of community in first half of the twentieth century. In the words of Zdravko Mlinar, globalization has radically altered experiences of proximity and social connectedness, shaking 'traditional territorial identities based on *contiguity*, *homogeneity*, and clearly (physically and socially) identifiable *borders*' (1992: 1, his emphases). In the new situation, various solidarities have developed that lack a territorial referent. They include transworld communities related to class, gender, race, religious faith, sexual orientation and youth, as well as (but not covered in detail here) a host of other shared concerns like disabilities, hobbies, political programmes and professions.

To be sure, some of these nonterritorial affiliations existed prior to contemporary large-scale globalization. For example, as noted in Chapter 3, adherents of the world religions have for centuries affirmed a notional unity with their co-believers everywhere, even though these long-distance communities usually never in practice had direct contacts with one another. Marcus Garvey's Universal Negro Improvement Association encompassed over 900 chapters across five continents in the mid-1920s (Leanne, 1994: 86–9). Transborder working-class solidarities gained some following in the late nineteenth and early twentieth centuries (Holthoon and Linden, 1988). Likewise, campaigners for female suffrage at this time exploited transborder support networks to good effect. In addition, several global associations of students and other young people were active in the first half of the twentieth century.

However, large-scale globalization since the 1960s has intensified challenges to the primacy of the nationality principle from nonterritorial communities. As supraterritorial spaces have spread, more persons have placed important aspects of their social affiliations in global as well as (and to some extent instead of) territorial groupings. Thus, for example, global communications, global organizations, global finance and the like have allowed ideas of the transworld *umma* of Muslims and the universal Christian church to be given concrete shape as never before.

To be sure, nonterritorial communities have, like nations, in practice housed considerable diversity. Thus, for example, differences in local and national circumstances have often complicated the development of trans-border class solidarity. Meanwhile gender politics have spawned multiple feminisms, including liberal, socialist, black, pacifist, radical and ecological strands. Indeed, some parts of the transworld women's movement have rejected the 'feminist' label altogether. Considerable diversity and various internecine disputes have also marked lesbian and gay networks. That said, differences can coexist with solidarity.

Class solidarities

Class is one area where contemporary globalization has encouraged some growth of nonterritorial community. In respect of global labour organizations, for instance, the ICFTU as of 1999 grouped 213 national trade union centres from 143 territories, while membership of the World Confederation of Labour spanned 113 countries. In addition to global union networks, supraterritorial working-class interests have also been embraced in certain new social movements, for example, concerning human rights. Both through formal institutions and in grassroots circles, various labour activists have used the Internet to build a 'new internationalism' (Lee, 1997). Occasionally local labour disputes such as the miners strike of 1984–5 in Britain have attracted transworld backing (Saunders, 1989). Sacked dockers from Liverpool in England toured 15 countries in 1995–6 to garner support for their cause (Waterman, 1998: 258). Workers across North America campaigned against the NAFTA accord in 1993 (Kidder and McGinn, 1995). (For further examples of transborder labour solidarity, see Kamel, 1990: ch 5.)

However, on the whole supraterritorial workers' communities have remained fairly weak. The illustrations just given have marked the exception rather than the rule. Most shop floors have known no trans-world organizations or Internet links. Indeed, in the contemporary situation of mobile global capital and considerable structural unemployment, wage earners in different parts of the world have sooner been set in competition against each another.

Underclasses have also constructed some transworld solidarities outside the labour movement. For example, representatives of the urban poor in Asia and Southern Africa have maintained community exchange programmes since the late 1980s, organizing themselves formally as Shack/ Slum Dwellers International in 1996 (Bolnick, 1999). Another small-scale initiative, the Participation Resource Action Network, has linked poor people across four continents (Gaventa, 1999). Thousands of transborder partnerships between North-based and South-based development NGOs have likewise championed the interests of the poor, although the NGO activists themselves have largely come from more privileged circles.

Indeed, the main contemporary growth in supraterritorial class bonds has transpired in business and governing circles. In this respect Susan Strange has written of 'a transnational managerial class . . . in which the life-styles of each [national fraction] resemble each other more than they do those of state officials or corporate managers who function only in a national milieu' (1994: 138). These supraterritorial nomads – comparatively small in number but very large in influence – have found their common home in airport lounges, mobile telephones, corporate computer intranets, transworld associations like the International Chamber of Commerce, and official global regulatory agencies (cf. Pijl, 1989; Sklair, 1995). They have included the more than 100,000 members of the 'Six Continents Club' of Inter-Continental Hotels. In a sense something like the global union of capitalists described (prematurely) on the eve of the First World War in Karl Kautsky's speculations on 'ultra-imperialism' has now taken shape (Kautsky, 1914).

Gender solidarities

Some of the most pronounced deterritorialization of collective solidarities has occurred since the 1960s in respect of gender. These bonds have built on differences between femininity and masculinity. Supraterritorial affiliations in terms of gender have developed mainly among women, although the 1990s also saw the emergence – halting, mainly reactive and on a much smaller scale – of a men's movement.

Recent decades have brought an unprecedented proliferation and growth of networks – local and transborder, grassroots and official – that are devoted specifically to the advancement of women's interests. Gender politics have turned matters such as physical abuses of women, reproduction strategies, equal opportunity between the sexes, and women's labour into 'global gender issues' (Peterson and Runyan, 1999). Four global women's conferences with attendance running into many thousands took place between 1975 and 1995. Women's groups have also figured prominently in the NGO Forums that were held almost annually in the 1990s alongside special UN meetings (Pietilä and Vickers, 1994). Like indigenous peoples, women's groups have on various occasions found support from global governance agencies that was lacking from a patriarchal state (Stienstra, 1994). More informally, women activists have developed much solidarity through the Internet (Harcourt, 1999).

Lesbian and gay solidarities

Another touchstone of growing nonterritorial community has related to sexual preference, in particular homosexuality and, on a smaller scale, bisexuality. True, same-sex desires are age-old, and some evidence suggests that these orientations may have genetic as well as social bases. However, apart from some shortlived gay activism in the early twentieth century, it is only in the time of accelerated globalization that lesbians and gay men have identified themselves as 'peoples'. In other words, sexual disposition has become a touchstone of collective identity, solidarity and strivings for self-determination (Adam, 1987; Cruickshank, 1992).

The historical concurrence of the lesbian and gay revolution with the growth of supraterritorial space is significant. As with the other cases already discussed, globalization has made room for lesbian and gay affiliations by loosening the hold of territorial communities. In addition, much 'coming out' has occurred at supraterritorial locations: on television and in film; through telephone switchboards; in global sports and music; with gay tourism and migration; by lobbying of suprastate institutions; via the 'queerplanet' and other computer conferences; and, unhappily, in response to the global AIDS epidemic and its attendant homophobic backlash. In territorial spaces lesbians and gay men have tended to be isolated and hidden from one another; yet in global arenas homosexuals can veritably claim, 'we are everywhere'. (See further Manalansan, 1997.) Various transworld and regional organizations have been established since the formation in 1978 of the International Lesbian and Gay Association (ILGA). Today the ILGA membership includes groups in over 60 countries.

Racial solidarities

Next to class, gender and sexuality, race has provided another important nonterritorial framework of community in the contemporary globalizing world. On these occasions collective solidarity has developed in relation to shared bodily features, especially skin pigmentation, and shared social experiences associated with those phenotypical characteristics.

Racial consciousness – in particular 'black'/'white' and 'yellow'/'white' dualisms – emerged as a significant social circumstance several hundred years ago and became pervasive throughout the world in the second half of the nineteenth century. As noted in Chapter 3, some racially based transworld solidarity developed a hundred years ago among Anglo-Saxons and Pan-Africanists. In contemporary times, global communities that put an explicit emphasis on race have mainly linked people of colour. However, some transborder coalitions of white supremacists have also developed, including through the Internet.

Shared experiences of racial discrimination were one important stimulus to the development of transborder Third World solidarity in the 1960s and 1970s. Global governance agencies and global communications greatly facilitated the activities of *inter alia* the Non-Aligned Movement and the Group of 77, both formed in the early 1960s. Global connections likewise lent much strength to the Anti-*Apartheid* Movement during its 35-year struggle against legalized racism in South Africa.

In addition, consultations between leading Africans and prominent African-Americans regained some prominence in the 1990s. For instance, a Policy Summit joining these circles at Abidjan in 1991 drew 1,500 participants. In another initiative, the first black governor of an American state hosted 25 African heads of government in the capital of Virginia in 1993 (Leanne, 1994: 2). Such conferences have *inter alia* generated substantial contributions from black Americans to education efforts in Africa. The Congressional Black Caucus and its foreign policy lobby TransAfrica, both formed in the 1970s, were influential in prompting the introduction of wide-ranging official US economic sanctions against *apartheid* in 1986 as well as US military intervention in Somalia and Haiti during the early 1990s (Johnson, 1998).

Alongside this overtly political activity, electronic mass media have played an important role in forging notions of supraterritorial black solidarity. On the Internet, for example, African-Americans have carved distinctive racial spaces like NetNoir and The Black World Today, in some cases including links to the broader African diaspora (Lekhi, 2000). In the context of global consumerism, many marketers have deliberately promoted 'black' music, 'black' writers, 'black' sitcoms and 'black' superstars. At a grassroots level, many members of the African diaspora have taken to donning 'native' dress as an identity statement. More negatively, globalization can advance supraterritorial black solidarities insofar as the pains of economic restructuring have tended – and are strongly perceived – to fall disproportionately on people of colour.

Religious solidarities

Contemporary history has furthermore witnessed a growth of confessionally based supraterritorial communities. This religious resurgence has encompassed Baha'i, Buddhist, Christian, Hindu, Islamic, Judaic, Sikh, and various so-called New Age faiths (Robertson and Garrett, 1991). As discussed in Chapter 8, some of this resurgence has had a revivalist character that challenges the prevailing rationalist knowledge structure.

True, the heart of a religious community may be located at a particular place. Thus, for example, *Eretz Yisrael* is home for revivalist Jews. The temple at Ayodhya has had core importance for Hindu revivalists in India.

Other nationalist campaigns, too, have focused on religious differences as a primary rationale for drawing boundaries between territorial communities.

However, some contemporary religious resurgence has given an explicit priority to shared faith instead of common territory and nationality. For example, Ayatollah Ruhollah Musavi Khomeini declared that his return to Tehran in 1979 after prolonged exile evoked no special emotion; his 'homeland' was Islam (Simpson, 1988: 29–30). The ensuing revolution in Iran found echoes across the world at greater speeds and (non)distances than in any previous Muslim revivalist movement (Esposito, 1990).

Accelerated globalization of recent times has given considerable stimulus to such supraterritorial religious bonding. Aeroplanes have taken the Pope anywhere and drawn *haji* to Mecca from everywhere. Transworld mass media and publishers instantly made the Rushdie affair a global event in 1989. Satellite broadcasts have enabled televangelists to preach global sermons. The Organization of the Islamic Conference, set up in the early 1970s, has taken a part in global governance. Muslims have maintained scores of web pages, while the Vatican site attracted over 300,000 hits from 70 countries at Christmas 1995 (*FT*, 19 February 1996: 13).

At the same time as being pursued through supraterritorial channels, the contemporary upsurge of collective identities rooted in religion has, like nationalist movements, often also been in part a defensive response to globalization. Thus religious revitalization has frequently waxed into a kind of nonterritorial cultural protectionism, where the nonbeliever is violently excluded. Indeed, certain former proponents of containment in the Cold War have seized on religious revivalism to construct a new manichaean planetary rift to supplant the East–West divide. This thesis holds that 'the clash of civilizations' is replacing conflict between states and nations as the predominant motif of world politics (Huntington, 1993).

Youth solidarities

Finally, a loose nonterritorial community has developed in the course of globalization with respect to youth. Nominally this category relates to a particular age group, though more fundamentally it encompasses lifestyles and phases of psychological development that are identified as 'young'.

Much global culture is youth culture. Global consumerism has linked young people across the planet through shared cult films, music hits, slang, and fashion trends. Satellite music television stations have since the 1980s come to reach several hundred million households on all inhabited continents. Global audio-visual media have arguably made many of today's youth more familiar with Hollywood's constructions of America than with many parts of their 'home' countries. Global backpacking has brought young people (mainly from wealthier circles in the North) into contact with their generational peers at all corners of the earth.

Yet it is not clear that these increased transworld contacts have created deep and lasting bonds of global youth solidarity. True, student activism of the late 1960s took encouragement from transborder support between Berlin, Chicago, London, Paris and Prague. Protest movements on a smaller scale in the 1990s (for example, surrounding meetings of the G7, IMF, World Bank and WTO) have likewise created global networks of young people. However, these communities have tended to be ephemeral, dying away after the global event ends.

In sum, the disruption, through globalization, of the equation of 'space' and 'territory' has encouraged the growth of various nonterritorial communities in contemporary history. In addition to the six types of affiliation discussed in more detail above, other transborder solidarities have focused, for example, on a particular disability, profession or recreational activity. In this way computer bulletin boards, telephone help lines and the like have encouraged the development of 'electronic tribes' of cancer patients, lawyers, football fanatics, etc. (Jones, 1994). Likewise, e-mail, global journals, multilateral research teams and transworld conference circuits have forged supraterritorial 'epistemic communities' that now figure centrally in many academic professions (Haas, 1992).

True, we must not exaggerate the extent and depth of supraterritorial affiliations. Globalists often celebrate the *potentials* of nonterritorial human solidarities more than their actual accomplishments. Nevertheless, it would be equally mistaken to reiterate today Heidegger's conclusion, spoken on the eve of contemporary accelerated globalization, that 'the frantic abolition of all distances brings no nearness' (1950: 165). On the contrary, transworld communities have come to figure significantly in the social networks of hundreds of millions of people.

Cosmopolitanism

Is this to say that contemporary globalization is paving the way for the realization of age-old liberal visions of a single universal community of humankind? The rise of supraterritoriality has given people all over the world unprecedented degrees of intimacy with one another. Global markets, global organizations, global mass media, global monies and global symbols (like photographs of earth from outer space) have given humanity common reference points as never before. As Anthony Giddens has observed, with globalization 'humankind in some respects becomes a "we", facing problems and opportunities where there are no "others" ' (1991: 27). To be sure, 'global village' metaphors must not be overplayed, but they have gained greater substance in current times.

Global humanitarian relief campaigns provide some notable evidence of increased cosmopolitan community. Wars, famines, epidemics and natural disasters have since the 1960s elicited transworld assistance with much greater frequency and on a much larger scale than transborder activities of earlier times. Global mass media in particular have often played a key role in mobilizing the so-called 'world community' to provide emergency relief. In July 1985, for example, satellite transmissions brought the Live Aid pop concerts simultaneously to half the countries of the world and yielded almost $4 billion in donations for 20 drought-stricken countries of Africa.

On a smaller scale, but with greater consistency over a longer term, other cosmopolitan solidarity has grown since the 1950s around the theme of 'development'. The specific content of this term has remained ambiguous and contested, but a broad transworld consensus has emerged that all of humanity should benefit from certain economic, political, cultural and ecological standards of living. Moreover, millions of individuals have undertaken acts of cosmopolitan solidarity (financial donations, voluntary labour, etc.) with the aim of assisting 'development' to a 'humane' condition everywhere and anywhere on earth. A smaller circle of people has been ready in addition to contemplate a fundamental reallocation of world resources in the name of global distributive justice.

Further increased cosmopolitan community has been evidenced through the growth in the second half of the twentieth century of a substantial transworld human rights movement. Universalism is of course embedded in the very concept of *human* rights, even when it is conceded that there are culturally specific variants of the underlying norms. The Universal Declaration of Human Rights of 1948 has gained the adherence of most of the world's states. Governments have also since the 1950s acceded in large numbers to UN-sponsored covenants and conventions on human rights as well as to region-specific African, American and European charters of human rights. The creation of a permanent International Criminal Court was a utopian fantasy before the 1990s. Outside official circles, millions of individual members have supported transborder human rights organizations like the Anti-*Apartheid* Movement, launched in 1959, and Amnesty International, formed in 1961.

Another area where globalization has increased cosmopolitan impulses lies in environmentalism. Global ecological issues have prompted the creation of a number of transworld associations and campaigns whose members work together in the (supposed) interest of humankind as a whole. For example, the Rainforest Action Network has included members in 74 countries, while Greenpeace has acquired branch organizations in 33 countries. Similarly, fears of common destruction in mechanized warfare have stimulated the recurrent growth since the middle of the nineteenth century of transborder peace movements.

Through the various campaigns just mentioned, cosmopolitan solidarity has gained unprecedented strength in the contemporary globalizing world. This is by no means to suggest that cosmopolitanism has displaced communitarianism as the principal dynamic of social solidarity. On the contrary, universalist sentiments and acts of solidarity with humanity as a whole remain secondary and fleeting in the everyday life of most people as we enter the twenty-first century.

Hybridization

Taken together, the different trends described so far suggest a fourth important shift in the construction of communities under conditions of accelerated globalization, namely, increased hybridization at the level of individuals. A hybrid identity draws from several different strands in substantial measure, so that no single marker holds clear and consistent primacy over others. For example, a person might hold several nationalities, or might be of mixed race, or might have a multifaceted sexual orientation, or might combine different class contexts. Likewise, hybrid persons can emphasize several strong aspects of their identity, with the result that, for instance, national loyalties, religious bonds and gender solidarities could compete and conflict.

Hybridization has not been new to the present period of accelerated globalization, of course. In earlier times, too, collective identities were in practice often not centred on single nations as completely and unreservedly as the previously cited quotations from Niebuhr and Emerson affirmed. For example, a century ago intimate contacts between colonizers and colonized induced many experiences of plural and in some ways contra-dictory identities on both sides of those encounters. Immigrants, too, were frequently torn between their original and adopted territorial homelands well before air travel and telephone calls allowed migrants to 'stay' in their place of birth from a distance.

However, the immediacy of the whole world in contemporary condi-tions of globalization has greatly multiplied and intensified experiences of being several selves at once. In the author's current place of residence, for example, the evening television news can, in a matter of minutes, emphasize notions of 'us' in relation to the Midlands, England, Britain and Europe. A Chinese family living in Mexico deposits its wealth in euros at a Saudi-owned bank located in Switzerland: where are their attachments? A Fijian citizen of Indian descent works in Paris for a US-based accountancy firm: who is she? What collective identity do we ascribe to the computer programmer (sitting beside me on a flight from Chicago to London) who moves between South Africa, Western Europe and North America, having no fixed address and never staying in any country for more than a fortnight? What do we make of prostitutes from Africa lining Tverskaya Street, Moscow, dressed in traditional Russian costume that hardly any local would today wear? In countless such situations, globalization has produced striking cultural mixes.

Global relations can in this way decentre the self. Fredric Jameson has spoken along these lines of a 'postmodern' condition where 'everyone "represents" several groups all at once' (1991: 322). Anthony Smith has depicted a global culture that is 'tied to no place or period . . . a true melange of disparate components drawn from everywhere and nowhere' (1990b: 177). James Rosenau has similarly described a 'turbulence' of multidirectional shifts in identity and legitimacy sentiments in the context of globalization (Rosenau, 1990). According to Lothar Brock, globalization has encouraged 'identity surfing', where people slide from identity to identity in borderless realms of unconnectedness (1993: 170).

These quotations depict more intense instances of hybridity than most people experience in their day-to-day lives at the start of the twenty-first century. Nevertheless, globalization has tended to increase the sense of a fluid and fragmented self, particularly for persons who spend large proportions of their time in supraterritorial spaces, where multiple identities readily converge. In more globalized lives, identity is less easily taken for granted; the self is much more up for grabs.

Hybridity presents significant challenges for the construction of community. How can we build deep and reliable social bonds when individuals have multiple and perhaps competing senses of self – and indeed often feel pretty unsettled in all of them? Moreover, hybridity can hardly be reconciled with a communitarian approach to social cohesion, where solidarity rests on neat group distinctions and oppositions.

Conclusion

The present chapter has shown that globalization has encouraged several important changes to the contours of community in the contemporary world (summarized in the Box below). Contrary to some expectations, the rise of supraterritoriality has not spelled the end of territorial solidarities centred on the nationality principle. However, the shape of many nations has changed, and the state has lost its previous near-monopoly on national projects. In addition, globalization has promoted the development of

Globalization and contemporary community in summary

Proliferation of nations
- persistent and in many cases reinvigorated state-nations
- growth of ethno-nationalism, including indigenous peoples' movements
- modest emergence of region-nations
- deepening ties within transworld national diasporas

Growth of nonterritorial communities
- class solidarities, especially in managerial and professional circles
- gender solidarities, particularly through a greatly expanded women's movement
- lesbian and gay solidarities
- racial solidarities, especially among people of colour
- religious solidarities, most strongly in revivalist movements
- spread of global youth culture

Some increase in universalistic cosmopolitanism
- humanitarian relief campaigns
- development cooperation efforts
- growth of human rights promotion
- emergence of global environmentalism
- periodic upsurges of peace activism

Greater hybridization
- more mixture of identities in global spaces
- more mobility between identities in global spaces

various nonterritorial affiliations, some growth of cosmopolitanism, and increased hybridization.

In short, then, the significance of globalization has lain not in eliminating nationhood, but in substantially complicating the geography of community. Globalization has facilitated an upsurge of so-called 'identity politics' that has since the 1960s eroded the position of the state-nation as the preeminent structure of community and promoted the rise of multiple alternative frameworks of solidarity. In the process, constructions of collective identities have tended to become more multidimensional, fluid and uncertain.

Yet, as noted at the outset of this chapter, a key continuity has underlain the various changes: namely, that of communitarianism. All of the national and nonterritorial communities discussed above have arisen and been sustained through processes of othering, that is, by separating groups and setting them in opposition in terms of difference. Even liberal cosmopolitanism has advanced – and sometimes forcefully imposed – particular constructions of 'development' and 'human rights' against cultures with different views. Insofar as communitarianism builds solidarity through denigration and exclusion of the other, it yields artificial cohesion for the in-group and violence towards the out-group. These harms are discussed further in Part III.

Chapter 8

Globalization and Knowledge

Main points of this chapter

- contemporary globalization has not substantially weakened the hold of rationalism on the social construction of knowledge, although some rationalism has become more reflexive
- the rise of supraterritoriality has encouraged some growth in anti-rationalist knowledges like religious revivalism, ecocentrism and postmodernism
- the growth of transworld relations has promoted some shifts in ontology, methodology and aesthetics

---

Together with frameworks of community, governance and production, the structure of knowledge is a fourth primary facet of a social order. How we understand is a key social question alongside (and interrelated with) issues of how we bond, how we regulate, and how we produce. Moreover, just as prevailing structures in regard to community, governance and production vary by setting, so too underlying frameworks of knowledge shift according to social and historical context. It is therefore important to consider whether and how globalization has affected knowledge patterns.

Questions of knowledge have already surfaced at a number of earlier junctures in this book. For example, in Chapter 2 we saw that global consciousness (that is, awareness of the world as a single place) is one of the main manifestations of supraterritoriality. In Chapter 3 we saw that ideas of globality have figured in the history of transworld relations for at least half a millennium. In Chapter 4 we saw that the predominant modern structure of knowledge, rationalism, has been vital to the creation of global spaces. Now, in the present chapter, we proceed to assess the consequences of contemporary globalization for rationalism and the character of knowledge more generally.

As mentioned in Chapter 1, several authors have linked globality with a purported decline or even demise of modern rationality. Martin Albrow has presented a particularly explicit and articulate statement of this thesis (Albrow, 1996). Certain other sociologists have linked globalization with the challenge to rationalism posed by contemporary religious revival movements, or what has popularly often been called 'fundamentalism' (Robertson and Chirico, 1985; Robertson and Garrett, 1991; Beyer, 1994).

Yet announcements of the death of modern rationality in the face of globalization are no less premature than proclamations of the end of capital, the state or the nation. True, as is elaborated in the first section below, global flows have in some ways made room for nonrationalist knowledges such as religious revivalism, ecocentrism and postmodernist thought. However, most knowledge that has circulated in global spaces to date has continued to exhibit the core rationalist attributes of secularism, anthropocentrism, scientism and instrumentalism. To this extent, contemporary globalization has tended to spread and strengthen the position of modern rationality.

This is not to say, though, that the rise of supraterritoriality has left rationalist knowledge untouched. On the contrary, as later parts of this chapter indicate, the new geography of social relations has contributed to several broad shifts in the attributes of modern reason. In respect of epistemology, for example, global problems such as ecological degradation and financial crises have encouraged a greater appreciation of the limitations and potential dangers of rationalism. In terms of ontology, contemporary globalization has fostered a different conception of 'the world' to which reason is applied, as well as different appreciations of speed and change. With regard to methodology, the spread of supraterritoriality has helped to promote new fields of study, new approaches to education, new literacies, and new kinds of scientific evidence. In the area of aesthetics, globalization has facilitated the emergence of new forms and appreciations of beauty.

To be sure, the growth of transworld spaces has not been the only cause of these contemporary developments in the social construction of knowledge. For one thing, local cultures have strongly influenced whether or not reactions against rationalism occur and, if so, in what form. In addition, contemporary shifts in knowledge have emerged partly out of developments within science, philosophy and religion themselves. However, in combination with other impulses, globalization has exerted some important influences on knowledge structures in contemporary history.

Epistemology: modern rationality and its critics

One key aspect of a knowledge system is the underlying notion of knowledge, or what philosophers formally call epistemology. Our epistemology (of which we are often only minimally conscious) tells us what counts as 'fact', 'explanation' and 'understanding'. In what ways, if any, has contemporary globalization altered conceptions of the character of knowledge?

Once again the answer is one of change and continuity. The growth of supraterritorial relations in recent history has in some respects stimulated a rise of anti-rationalist epistemologies, in forms including religious revivalism, ecocentrism and postmodernism. However, in the main globalization has thus far reinforced and extended the hold of modern notions of reason. At the same time, contemporary globalization has also encouraged turns toward greater reflexivity in some rationalist thinking. In reflexive rationality the main precepts of rationalism continue to reign supreme, but people subject this epistemology and the knowledge that results from it to more critical examination.

Persistent rationalism

Rationalism has ranked as the most powerful epistemology in modern social relations. Yet, like any other construction of knowledge, the rationalist perspective is socially and historically bound. It ascended in particular places (starting with the North Atlantic area), in particular social circles (starting with middle-class intellectuals), and in particular times (especially from the eighteenth century onwards). In turn, we could expect rationalism to give way to other epistemologies when sociohistorical conditions become ripe for such a transformation.

Has the contemporary rise of supraterritoriality constituted the occasion for a transition to post-rationalist epistemology? Have this reconfiguration of geography and accompanying shifts in production, governance and community made modern rationality unsustainable? Although rationalism has figured as a major cause of globalization, has, the contemporary reorganization of social space rebounded to undermine that knowledge structure?

Such a proposition is difficult to sustain, particularly since rationalism has remained integral to most supraterritorial relations. For one thing, global communications technologies have well served modern science and its chief production sites, like universities and research institutes. Global markets, global production, global finance and global organizations have likewise mainly reproduced secular and instrumental thinking. Global ecological problems and prevailing policy responses to them have reflected a persistence of anthropocentric attempts to subordinate nature to human purposes with science and technology. Similarly, most global consciousness has had a decidedly secular character.

Moreover, the currently most influential approaches to globalization, summarily described in Chapter 1, have rested firmly on rationalist premises. Both neoliberalism and reformism have exhibited a thoroughly secular, anthropocentric, techno-scientific and instrumentalist orientation to knowledge. Among radical perspectives, socialist views on globalization, too, have involved a rationalist epistemology. By comparison, nonrationalist approaches to knowledge like traditionalist religion and postmodernism have had far less influence.

In these ways contemporary globalization can be associated with a further ascendance of rationalism to unprecedented strength. Indeed, religious practices have declined across much of the planet during the period of accelerated globalization, particularly in the OECD countries where supraterritoriality has become most widespread. (Continuing high levels of church attendance in the USA have formed an exception in this regard.) The thinking of global managers has in most cases been as anthropocentric as knowledge comes. Capitalism and bureaucratism – both of them substantially advanced through contemporary globalization – each involve intensely instrumentalist orientations. In short, the growth of global relations has in various ways extended rationalist knowledge to more parts of the world and to more parts of our lives.

Indeed, people who construct knowledge in secular, anthropocentric, techno-scientific, instrumental terms have generally exercised the greatest power in global spaces. Rationalist epistemology has reigned supreme in global enterprises, global governance agencies and the more influential parts of global civil society like think tanks and professional NGOs. People who espouse Hindu revivalism, deep ecology or an ultra-relativist postmodernism have had little career in British Petroleum (BP), the Bank for International Settlements, or Amnesty International.

Religious revivalism

On the other hand, supraterritorial spaces have in some respects also accommodated nonrationalist epistemologies and have in some cases even encouraged anti-rationalist movements. For instance, the decades of accelerated globalization have witnessed numerous instances of religious revivalism, where believers seek to regain their faith's original, premodern truth. This 'fundamentalism' has appeared across all of the major world religions (Kepel, 1991; Marty and Appleby, 1991). For one thing, charismatic and evangelical movements have proliferated in Protestant circles across the world (Poewe, 1994). Meanwhile many quarters of

Eastern Orthodoxy and Roman Catholicism have experienced heightened conservatism, the latter especially under the pontificate of John Paul II, starting in 1978. Concurrently, Islamic revivalism has attained considerable strength in many parts of Central, South West, South and South East Asia as well as North Africa. Judaic revivalism of groups like *Gush Emunim* ('Bloc of the Faithful'), founded in 1974, has motivated many Jewish settlers in territories occupied by Israel in the Six-Day War of 1967. In India the *Rashtriya Swayamsevak Sangh* (RSS), the *Vishwa Hindu Parishad* (VHP) and the *Bharatiya Janata Party* (BJP) have sought to Hinduize politics and radicalize Hinduism. Meanwhile various forms of Buddhist revival have unfolded in Mongolia, Sri Lanka and Thailand.

Contemporary globalization has encouraged religious revivalism in several ways. On the one hand, many of these anti-rationalist strivings can be understood in part as defensive reactions against encroachments by global forces on established cultures and livelihoods. This point has been previously elaborated in discussions of traditionalist discourses and transborder religious communities. Yet at the same time, as also noted in Chapter 7, a number of revivalist movements have exploited global relations to advance their causes. To give further examples in this regard, the leading mullah in Tajikistan has maintained many of his communications by fax and cellular telephone (Juergensmeyer, 1993: 5). Meanwhile Ayatollah Khomeini used world service broadcasts to pronounce his *fatwa* against the author Salman Rushdie in 1989.

However, we should not overestimate the scale of religiously based antirationalism under contemporary globalization. George Weigel has surely exaggerated in asserting that 'the unsecularization of the world is one of the dominant social facts of life in the late twentieth century' (cited in Huntington, 1993: 26). True, several religious revival movements have attracted large followings and exerted notable political influence. However, on the whole religious revivalism has enlisted only a small proportion of the world's population and stimulated relatively few major policy changes.

Moreover, these religious upsurges have not been new to contemporary times of globalization. Revivalist reactions against the secularist character of modern rationality have emerged from time to time ever since the Enlightenment. For example, the 1920s saw the creation of the Hinduist RSS and the rise of Islamic revivalism in a number of anti-colonial struggles (Peters, 1979). An earlier phase of Protestant 'fundamentalism' in the USA culminated in the mid-1920s with a court challenge (in the Scopes trial) against teaching Darwinian ideas of biological evolution.

Indeed, just as previous rises of religious revivalism have proved temporary, little evidence today suggests that recent increases are on course to displace rationalism as the dominant epistemology in our globalizing world. Transborder relations have helped to stimulate and sustain some renewals of anti-rationalist faith, but global networks have more usually promoted activities involving rationalist knowledge. Contemporary revivalist movements have largely replayed a long-term tendency – one that well predates contemporary globalization – whereby certain religious circles have from time to time revolted against modern secularism.

Meanwhile today, as during much of the past two centuries, many if not most influential religious thinkers have sought to marry faith and reason, that is, to combine and reconcile experience of the transcendent with scientific and instrumental knowledge. Thus, for example, the executive director of a global bank might be a techno-scientific economist by day and a practising Buddhist after hours. Modernizing tendencies in Islam have rivalled revivalist movements. Likewise, reform Judaism has on balance exerted as much influence as revivalist Judaism. Many if not most Christians, Confucians and Hindus, too, have sought to adjust their religious understanding to accommodate modern rationality. In short, revivalist anti-rationalism has been a minority tendency even in many religious circles.

Ecocentrism

Next to religious revivalism, ecocentrism has formed a second notable reaction in contemporary history against prevailing rationalist epistemology. The term 'ecocentrism' is borrowed from Robyn Eckersley (1992), although it is here applied to a wider range of authors and arguments. Whereas religious revivalists have taken principal aim against the secularist character of modern rationality, ecocentrists have in the first place opposed anthropocentrism and the attendant drive to control nature for human ends. In ecocentrist knowledge, humanity exists within – and as but one part of – a larger life system. *Homo sapiens* is subordinate to nature rather than vice versa, and human desires need to be renounced in favour of ecological health when the two conflict.

Ecocentrism has taken a number of guises in contemporary history. For example, many indigenous peoples have as part of the assertion of their collective identity promoted notions of aboriginal knowledge where human beings are integrated within and subservient to a natural order. Ecocentrist premises have also underlain notions of 'deep ecology', which reject the 'shallow' environmentalism of those who advocate so-called 'sustainable development' using rationalist knowledge frameworks (Naess, 1976; Devall and Sessions, 1985). From another angle, ecofeminists have identified rationalism with masculinism and have opposed both forces in terms of their purported violence against nature (Warren, 1996). For his part, the inventor James Lovelock has popularized the so-called 'Gaia' notion that regards planet earth as a living creature to which people owe their greatest responsibility (Lovelock, 1979). Various grassroots environmentalists like anti-road campaigners and animal liberation groups have likewise understood the world in ecocentrist terms.

Globalization has not been the only circumstance to promote the rise of ecocentrist knowledge, but the growth of supraterritorial relations has played an important part. In particular, global ecological changes have raised awareness of the damages that anthropocentric rationalism can inflict. An appreciation of humanity's dependence on ecological conditions is heightened in the light of developments (like climate change and biodiversity loss) from which there is no escape, short of leaving the planet. In addition, some people have been drawn to ecocentrist thought by the ecological irrationality of much global economic activity. In this vein it might be asked why we ship foods between continents, at a cost of considerable air and sea pollution, when adequate (and often more nutritious) supplies could usually be available from local production. Finally, much as some religious revivalists have exploited global communications and transborder associations to further their causes, so some ecocentrists have benefited from the supraterritorial political activities that globalization makes possible.

Yet we must not exaggerate the scale of ecocentrist challenges to rationalism in the contemporary world. Aboriginal knowledge, deep ecology, ecofeminism and the Gaia hypothesis have, even collectively, attracted relatively small followings. Nor do present trends suggest that ecocentrism is on the way to becoming more than a marginal epistemology. Insofar as ecological sensitivities have gained ground in the context of globalization, policymakers have mainly opted for a rationalist response of 'sustainable development'. This strategy seeks to perpetuate humanity's subordination of nature and to find techno-scientific solutions to environmental problems.

Postmodernism

In addition to religious revivalism and ecocentrism, the time of accelerated globalization has also witnessed a rise of so-called 'postmodernist' epistemologies. These perspectives on knowledge, briefly introduced in Chapter 1, have generally retained the secular and anthropocentric orientations of rationalism. However, postmodernists have rejected scientific claims concerning objective facts as well as instrumentalist notions that the primary purpose of knowledge is technical problem-solving.

Against rationalism, postmodernism adopts an anti-universalist and anti-essentialist view of knowledge. Instead, this alternative epistemology regards all knowledge as bound to its time and place, as well as the particular person who constructs it. Every truth is therefore contingent upon its context. No understanding transcends its specific personal, cultural and historical setting. For postmodernists, rationalist notions of scientific objectivity are – like any other knowledge claim – a myth with no absolute truth about them (Anderson, 1990). It is social power relations – rather than any fundamental truth – that have elevated rationalism over other modes of knowledge in modern contexts.

Logically, it is possible to conclude from the relativism of postmodernism that all knowledges are equally valid. Some postmodernists have indeed adopted an ultra-sceptical position toward knowledge, where no grounds other than personal whim are available for ranking certain values and beliefs over others. At this extreme, fascism could not be condemned relative to liberalism, and no basis would exist to distinguish good art from bad. In such a situation postmodernism would replace the objectivism of rationalism with an 'anything-goes' subjectivism.

However, postmodernists do not – as some of their critics charge – have to take the rejection of objectivism to a nihilistic conclusion. On the contrary, many proponents of this alternative epistemology have advanced strongly held value claims about culture and politics. Postmodernist philosophers like Michel Foucault and Julia Kristeva have taken very overt and public normative stances. Some feminists have integrated postmodernist knowledge into a struggle against gender hierarchies (Peterson, 1992). Postmodernist security studies have employed the epistemology in critiques of military violence (Campbell and Dillon, 1993). In contrast to religious revivalists, however, postmodernists regard their truths as contingent and contestable.

As mentioned in Chapter 1, postmodernism has attracted most of its explicit adherents in academic circles and the arts. Among academics the exponents have concentrated mainly in the humanities (especially Literary Criticism and Philosophy) and on the fringes of social research (including Anthropology, Geography, Linguistics, Politics and Sociology). In the arts postmodernism has reshaped significant parts of architecture, cinema, literature, music, painting, sculpture and theatre.

The contemporary growth of postmodernist epistemologies can be connected to globalization in several ways. For one thing, global relations have, by eliminating territorial buffers, intensified intercultural contacts and heightened general awareness of cultural diversity. Many people have thereby come – in line with postmodernist precepts – to regard their knowledge as socially and historically relative. Persons who have experienced intense hybridization of the kind described in Chapter 7 seem to have been especially susceptible to postmodernist relativism. Indeed, exponents of postmodernism have included disproportionate numbers of migrants and exiles.

Globalization has also promoted postmodernist thought through the technologies of supraterritorial communications. For example, mass media reports of world news have often involved obvious manipulations of 'facts'. After all, the story depends largely on where the camera is pointed. Computer-generated 'virtual realities' have likewise blurred lines between fact and fiction. Indeed, by increasing communication through images as opposed to verbal exchanges, global relations have perhaps given more reign to 'irrational' unconscious associations in human thought (Lash, 1990: ch 7).

In addition, globalization has encouraged the rise of postmodernist epistemology through consumer capitalism. The consumerist mindset is oriented more to ephemeral experiences than to fixed facts. As a way of knowing the world, consumerism (through shopping, tourism, etc.) gives greater weight to sensation than to science. Also, against instrumentalist logic, consumerism accords higher priority to gratifying desires than to solving problems.

All of this said, we should not overestimate the novelty and power of postmodernist epistemologies in the contemporary world. Like religious revivalist movements, relativist philosophies date back well before the onset of accelerated globalization. The nineteenth-century nihilism of Friedrich Nietzsche gives but one prominent example. Moreover, to this day fully-fledged postmodernist thought has figured mainly on the margins of social life. The overwhelming majority of academics, entrepreneurs, officials and civil society organizers have stayed with a rationalist orientation.

Reflexive rationalism

Thus, in spite of various important challenges, rationalist knowledge has retained primacy in contemporary times of growing global relations. Yet this prevailing epistemology has not come through the twentieth century unchanged. In particular, modern rationality has in recent history often become more reflexive.

A number of sociologists have invoked the term reflexivity to describe rationalist thought that is acutely self-conscious, self-searching and self-critical (Beck, 1994; Giddens, 1994). Reflexive rationalists 'think about what before they did unthinkingly' (Smart, 1999: 33). Reflexivity brings less confidence in rationalist knowledge claims and reduced faith in the modern project of perpetual progress through the application of human reason.

Reflexive rationalism is still rationalist. It rests on the old and well-tried core tenets of secularism, anthropocentrism, scientism and instrumentalism. However, reflexivity takes away the conviction element: modern knowledge is no longer taken for granted. Thus many modernist thinkers today, while still regarding rationalism as the most promising epistemology currently available, have also recognized its limitations and flaws. With this attitude, reflexive rationalists tend to be less dismissive of alternative knowledges and more ready to experiment with different epistemologies (for example, in unconventional approaches to health care).

Indeed, reflexive rationalism and postmodernism overlap at points. Like postmodernists, reflexive rationalists view knowledge as uncertain and contingent. Also like postmodernists, reflexive rationalists see that modern reason can have harmful outcomes, for instance, in the form of military-industrial complexes and ecological degradation.

Yet the two epistemologies also part ways. In particular, postmodernists regard rationalism as irredeemable and actively pursue alternative epistemologies, whereas reflexive modernists conclude that, for all its limitations, rationalism is still the best game in town and indeed can be reformed. In the latter vein André Gorz has called for a 'rationalization of rationality', and Ulrich Beck has prescribed a 'new modernity' of more self-critical and self-limiting science (Gorz, 1988: 1; Beck, 1986). Thus reflexive modernists seek a regeneration of rationalism in forms where it does not promote ills such as centralized power and the suppression of cultural diversity. In contrast, postmodernists doubt that such corrections are possible.

Reflexive rationalism is not completely new to recent history, of course. A sceptical bent has been intrinsic to modern rationality. Science has constantly questioned and perpetually revised knowledge in the light of new information and analysis. To be modern is in part to 'stand outside' of and critically reflect upon one's being.

Yet the self-monitoring aspects of rationalism have gained unprecedented intensities in contemporary history. Anthony Giddens has in this light characterized the current situation as one of 'high modernity' marked by extreme reflexivity (1991: 28–9). In these circumstances people have become less trusting of science and technology. Thus, for example, we witness recurrent food scares and widespread calls for greater spirituality in modern life. Even many professional scientists have retreated from claims to hold objective facts and full truths: the scepticism of science has turned upon science itself (Beck, 1986: 155). The enlightened are questioning their Enlightenment. Modernists are questioning modernity.

Globalization has not been the only force behind the growth of reflexive rationalism, but this rearrangement of social space has encouraged this turn in knowledge in several ways. For one thing, much as with the spread of postmodernism, the rise of supraterritoriality has promoted heightened reflexivity by intensifying cross-cultural encounters. Global travel, electronic communications and transworld marketing of artefacts such as Rastafarian music and certain alternative therapies have made rationalists more aware that the world contains a plurality of knowledge systems, each with its own internal coherence. For many people the posited hierarchy of 'reason' over 'folk wisdom' has become more qualified in consequence.

Computer technologies at the heart of globalization have also injected uncertainties into the rationalist project. On the one hand, digital computers have enabled people to access much more information and to manipulate it faster and in more complex ways. These capacities have often advanced the rationalist cause of subordinating natural and social forces to human purposes. On the other hand, computers have also generated more data than human minds can effectively monitor and control. Furthermore, we face the prospect of increasingly sophisticated artificial intelligence that operates with relative autonomy from human decision. Already, for instance, self-monitoring computer programmes have contributed to 'irrational' runs on currencies and stock markets.

As these undesirable outcomes of electronic finance illustrate, globalization can encourage greater reflexivity insofar as transworld relations have produced harms that call into question the rationality of rationality. Other examples include the destructive potential of supraterritorial weapons, the damage of anthropogenic global ecological changes, and the cruelty for vulnerable social circles of liberalized global markets. Such threats (which are elaborated in Part III) have prompted many rationalists to reflect that reason can sometimes be the problem rather than the solution.

To repeat, however, reflexivity marks a shift within rather than a change of knowledge structure. In reflexive rationality, 'reflexive' is the adjective and 'rationality' is the noun. Although reflexive rationalists may show greater openness to alternative knowledges than traditional 'conviction rationalists', they remain rationalists. High modernity is still modernity.

Giddens and others have sometimes spoken of 'high modernity' as being also 'late modernity'. This characterization intimates that reflexive rationalism could mark the start of a transition to some kind of postmodern knowledge. Indeed, as noted above, reflexive and postmodernist epistemologies do have some notable overlap. Yet it is too early to draw the further implication that increased reflexivity is taking rationalism toward the historical exit door.

On the contrary, we do well to remember that much rationalism at the dawn of the twenty-first century has not acquired a heightened reflexive character. There is still plenty of evangelical scientism about. Many a manager bows before the shrine of productivity, and many an economist kneels at the temple of efficiency. Many people still regard science and technology as the salvation of our earthly lives. Globalization has (so far) not on the whole displaced that faith.

Ontology

Next to its effects on epistemology, globalization has also contributed to some interesting and important turns in respect of other aspects of knowledge. Several of these developments relate to ontology, that is, the broad way that we define 'reality'.

All cultures and individuals hold particular conceptions of the entities and relationships that constitute their world. Key ontological concerns include the character of God (if any), life, the self, time and space. Our notions of such conditions form a backdrop to, and shape, our every thought and purposeful action, even if we may only rarely, if ever, express these ideas explicitly. Shifts in our mental constructions of reality may also occur so subtly as to be little noticed.

Space

Has contemporary globalization generated changes in ontology? In the first place we might consider whether, and how far, the rise of supraterritoriality has altered conceptions of space. Have our ideas of 'place' become different?

As noted in Chapter 2, a number of social thinkers including Heidegger, Harvey, Castells and Ruggie have redefined geography in post-territorialist terms. The present book adds to that trend. To the extent that these academic reconceptualizations of space strike a chord with the population at large, the accounts are articulating a broader ontological shift.

Incipient new ideas of space have indeed emerged in wider circles than a cluster of social theorists. We saw in Chapter 3 that an awareness of globality has in recent history become commonsense for a notable proportion of humanity. The sociologist Roland Robertson has in fact defined globalization as a growth in 'the scope and depth of consciousness of the world as a single place' (1992: 183). The different conception of space articulated in the present book will resonate with far more people today than it would have done fifty years ago.

Current widespread talk of 'virtual reality' seems revealing in this regard. We recognize that images on screen are 'real', yet they do not fit conventional understandings of geographical 'reality'. We are therefore driven to construct alternative, post-territorialist definitions of space, in order to restore a fit between our understandings and our experiences. Such an ontological shift allows us to move cyberspace and other global phenomena from virtual to actual reality.

However, this shift to a post-territorialist understanding of space is far from complete. Many people at the start of the twenty-first century still equate 'space' and 'geography' with 'territory'. Perhaps global maps of reality will one day be as obvious to people as territorial maps have been in modern history. Then we would no longer need, as in the present book, to express post-territorialist ontology with constant references back to old terminology, that is, invoking notions of supra*territoriality* and trans-*border* relations. The vocabulary of globality would at this point be able to stand on its own. For the moment, though, nonterritorialist concepts of space remain relatively novel and far from fully developed.

Time

Next to conceptions of space, notions of time are another area where the rise of supraterritoriality has prompted some ontological shifts. As noted in Chapter 2, globalization involves a qualitative change in the relations of space and time insofar as it dissolves the connection (within the confines of our planet, at least) between time and distance. As a result, people living more globalized lives are less inclined to think of time with reference to distance. For example, we do not, as in many premodern contexts, understand a day in terms of the time it takes to travel to the next village or some other destination. In addition, the hour has today lost its once close connection with the railway timetable.

Globalization has tended to shift the ontology of time from a link with distance to a connection with speed. For example, air travellers usually think more about how fast than how far they are going. With fax and e-mail we are more concerned with the speed than with the distance of communications: it is not how far a correspondent has to respond, but how quickly they answer. In global production the issue of how swiftly suppliers can deliver ('just in time') often has little to do with how far they have to deliver. By in these and other ways putting greater stress on speed, globalization has contributed to a general acceleration of life.

In addition, globalization has tended to heighten our experience of the fullness of time. By removing the buffers previously afforded by distance, supraterritorial connections have allowed ever more activity to crowd into a person's time. A day becomes a deluge of telephone calls, e-mails, channel hopping between radio and television transmissions, electronic money transactions, etc. In a word, life becomes far more 'busy'.

The combination of faster and fuller time in a highly globalized life can present substantial coping challenges. In this regard it is probably no accident that stress and supraterritoriality have grown concurrently in contemporary history. Indeed, like notions of 'globalization', the concept of 'stress' has in recent decades spread to countless languages across the world.

Methodology

Along with epistemology and ontology, methodology is a third area of knowledge where we might look for effects of globalization. Methodology refers to the ways that we build knowledge: that is, the principles and procedures of inquiry. It involves questions both of general approach to knowledge construction and of specific research tools.

Globalization has *not* made general impacts on several core methodological issues in social inquiry. For example, concerning the agent-structure question (discussed in Chapter 4), globalization has not prompted a mass conversion of voluntarists into structuralists, or vice versa. Likewise, the rise of supraterritoriality has not turned materialists (those who root social causation in economics and/or ecology) into idealists (those who explain social relations in terms of cultural and/or psychological forces), or vice versa. Nor has increased globality induced general changes of perspective on the relationship between facts and values; nor has it altered views on the links between theory and practice. These methodological issues (which I have explored at greater length in Scholte, 1993b) are not directly connected to the shape of social space. Thus globalization is a new subject of study around which long-running debates about methodology can be replayed (Taylor, 1996; Germain, 1999). However, the contemporary shift in geography has not changed the balance in these arguments, let alone resolved them.

Globalization has arguably had more direct implications for several other methodological issues. As elaborated below, these impacts have related to the role of academic disciplines, to processes of teaching and learning, and to the nature of empirical evidence.

Disciplinarity

The growth of supraterritorial problems has accentuated the need to transcend conventional academic divides when undertaking social inquiry. Some theorists have called for *multi*disciplinarity, where researchers from several fields each contribute their own approach to a joint investigation. Others have appealed for greater *inter*disciplinarity, where researchers take the additional step of integrating principles and tools from different fields of study. Some academics have gone still further and argued for *post-*

disciplinarity, namely, the creation of substantively new methodologies that do not rely on separated fields of study. The so-called 'world-system approach', associated especially with the work of Immanuel Wallerstein, provides one example of post-disciplinarity (Wallerstein, 1991).

The rise of supraterritoriality has contributed to some retreats from discipline-bound research inasmuch as academic divides have often hampered rather than advanced knowledge of transworld relations. Global communications, global economic restructuring and global ecological degradation are among a number of contemporary issues that can be only partially – and often but poorly – understood through single disciplines. Little wonder, then, that recent history has seen the emergence of interdisciplinary enterprises such as Media Studies, International Political Economy and Environmental Sciences. The US Committee on the Human Dimensions of Global Change has concluded that 'the need to understand global change may well become a powerful force for change in the existing structure of scientific disciplines' (Stern, 1992: 33). Likewise, several world-system theorists have cited globalization as a justification for their post-disciplinary approach to social enquiry (Taylor, 1996).

However, we must not exaggerate recent moves away from disciplinarity. So far, exhortations to transcend the old academic divides have well exceeded actual multidisciplinary, interdisciplinary and post-disciplinary research practices. Like contemporary social inquiry in general, most studies of global issues have drawn from a single field: either Anthropology, or Economics, or Geography, or Law, or Politics, or Sociology. Several nondisciplinary academic journals for the study of global problems have appeared, such as *Review* and *Global Social Policy*; yet most professional research continues to be funnelled through discipline-related organs. Similarly, most academic conferences have remained tribal conclaves on disciplinary lines. Most academic funding has continued to flow through disciplinary channels, and respect of disciplinarity normally still provides researchers with a faster track to promotion than alternative approaches. In short, some minor inroads aside, disciplinary methodology remains quite firmly entrenched in the contemporary globalizing world.

Teaching and learning

Other methodological shifts prompted in part through globalization have related to education processes. For example, the growth of supraterritoriality in publishing has meant that millions of schoolchildren and students now acquire part of their learning from transworld textbooks. A number of academics including Paul Samuelson in Economics, Kenneth Waltz in International Relations, and Anthony Giddens in Sociology have in this way become global teachers.

At an institutional level several colleges and universities have embarked on transborder franchising of entire courses. For instance, Monash University in Melbourne has marketed its programmes in standardized packages throughout Asia (Waters, 1995: 172). Several UK-based institutions have embarked on similar enterprises. In addition, universities can – thanks to air transport, faxes and the Internet – use academics in different countries or continents as external examiners for their programmes. At secondary-school level the International Baccalaureate (IB) has emerged as a supraterritorial diploma: it draws from no country and is recognized across countries.

Meanwhile mass air travel has in recent history facilitated large increases in study abroad activities. Children from wealthier families can today expect at least one school trip overseas as part of their secondary education. Hundreds of thousands of university students in the North have completed a period of study abroad, albeit that complications of credit transfer and grade translation often still arise. At postgraduate level a few institutions have begun to experiment with transborder programmes, where students spend different parts of their course in different countries or continents.

Other 'distance learning' has developed on 'virtual campuses' via television and computer networks. For instance, the Open University in Britain, the Télé-Université in Québec and Item/Seis in Mexico have beamed prerecorded lectures and demonstrations to their students by satellite. Many other teachers have used the Internet as a classroom tool, with websites at least partially displacing books and journals as reading material.

Indeed, the technologies of globalization have substantially broadened the character of literacy. In many lines of work the ability to use computer applications has become as important as the ability to read and write with paper and pen. In addition, television, film and computer graphics have greatly enlarged the visual dimensions of communication. Many people today 'read' the globalizing world without a book. Sociologists Scott Lash and John Urry have in this regard contrasted the 'literary paradigm' of modernism with a 'video paradigm' of postmodernism (1994: 16). In the world of electronic mass media, journalists, advertisers and disk jockeys have come to rank among our principal teachers.

Finally, the growth of supraterritorial spaces has spurred the development of English as a global lingua franca. English has served as the chief medium of verbal communication in transborder relations. The language is now spoken by 1.7 billion people across the world (BT, 2000: 10), including many who have never set foot in a country to which English is native. We might even distinguish a 'global dialect' of English, namely, the version that is spoken in tourist resorts and professional conferences. This 'global English' uses vocabulary and turns of phrase that have little currency on the streets of Glasgow and Omaha. The supraterritoriality of English has spawned several diplomas such as TOEFL (Teaching of English as a Foreign Language) and has raised the Cambridge Proficiency Examination to a transworld standard. At the same time, native speakers of English have found it increasingly easy to get by in the world without learning other languages. (See further Pennycook, 1994.)

Evidence

While widening the scope of literacy, the technologies of globalization have also enlarged the amounts and types of empirical evidence that are available to researchers. Air travel, telecommunications and computer networks have enabled investigators to gather data in no time from any and all corners of the planet. An era of global research has dawned (for those who can obtain the required funding).

The Internet in particular has changed the character of research. Increasingly, academic writings (like the present book) include references to on-line sources. No longer is a 'document' limited to paper sheets with static, monochrome text. In some ways the Internet approximates the 'world brain' that H. G. Wells anticipated more than sixty years ago as 'an efficient index to *all* human knowledge, ideas and achievements . . . a complete planetary memory' (1938: 60).

Digital information processing has also enabled researchers in our globalizing world to handle much greater quantities of data. Large-scale number crunching and bulging bibliographies have become the order of the day. Whether greater wisdom has resulted is another matter, of course. In the information age it is arguably often harder to see the wood for the trees.

In sum, then, when it comes to methodology globalization has: (a) created greater urgency to abandon narrow disciplinary studies; (b) altered some aspects of education processes; and (c) increased amounts of empirical material and the ways that researchers handle evidence. Yet these developments have not substantially altered the kinds of knowledge that result from academic endeavours or from learning generally. As noted earlier, rationalism has remained the prime order of the day in global knowledge.

Aesthetics

What, finally, of aesthetics? Has globalization affected prevailing appreciations of beauty or, to put it another way, the ways that we know art? As the next paragraphs indicate, beauty has exhibited some different facets in supraterritorial spaces. However, older ideas of what constitutes art have not disappeared in the process.

To begin with, globalization has helped certain art forms to obtain worldwide currency. Electronic mass media and global markets in particular have promoted some kinds of music, dance, film, dress and cuisine to the top of fashion across all continents. Ronaldo's turns on the football pitch, Andy Warhol's images, and tinted-glass office blocks have become transborder marks of beauty, unconnected to any specific country and appreciated (in some circles, at least) the world over.

Much as globalization has encouraged greater hybridization in collective identities, as discussed in Chapter 7, so transworld spaces have also provided increased possibilities for intercultural combinations in the arts. For example, an Indian sitarist has linked up with an American guitarist to produce a new variant of jazz (if it can still be called that). British Airways has replaced its old Union Jack tail design with a mix of compositions drawn from diverse corners of the world. An evening's entertainment in a global city can readily encompass an Ethiopian meal, a Russian play and transport by Korean car with American pop music on the stereo. In Berlin, home to people from 181 countries, *Multikulti* radio issues broadcasts in 19 languages (Velea, 1996). Beauty has thereby increasingly lain in blends as well as in the 'purity' of traditions.

In addition, the rise of supraterritoriality has contributed to the creation and spread of certain new forms of beauty. For instance, computer-generated images and global brand symbols have often fallen outside pre-existent categories of art. Global relations have also tended to endow speed with beauty, *inter alia* in the sensation of jet travel, the pulse of electronic music and the flurry of still motion on television and cinema screens.

Together, these three trends – of importations, combinations and new creations – have arguably brought greater diversity and flexibility to appreciations of beauty. David Harvey has on these lines described 'the ferment, instability and fleeting qualities of a postmodernist aesthetic that celebrates difference, ephemerality, spectacle, fashion, and the commodification of cultural forms' (1989: 156). On the other hand, contemporary times of globalization have also witnessed many a traditionalist reaction against new turns in the arts.

Conclusion

So, as with production, governance and community, we can identify a number of repercussions of globalization for knowledge (summarized in the Box below). In regard to epistemology, the rise of supraterritoriality has encouraged several anti-rationalist reactions as well as promoted greater reflexivity within rationalism. With respect to ontology, spreading globality has prompted some shifts in conceptions of space and time. In terms of methodology, the growth of transworld networks has furthered some altered approaches to research, teaching and learning. As for aesthetics, globalization has introduced some different experiences of beauty. From all of these angles the new geography has encouraged greater pluralism and contestation in the construction of knowledge.

Yet once again – as in preceding investigations of production, governance and community – we discover that, thus far, the new post-territorialist geography has on the whole affected the margins more than the core when it comes to structures of knowledge. Rationalist epistemologies have retained primacy in global realms and contemporary social relations

Globalization and knowledge in summary

Epistemology
- global relations have largely reproduced rationalist knowledge
- the rise of supraterritoriality has in some ways also encouraged anti-rationalist reactions such as religious revivalism, ecocentrism and postmodernism
- globalization has promoted a growth of reflexive rationalism

Ontology
- globalization has altered notions of space
- supraterritorial relations have shifted several qualities of time

Methodology
- global problems have intensified the need for inter- and post-disciplinary modes of inquiry
- many educational tools and programmes have gained transworld circulation
- supraterritorial spaces have increased the importance of visual literacies
- English has become a transborder medium of communication
- technologies of globalization have generated greater quantities and different qualities of empirical evidence

Aesthetics
- transborder relations have facilitated the worldwide spread of certain forms of art
- globalization has encouraged increased hybridization in art
- transworld spaces have helped to produce new categories of art

generally. Apart from constructions of space and time, globalization has not had major direct repercussions for ontology. Discipline-based methodologies have continued to thrive in our globalizing world, and most shifts in education practices have affected form more than content. New types of art have in general supplemented rather than displaced the old. Knowledge has arguably witnessed greater creative ferment in our globalizing world, but overall structures have not radically altered.

This general conclusion of change within continuity has applied throughout Part II of this book. In each of the last four chapters we have found important shifts: in production, in governance, in community and in knowledge. To this extent contemporary globalization has certainly not marked 'the end of history'. On the other hand, we have also found underlying continuities: of capitalism, of bureaucratism, of communitarianism and of rationalism. A more global world could in principle bring deeper structural transformations in these areas; however, forces in the (thus far) predominantly neoliberal course of contemporary globalization have favoured the pre-existent social order.

Part III
Policy Issues

Having elaborated a concept of globalization, having traced the historical course of the trend, having examined its causes, and having traced the consequences of this reorganization of space for wider social structures, we have developed a substantial basis from which to assess costs and benefits of the new geography. Who has been winning and who has been losing from contemporary globalization, and in what ways? In the light of such a balance sheet, has the rise of supraterritoriality to date been a good and/or a bad thing? Inasmuch as globalization has caused harms, what corrective measures might be taken?

This book highlights three main measures of a good society: human security, social justice, and democracy. The next chapters examine these three broad questions in turn. Chapter 9 considers the implications of the rise of supraterritoriality for human security, that is, the types and levels of safety and confidence that people do and do not experience in society. Chapter 10 assesses the repercussions of recent decades of accelerated globalization for social justice, that is, the forms and intensities of arbitrary hierarchies between people (in terms of class, gender, race, etc.). Chapter 11 explores the consequences of spreading transworld relations on democracy, that is, the ways and degrees that people are able to shape their collective destiny.

In each case contemporary globalization is found to have yielded both positive and negative outcomes. As a *critical* introduction, this book places greatest emphasis on the downsides, particularly as they are largely avoidable. In other words, the harms have resulted not from supraterritoriality as such, but from the policies that we have adopted towards it.

Chapter 12 then considers what alternative policies might be available to counter the insecurities, injustices and democratic deficits that have flowed from currently prevailing (that is, mainly neoliberal) approaches to globalization. Contemporary social forces and political constellations give few prospects to radical strategies such as traditionalism or global socialism. However, a host of reformist measures – some of them quite far-reaching – could make our globalizing world a happier place.

Chapter 9

Globalization and (In)Security

Main points of this chapter

- globalization has had important repercussions for various dimensions of human security: military, ecological, economic, cultural and psychological
- on each of these dimensions the consequences of globalization have been both positive and negative
- the considerable negative impacts have not been intrinsic to globalization, but have resulted chiefly from neoliberal policies toward the trend

---

To start a normative evaluation of globalization, the present chapter highlights questions of security. In what ways and to what extent has contemporary globalization increased or decreased people's safety and confidence? Absolute security is of course not available: no social order can remove all uncertainty, danger, destruction and death. However, different circumstances can provide greater or lesser degrees of relative security. Therefore the question is in what ways globalization can enhance and/or undermine security, and whether we have maximized the potential benefits and minimized the possible threats.

The discussion below examines various aspects of security: military, ecological, economic, psychological and cultural. Traditionally, analyses of 'international relations' have presumed that security in world affairs entails no more than the preservation of states' territorial integrity and the absence (or at least limitation) of armed conflict. However, the contemporary growth of global communications, global production and markets, global money and finance, global social ecology and global consciousness has helped to broaden the security agenda beyond military matters alone. Today notions of security in world politics tend also to encompass guarantees of ecological integrity, subsistence, financial stability, employment, cultural identity, social cohesion, and knowledge (cf. Booth, 1991; Krause and Williams, 1997; Thomas and Wilkin, 1999).

The rest of this chapter addresses these multiple dimensions of security in turn. As might be expected, the balance sheet has both positive and negative entries. Accelerated globalization of recent decades can in some respects be linked to reduced warfare, to heightened ecological sensitivity, to greater material prosperity and to cultural innovation. On the other hand, the rise of supraterritoriality can also be linked to more destructive military capabilities, to increased environmental degradation, to persistent poverty, to greater financial instability, to more precarious job tenure and working conditions, to cultural extinctions, to greater social fragmentation, and to increased anxiety about the status of knowledge.

As a critical introduction, the present account on the whole places more emphasis on the downsides than on the benefits of globalization as that trend has unfolded thus far. The priority is put on making things better. The insecurities associated with the rise of supraterritoriality in contemporary history have indeed been great. These ills are all the more regrettable insofar as they might be substantially reduced. In other words, the problems have in the main resulted not from globalization as such, but from the particular courses of globalization that we have taken to date. The following evaluation is therefore principally an indictment of established (mainly neoliberal) policies and not a rejection of globalization per se. A different approach to supraterritoriality should allow us to reduce the harms to human security without losing the benefits.

Peace

As noted in Chapter 6, globalization would seem to discourage warfare insofar as armed conflict between states for control of territory serves little purpose for most supraterritorial concerns and interests. In those parts of the world where globalization has gone furthest, governments face – and are to a considerable degree dependent on – powerful transworld markets and communications networks whose operations would be greatly disrupted by military adventures. In addition, many citizens – including powerful élite circles in particular – have developed commitments to global issues and attachments to global communities, ties that make them less disposed to support old-style campaigns to conquer territory.

Thus it is arguably in part (albeit not only) owing to large-scale globalization that the OECD states have not gone to war against each other since 1945. Military conflict between states in East Asia, the European Union and North America also seems unlikely in the foreseeable future. To this extent neoliberals have had cause to applaud a link between globalization and greater peace.

In addition, the growth of suprastate governance has brought some greater possibilities of arms control. For example, a number of multilateral treaties (some with regional scope and others with transworld coverage) have restricted the testing and deployment of nuclear warheads. The nuclear non-proliferation treaty (NPT) regime, established in 1968 through the IAEA, has discouraged (albeit not with total success) the spread of nuclear weapons to more state arsenals. At the end of 1999 a total of 129 states had ratified the Chemical Weapons Convention of 1993, adminis- tered since 1997 through a permanent Organization for the Prohibition of Chemical Weapons (OPCW, 1999). Global controls have also advanced for biological weapons and land-mines. The transborder campaign against land-mines in particular has demonstrated that substantial popular sup- port can be mobilized for tighter control of global production and trade of arms (Price, 1998).

Suprastate governance has also opened new means of conflict manage- ment. Since the 1950s the UN has developed so-called peacekeeping operations in inter-state conflicts, and in the 1990s the organization substantially expanded humanitarian assistance in civil wars (Weiss *et al.*, 1994; Minear and Weiss, 1995). Some of these efforts have had limited success, but various positive UN contributions to conflict limitation have developed as well, for example, in Cambodia, Cyprus and Namibia. Meanwhile regional governance bodies like the Organization of African Unity (OAU) and the Organization for Security and Cooperation in Europe (OSCE) have undertaken conflict management initiatives in their respective areas. Transborder humanitarian NGOs have often assisted both transworld and regional official agencies in alleviating the harms of war.

However, the rise of supraterritoriality has not enhanced our security from military dangers in every respect. After all, 'peace' has prevailed between major states since the mid-twentieth century under a spectre of destruction such as people have never before experienced. In spite of the end of the Cold War, and even after full implementation of the START I and II agreements, the world will still have enough nuclear warheads to eliminate the entire human race. Global weapons such as fighter jets, missiles and spy satellites have sown insecurity in the target populations, whether or not those tools have been activated. In addition, the holders of such weapons have lived with a constant anxiety that prospective enemies could acquire similar capabilities – or worse, develop still more sophisti- cated technologies for supraterritorial attacks. A Comprehensive Test Ban

Treaty in respect of nuclear weapons was signed in 1996; however, after the US Senate's refusal to ratify, it is doubtful whether the agreement will ever enter into force.

Moreover, interstate warfare has persisted outside the North. Recent decades have witnessed several armed conflagrations between states, including Vietnam and Cambodia, Iran and Iraq, Ecuador and Peru, Eritrea and Ethiopia. Indeed, global reach with 'rapid reaction forces' and the like has facilitated military interventions by states of the North in conflicts in the South and the East. The US government in particular has despatched armed forces to the Balkans, the Caribbean, Central America, the Horn of Africa and the Persian Gulf. Territorial interests still drove the British government to war with Argentina over the Falklands/Malvinas in 1982. Nor has a half-century of large-scale globalization ended the state of war on the Korean peninsula, where the will for territorial reunification under a single nation-state has persisted, irrespective of South Korea's deep involvement in transworld relations. Meanwhile, as mentioned earlier, widespread ethnic and religious revivals encouraged by globalization have promoted a substantial rise in intrastate warfare outside the North: in Afghanistan, Angola, Indonesia, Russia, Sri Lanka, Sudan, former Yugoslavia, etc.

Globalization and militarization have also been closely interlinked in other ways. For example, the telephone was used on the battlefield within two years of its invention (Young, 1991: 49). Likewise supraterritorial connections by radio and laser have acquired important military purposes. Computer networks were first developed in the US armed forces in 1969 and have become a key tool of contemporary warfare for major states. Many future military operations may focus on invading computer systems as much as on occupying territorial domains. Global finance largely paid for the Gulf War of 1990–1, whose oil fires also provoked a major global ecological scare. Global companies have figured prominently in the production of military equipment, while global traders have supplied arms both to many weak states and to the rebels who have risen against them. Global organization has featured in military alliance structures such as NATO, in the transborder paramilitary activities of various so-called 'terrorist' groups, and in armed violence pursued by transborder criminal networks.

In short, the rise of supraterritoriality in no way inherently reduces military threats to human security. Indeed, it is conceivable that general warfare between major states could recur in spite – or even because – of globalization. As is elaborated below, adjustment to global relations can produce many pains in terms of ecological damage, increased poverty, job losses, deterioration of working conditions, cultural destruction and social division. In certain circumstances such heightened insecurities could encourage a return of large-scale interstate warfare. On this count, too, equations of globalization and peace might prove to be dangerously complacent.

Ecological integrity

As stressed earlier, security in world politics involves more than military matters. Human safety also depends crucially on maintaining a viable relationship between people and their natural surroundings. It goes without saying that human life requires certain atmospheric, hydrospheric, geospheric and biospheric conditions. We need breathable air, potable water, arable soil and coexistence with other life forms.

Thanks in good part to global ecological developments, environmental issues have risen to considerable prominence on the widened contemporary security agenda. Countless civic groups, think tanks, official agencies and firms have since the 1960s put the spotlight on environmental questions as never before. On the whole, this greater sensitivity to ecological concerns has tended to heighten awareness of the fragility of life and associated feelings of insecurity.

True, the technologies associated with globalization have offered *homo sapiens* unprecedented capacities to manipulate natural forces for human purposes. For one thing, as stressed throughout this book, global relations have allowed people largely to escape the constraints of territorial geography. In addition, telecommunications, digital data processing, satellite surveillance and the like have provided highly sophisticated tools for anticipating natural disasters and monitoring ecological trends.

On the other hand, the technologies of globalization have tended to be highly polluting. Aeroplanes have dirtied the skies, and the motor ships that support global trade have dirtied the seas. Much of the electricity to run global communications has been generated with nuclear and fossil fuels whose by-products contaminate air, land and sea. Contrary to some expectations, computers have tended in practice to increase rather than decrease paper use, thereby adding pressure on forests. Rapid turnover in global consumer goods has added massively to non-degradable solid waste, however well intentioned recycling activities might be. Meanwhile spent rockets and satellites have been creating a junkyard in outer space.

Global capitalism has often undermined ecological security in other ways, too. For instance, some companies (especially producers of toxic substances like pesticides and heavy metals like zinc) have 'gone global' in part to locate their operations at sites where environmental regulations are less stringent (Heerings and Zeldenrust, 1995: ch 4). Likewise, as governments and consumers in the North have restricted or banned a number of tobacco products, pharmaceuticals and pesticides, global marketing has created new outlets for many of these goods in the South and the East. Nearly a third of pesticides exported from the North have been outlawed, unregistered or withdrawn in the country of manufacture (TWG, 1993: 106). Global trade in toxic wastes (so-called 'pollution flight') has also posed dangers for populations in the South. One source on 'garbage imperialism' has calculated that firms made over 500 attempts between 1989 and 1994 to export a total of more than 200 million tons of waste from the OECD countries to the South (Bellamy Foster, 1994). Transborder lending, too, has sometimes promoted environmental degradation as, for example, governments have intensified exports beyond sustainable levels in order to obtain foreign exchange earnings for debt repayment (Miller, 1991). Likewise certain ministries have abandoned environmental projects and policies in an effort to achieve fiscal targets connected with globally sponsored structural adjustment programmes (Reed, 1996).

Meanwhile each of the major anthropogenic global environmental changes of contemporary history has presented threats (imminent and/or long term) to ecological integrity. Transboundary air pollution could, it is feared, destroy forests and lakes. Nuclear accidents and thinned ozone yield the spectre of an increased incidence of cancer. Declining biological diversity might take the earth to a species depletion threshold beyond which the entire biosphere would collapse. Rising sea level associated with climate change could submerge highly populated coastal areas and small island countries. Large-scale contamination of soil and freshwater could threaten human subsistence.

Given such prospects, the emergence of global social ecology has, not surprisingly, produced a succession of popular scares. For example, rapid growth in world population led in the late 1960s to widespread fears of a 'time bomb'. The global oil crisis of the 1970s fed worries of an impending exhaustion of many vital natural resources. Globally transmittable diseases like HIV/AIDS and BSE have produced a succession of popular panics in the 1980s and 1990s. Further anxiety has accompanied the spread of genetically engineered foodstuffs through the transborder markets of agribusiness and biotechnology firms. In a word, then, global environmental issues have become a prime source of insecurity in the contemporary human condition.

To be sure, as mentioned in Chapter 6, we have developed some potentials for global governance of environmental matters. In this respect the ozone regime established through the 1985 Vienna Convention and the 1987 Montreal Protocol has proved particularly successful. By 1997 world production of the most ozone-depleting substances had fallen to 76 per cent of the 1988 level (Edwards, 1999: 22). Meanwhile the Global Environment Facility (GEF) – operative since 1994 and administered between UNDP, UNEP and the World Bank – has pledged some $2 billion to help poor countries make investments that benefit ecological integrity. That said, $2 billion spread across a decade and across the world is pretty modest in relation to the challenges at hand.

More generally, too, the advance of global environmental care must not be exaggerated. For example, implementation of the 1992 Framework Convention on Climate Change has proceeded with painful slowness. Various proposals have circulated for carbon taxes, tradable permits in greenhouse gas emissions, and other 'clean development mechanisms' to reduce global warming. However, half a dozen UN conferences through the 1990s on climate change have yielded limited concrete results. As for connections between global trade and environmental degradation, we are still far from a 'green round' of WTO negotiations, where ecology would take precedence over growth rather than the other way around. Nor has general backing yet developed for a World Environment Organization that would work on a par with the WTO and other global governance agencies (Newell and Whalley, 1999).

Subsistence

Champions of neoliberal globalization have suggested that transworld production, markets, monies and finance will, by the magic of *laissez-faire*, automatically yield material prosperity for all. To be sure, global operations have provided economies of scale for many producers and wider choices of goods for many consumers. Global travel, telecommunications, radio and television have enriched the life experiences of hundreds of millions of people.

Yet has spreading supraterritoriality brought freedom from poverty, even by crude material indicators (that is, leaving aside the greater complexities of poverty, including its subjective dimensions)? Certainly world poverty has, by some measures, declined during the period of accelerated globalization. For example, in terms of UNDP's Human Development Index, the proportion of the world's population living in destitution more than halved between 1960 and 1992 (UNDP, 1994: 1–2). In sheer numbers, more people escaped from poverty in the second half of the twentieth century than in the preceding 500 years (UNDP, 1997: 2).

In the South, home to most of the world's poor, average per capita income more than doubled between 1950 and 1980 (Nyerere *et al.*, 1990: 32). Average life expectancy in the South lengthened by 17 years between 1960 and the mid-1990s (*FT*, 2 February 1996: I). Infant mortality fell by more than half between 1960 and 1994, while the proportion of one year-olds immunized rose from 70 per cent in 1990 to 89 per cent in 1997. Adult illiteracy declined from nearly 60 per cent in 1970 to 35 per cent in 1994. The share of the world's population with access to safe water rose from 40 per cent in 1990 to 72 per cent in 1997 (DFID, 1997: 13; UNDP, 1999: 22). Advances of these kinds have been especially pronounced in the so-called 'newly industrializing countries' (NICs) in parts of East and South East Asia and Latin America. For instance, a million people made an exit from poverty in Chile in the early 1990s alone (Frei, 1995).

Some of these reductions in poverty might be partly linked to globalization. Between the 1970s and the late 1990s, the prosperity of the NICs generally unfolded hand in hand with their increased involvement in global investment, production and markets. The gross national product of China tripled between 1978 (the year of 'opening up' to global commerce) and 1993. The ranks of the indigent in China declined by more than half between 1978 and 1985, and from 280 million in 1990 to 125 million in 1997 (Rohwer, 1992: 4; AP, 1999b).

However, half a century of accelerated globalization has clearly not eliminated poverty from the face of the earth. On the contrary, although the abject poor have decreased since 1960 as a proportion of the world's population, their absolute number has grown. The World Bank has estimated that the number of people living on less than the equivalent of $1 per day rose from 1.2 billion in 1987 to 1.5 billion in 1997 (AP, 1999b). During the 1980s, 37 of the world's poorest countries experienced cuts in health budgets (Krause, 1996: 228). As of the mid-1990s, around a seventh of the world's population (828 million people) was chronically malnourished (FAO, 1998). More than 80 per cent of this hunger resulted from long-term poverty rather than from emergency situations (Speth, 1992: 149).

In spite of concerted efforts to promote 'development' – many of them through global agencies – most lands of the South have not become NICs. Next to the exceptions, 70 other countries experienced no increase in per capita income between 1980 and the mid-1990s, and 43 countries had a lower per capita income in the mid-1990s than in 1970 (UNDP, 1996: 1). The scale of poverty in Sub-Saharan Africa was as great in the mid-1990s as in the mid-1960s (UNCTAD, 1995: 11).

Poverty has also persisted – and sometimes even increased – outside of the South in the time of full-scale globalization. Indeed, some of the most striking growth of poverty occurred during the 1990s in certain so-called 'transition countries' of Eastern Europe and the former Soviet Union. Life expectancy actually declined in seven of these countries after 1989 (UNDP, 1999: 79). Meanwhile slum dwellers in Chicago's South Side have endured deprivations alongside the destitute of Lima. Between the early 1980s and the mid-1990s, child poverty rose by a third in the USA and by half in Britain (Jolly, 1995).

Some of this poverty can be partly attributed to globalization. For example, vulnerable circles in the South, the North and the East have all suffered from cuts to state welfare provision in the course of economic restructuring to accommodate global capitalism. When faced with a choice between sustaining social policy and improving global competitiveness, governments have tended to favour the latter. Neoliberals have argued that such retrenchment is an unavoidable painful transition before a liberalized global economy can yield greater prosperity for all; however, critics have questioned whether structural adjustment must as a matter of necessity hit the poor, and hit them so hard.

Indeed, it is now widely accepted that official measures are needed to counter the frequent harmful impacts on vulnerable circles of economic restructuring in the face of globalization. 'Adjustment with a human face' moved from being a fringe slogan in the 1980s to becoming a core policy principle in the 1990s. Social safety nets are now a normal feature of structural adjustment packages supported by the IMF and the World Bank. In fact, in the Asia crisis of 1997–9 the two institutions departed from their traditional fiscal conservatism to advocate substantial public-sector deficits, with a view to protecting food security, primary health care, basic education and employment. Since 1996 the World Bank has, through a Structural Adjustment Policy Review Initiative, joined with over a thousand civic associations to explore various possible connections between neoliberal economic restructuring and poverty (SAPRI, 1999). Meanwhile the IMF in 1999 changed the name of its Enhanced Structural Adjustment Facility (ESAF) to the Poverty Reduction and Growth Facility (PRGF). It is too early to tell what practical beneficial effects for the poor these recent changes in orientation may hold, but the new language is a promising start.

Prevailing approaches to global trade, too, may have certain detrimental effects on poverty alleviation. For example, 'free' global markets in primary commodities have on the whole given the poor countries that most rely on these exports steadily declining terms of trade since the 1970s (Coote, 1996). World prices of primary commodities in the mid-1990s stood at the lowest level since the 1930s (ul Haq, 1995: 29). Moreover, a study by UNCTAD has concluded that the world's 48 poorest countries will collectively lose $300–600 million per annum as a result of reduced exports and increased food imports under the Uruguay Round agreements (Went, 1996: 126). Meanwhile trade liberalization in the context of structural adjustment has deprived many poor states of one of their chief sources of tax revenue (namely, customs duties), thereby increasing the squeeze on public-sector resources for poverty alleviation.

Meanwhile the debt crisis surrounding global loans to the South has severely undermined poverty alleviation efforts in many countries since the early 1980s. The transborder debts of the South grew sixteenfold between

1970 and 1997, to nearly $2.2 trillion. Most of the $1.3 trillion in increases between 1980 and 1994 involved an accumulation of unpaid interest rather than fresh credits (Childers, 1994: 10; World Bank, 1994: 192). By 1996 41 of the world's poorest countries between them had accumulated some $250 billion in transborder debts, a burden that severely limited their governments' capacities to attack poverty. In Latin America during the debt crisis of the 1980s, the ranks of indigent people expanded from 130 to 180 million (Bello *et al.*, 1994: 52). By now even the most hard-nosed bankers concede that the debt burdens of many poor countries are unsustainable and have had damaging impacts on vulnerable circles.

Several initiatives of the 1990s brought some reduction of transborder debts in the South. In respect of commercial loans, for example, 15 governments between 1989 and 1996 concluded so-called 'Brady deals' that convert some of their bank debt into bonds at lower interest rates. In respect of bilateral borrowings by Southern governments from Northern states, the Paris Club of official creditors has since 1988 developed a sequence of relief measures for low-income countries. These schemes have involved partial debt cancellation, long-term rescheduling of remaining loans, and interest rate reductions. Finally, in the mid-1990s the IMF and the World Bank jointly formulated the Highly Indebted Poor Countries Initiative (HIPC) for relief on debt owed to multilateral institutions. The HIPC programme was enhanced in 1999 with larger funds, less stringent eligibility criteria and faster delivery of relief. In sum, then, long and dogged efforts to address the debt crisis of the South have borne some fruit.

Yet this progress in reducing the transborder debt burdens of poor countries must not be overestimated. On the whole the relief has been small, slow and grudging. On bilateral debts, application of the so-called 'Toronto' (1988), 'enhanced Toronto' (1991) and 'Naples' (1994) terms has been limited. It remains sadly telling to contrast this record with the scale and speed of reactions to crises in global financial companies. For example, far more money was mobilized far more quickly to rescue the Long Term Capital Management hedge fund in 1998 than has been garnered to support the HIPC initiative.

Other instabilities of global finance have also afflicted the poor. In Indonesia, for example, concerted efforts reduced the count of destitute people from 70 million (60 per cent of the populace) in 1970 to 25.9 million (13.7 per cent of the populace) in 1993. However, the Asia crisis of 1997–9, induced largely by developments in global capital and currency markets, may have put up to 130 million Indonesians in poverty by early 1999 (AP, 1999a). The economic crisis in Russia in 1998 – again substantially a consequence of global financial flows – likewise swelled the ranks of the poor in that country.

Of course globalizing capitalism has not been the only force behind persistent and sometimes growing poverty in recent history. Local social structures, national policies, natural calamities and other forces have also played their parts. However, the poverty-alleviating potentials of global relations have been far from maximized, and in some ways supraterritorial links have to date worsened the lot of many poor people.

Financial stability

The volatility of global financial markets has heightened insecurity among the world's wealthy and poor alike. A long string of currency swings, stock and bond market crashes, and derivatives debacles (described in Chapter 5) has left investors in a perpetually anxious state. Such insecurities have generated a new 'science' of risk management, with practitioners grouped in a Global Association of Risk Professionals.

Indeed, the destructive volatility of transborder banking, securities and derivatives provoked much discussion in the late 1990s about reform of global financial governance (cf. Eichengreen, 1999; Bryant 2000). Already some steps have been taken: (a) to increase disclosure and transparency of relevant statistics; (b) to impose greater prudence on transborder banking; and (c) to encourage more stability in global securities and derivatives markets.

Regarding transparency, many experts hope that global financial markets will become less volatile when relevant macro- and micro-economic information is of good quality and readily available. To this end the IMF established a Special Data Dissemination Standard in 1996 and a General Data Dissemination System in 1997. Both are freely available on the Internet at http://dsbb.imf.org. In 1999 the International Federation of Accountants, the IMF and the World Bank launched an International Forum on Accountancy Development that aims to build accounting and auditing capacity in the East and the South. Meanwhile the International Accounting Standards Committee has recently formulated transworld standards on accounting specifically for financial instruments (Bryant, 1999: 22).

Regarding prudence in transborder banking, the Basle Committee on Banking Supervision of the BIS has issued multiple recommendations, guidelines and standards since its establishment in 1975. Prominent among these measures is the Basle Capital Accord – first adopted in 1988 and subsequently modified several times – which has provided a framework for assessing the capital position of banks as they engage in large-scale global lending. In 1997 the Basle Committee moreover published a set of *Core Principles for Effective Banking Supervision* (BIS, 1997). Meanwhile a

Financial Action Task Force of the OECD has worked since 1989 to counter money laundering with strengthened national regulation and closer multilateral cooperation (Reinicke, 1998: 156–72; Wiener, 1999: ch 3).

A number of other governance initiatives have aimed to increase stability in wider global finance. The International Organization of Securities Commissions, the International Association of Insurance Supervisors, the OECD Committee on Financial Markets, the BIS Committee on Payment and Settlement Systems, and the BIS Committee on the Global Financial System have between them developed a host of principles and standards for risk management in transworld foreign-exchange, securities, derivatives and insurance markets. Since 1996 the Basle Committee, the IAIS and IOSCO have coordinated a Joint Forum on Financial Conglomerates that enhances cooperation among bank, securities and insurance supervisors (given that global financial companies have increasingly operated across the three sectors). On the initiative of the G7, a Financial Stability Forum was established among major state and multilateral authorities in 1999 'to promote international financial stability, improve the functioning of markets, and reduce systemic risk' (FSF, 1999).

Yet such initiatives have to date not brought adequate stability to global finance. Crises have persisted – if anything with greater frequency and greater intensity. Moreover, the harms have extended far beyond the investors who knowingly take risks. Indeed, the greatest pains of global financial instability have often hit highly vulnerable social circles, as recent crises in Asia and Russia have shown.

Meanwhile momentum behind more ambitious reforms of global financial governance has remained limited. During the height of market turmoil in 1997–8 some proposals circulated to convene a new Bretton Woods-like conference in order to overhaul existing suprastate institutions. However, with the return of relative calm in 1999, opinion shifted back to incrementalism – until the next crisis, at least.

Employment

Security is for most people closely connected with security of work. The impact of globalization on employment has attracted many claims and counterclaims. Much of the debate has centred on job security, that is, whether or not global capitalism is providing, or can provide, waged positions for everyone in the world workforce who needs or wants them. As noted in Chapter 1, many critics have charged that globalization has created major job losses. Others including neoliberals have mainly attributed problems of unemployment to other factors, such as new labour-saving technologies, inadequate education and training, or unsustainable levels of wages and benefits. When neoliberals accept that a link could exist between globalization and unemployment, they usually regard job losses as a temporary pain of economic restructuring in response to the liberalization of world trade and investment. Following successful adjustment, say the optimists, employment prospects will improve.

Champions and critics of globalization alike agree that unemployment constitutes a major world challenge for the twenty-first century. According to UN estimates, the world labour pool of 2.8 billion people in the early 1990s included about 800 million unemployed (120 million of them officially registered as such) and over 700 million underemployed (Simai, 1995: 4). Apart from the NICs, most countries in the South have suffered dire shortages of opportunities for waged labour. The end of central planning has also brought large-scale unemployment to the so-called 'countries in transition'.

In the North, the period of accelerated globalization has seen a move from effective full employment in the 1960s to persistent unemployment (often in double-figure percentages) in the 1980s and 1990s. Unskilled male workers have been particularly vulnerable (Wood, 1994). Many more wage earners (estimated at 15 million across the OECD countries in 1994) have endured involuntary part-time employment (ILO, 1995). Concurrently, a large proportion of workers in the North have experienced continual worries about their job security in the short or medium term. Even corporations in Japan have since the early 1990s abandoned their traditional commitment to lifelong employment for their staff. Across the North the goal of full employment has largely disappeared from macroeconomic policy.

However, are these unhappy trends of the last quarter of the twentieth century a result of globalization? To be sure, the balance sheet on globalization and employment has shown some positive entries. For example, significant expansion of the payroll has occurred in service industries such as retail trade, finance, communications, and information technology. As seen in Chapter 5, these sectors have lain at the heart of supraterritorial capitalism.

Meanwhile global enterprises in these and other sectors have often created new jobs at their host sites. By 1992 transborder corporations directly employed some 29 million people outside their country of origin (ILO, 1995). Particularly in the South, jobs with global companies have often involved higher wages, better training and greater benefits than local employers would offer. Countless other workers have indirectly gained a livelihood from FDI, that is, through subcontracting and other services to transborder firms.

Yet the job-creating effects of globalization have remained modest on the whole. As of the late 1990s, all the EPZs across the world had between them generated only 27 million jobs (UNDP, 1999: 86). Another calculation, by a socialist critic, has put this figure as low as 4 million (Harris, 1998–9: 27). Total increased employment in the South from exports to global markets averaged less than 700,000 new jobs per annum over the 30-year period from 1960 to 1990 (Wood, 1994: 13). As of 1992, global companies collectively employed only 73 million people, amounting to less than 6 per cent of the overall world payroll (ILO, 1995: 45).

In certain other ways contemporary globalization has had positively detrimental effects on employment security. For example, some job losses have occurred in the North when firms have exploited the possibilities of global organization, global communications, global production and global finance to move their manufacturing plants to low-wage sites in the South and the East, particularly in the NICs and in EPZs. Such relocations are estimated to have reduced demand for unskilled labour in the North by some 6–12 million person-years between 1960 and 1990 (Wood, 1994: 11).

This trend seems likely to continue. The World Competitiveness Project at the International Institute for Management Development has affirmed that, on account of differential labour costs and trade liberalization through the WTO, 'an outflow of manufacturing operations from western economies seems inevitable' (*FT*, 30 September 1994). Similarly, in a survey of 10,000 firms in Germany in 1993, one in three respondents said that they planned to transfer production to Eastern Europe or Asia in order to take advantage of lower labour costs and environmental standards (Axford, 1995: 118).

However, it would be simplistic to affirm, as some critics have maintained, that growing unemployment in the North has arisen solely or even mainly as a result of relocation by global firms to the South and the East. After all, many of the 29 million jobs directly attributable to inward FDI have appeared in the OECD countries (when, for example, a Japan-based company has invested in the European Union). Moreover, many global enterprises have established facilities in the South and the East not as a relocation strategy from the North, but as an expansion strategy in order to produce locally for so-called 'emerging markets'.

Meanwhile many layoffs in the North have resulted largely from the introduction of labour-saving technologies such as digital computers and robotics. For instance, 'jobless growth' in many manufacturing industries has seen production rise while employment levels fall. In this vein the Ford Motor Company in the USA cut labour hours by 47 per cent during the 1980s while raising productivity by 57 per cent (Harris, 1998–9: 27). Likewise, major staff cuts have occurred in telecommunications as automated technologies steadily replace human labour. For instance, British Telecom eliminated 19,000 jobs in a single day in 1992. Telia in Sweden reduced staff from 48,000 in 1990 to 33,000 in 1996, and AT&T announced in 1996 that it was shedding 40,000 jobs (*FT*, 25 March 1996: 23; 9 July 1996: 21).

In short, although certain direct links have existed between job losses in the North and job gains in the South, some critics of globalization have exaggerated the connection. 'Lost jobs' in the OECD countries have often gone not to the South and the East, but to machines.

That said, several other important connections can be drawn between contemporary globalization and the growth of unemployment in the North. First, the expanding financial, information and communications sectors of global capitalism have generally required smaller workforces than older extractive and manufacturing industries. For example, with its payroll of 15,000 the IT giant Microsoft has employed far fewer people than the largest manufacturers of earlier generations. Capital-intensive, highly automated new sectors of the economy seem unlikely to satisfy the growing demand for waged work.

In addition, corporate mergers and acquisitions have often resulted in substantial job losses. As seen in Chapter 5, M&A activities have proliferated in good part as a response to global market competition and consolidation. In the pharmaceuticals sector, for instance, the fusion of Glaxo and Wellcome brought an 11 per cent shrinkage of the payroll, while Pharmacia and Upjohn closed 40 per cent of plants in the context of their merger (*FT*, 5 March 1996: 23; 7 March 1996: 1). When Chase and Chemical Banks merged, 12,000 people became redundant (*FT*, 1 April 1996: 23). As one quip has it, global competition has tended to make companies 'lean and mean' (Harrison, 1994).

Contemporary globalization has further encouraged structural unemployment insofar as the massive growth of finance capital has shifted much investor interest from job-creating projects in the 'real' economy to financial instruments as objects of investment in their own right. Debt instruments, equities and currency speculation have enticed investors with promises of high and fast returns. By comparison, investment in more labour-intensive 'real' production has in contemporary capitalism tended to yield lower profits over a longer term. True, casino capitalism has generated some expansion of payrolls in the financial sector. However, today's banking, securities and derivatives businesses are largely automated, and mergers in the sector during the 1990s brought substantial job losses in a number of firms. In any case, the extra employment created through the expansion of finance capital has probably been considerably smaller than the job growth that could be had were investments to be placed in 'real' production.

Finally, globalization has often undermined job security in the context of structural adjustment programmes. Most of these policy packages agreed by governments with the IMF and the World Bank have prescribed a significant contraction of the civil service. In most cases no accompanying measures have redeployed the redundant officials in new jobs. Likewise, privatization and liberalization policies at the heart of neoliberal structural adjustment have often brought job losses when local trade and industry are exposed to global competition. Proponents of conventional structural adjustment programmes have argued that rejuvenated market forces will correct these employment problems in the medium and long term. However, little evidence has as yet emerged in the South and the East to substantiate this claim.

In sum, globalization has had several unhappy implications for job security. To be sure, these consequences should not be exaggerated. For example, there is little sign that we are moving to the so-called 'jobless future' (Aronowitz and DiFazio, 1994). Nor has globalization been the sole cause of growing un(der)employment in contemporary history. Nevertheless, the globalizing economy has thus far reduced certainty of job tenure for most people in work, and the new geography has to date come nowhere close to generating the positions needed to address structural deficits in world employment opportunities. High-level meetings like the G7 Jobs Summits at Detroit in 1994 and Lille in 1996 have been pretty inconsequential. Nor have ILO initiatives and the World Summit for Social Development done much beyond publicize a need for job creation within globalization.

Working conditions

Accelerated globalization in recent decades has affected not only the opportunities for waged employment, but also the conditions of work. The balance sheet in this respect has had some decidedly negative entries. Within a neoliberal policy framework, the rise of supraterritorial capitalism has put significant downward pressures on wages, benefits and safeguards, particularly in the North and especially for unskilled and semi-skilled labour. In similar ways, neoliberal globalization has weakened the previously considerable power of trade unions in much of Latin America and has arguably also discouraged improvements in working conditions elsewhere in the South.

To put the point in Gramscian terms, globalization has been a key force in the decline of the so-called 'Fordist' social contract in countries of the North. Fordism developed from the 1910s and peaked between the 1940s and the 1960s. It rested on an implicit trilateral pact between government, corporate business and organized labour. For their part, the trade unions delivered acquiescent and more productive workers to business. On its side, corporate business delivered higher wages, benefits and protections to workers. Completing the triad, the state delivered union protection and wide-ranging social welfare to workers as well as guarantees of property rights and various services to business. With these arrangements, Fordism produced 'the affluent worker' who had sufficient income and leisure time to consume mass-produced goods. To be sure, the fruits of Fordism were restricted to a minority of the world's workers: unionized white men in the North were the prime beneficiaries. Moreover, the labour in question often centred on tedious assembly-line work. Nevertheless, Fordism marked a notable advance over earlier social contracts and held out the promise of more progressive capitalism.

In contrast, contemporary globalization has been associated with the displacement of Fordism by what neo-Gramscian theorists have called a 'post-Fordist' regime of accumulation. This new situation has been distinguished by 'flexibilization'. The 'flexible' worker lacks a job for life, but instead moves and retrains to meet altered market demands. To facilitate such mobility most OECD governments have loosened laws on hiring and firing. Post-Fordist workers are also expected to be 'flexible' in respect of hours, wages, benefits, health and safety standards, etc. 'Flexible' jobs are often casual, part-time and temporary, with few if any benefits beyond the (often low) wages offered. The workers involved frequently lack collective bargaining arrangements and other union protections. Under these conditions many households have needed more than one wage to make ends meet.

On all of these counts, the move from Fordism to post-Fordism has entailed a significant deterioration in working conditions, especially for less skilled labour. Many workers who have lost jobs on Fordist terms have returned to employment in 'flexible' positions. Most wage earners born after 1960 have never known Fordist securities during their working lives. Flexibilization has gone further in the UK and USA than in continental Europe and Japan, but the trend has not bypassed any OECD country. (For more on Fordism and post-Fordism, see Cox, 1987: ch 9; Amin, 1994.)

Increased insecurity in the workplace has readily spilled over to affect other aspects of life. The stresses induced by unceasing pressures for greater productivity and worries about job security can heighten tensions in the household and on the street. It would be difficult to demonstrate precisely that flexibilization has fuelled domestic strife, uncivil driving, hooliganism and other violence; and no doubt other factors have also played their part. However, it seems reasonable to posit that insecurity at work has fed insecurity elsewhere.

In addition, the demands of flexibility in waged labour have tended to reduce the time and energy that people have available to execute unpaid caring duties. The consequences for children and the infirm can be particularly unhappy, as well as for women, who tend to bear the bulk of domestic caring tasks. The state has rarely stepped in to fill the shortfalls in care, given the downward pressures on public-sector welfare programmes described in Chapter 6. The repercussions of inadequate child rearing for the next generation may include asocial behaviour and unstable intimate relationships.

Globalization has promoted this in many respects damaging shift to flexible labour in three general ways. First, some of the greatest flexibilization has occurred in the leading sectors of supraterritorial capitalism. Major demands for 'flexibility' have fallen on support staff in the retail, financial, information and communications industries: that is, on shop assistants, bank clerks, data key punchers, telephone operators, and so on. Few of these workers have gained substantial wages and benefits, good promotion prospects, or long-term job security.

Second, flexibilization has generally accompanied the shift of jobs in the globalizing economy from older industrial centres in the North to new sites in the South and the East. As noted earlier, the scale of this transfer must not be overestimated. However, on those occasions when it has occurred, positions in the North with higher remuneration and greater worker protection have generally given way to lower-paid jobs in the South with longer hours, less collective bargaining, and weaker health and safety standards. More generally, too, transborder companies have not given their employees in the South and the East the sorts of guarantees that workers in the North obtained under Fordist arrangements. Employees in the subcontracted firms that serve global corporations have often fared still worse.

Third, much flexibilization has unfolded under the spectre of 'global competition'. Managers have pushed for 'flexible' labour in good part because they believe, rightly or wrongly, that higher guarantees to employees will undermine a firm's position in global markets. For their part, workers have accepted 'flexible' contracts in good part because they believe, rightly or wrongly, that demanding higher conditions of service will send jobs elsewhere in the world. Labour in the North has been constantly reminded that alternative workforces are available in China, Mexico and Slovakia. As a result, globalization has promoted what critics have decried as a 'race to the bottom' of labour conditions.

Drawing from such concerns, various initiatives of recent years have aimed to achieve better labour standards in a globalizing economy. For example, the core conventions of the International Labour Organization have attracted larger numbers of adherents. The ILO has furthermore developed new codes like the 1996 Convention on Home Work that seeks to protect homeworkers (a largely female sector) with minimum wages and conditions (HomeNet, 1999). On the whole, however, the ILO has yet to pursue global labour rights with the degree of vigour that the WTO and the IMF have pursued trade and financial liberalization.

For their part, transworld trade rules have as yet included little in the way of labour standards. True, revisions to the Generalized System of Preferences effective from 1995 have involved some elements of a social clause (Jordan, 1995: 28). However, attempts in 1996 to incorporate a Working Party on Worker Rights into the WTO were rebuffed, with particularly strong resistance from governments of the NICs. Indeed, many in the South have worried that appeals to 'social protection' are a ruse to sustain Northern advantage in world trade (John and Chenoy, 1996). Much like the WTO, the proposed (and for now abandoned) MAI protected capital mobility and property rights, but neglected to safeguard labour rights.

At a regional level, the European Community adopted a Charter of the Fundamental Social Rights (otherwise known as the Social Charter) in 1989 and included a Social Chapter in the Maastricht Treaty two years later (Purdy, 1997). The Social Charter has enshrined principles such as equal treatment for women at work, works councils and EU-wide collective bargaining with transborder companies. Elsewhere the North American Free Trade Agreement of 1994 included a side accord regarding labour rights and standards, although these provisions have even fewer teeth than the EU measures. In South America the *Mercado Común del Sur* (Southern Common Market) (MERCOSUR) has had a social committee that includes trade union representation, but this organ, too, has been quite marginal.

Finally, global companies themselves have also taken some modest initiatives to promote labour standards, particularly following adverse publicity from consumer campaigns. For example, firms including Disney, Levi Strauss and Mattel have since 1991 established in-house codes of conduct for their factories in the South and undertake workplace inspections to check compliance (Cavanagh, 1997: 99; Justice, 1999; UNDP, 1999: 100). However, voluntary self-regulation by a few individual transborder enterprises is hardly satisfactory.

In sum, despite some mild countervailing measures in recent years to enhance labour standards, on the whole flexibilization through globalization has had substantial adverse repercussions for security in work. Moreover, the economic logic of flexibilization has arguably been deeply flawed as well. Lower labour guarantees could yield less rather than greater competitiveness. Well-trained, well-remunerated, well-protected workers could provide a more motivated, reliable and productive labour force. To this extent the 'race to the bottom' in wages and other working conditions would operate not only against human security, but against efficiency as well.

Identity

Human security is not only a material question of military, ecological and economic conditions; it has psychological and cultural dimensions as well. Identity figures in this respect owing to the importance for security of an assured sense of self: a comfortable concept of who one is and a confidence that society will respect and preserve this way of being.

Contemporary globalization has in some ways provided wider scope for the discovery and expression of identity. Territorialist geography arguably entailed a restrictive bias toward national identities. In contrast, as indicated in Chapter 7, supraterritorial spaces have created more room for the expression of other elements of identity, such as class, disability, gender, generation (especially youth), minority nationalities, profession, race, religion and sexual preference. Globalization has thereby encouraged a shift from the straightjacket of one-dimensional state-centred nationhood (as tended to prevail in the mid-twentieth century) to a greater pluralism. Many people have found a more secure and 'genuine' sense of self as a result.

On the other hand, the turn toward alternative, multidimensional and hybrid identities has removed the security of simplicity and predictability that marked a territorialist world where each person tended to be neatly defined by a single national identity connected to their state. The sense of self can become ambiguous and unsteady when people hold several national identities at once: for example, the nationality of their state; the nationality of their country of origin (in the case of migrants); the nationality of a substate ethnicity; and so on. Further uncertainty can arise when the national self coexists uneasily (and perhaps in contradiction and competition) with class, religious and other identities. In these ways the globalizing world has left some people feeling torn and lost.

Contemporary globalization has also sometimes undermined the security of identity through cultural destruction. Various cultures have succumbed to an invasion of television, transworld tourism, global English, notions of universal human rights, global consumerism and other supraterritorial interventions that have contradicted local traditions. For example, radio made little time for the 'long songs' of the Dayak people in Sarawak. As a result this age-old cultural form was obliterated in less than 20 years after the introduction of the wireless (Rubenstein, 1991). In addition, dams, roads and other major infrastructure projects financed by global institutions and/or built by global contractors have severely disrupted a number of indigenous ways of life. Indeed, to date transworld economic agencies like the BIS, IMF, IOSCO, OECD, WTO and World Bank have tended to be culturally blind, an approach that has arguably contributed to some wanton destruction of lifeworlds. In these respects some observers have worried that globalization can crush cultural diversity along with biological diversity. Up to half of the languages currently spoken in the world are already threatened with extinction, and some linguists forecast that over 90 per cent could die out during the next century (Wurm, 1996).

That said, cultural preservationists have discovered on various occasions that the technologies of globalization can be used to reinvigorate otherwise declining or dormant identities. For example, video productions have contributed to a revitalization of Bedouin culture in Egypt (Abu-Lughod, 1989). Television has fostered self-assertion among Aborigines in Australia and among Catalans in Spain. Satellite broadcasts have furthered the survival of the Inuktituk language in the Canadian Arctic. Radio has fuelled Maori identity politics in Aotearoa (the indigenous name for New Zealand) (Dowmunt, 1993).

Thus globalization has not, as some observers have asserted, been a force of simple homogenization, where one culture sweeps away all other identities. The rise of supraterritoriality has undermined some ways of being with 'westernization' and 'Americanization'. Yet transborder relations have also promoted alternative cultures. More than homogenization, the overall impact of globalization on identity has been one of destabilization. As such, the new geography has fostered considerable insecurity.

Social cohesion

A secure sense of identity is usually closely connected with a secure sense of belonging and related expectations that a person will both receive support from and contribute support to a wider collectivity. Recognizing the importance of these bonds, the 1995 World Summit for Social Development promoted social integration as a leading theme next to poverty reduction and employment creation.

Contemporary globalization has arguably enhanced social cohesion insofar as the trend has, as described in Chapter 7, encouraged growth both of multiple transworld solidarity networks and of cosmopolitan commitments. True, the liberal-internationalist vision of a single universal community of humankind, underpinned by a world state, is nowhere in prospect. However, global organizations, global communications, global consciousness and the like have yielded unprecedented capacities and readiness to build transborder bonds between women, indigenous peoples and so on. The contemporary expansion of transworld humanitarian relief efforts provides further evidence of growing social cohesion beyond the state.

Yet what of social integration in local communities? Arguably supra-territorial relations have often weakened intimacy and mutual support within neighbourhoods. People who are glued to television and computer screens may have virtual bonds across the planet but little or no acquaintance with the persons living next door. Similarly, globally mobile companies tend (exceptions duly noted) to hold limited long-term commitments to the locality where their facilities are situated at any particular time. Flexible workers, too, often have restricted opportunities to plant roots in a locality before the labour market calls them elsewhere.

On a larger scale, globalization has undermined the modern territorialist premise that social cohesion is guaranteed through the state-nation-country-society. On that principle previous generations have assumed that every 'people', each tied to its territorial homeland, could and should secure social integration through a sovereign state. However, as stressed throughout this book, the growth of global spaces has made it impossible to parcel the world into discrete territorial units with neatly separated peoples, each ruled by a sovereign authority.

Meanwhile, globalization has also fuelled various divisive communitarian dynamics. The proliferation of ethnic revivals, xenophobia and other reactions was noted in Chapter 7. Nonterritorial solidarities, too, have often rested on the exclusion of a certain 'other': that is, a different class, a different race, and so on. Religious revivalists, radical feminists and others have usually created cohesion of the in-group largely by stressing separation from and conflict with 'outsiders'. In other words, these transborder communities have needed to fragment the societal whole in order to integrate their slice of the world population. Overall social cohesion – both within countries and on a world scale – has readily suffered as a result.

On a more positive note, the period of accelerated globalization has seen some initiatives to develop 'socially responsible business' and 'corporate citizenship' as a way to tighten the social fabric. As *The Economist* has put it, 'tomorrow's successful company cannot afford to be a faceless institution that does nothing more than sell the right product at the right price' (Thomas, 1999). Courses and research centres on business ethics have proliferated since the mid-1980s. For example, the California-based World Business Academy, launched in 1987, has promoted 'a better world through business', as has the UK-based New Academy of Business, started in 1995 (NAB, 1999; WBA, 1999). Outside the MBA classroom, companies have formed several social policy forums, including the Business Council on National Issues in Canada and the European Business Network for Social Cohesion. Some management consultants have heralded 'new ways of business' as offering some of the most positive and powerful possibilities for tightening the social fabric (Harman and Hormann, 1990; Ray and Rinzler, 1993).

However, to date these business initiatives have on the whole made limited progress beyond rhetoric. Few Chief Executive Officers (CEOs) – that is, the corporate decision takers as opposed to their public relations staff – have participated with any regularity and prominence in public forums on social policy. For example, George Soros has been an exception in this regard among global financiers. The worry remains that many companies have signed up to 'social responsibility' slogans merely as a marketing ploy and/or to parry calls for greater regulation of global capital.

Indeed, many reformers have looked to transborder NGOs more than global business to enhance social cohesion. These 'third sector' organizations have provided much relief and rehabilitation in emergency situations of various kinds. Global NGOs have also filled many gaps in social services in countries with weak states and markets. Finally, as indicated before, transborder civic associations have often helped to forge social solidarity beyond the state of a sort that is suitable to – and indeed necessary for – a globalizing world.

To be sure, we should be wary of blanket claims regarding the supposed supreme appropriateness, innovation, efficiency and virtue of nonprofit agencies in supplying social services. NGOs have proved more successful in some places and activities than in others. Moreover, one NGO is more competent than the next. The third sector offers no magic bullet (Edwards and Hulme, 1995).

Moreover, the question remains whether NGOs have been applying plaster to the crumbling buildings of a neoliberal order or providing foundations for socially sustainable globalization. As one long-time critical observer asks, has the third sector merely been strengthening ladles for the global soup kitchen (Fowler, 1994)? In the words of another author, are NGOs but a changing fashion, or do they fashion change (Devine, 1996)?

In sum, globalization has made territorialist and statist approaches to social integration unviable, and no adequate workable alternative has yet been devised. This void has, it would seem, encouraged some inhabitants of our globalizing world to conclude that 'there is no such thing as society'. This negativism has arguably encouraged a general decline in social responsibility, with particularly unhappy consequences for vulnerable circles.

Knowledge

A final aspect of security that needs to be evaluated in regard to globalization concerns the confidence that people feel in the knowledge that they hold. As indicated in Chapter 8, the growth of supraterritorial relations has contributed to several shifts in prevailing structures of understanding. On balance, these developments have tended to heighten human insecurity.

True, the growth of religious revivalism described in Chapter 8 has provided adherents with, for them, secure truths. Revivalists among Buddhists, Christians, Hindus, Jews and Muslims have all enjoyed the comfort of believing that they hold an indisputable knowledge. Likewise, secular fundamentalists who endorse an uncritical rationalism have felt sure in the gospel of science, the dogma of efficiency, and the cult of progress.

Yet each of these absolutisms has maintained its truth claims in part by denying a hearing to alternative beliefs. Fundamentalism has thereby tended to breed violence between contending dogmas. Thus, for example, revivalist Sikhs have clashed, sometimes with force of arms, against Hindus. Revivalist Hindus have sought to silence Muslims in India. Revivalist Muslims have aimed to eliminate the state of Israel, while revivalist Jews have tried to marginalize Christian and Muslim Arabs in Palestine. In these cases and more, the intellectual security of absolutist knowledge for some has come at a cost of physical insecurity for others, sometimes with deadly consequences.

Like religious fundamentalists, devout rationalists have generally also had little ear for alternative forms of knowledge. The 'imperialism of science' has thereby constituted a threat to circles like indigenous peoples and religious traditionalists who have found their security of knowledge in nonrationalist thinking. True, globalization has, as seen in Chapter 8, opened some additional possibilities for different epistemologies to develop. However, supraterritorial spaces have at the same time given rationalists extra tools with which to marginalize and silence rival modes of understanding. For example, cyberspace, transworld publications and global conferences have served rationalist academics far more than holy persons and other nonrationalist teachers. Secularism has dominated in global foundations and think tanks. Technocracy has dominated in global governance. Instrumentalism has dominated in global business. These circumstances of the globalizing world have made it harder for nonrational knowledges to survive.

Meanwhile, insofar as it has encouraged the rise of reflexivity, globalization has also tended to undermine the security of knowledge among rationalists. Part of the secular intelligentsia has thereby lost positivist certainties and Enlightenment confidence. Most rationalists are uncomfortable with the indeterminacy of truth in post-positivist epistemology. Even self-proclaimed relativists often carry too much residual rationalist baggage to feel genuinely at ease with knowledge that has no validity beyond its particular personal, social and historical context. Meanwhile most rationalists have recoiled from what they see as the 'meaninglessness' of postmodernist epistemology. Indeed, in academic circles scientists have often mobilized to suppress postmodernist challenges to rationalism with as much determination as they have opposed traditionalist myths.

Hence none of the major turns in knowledge structures encouraged by globalization has done much to enhance human security. Fundamentalism (both religious and secular) has provided confidence to some at a cost of violence to many. Meanwhile reflexive rationalism has tended to sow unsettling doubt, and postmodernism has tended to remove certainty altogether.

Conclusion

Considering the various evaluations above together (as summarized in the Box overleaf), accelerated globalization has not, on the whole, brought satisfactory levels of security to social life. The altered geography of contemporary world politics has, to date, had significant negative implications for peace, ecological integrity, poverty, employment, self-confident identity, social cohesion and secure knowledge. As noted at the start of this chapter, we cannot expect any social order to provide absolute security. However, we have good cause to ask whether globalization needs to produce as much insecurity as it has tended to do so far.

The significance of globalization for human security must of course not be overplayed. Other social forces have also contributed. For one thing, as seen in Chapter 4, globalization has itself been a product of various developments in knowledge and production structures, technological changes and governance measures. In addition, local and national circumstances have often also contributed to environmental damage, social fragmentation, and so on.

Nor have the negative consequences of globalization for security described in this chapter been intrinsic to transworld relations. As is argued in Chapter 12, different approaches to globalization – in particular a move away from neoliberal policies – might yield more desirable outcomes. Nevertheless, in contemporary history the growth of supra-territorial spaces has contributed significantly to the sorts of heightened insecurities that have prompted Ulrich Beck to characterize our present condition as a 'risk society' (Beck, 1986, 1999).

Globalization and (in)security in summary

Peace
- global interconnectedness has created significant disincentives to war
- global governance has increased possibilities of arms control and conflict management

but
- technologies of globalization have added to the destructive capacities of war
- global reach has facilitated military interventions from North into South
- global arms markets have supplied extra means of destruction
- globalization has fuelled violence in the context of ethnic and religious revivalism

Ecological integrity
- global consciousness has promoted greater ecological awareness
- technologies of globalization have improved means to monitor environmental change
- several suprastate mechanisms have enhanced environmental conservation

but
- many global activities are heavily polluting
- global restructuring has placed downward pressures on environmental standards
- global ecological changes have generated much uncertainty and fear

Subsistence
- global capitalism has contributed to rapid welfare rises in the NICs

but
- comparatively few countries have achieved NIC status
- economic restructuring in the face of globalization has often increased poverty
- the debt crisis of the South has severely compromised poverty alleviation efforts
- existing global trade regimes have had detrimental effects on poor countries

Financial stability
- global finance has mobilized large sums of capital for investment

but
- the volatility of global financial markets has added considerably to feelings of economic insecurity
- crises in global finance have harmed vulnerable circles as well as investors

(Un)employment
- global companies and industries have generated millions of new jobs

but

→

$\longrightarrow$

- global corporate relocation has brought job losses and fears for job security
- global capitalism is generally less labour intensive than older areas of production
- global finance capitalism has diverted investment from the 'real' economy
- economic restructuring in the face of globalization has brought job losses

Working conditions
- global companies have often improved terms of service for workers in the South

but
- globalization has undermined the Fordist social contract with flexibilization
- no adequate guarantees of workers' rights under global capitalism have been developed

Identity
- global links have increased possibilities to develop multiple aspects of self
- technologies of globalization have reinvigorated some declining cultures

but
- global relations have also often suppressed traditional cultures
- the ambiguities and contradictions of a multidimensional self can be unsettling

Social cohesion
- globalization has enabled the growth of various transworld solidarities
- transborder NGOs have often supplied basic social services

but
- supraterritorial connections have sometimes undermined the cohesion of localities and state-nations
- notions of socially responsible global business have progressed little beyond rhetoric
- nonterritorial communities have often been highly exclusionary

Knowledge
- globalization has sometimes encouraged fundamentalism that offers apparently secure truths

but
- fundamentalism has generally involved violence toward alternative knowledges
- global channels have often facilitated the imposition of rationalist dogmas
- reflexive rationalists have lost positivist certainties and Enlightenment confidence
- few feel secure with the postmodernist alternative of indeterminate knowledge

Chapter 10

Globalization and (In)Justice

Main points of this chapter

- globalization has had significant effects on various types of social stratification, including with respect to class, country, gender, race, the urban/rural divide, and age
- although contemporary globalization has helped to narrow social hierarchies in certain respects, on the whole it has tended to widen gaps in life chances
- these injustices are not inherent to globalization, but have mainly flowed from neoliberal approaches to the new geography

Human security is closely related to questions of social equity. To the extent that society is not just, there is less likely to be peace, adequate care for the environment, poverty eradication, labour protection, unencumbered development of identity and knowledge, or social cohesion. Conversely, to the extent that people feel insecure, they are less likely to relinquish any unfair social advantages that they might have.

This is not the place to engage in lengthy and complex philosophical debates regarding the precise grounds for determining (in)equity in social life. A number of criteria could be used. For example, some deem that fairness is achieved when all persons in a society enjoy the same conditions of life. In contrast, others define social justice in terms of the guarantee of certain minimum entitlements for all members of a society.

The present assessment of social equity in contemporary globalization adopts a third approach, identifying justice principally in terms of the absence of arbitrary privilege and exclusion. From this perspective, unequal outcomes between individuals can be fair, provided: (a) that all parties have minimum acceptable living conditions; and, more particularly, (b) that such inequality does not result from structural hierarchies of opportunity that accord some parties an inbuilt advantage over others (for example, by accident of birth). Issues concerning the effects of globalization on minimum living standards are addressed in the previous chapter on human security; hence the present chapter concentrates on the question of social hierarchies in the context of globalization.

Historically, many kinds of arbitrary privilege have arisen in social relations. Examples include dominance and subordination on the basis of class, country, gender, race, urban/rural divides, and age group. In relation to class, for instance, persons born into some socioeconomic circles have generally had fewer life chances than those born into others. Likewise, in terms of countries, individuals in the South or the East who have equivalent personal capacities and make similar efforts as persons in the North have tended to harvest fewer fruits, simply by virtue of living in one zone of the planet rather than another. In addition, patriarchal gender relations have generally given men built-in privileges in social life relative to women. Socially constructed racial hierarchies have usually advantaged white people over people of colour. Meanwhile across the world urban-centred development strategies have tended to marginalize rural sectors. In terms of age, vulnerable groups such as children and the elderly have readily seen their interests systematically subordinated to those of people in mid-life who occupy most decision-taking offices.

Equity does not – in the perspective adopted here – demand that social categories be eliminated and that all people become the same. Such uniformity is neither attainable nor desirable. However, it is manifestly unfair when an embedded stratification of social positions largely determines whether or not people gain access to the resources they need to develop their potential. Thus there is no justifiable reason why children from wealthier circles should have more life chances than children born into poorer circles, or why men should have greater opportunities than women on grounds of gender, or why rural inhabitants should be structurally disadvantaged relative to town dwellers. Greater rewards for greater accomplishments can be defended, but justice demands that all parties have equivalent possibilities to produce those greater accomplishments.

Needless to say, globalization does not constitute the original source of social inequity. Stratification by class, country, gender, race and other social categories predates the contemporary rise of supraterritoriality by several generations or even many centuries. Hence the question is how globalization has affected the forms and the intensity of social hierarchies in contemporary history. In what ways and to what extent has the spread of transworld relations either loosened or sustained – or perhaps even hardened – arbitrary subordinations in social life?

As in the case of human security, the record is mixed, but with disturbing negative aspects. Some developments in contemporary globalization have reduced structurally imposed handicaps on people. For example, as elaborated below, contemporary global capitalism has in general increased opportunities for women to engage in waged employment. However, the recent growth of supraterritorial spaces has – under prevailing neoliberal policies – usually distributed costs and benefits in ways that favour the already privileged and further marginalize the already disadvantaged.

As a result, global relations have, to date, tended on the whole to widen resource gaps and reinforce social hierarchies, especially those related to class, country and urban/rural divides. Class stratification has meant that investors, managers, professionals and certain skilled workers have profited far more from globalization than less trained workers. The 'lower' classes have indeed often seen their position deteriorate in absolute terms. In regard to countries, embedded hierarchies have thus far channelled the benefits of globalization disproportionately to lands of the North relative to those of the South and the East. With its highly urban-centric character, contemporary globalization has also tended to accentuate the marginalization of rural areas. The record with regard to gender, race and age stratifications is more ambiguous or mixed, but neoliberal globalization has in some respects clearly operated against women, people of colour and the elderly.

In view of these trends, observers from a wide variety of political persuasions have noted, with Jane Marceau, that:

> while reordering the world of production is well underway, much less progress is being made in . . . the social distribution of the resulting profits.

> (1992: 473)

Not surprisingly, therefore, the growth of global relations has unsettled many consciences and sparked resistance from a number of subordinated circles.

To be sure, (neoliberal) globalization has not been the sole cause of persistent and in some cases growing social injustice in today's world. However, the rise of supraterritoriality has contributed to these regressive trends in at least four important general ways. First, classes, countries, sexes, races, urban/rural sectors and age groups have had unequal opportunities to access purportedly 'free' and 'open' global spaces. Second, on its mainly neoliberal course, contemporary globalization has often undermined the redistributive mechanisms that were built up through the state during the first three-quarters of the twentieth century. Third, global regimes (that is, the rules and institutions that govern supraterritorial communications, markets, finance and the like) have thus far generally underwritten an allocation of benefits and harms that favours the already advantaged. Fourth, contemporary globalization has substantially undermined the capacity of traditional, territorially based social movements like trade unionism and anti-colonialism to campaign for a fair distribution of capitalist surpluses. More positively, though, globalization has often facilitated a growth of new social movements that have highlighted questions of gender justice, racial equity, children's rights and a purported 'right to development' for all countries.

The rest of this chapter examines the dynamics of (mal)distribution under globalization in more detail. Most research on globality and social equity has addressed stratifications associated with class, North–South divisions and gender; thus these three types of hierarchies are discussed at greater length below. Less evidence is currently available regarding the implications of globalization for race, urban/rural divides and age; hence remarks on these matters are more brief.

Throughout the discussion below it becomes apparent that social inequity is no more intrinsic to global relations than to territorial geography. Yes, hierarchies between classes, countries, sexes, races, urban/rural divides and ages have often persisted and grown in the context of contemporary globalization. However, these trends have mainly resulted from *laissez-faire* policies toward globalization and are not inherent in globalization itself. Different approaches could yield more just outcomes.

Class stratification

As noted in Chapter 1, many critics have alleged that contemporary globalization has intensified class hierarchies. 'Class' refers here to the division of a population in respect of different roles in the production process. In contemporary capitalism, for example, people tend to contribute to production primarily as investors, managers, professionals, skilled manual workers or untrained manual workers (including home-makers). This division of labour is often further reflected in associated differences of customs, dress, language, art forms, etc.

Class diversity is to be accepted and indeed welcomed; however, it is unjust when class categories generate unequal life chances. Certain forms of work may warrant higher rewards owing to the greater expertise and/or exertion demanded. However, class distinctions must not restrict social mobility, educational opportunities, access to public services, and so on. In these situations class *difference* becomes class *hierarchy*.

Class inequity existed long before the current period of accelerated globalization, of course; yet how has the growth of supraterritorial capitalism affected these inequalities? Certainly the general distribution of income and assets between socioeconomic groups has become more skewed during recent decades. Across the world the overall pattern of resource distribution has tended to shift since the 1960s from the shape of an egg to that of a pear. In other words, fewer people have occupied the top, and more people have slipped toward the bottom.

In the USA, for example, differences in household income between the top fifth and the bottom fifth of the populace narrowed between 1947 and 1973, but then increased by more than 50 per cent between 1973 and 1996 (Burtless *et al.*, 1998: 3). During the 1970s and 1980s, real incomes of the top 30 per cent of earners in the United States rose, while those of the bottom 70 per cent declined (Santamäki-Vuori, 1995: 42). By 1991 the richest 10 per cent of the US population owned 83.2 per cent of assets (Robinson, 1996a: 23).

Wealth gaps of this kind have grown in recent decades across almost all the OECD countries, albeit usually not as much as in the USA (Ghai, 1994: 30–2; UNDP, 1999: 37). Less trained workers (that is, people with no more than general secondary education) have especially suffered. Involvement in high-tech industries – many of them integral to globalization – has enhanced the position of certain workers. However, in the North the demand for low-trained labour dropped around 20 per cent between 1960 and 1990 relative to that for skilled labour (Wood, 1994: 11). Much of this reduced demand occurred as global production and markets shifted some manufacturing from the North to the South and the East. In these circumstances wage differentials have widened in the OECD countries between more trained labour (professionals, managers, technicians) and less trained labour, after the gaps had decreased during the third quarter of the twentieth century.

In the East, meanwhile, most countries in transition from state socialism to market economies have experienced a steep ascent to wealth for a few and a rapid descent to poverty for many. In Russia, for instance, the richest fifth of the population saw its proportion of national income rise from 32.7 per cent in 1990 to 46.7 per cent in 1997, while the poorest fifth had its share decline over the same period from 9.8 to 6.2 per cent (UNDP, 1998: 8). Across most of Central and Eastern Europe and the former Soviet Union, a limited circle has reaped major material gains from the new connections to global capitalism, while the majority of people have seen their standard of life worsen.

At the same time countries of the South have developed some of the world's greatest income inequalities during the period of accelerated globalization. To take the most extreme example, in the early 1990s the wealthiest fifth of the population in Brazil earned 26 times as much as the poorest fifth (UNDP, 1991: 34). Many cities of the South today house the ugliest of shantytowns in the shadows of the shiniest of skyscrapers. That said, exceptions also exist where, for example, the Gini coefficient (a standard measure of income inequality) in Malaysia declined from 0.49 in 1980 to 0.45 in 1993 (UNDP, 1999: 88).

At the very tip of world class stratification sit the superrich, the 'hinwis' from the South, the East and the North. As of the mid-1990s, the value of the assets of 358 billionaires exceeded the combined annual incomes of countries with 2.3 billion inhabitants, or the poorest 45 per cent of the world's population (Speth, 1996: 33; UNDP, 1996: 2). Even allowing for the objection that assets are not directly comparable to income, this calculation points to a deplorable uneven distribution of world resources that goes well beyond anything that can be justified on grounds of special skill and exertion. Against this backdrop, the *Human Development Report* has spoken of 'a breathtaking globalization of prosperity side by side with a depressing globalization of poverty' (UNDP, 1994: 1).

Moreover, class inequity has reverberated beyond the wealth gap. For example, many countries across the world – especially though not exclusively in the South and the East – have in recent history witnessed a relative if not absolute general deterioration in publicly provided education. The alternative of private instruction or other supplements has generally only been available to wealthier households. As a result, class-based inequalities in educational opportunities have tended to increase. Widespread deterioration across the world in public health, public housing and public transport has likewise tended to impact more heavily on 'lower' than 'higher' classes, thereby strengthening hierarchies between them.

Yet how far, if at all, can deepened stratification of classes in contemporary history be attributed to globalization? The two developments have unfolded concurrently, but has the rise of supraterritoriality *caused* the increases in class gaps? Neoliberals tend either to ignore questions of class or to declare that uneven life chances between socio-economic groups are inevitable. Some authors of a neoliberal persuasion have explicitly rejected the proposition that liberalization could increase class inequality (cf. Burtless *et al.*, 1998: ch 4). At another extreme, many radical critics have regarded deepened class hierarchies as an inherent and incorrigible evil of global capitalism.

Neither of these positions is tenable. Globalization has indeed figured in the contemporary growth of class stratification; however, this outcome is not inherent to supraterritorial social relations. The problem has lain not in globality as such, but in the prevailing neoliberal approach to managing the new geography. Policymakers have generally pursued stabilization, liberalization, deregulation and privatization without specific attention to issues of class justice.

One major way that globalization has widened class gaps in contemporary history relates to access. 'Free' global markets have by no means been 'open' to all. As indicated in Chapter 5, supraterritorial spaces have generated considerable surplus; however, different classes have had substantially different opportunities to tap that accumulation. Propertied circles, professionals and certain skilled workers have had far better chances to acquire the means (such as fax, air travel and financial advisers) to participate actively in global capitalism. Class divides have substantially skewed access to the Internet as well (Loader, 1998). Offshore banking and securities have mainly been reserved to the super-rich, such as 78,000 citizens of Saudi Arabia who as of the mid-1990s had an average of $5.4 million each invested in global finance (FT500, 1997: 46). In contrast, salaried workers have tended to stay onshore, while most residents of today's world have lacked any bank account whatsoever. Several billion people have consumed global products, but only a small minority has owned the resultant profits.

A second way that globalization has generated greater class divisions follows from the decline of the redistributive state described in Chapter 6. Earlier in the twentieth century, a number of mechanisms were developed through the state to lessen class stratifications. Keynesianism in the North and various forms of socialism elsewhere in the world went some way to extract from the rich that part of wealth accumulation which derived from class privilege. Governments used instruments such as progressive taxation, wage controls, price manipulations and improved public services to redirect much of that surplus to less advantaged socioeconomic circles. As a result, people from subordinated classes often gained increased opportunities to realize their potentials. To be sure, Keynesianism and socialism in practice frequently fell short of their promise to remove injustice based on class. At a minimum, however, the redistributive state that peaked in the third quarter of the twentieth century prevented class gaps from growing.

As indicated in Chapter 6, the huge expansion of globally mobile capital in contemporary history has constrained states to abandon many of their redistributive policies. Across the world, governments have retreated from progressive taxation (Tanzi, 1996). Top tax brackets fell in the OECD countries from an average of 52 per cent in 1985 to 42 per cent in 1990 (UNDP, 1999: 93). Widespread introductions and increases of value-added tax (VAT) have had a particularly regressive effect, especially when applied to essential goods like basic clothing and staple foods. Liberalization and deregulation have attenuated or terminated many redistributive wage and price policies. Fiscal austerity to improve 'global competitiveness' has often meant reductions in the amount and quality of state-provided education, housing, nutrition, health care, pensions and unemployment insurance. In sum, neoliberal globalization has tended to erode the protective shield of the redistributive state. As Ethan Kapstein has put it, 'just when working people most need the nation-state as a buffer from the world economy, it is abandoning them' (1996: 16).

Emergent suprastate frameworks have not filled the regulatory gaps left by states in respect of countering arbitrary class hierarchies. On the contrary, global economic institutions such as the IMF, the OECD, the WTO and the multilateral development banks have figured as major promoters of neoliberal policies during the 1980s and 1990s. Indeed, many states have embarked on deregulation, liberalization, regressive tax reform and fiscal austerity in the context of structural adjustment programmes sponsored by suprastate agencies. Meanwhile these institutions have generally given short shrift to proposals for redistributive global taxes or a major clampdown on what in effect amounts to tax evasion by the wealthy through offshore finance facilities. Regional bodies, too, have mainly concentrated on market liberalization, with at best secondary attention to questions of class justice. For its part the ILO has focused on securing minimum workers' rights rather than pursuing a more ambitious agenda of class equity.

Nor have social movements been able to mount effective opposition to growing class gaps in the context of neoliberal globalization. The main traditional force for class equity, the trade union movement, has experienced substantial drops in membership as old industries decline and new 'flexible' labour practices largely exclude collective bargaining. Moreover, trade unions have – notwithstanding some notable exceptions (cf. Munck and Waterman, 1999) – tended to persist with national and territorial campaigns. Such a strategy is decidedly inadequate when a large proportion of capital is globally mobile. In some countries where organized labour has retained important strength, bureaucratization, close ties with ruling circles and self-aggrandizement of leaders have undercut trade union credibility. Meanwhile new global social movements (for example, of consumer advocates, environmentalists, human rights activists and women) have tended to give only secondary if any attention to issues of class equity.

In sum, contemporary globalization has indeed contributed to a greater entrenchment of class hierarchies. Even a bastion of neoliberalism such as the WEF has acknowledged a challenge of 'demonstrating how the new global capitalism can function to the benefit of the majority and not only for corporate managers and investors' (Schwab and Smadja, 1996). Access to global spaces has been highly uneven on class lines. Global capital has prompted states to undo many policies that previously reduced arbitrary class inequalities. Global regimes have not installed redistributive mechanisms to replace those lost at state level. Global social movements have generally underplayed questions of class stratification. None of these dynamics of social injustice is inherent to globalization, but prevailing neoliberal policies have had the general effect of reinforcing and widening class gaps.

Country stratification

Arbitrary class hierarchies are of course not the only form of social injustice in the contemporary globalizing world. In addition, for example, theses concerning imperialism have since the nineteenth century high-lighted a purported inequitable stratification of countries alongside that of classes. The modern world order, these accounts affirm, has unfairly discriminated against the 'South' (also termed the 'periphery', 'Third World', 'underdeveloped countries', etc.) and the 'East' (also called the 'semi-periphery', 'Second World', etc.) in favour of the 'North' (alternatively named the 'core', 'centre', 'First World' or 'developed countries').

To be sure, like any analytical categorization, the distinction of a North, a South and an East in world affairs involves substantial simplification. In practice the North, the South and the East have each contained consider-able diversity. For example, the 'poor' South is normally taken to include the huge oil wealth of Kuwait and the major derivatives market of Singapore. Meanwhile the 'rich' North is normally taken to include the slums of New York City and marginalized farmers of Sicily. Indeed, poor people arguably form something of a 'South' within the North, and élites could be said to constitute a 'North' within the South and the East. It would clearly be perverse if 'international redistribution' meant further enriching the wealthy of the South by further pauperizing the poor of the North.

Similarly, a country can contain large internal welfare disparities between regions. In Argentina, for instance, Chubut Province is much poorer than Buenos Aires Province. In India the state of Bihar has a far higher poverty level than Kerala. In England widespread wealth in the South East contrasts with widespread need in the North East. China's economic boom of recent decades has concentrated on the coastal provinces while many interior regions have remained stagnant. Owing to such differentials, too, analysis in terms of country units involves con-siderable simplification.

Yet social hierarchy within countries does not negate the fact of a concurrent hierarchy between countries. Although the notion of a North–South divide may be crude, it does capture an important general config-uration of modern world politics. People living in lands whose govern-ments are members of the Group of Seven, the OECD, the BIS and NATO have manifestly held structural advantages over inhabitants of countries that have lain outside such clubs. Resource distribution, laws, institutions and inherited prejudices are such that the 'average' person born into a country of the South (where the 'South' has since 1989 arguably included much of the post-communist East) has had fewer life chances than the 'average' person born into a country of the North. Even when an individual from the South and an individual from the North have had equivalent personal means, the resident of the North has generally been able to obtain greater gains from those resources. In these important senses a North–South divide has imposed a significant arbitrary hierarchy of opportunity in modern world history.

How has contemporary large-scale globalization affected injustice on North–South lines? Has the end of territorialism meant the end of stratification based on territorial units? Or have critics been right to attack globalization as a new imperialism of the North over the South? Evidence suggests that globalization to date has often reinforced arbitrary hierarchies between North and South. However, as with class inequities, unjust outcomes in respect of North–South relations have resulted from the (mainly neoliberal) policies that have been adopted in respect of global spaces rather than from supraterritoriality per se.

The general welfare gap between the South and the North has grown during the period of accelerated globalization. True, as seen in Chapter 9, populations in both the North and the South have, on the whole, experienced improvements in material conditions during these decades. Yet the advances have been greater in the already privileged North. To take one general indicator, aggregate income in 1960 of the countries with the richest fifth of the world's population was 30 times as great as aggregate income of the countries with the poorest fifth. By 1997 this ratio had grown to 74:1 (UNDP, 1999: 3). As noted in the last chapter, a few previously 'less-developed' countries have during this period become NICs; however, most lands of the South have seen little improvement – if not an actual decline – in the general welfare of their populations. These misfortunes can be partly attributed to local and national circumstances of the countries concerned, but globalization has also played a part in deepening North–South inequality.

For one thing, uneven access to global spaces has widened North–South differentials. Pre-existent stratification has meant that, like subordinated classes, disadvantaged countries have been less able to share in the gains of supraterritorial capitalism. For example, the great bulk of the infrastructure for global communications has been situated in the North. Today countries with the richest fifth of the world's population have 74 per cent of all telephone lines, while the poorest fifth have a mere 1.5 per cent (UNDP, 1999: 3). As of the mid-1990s there were more telephones in Tokyo than in the whole of Africa (*FT*, 7 June 1996: 3). The OECD countries accounted for 94 per cent of the market in packaged computer software in 1994 (UNDP, 1999: 69). With regard to global companies, the North at the beginning of the 1990s held over three-quarters of the accumulated stock of FDI and attracted 60 per cent of new FDI flows (Hirst and Thompson, 1996b: 63). Moreover, when FDI has gone to the South, it has concentrated in ten countries, bypassing the vast majority. Likewise, global products have mostly circulated in the North. For instance, consumers in 13 countries of the North have accounted for 80 per cent of the world market in music recordings (*FT*, 2 September 1996: 2).

In respect of money, the US, European and Japanese currencies have dominated global transactions, not the Brazilian real or the Thai baht. While residents of the North have acquired several hundred million global credit cards, the 1.2 billion inhabitants of China between them held only 14 million of these plastic passes in the mid-1990s (*FT*, 19 September 1996: 37). Although many offshore finance centres have been 'located' (if sometimes only with brass plates) in the South, the tax advantages of these operations have accrued principally to already wealthy 'hinwis' who mostly reside in the North.

In global financial markets the South long ago lost the substantial stream of transborder commercial bank loans that temporarily flowed its way during the 1970s. In the mid-1990s clients based in the North obtained nearly 90 per cent of new global borrowing (OECD, 1996a: 5). On a similar pattern, nearly three-quarters of both equity value and derivatives business were concentrated in the USA, Japan and Britain as of 1993 (Kidron and Segal, 1995: 70–1). At the end of the 1990s only 25 governments of the South had a credit rating that gave them access to global bond markets (UNDP, 1999: 31). To the (limited) extent that financial trading sites have developed in so-called 'emerging markets' of the South, transworld electronic transfers have ensured that investors based in the North frequently own most of the assets and reap most of the profits. Moreover, when largely globally induced financial crisis has hit the South – for example, in Latin America 1994–5, Asia 1997–8, Russia 1998 and Brazil 1999 – investment houses based in the North have instantaneously withdrawn enormous funds.

Skewed access that favours the North over the South has also prevailed in global governance, especially in regard to economic matters. For example, the G7 governments currently control more than 45 per cent of votes on the IMF Executive Board, while 43 governments in Africa between them control less than 5 per cent (IMF, 1999: 194–7). In contrast, the WTO works on the principle of one-state-one-vote; however, many governments of the South have lacked the resources to maintain a permanent delegation in Geneva to monitor and intervene in the organization's day-to-day proceedings. Meanwhile most of the South has had no representation whatsoever at the BIS and the OECD.

Next to problems of uneven access, contemporary globalization has also furthered a growing North–South gap insofar as neoliberal policies have discouraged public-sector interventions to counter this inequality of opportunity. During the third quarter of the twentieth century many states of the South attempted to promote 'development' with measures (like tariff protection for infant industries) that sheltered local producers from world market competition. At the same time most states of the North expanded programmes of official development assistance as a means to redistribute wealth between countries.

Neoliberal critics have rejected 'inward-looking' macroeconomic strategies and sometimes also 'foreign aid' as unhelpful disruptions to inherently progressive forces of the 'free market' (Bandow and Vásquez, 1994). On the neoliberal wave of the late twentieth century, states across the South have (to varying degrees) reoriented their policies toward the world economy from protectionism to liberalization. Meanwhile, fiscal constraints and the rigours of global market competition have encouraged most governments in the North to reduce concessionary resource transfers to the South. By 1995 ODA amounted to only 0.27 per cent of the GNP of the OECD countries, the lowest proportion since such statistics were first collected in 1950 (*FT*, 6 February 1997: 5). Moreover, with the addition of clients in the post-communist East, these smaller sums of ODA have since the 1990s been spread across more recipients.

Neoliberals have rightly attacked certain shortcomings in statist approaches to 'development' and the often less than optimal use of ODA. State ownership, government subsidies and statutory trade barriers have frequently encouraged inefficiencies and – through various forms of corruption – greater rather than less social injustice in the South. However, it is far from clear that the neoliberal prescription simply to withdraw public-sector management of cross-border resource movements improves matters. After all, certain kinds of state steering have arguably allowed countries like the so-called 'Asian tigers' to narrow welfare gaps between themselves and the North. Moreover, while preaching liberalization to the South, OECD governments have retained many subsidies and other interventions in the market that have helped to preserve and enlarge their advantages over poor countries. As on earlier historical occasions, 'free trade' has paraded in contemporary neoliberal globalization as an ideology of the strong whom it favours.

As for global regimes, these frameworks have on the whole promoted neoliberal formulas with little regard to the detrimental effects that such policies might have on resource distribution between the North and the South. In the area of global communications, for example, institutions like the ITU, UNESCO and the WTO have concentrated their efforts on promoting 'free' flows of information. Thus the global regulators have accorded their main priority to harmonizing technical standards and reducing statutory trade restrictions. Only secondary if any consideration has gone to public policies that would improve the South's access to telecommunications and electronic mass media. Indeed, when UNESCO in the late 1970s and early 1980s attacked arbitrary North–South hierarchies with its proposals for a New World Information and Communications Order, dominant states in the North suppressed the initiative. Neoliberal governments in Britain and the USA went as far as to withdraw from organization in 1984. The installation of a new leadership at UNESCO in 1987 brought a return to a more orthodox policy direction, though as of 1999 Washington had still not rejoined the agency (Wells, 1987; Imber, 1989).

Like supraterritorial rules governing communications, the global trade regime centred on the GATT/WTO has focused primarily on liberalization, with limited regard to the possibility that 'free trade' might work against an equitable distribution of opportunities between countries. A so-called 'open' field favours the strong market players, who have been disproportionately situated in the North. Moreover, the GATT/WTO regime has over the half-century of its existence generally proved quickest to liberalize in areas like (most) manufactures and intellectual property where North-based interests hope to exploit opportunities in the South. Progress has tended to be slower in areas like agriculture and textiles where trade liberalization would give South-based interests greater opportunities in the North.

Economists are agreed that most of the income gains from the 1994 Uruguay Round agreements will accrue to the already advantaged North (Dubey, 1996: 14–16; Whalley, 1996: 428). For example, a study commissioned by the OECD and the World Bank calculated that the North would acquire 63.4 per cent of the income gains and that the new arrangements would also increase the income gap between Africa and all other regions (Goldin, 1993: 142, 205). Already the annual export earnings (in current dollars) of Sub-Saharan Africa declined from \$50 billion in 1980 to \$36 billion in the early 1990s (Svedberg, 1993: 21).

The TRIPS agreement is also widely regarded as increasing South–North gaps (South Centre, 1997). Indeed, most governments of the South signed this accord before they adequately understood its terms and implications. TRIPS has raised the cost of access to advanced technologies and medicines beyond the reach of many poor countries. Moreover, global patents on genetic material – henceforth to be guaranteed through the WTO – have given 'bio-prospectors' from the North control over, and income from, many varieties of plant life that originated in poor countries

(Shiva, 1997). The *Human Development Report* has spoken in this context of 'a silent theft of centuries of knowledge' (UNDP, 1999: 68).

True, several suprastate initiatives have stabilized prices and improved access for exports of the South to the North. In this vein, the Generalized System of Preferences (GSP) of the GATT has since the late 1960s offered some Southern producers better access to Northern markets in certain goods. Similarly, a succession of Lomé Conventions between the EU and 71 African, Caribbean and Pacific countries has since 1975 aimed *inter alia* to stabilize export earnings from the South to Western Europe. In addition, a Compensatory and Contingency Financing Facility was established through the IMF in 1988 for countries that experience temporary shortfalls in export earnings. However, the overall impact of these schemes has remained modest.

In the voluntary sector a number of so-called 'alternative' trading organizations have linked producers in the South directly with nonprofit buyers in the North, thereby increasing the suppliers' earnings. Examples of such transborder NGO initiatives include TWIN Trading and Traidcraft Exchange. Another alternative trade scheme, PEOPLink, has since 1995 used the Internet to sell the crafts of grassroots artisans from 30 countries of the South (PEOPLink, 1999). An International Federation for Alternative Trade was launched in 1989 and a decade later grouped 142 associations in 47 countries (IFAT, 1999). Nevertheless, these inspirational efforts have accounted for only a miniscule proportion of total world trade.

Moreover, proposals for a more comprehensive redistribution of the gains of world commerce have stalled. Reform of North–South trade lay at the heart of the unsuccessful campaign of the 1970s for a so-called New International Economic Order (Bhagwati, 1977; Sauvant and Hasenpflug, 1977). Even OPEC's quadrupling of oil prices in 1973 only reestablished the earlier level relative to manufactures, and the rate per barrel subsequently fell back to pre-1973 prices (Singer, 1995: 23). Many Northern agricultural subsidies remain in place, and steps to dismantle the protectionist Multi-Fibre Arrangement have likewise dragged for years. In the 1990s barriers to trade in the North were estimated to cost the South twice the value of all development aid (Carlsson *et al.*, 1995: 166). 'Generosity', indeed.

Further inequities in North–South relations have developed out of the regimes that govern global finance. In this issue-area, too, regulators have accorded top priority to liberalization rather than equity (or they have assumed simplistically and uncritically that justice flows automatically from an 'open' economy). Neoliberal policies have mainly removed statutory restrictions, for instance, on foreign exchange transactions, capital flows between countries, foreign ownership of financial assets, and so on. Some other initiatives in global financial governance have sought to reduce the risks of systemic breakdown as a result of banking crises. Examples of these market safety measures include the BIS capital adequacy standards and IMF/World Bank sponsorship during the 1990s of financial sector reform in a number of countries. Certain other suprastate measures have sought to counter misbehaviour by rogue traders on global securities and derivatives markets.

However, the regulation of global finance has to date neglected questions of structurally unequal access between countries. When the allocation of global loans and bonds is left to 'market forces', then credit goes disproportionately to borrowers with the greatest means to repay. Moreover, in the market higher credit risks attract higher borrowing costs, so that the countries most in need of funds have tended to pay the highest charges.

The North–South distribution of pains in global finance has likewise been unjust. Consider the approach adopted through the IMF and the London Club to 'resolve' the global commercial debt crisis of the 1980s. The losses fell far more heavily on borrowing governments in the South than on lending banks in the North. Indeed, in 1990 the interest on transborder debt due from the South to the North ($112 billion) amounted to nearly three times the flow of bilateral ODA from the North to the South ($41 billion) (Harrod, 1992: 106). Notwithstanding various initiatives since the late 1980s to reduce the burden of debt repayments, the scale of net South-to-North transfers in respect of official and commercial global loans has exceeded anything previously witnessed, including during colonial times.

In the 1990s governments, firms and peoples of the South have borne the brunt of the pain in financially induced economic crises in Asia, Latin America and Russia. Multilateral financial agencies have usually centred the blame for these misfortunes on flaws in the domestic laws and institutions of the affected countries. Accordingly the lion's share of recovery costs and corrective measures have applied to the South. Meanwhile global regulators have generally underplayed the role in these crises of liberalized transborder capital flows. Hence global banks and investment companies (who hold mainly North-based funds) have avoided even the idea of contributing to the public costs of these downturns in 'emerging markets', for example, in terms of the alleviation of increased unemployment and destitution. Along similar lines, if a global bond-rating agency downgrades a poor country on the basis of faulty intelligence, the unfortunate victim has no way to recoup the damages that it suffers in terms of increased interest charges on its transborder debt.

The preceding remarks concerning global regimes are not meant to discount initiatives throughout much of the United Nations system since the 1960s to address issues of North–South inequity. Bodies like the UN

Conference on Trade and Development (UNCTAD, launched in 1964) and UNDP, created in 1965, have produced valuable research on North–South relations. These agencies have also helped more generally to keep questions of social justice on the global agenda. Yet since the 1980s UN agencies have generally taken the backseat in multilateral economic governance. The initiative has clearly lain with the Bretton Woods institutions and other agencies like the OECD and the WTO that have operated outside the UN purview.

Since official channels have largely failed to address – and indeed have often exacerbated – unjust distribution between the North and the South under contemporary globalization, one might expect social movements to have risen up in protest. After all, starting in the 1920s a global anti-colonial coalition powerfully linked nationalists and socialists from across the South, along with various supporters in the North. Yet this progressive alliance largely dissipated after formal decolonization. To some extent certain religious groups and development NGOs have taken the struggle against what was once popularly called imperialism forward into the twenty-first century. Owing in good part to these efforts, many people would today broadly accept that countries have a 'right of development'. Yet active participation in the development movement has on the whole remained limited. Meanwhile, other new social movements (for example, in respect of consumer protection, environmental conservation, and human rights) have usually not put questions of North–South equity high on their agenda.

On the whole, then, accelerated globalization has – especially in the 1980s and 1990s – had unhappy consequences for the distribution of human life chances between countries. Inhabitants of the already privileged North have amassed a disproportionate share of the fruits of contemporary globalization, largely on account of the accident of their country of birth. Currently prevailing state and suprastate policy frameworks have sooner reinforced than countered this inbuilt inequality of opportunity, and to date social movement protests against growing North–South gaps have generally been weak and ineffectual. However, to repeat the key point, this dismal trend in injustice between countries has not been inherent to globalization. In particular, stronger social movements and alternative regulatory arrangements could yield more just outcomes.

Gender stratification

In addition to highlighting problems of class and country hierarchies, a number of critics of contemporary globalization have (as noted in Chapter 1) alleged that the process has tended to perpetuate, if not exacerbate, the subordination of women relative to men. A number of feminist analyses in particular have highlighted the significance in globalization of gender inequity, that is, injustice that results from particular social constructions of femininity and masculinity. It is clearly arbitrary and unfair that biological differences between sexes become grounds for social inequalities.

Like 'class' and 'North/South', 'gender' refers to broad social patterns. Thus, just as certain individuals from underprivileged classes have beaten the odds to reach positions of influence, and just as certain countries from the South have attained accelerated 'development', so certain women have overcome gender obstacles to become leading managers, politicians and professionals. Yet exceptions at the level of individual women – as exceptions – sooner demonstrate than disprove the existence of social hierarchies on gender lines. Moreover, the 'successful' women have often had to adopt masculine behaviours in order to make their accomplishments.

The structural dominance of men over women is of course hardly new to the contemporary period of accelerated globalization. 'Patriarchy' (as some commentators prefer to call this gender subordination) has a long history and had become embedded in most social contexts across the world before the rise of supraterritoriality accelerated in the 1960s. Globalization is no more the original source of gender injustice than it has been the wellspring of class or country stratification. Yet has contemporary globalization intensified gender injustice, like it has often widened class gaps and North–South hierarchies?

Connections between globalization and gender trends are rather difficult to specify empirically. Researchers have only recently begun systematically to assemble gender-based social data; hence we can trace few precise statistical indicators historically from before, and then across, the period of accelerated globalization. That limitation noted, available data suggests that the contemporary growth of transworld relations has had mixed consequences for gender justice.

In a positive vein, it appears that some significant reductions have occurred since 1970 in gender gaps with respect to health and education (UNDP, 1995: 3). For instance, the worldwide rate of girls' enrolment in secondary school rose from 36 per cent in 1990 to 61 per cent in 1997 (UNDP, 1999: 22). In many parts of the world women have also gained greater access to paid employment. For example, participation in waged labour rose in the OECD countries from 48.3 per cent of women in 1973 to 60 per cent in 1990 (Simai, 1995: 12). In Western Europe between the 1970s and the 1990s, male jobs declined by one million while female employment grew by 13 million. Moreover, between 1978 and 1988 the median wage of women workers in the North rose from 43 per cent to 54 per cent of the level for men (Lang and Hines, 1993: 74). In countries such as Germany, Sweden and the USA, women have since the 1960s obtained a larger proportion (albeit still a clear minority) of professional and managerial posts (Esping-Andersen, 1990: 212).

However, such improvements have not yielded full equity. When researchers calculated a gender-related development index (GDI) for the 1995 *Human Development Report*, women had equal opportunities with men in none of the 130 countries covered (UNDP, 1995: 2). A survey taken around 1990 found that only 6 of 96 governments in the South made explicit reference to women's issues in their national economic policies (Vickers, 1991: x). Very often women still do not receive equal pay with men for the same work. In the former communist countries the position of women has generally deteriorated – both in absolute terms and relative to men – in respect of reproductive rights, employment opportunities, caring burdens and participation in representative institutions (Einhorn, 1993; Funk and Mueller, 1993; Moghadam, 1993). In the 1990s almost 70 per cent of the world's poor people were female, and many girls in the South still lacked access to formal education (UNDP, 1995: 36; Rivera *et al.*, 1995: 12).

Yet what specific role, if any, has globalization played in the continuities and changes of contemporary gender hierarchies? In regard to employment, supraterritorial capitalism has in several respects given a significant boost to women's opportunities to undertake paid work. For one thing, female labour has figured prominently in the expanding service economy of global information, global communications, global retailing and global finance. Women have also occupied a large proportion of jobs in global manufacturing operations. For example, 4 million women held positions in 200 EPZs in the South alone as of 1994, up from 1.3 million in 1986 (Joekes and Weston, 1994: 37). Moreover, in the 1990s women in the *maquiladora* plants began to rise to some management positions (Suárez Aguilar, 1999).

That said, increased access for women to wage labour through global markets has also had less than happy aspects. After all, many of the new feminized workplaces in finance, information and communication industries have had the quality of 'electronic sweatshops': highly stressful and poorly remunerated. Largely owing to occupational sex-typing in global finance, men have taken most of the high salaries in management and on the trading floor, whereas women have provided most of the low-paid clerical support in the backroom (McDowell and Court, 1994). Any peek into an airport business class lounge reveals that women have gained relatively few places in global management circles.

True, jobs in global production through EPZs have often offered women better pay and benefits than other work (Lim, 1990). Yet many of the positions have come with highly 'flexible' labour conditions. Moreover, the 1990s have witnessed some 'remasculinization' of the *maquiladora* workforces: partly due to a shortage of female labour; and partly owing to increased automation of the plants (with the stereotypical assumption that only men can handle heavy machinery) (Runyan, 1996: 240; Suárez Aguilar, 1999).

Still more dubious turns in gendered employment patterns have arisen in informal sectors of the global economy. Expanded global markets in domestic servants, mail-order brides and prostitutes have also enlarged job 'opportunities' for women (Pettman, 1997; Skrobanek *et al.*, 1997; Kempadoo and Doezema, 1998). For example, between 1988 and 1992 some 286,000 Filipinas and 50,000 Thai women arrived in Japan as 'entertainers' (Pettman, 1996: 197). Many migrant female domestic workers have suffered bodily violence as well as unacceptably arduous labour, although these problems have not as yet been systematically documented on a world scale.

Finally, women who have gained paid employment in the global economy have usually not lost other labour burdens in the process. Most have retained at least a second (unremunerated) job of family care. Some have furthermore kept a third job of household food cultivation. Such workloads have generally left the women concerned with little time or energy to mobilize politically to improve their lot.

In sum, then, globalization to date has had mixed results for gender justice in respect of employment opportunities. On the one hand, global markets have substantially increased women's access to paid labour. On the other hand, particularly in the North, the terms attached to these jobs have generally been inferior to the conditions obtained by the preceding generation of (mainly male) workers. Meanwhile women across the world have tended to retain unpaid household chores as they have acquired waged work outside the home.

On issues other than employment, contemporary globalization has generally done little to reverse gender-based hierarchies of opportunity. For example, global finance has if anything exacerbated the exclusion of women from credit markets relative to men (Staveren, 2000). True, several bilateral and multilateral agencies have, together with grassroots groups, promoted innovative micro-credit schemes that have in particular offered poor women in the South increased borrowing facilities. However, the sums involved in these programmes have been tiny next to the huge flows of mainstream – 'malestream' – global finance capital.

Similar gender stratification has persisted elsewhere. In regard to global communications, for instance, various studies have shown that, in almost all countries (a few like France and Turkey being exceptions), men have formed a large majority of Internet users (Lake, 1994). As of the late 1990s, women made up 38 per cent of users in the USA, 25 per cent in Brazil, 16 per cent in Russia and 4 per cent in Arab countries (UNDP, 1999: 62). On the other hand, some recent evidence suggests that gender gaps in Internet access are closing, at least in the USA (Lekhi, 2000). Men have also constituted the vast majority of directors and producers in the mass media, thereby exerting disproportionate influence on constructions of gender through global communications (UNESCO, 1987). Women have figured no more prominently in the leadership of regional and global governance agencies than in the upper ranks of the state. For example, at the IMF, as of 1997, 31 women constituted 10 per cent of managerial staff, while 593 women constituted 86 per cent of support staff (IMF, 1998: 101). Although no precise census is available, casual observation suggests that women and men have shared considerably more equally in policymaking through transborder NGOs. On the other hand, men have dominated other sectors of global civil society like business associations, think tanks and trade unions.

Along with unequal access to supraterritorial spaces, contemporary globalization has also perpetuated and sometimes deepened gender hierarchies in the second general way named earlier, that is, through neoliberal restructuring of the state. True, gender discrimination has recently become a more explicit concern in many national economic and social development plans. A few states have designated special ministers or even (in the case of Uganda, for example) created a distinct ministry specifically to address the status of women. However, the contraction of state services in line with neoliberal prescriptions has tended to hurt women more than men. As the principal homemakers and carers, women have suffered disproportionately when the state has cut benefits for vulnerable citizens, reduced spending on health and education, decreased subsidies on food, lowered maternity and child care entitlements, and so forth. In spite of extensive academic research on these negative gender impacts (as referenced in Chapter 1), to this day programmes of neoliberal economic reform only rarely make even a passing mention of gender issues. Meanwhile, although relevant data are not available, the suspicion must be that gains in ownership and income from privatization have generally flowed disproportionately to men.

Trends in the treatment of gender stratification by global regimes have shown some positive signs, but the overall impact has again been mixed. In terms of progress, a number of suprastate legal instruments have put the spotlight on gender hierarchies. Examples include the 1979 Convention on the Elimination of All Forms of Discrimination Against Women (CEDAW) and several equal opportunity directives of the EU. The UN Convention for the Suppression of Traffic in Persons and the Exploitation of the

Prostitution of Others, approved by the General Assembly in 1949, has over the years attracted 70 state ratifications (UNDP, 1999: 103). The United Nations and its specialized agencies have also run a number of programmes to combat gender subordination, particularly through the UN Decade for Women in 1976–85 and four global conferences on women between 1975 and 1995 (Pietilä and Vickers, 1994; Winslow, 1995). Multilateral development programmes have also targeted certain projects specifically to meet women's needs. For example, the World Bank spent $1 billion on education and training of women in 1995, triple the amount expended annually under this heading in the 1980s (Balleroni, 1995).

However, women-centred initiatives have on the whole remained relatively marginal in global governance. Most suprastate agencies have at best relegated gender issues to a small and marginal office. For example, the United Nations created a fund for women in development at the launch of the Decade for Women, but twenty years later this programme, called UNIFEM, had an annual budget of only $11.6 million (Jepsen, 1995). No World Gender Organization has emerged to complement the ILO on labour issues or UNDP on North–South questions. Meanwhile, global economic institutions like the World Bank have generally shown at best limited recognition of gender issues as they have promoted policies of neoliberal restructuring (O'Brien *et al.*, 2000: ch 2).

Contemporary globalization has had some distinctly hopeful consequences for gender justice through the rise of supraterritorial social movements. As noted in Chapter 3, campaigns for women's rights have involved transborder networks since the late nineteenth century. However, global movements for gender justice have especially proliferated and grown in recent decades, as evidenced by the attendance of over 30,000 women at the Fourth United Nations Conference on Women, convened at Beijing in 1995 (Mawle, 1997: 155). A number of transborder mobilizations in respect of development cooperation, ecological sustainability and human rights have also emphasized concerns about gender hierarchies (Bunch and Reilly, 1994). To date, however, most of these initiatives have found it difficult to move people beyond a recognition of women's subordination to a commitment to implement concrete corrective steps.

In summary, contemporary globalization has had mixed impacts on gender equity. In a positive direction, global capitalism has increased women's opportunities for paid employment; global governance has introduced a number of legal and institutional initiatives to promote the status of women; and global civil society has provided increased means to mobilize for gender equity. On the negative side of the balance sheet, gender stratification has limited women's access to many other global spaces; much female labour in the global economy has had poor conditions; and the costs of neoliberal global economic restructuring have tended to fall disproportionately on women. Thus globalization has shown potentials to do both good and ill for gender justice. The challenge for future action is to expand the gains and reduce the harms.

Other stratifications

Most research and argument about contemporary globalization and justice has highlighted social hierarchies related to class, country and gender. However, stratification in supraterritorial relations has extended to other social axes as well. Casual observation readily suggests that further arbitrary subordinations have existed in global spaces with respect to race, urban/rural divides and age groups. Regrettably, little specific data and analysis is currently available on the disproportionate effects of transborder flows along these lines. The relative brevity of the following remarks reflects this paucity of research and is not meant to suggest that racial, urban/rural and age discriminations are necessarily less severe or less important than those related to class, country and gender.

Indeed, the different categories have often overlapped and reinforced one another. For example, racial hierarchies have frequently figured in North–South stratification. Likewise, class stratification has readily accentuated the marginalization of rural cultivators. Gender and age hierarchies have combined to make the position of girls still more vulnerable than that of boys.

To be sure, categories of race, urban/rural divides and age are as ambiguous and contested as those of class, North/South divides and gender. Nevertheless, it is apparent that, on the whole, people of colour have – both within and between countries – generally had smaller life chances than white people. Likewise, exceptions duly noted, rural people have more usually suffered deprivation than city dwellers in the contemporary world. Across the continents, too, vulnerable age groups have often lacked adequate social protection, so that children and the elderly have experienced higher incidences of malnutrition, preventable illnesses and abuse than able-bodied adults.

Contemporary globalization has affected these hierarchies in the same broad ways that have been distinguished above with regard to class, country and gender. In terms of access to global spaces, for example, a number of critics have argued that contemporary capitalism is marked by 'global *apartheid*', where race forms a principal, arbitrary determinant of inclusion and marginalization (Falk, 1993; Mazrui, 1994; Alexander, 1996). Unfortunately, research to date has produced little precise data to demonstrate racial hierarchies in access to global communications, global products, global finance and the like. Nor has a 'race and development indicator' appeared to complement similar statistics (problematic though they may be) for countries and sexes. Nevertheless, studies suggest that African Americans and Latinos have perceived greater threats from globalization to their wages and employment than other racial groups in the USA (Dawson, 1999). Racial stratification has arguably also been manifest when the mainstream mass media continually portrays black Africa as only weak, poor and violent. Substantial anecdotal evidence suggests that people of colour have experienced institutional racism in the hiring and promotion practices of some global organizations.

As for the dominance of the town over the countryside, rural communities have tended to be marginalized in contemporary globalization relative to urban centres. Thus when the NICs have taken advantage of global production and markets to advance 'development', their cities have usually taken the lion's share of the benefits, while much rural poverty has remained relatively untouched. In all countries – North, South and East – global communications, global markets, global finance and global organizations have used metropolitan centres as their primary nodes. It may well be that, as the Unwiring the World Project at the Massachusetts Institute of Technology Media Lab has enthusiastically declared, 'it can now be cheaper to have first-class communications in the rural village than in Manhattan' (MIT, 1999). Yet, in relation to incomes and resources, the cost remains well out of the reach of most of the world's rural people.

Meanwhile global agro-food industries have tended to weaken the often already precarious position of small-scale cultivators across the world. The big corporate players have commanded high technologies, large credit facilities and advanced management techniques that traditional farmers have lacked. True, some smallholders have exploited the opportunities of globalization to their benefit. For example, peasants in the interior of South Sumatra have used radio reports on the BBC world service to determine the optimal moment, in terms of prices, to take their produce to market (Galizia, 1993). Yet such enterprising initiatives have been no match for the sophisticated market intelligence available to global companies. Meanwhile other farmers in the South have used the possibilities of global marketing to supply affluent consumers in the North with speciality crops and off-season fruits and vegetables (Llambi, 1994). However, this practice has dubious ecological rationality and can moreover reduce local food security when the cultivators in question neglect their staple crops and become dependent on (relatively expensive) imports.

In terms of age groups, contemporary globalization has in some ways tended to exclude older generations. For example, many workers over 40 have found it difficult to retool their skills in the face of global economic restructuring. As a result, permanent unemployment has loomed for substantial numbers of middle-aged people, especially in the rust belts of the North and the former centrally planned economies. In addition, many (though by no means all) older persons have found computer technologies daunting, thereby producing a considerable age bias in cyberland.

In contrast, the technologies of globalization have in some ways offered children counterweights in their general subordination to adults. For instance, many young people have acquired more highly developed audio-visual literacy than older generations. Youth have likewise tended to access computers and advanced telecommunications with greater ease than their parents and teachers. In certain cases children have even used global communications to assert an autonomous voice in world politics. For example, the 2B1 Foundation (www.2b1.org) has aimed to give young people across the world some initiative in designing a digital global civilization. For children, then, global communications can offer opportunities of empowerment.

On the other hand, as already seen earlier with respect to class and gender, neoliberal economic restructuring in the face of globalization has often hurt vulnerable social circles. For example, people of colour have constituted a disproportionately high share of low-paid and unemployed workers; thus when 'global competition' has prompted reductions in state welfare entitlements, the pains have often been racially skewed. On the age front, the young and the elderly have been particularly vulnerable during economic restructuring in the East and the South. Indeed, the harmful repercussions for children of the 1980s global debt crisis led the United Nations Children's Fund (UNICEF) to spearhead calls for 'adjustment with a human face' (Cornia *et al.*, 1987–8). More recently, the Asia crisis of the late 1990s brought decreased school attendance and increased child malnutrition in some areas (Brown, 1999).

Meanwhile neoliberal restructuring of agriculture – largely sponsored by the Bretton Woods institutions and the WTO – has had mixed impacts on vulnerable smallholders. On the one hand, the liberalization of agricultural marketing has in some countries like Uganda freed cultivators from inefficient and oppressive state bureaux that previously denied farmers adequate earnings for their cash crops. On the other hand, structural reforms in Mexico have seen the government withdraw a number of crucial supports for poor farmers (Myhre, 1994). More generally, critics have worried that liberalization of agricultural trade through the WTO is favouring the strong corporate market players and making no provision to help millions of 'inefficient' cultivators, especially in the South, to develop new livelihoods.

Fewer doubts exist regarding the benefits of the global human rights regime as an instrument against race and age discriminations. For example, concerted efforts through the United Nations against *apartheid* helped to bring down the racist order in South Africa. Meanwhile the International Convention on the Elimination of All Forms of Racial Discrimination, supported by a Committee on the Elimination of Racial Discrimination (CERD), has since 1969 promoted racial equity in the world generally. Children's entitlements have been included in the global human rights regime through the Convention on the Rights of the Child, adopted by the UN General Assembly in 1989. This Convention, overseen by another Geneva-based committee of experts, obtained ratifications in record time and is now, with over 190 state signatories, 'the most universally embraced human rights instrument in history' (UNICEF, 1998: 21). However, poor resourcing in terms of limited funds and personnel has restricted the enforcement powers of these two treaty regimes.

Global governance agencies have also promoted the position of children in other ways. For example, the UN-sponsored World Summit for Children in September 1990 attracted 71 heads of state and government and agreed several dozen specific targets for improving the lot of children before the turn of the century (UNICEF, 1991: 72–4). Thanks largely to the efforts of UNICEF and the World Health Organization, child immunization coverage in the South increased from 15 per cent in 1980 to 80 per cent in 1990, saving over 12 million lives (UNICEF, 1991: 1, 3, 14). UNICEF has furthermore promoted breast-feeding, basic health and education for children, safe water and sanitation, care and support for mothers, high-quality family planning information and services, and the protection of children from abuse in households, workplaces, city slums and war.

On the whole, however, global policymakers have not had children in their sights. Outside UNICEF, global governance agencies have rarely highlighted the specific needs of young people. It seems telling when a porter at the Marriott Hotel in Manhattan reports that he has never in his many years of employment seen a child lodging among the global managers (Escorcia, 1999). Meanwhile no quarter of transworld governance has attended at length to the distinctive problems of older age groups in globalization.

Transborder social movements have complemented global governance programmes to combat racism and promote child welfare. The Anti-*Apartheid* Movement was an influential civic voice in the struggle for racial equity in South Africa. Transworld campaigns against child labour have also booked some successes. On the other hand, no global advocacy of note has promoted questions of social justice related to the elderly and marginalized rural populations.

Conclusion

As summarized in the Box overleaf, the preceding examination of various forms of social stratification suggests that contemporary globalization has tended in general to perpetuate and sometimes also to accentuate the inequities that result from arbitrary hierarchies of life chances among people. Classes, countries, sexes, races, urban/rural districts and generations have had structurally unequal opportunities to shape the course of globalization, to share in its benefits, and to avoid its pains. Even the organizers of the WEF have conceded that globalization has produced 'winner-take-all situations' where 'those who come out on top win big, and the losers lose even bigger' (Schwab and Smadja, 1996).

Yet these general conclusions require several important qualifications. For one thing, as said at the outset of this chapter, globalization has not been the original cause of these stratifications. Nor has the rise of supraterritoriality been the only circumstance promoting social injustice in contemporary history. Nor have global relations – as a particular kind of social geography – intrinsically discriminated between classes, countries, sexes, races, urban and rural areas, and age groups. Yes, globalization can sustain and even increase social inequity, but such results only emerge *when globalization is managed with policy frameworks that encourage unfair outcomes.*

In short, it is not globalization per se that matters so much as the ways that we handle the trend. As seen in Part II of this book, the growth of supraterritorial spaces has involved new forms of capitalism and new forms of governance. Capitalism has always held potentials both for social progress and for social injustice. The mix of actual results has depended largely on the mode of regulation employed. Contemporary globalization has promoted greater unfairness not because of the new geography itself, but mainly because of the accompanying broad policy shift from welfarism to neoliberalism. The implicit neoliberal assumption that 'free' markets maximize equity as they maximize efficiency is critically flawed. As shown above, most recent indicators suggest that neoliberal preoccupations with competition, productivity and economic growth have had severe equity costs.

To indict neoliberalism is not to advocate a return to old-style welfarism. The new contours of governance consequent upon globalization have rendered that statist approach unsustainable. However, neoliberalism is not the only policy approach available to our globalizing world. The challenge – as elaborated in Chapter 12 – is to formulate and implement workable alternatives.

Inequities of contemporary globalization in summary

Stratified access to global spaces
- concentration of global communications on professional and propertied classes, countries of the North, urban dwellers and younger generations
- increased opportunities for women's employment, albeit often on lower terms and conditions than men
- global money and credit disproportionately available to already privileged circles
- offshore finance facilities effectively reserved to the wealthy
- concentration of global investments in the North and in cities
- predominance in the management of global organizations of middle-aged, white, urban men from the North and propertied classes

Decline of the redistributive state
- retreats from progressive taxation, with consequent widening of class gaps
- reduction in state-supplied social services, with disproportionately harmful effects on children, the elderly, women, people of colour and less advantaged classes
- contraction of ODA under the pressures of 'global competition'

Social hierarchies in global regimes
- many global economic institutions have given at best passing attention to issues of social equity
- the 'free flow of information' principle in global communications has favoured dominant social circles
- the Uruguay Round and the WTO have advantaged North-based interests
- the management of crises in global finance has generally favoured creditors (mostly in the North and usually wealthy) over debtors (mostly in the South and often poor)

Resistance to arbitrary hierarchies through global social movements
- persistent reliance on mainly territorial and national organization has weakened the labour movement in the face of global capital
- transborder NGOs and religious groups have highlighted inequities in North–South relations
- transborder women's networks have promoted awareness of gender justice issues
- transborder human rights movements have advanced causes of racial equity and the protection of children

Chapter 11

Globalization and (Un)Democracy

Main points of this chapter
Globalization and democracy through the state
Democracy in multilayered governance
Democracy through the global marketplace?
Democracy through global communications?
Democracy through global civil society?
Conclusion

Main points of this chapter

- globalization has undermined conventional liberal democracy, with its focus on national self-determination through a territorial state
- devolution to substate agencies in the context of globalization has potential democratizing effects, but these benefits do not flow automatically
- suprastate regimes (both regional and global) have developed substantial democratic deficits
- nonofficial supraterritorial channels (global markets, global communications and global civil society) have sometimes enhanced, but frequently also undermined democracy

---

From the perspective adopted in this book, democracy ranks with human security and social justice as the third main normative concern of social relations. These three conditions can often (though not always) substantially reinforce each other. For example, people who enjoy security arguably have greater possibilities to participate in a working democracy, and democratic governance is likely to promote greater equity. Conversely, shortcomings in respect of human security or social justice have frequently paralleled deficits in democracy.

For as long as globalization has been observed, commentators have reflected on its implications for democracy. Indeed, the term 'globalism' was in its first usage coupled with a purported process of worldwide democratization. Back in the 1940s Reiser and Davies anticipated stark alternative futures of 'global slavery or global freedom'. They urged coming generations 'to build a democratic world order on a planetary scale' (1944: xi, 57). How have actual developments unfolded over the 60 years since then?

To make an assessment of globalization and democracy we need first to clarify the latter term. This is not to suggest that democracy is (any more than security or equity) susceptible to a single and fixed definition. On the contrary, notions of 'rule by the people' have been highly diverse and elastic. Nevertheless, a working definition is required to lend precision and coherence to the present discussion.

Here democracy is understood to prevail when the members of a polity determine – collectively, equally and without arbitrarily imposed constraints – the policies that shape their destinies. In democratic governance, people reach joint decisions using processes that are open to all and free of peremptory exercises of top-down power. In one way or another democratic governance is participatory, consultative, transparent and publicly accountable.

The qualification 'in one way or another' is important. In practice people have devised many different ways to fulfil the general criteria of democracy. No single set of customs and institutions provides a formula for democracy that is relevant and workable in all times and at all places. The manner in which a society conducts democratic governance is historically and culturally contingent. The heart of democracy lies in open, equal, collective decision-taking; however, the ways that these principles are honoured can vary enormously.

Thus democracy as a general condition needs to be distinguished from, for instance, liberal democracy as the currently dominant approach to 'rule by the people'. In the conventional liberal conception, democracy has existed when people are grouped in national states that hold 'free and fair' competitive elections to representative rule-making bodies. Liberal democracies also have multiple political parties, an independent mass media, educated citizens, and the rule of law.

Yet the liberal formula of democracy offers but one model of democracy. This approach might not be suitable – or optimal – in all sociohistorical contexts. Indeed, if pursued in inappropriate circumstances, liberal-democratic practices could, paradoxically, mask and sustain authoritarian conditions.

If democracy is contingent, and if (as seen in Chapter 6) globalization has brought some significant shifts in governance, then it might well follow that conventional liberal conceptions of democracy – centred as they are on the national state – have become inadequate. In the 'commonsense' of the Westphalian international system, democracy would exist when people group themselves as distinct nations living in discrete territories ruled by sovereign states that are subject to popular control. Yet global relations have promoted non-national as well as national communities. Globality has transcended territory and thwarted state sovereignty. As such, globalization has undercut liberal democracy through the state and created the need for supplementary – and in the long run perhaps even wholly different – democratic mechanisms.

Other authors have advanced similar claims. For example, Rob Walker has urged that 'we may ask what democracy could be if not rooted in a territorial community' (1995: 323). Tony McGrew has affirmed that under globalization 'the core principles of liberal democracy . . . are made distinctly problematic' (1997a: 12). Murray Low has noted that, if traditional democratic theory rested on a politics of bounded places, then globalization requires a new vision and mechanisms of democracy that are not organized around areal space (1997: 241–4).

The rest of this chapter elaborates the argument that, while contemporary globalization has encouraged some innovations in democratic practices, on the whole the new geography has to date made governance less democratic. That said, as with the negative security and equity consequences of globalization discussed in the last two chapters, the detrimental effects in regard to democracy have not been inherent to supraterritoriality. Democratic deficits have resulted from the prevailing ways that we have handled globalization. Alternative approaches could be more democratic.

The first section below indicates how contemporary globalization has generally weakened democracy through the state. The second section considers democratic deficits in the substate, regional and transworld realms of post-sovereign governance. The third section queries the neoliberal claim that 'free' global markets promote democracy. The fourth section qualifies the assumption found in many circles (neoliberal, reformist and radical alike) that the spread of global communications has advanced democracy. The fifth section scrutinizes the widespread belief that the growth of global civil society has promoted popular self-government.

Globalization and democracy through the state

Accelerated globalization of recent decades has unfolded in tandem with a notable growth of liberal democracy in many states where it was previously absent. A so-called 'third wave' of democratization has – especially in the late 1980s and early 1990s – engulfed much of Africa, Asia, Latin America and the former Soviet bloc. In 1998 a Freedom House survey found that 117 of the world's 191 countries held regular competitive multiparty elections (Karatnycky, 1999: 114). Thus to many (especially neoliberal) eyes, contemporary globalization has gone hand in hand with democratization.

Several connections can indeed be drawn between supraterritorial relations and the spread of liberal democracy to more states in the late twentieth century. For example, global human rights campaigns and other transborder civic associations pressed (with some effect) for an end to many authoritarian governments, such as communist regimes in Central and Eastern Europe and military regimes in Latin America (Keck and Sikkink, 1998: ch 3). The global mass media gave sympathetic publicity to democracy movements in China, Czechoslovakia, South Africa and elsewhere. Regional and transworld agencies have supplied various forms of democracy support: for instance, civil society development through EU programmes; election monitoring through the UN; and 'good governance' promotion through the Bretton Woods institutions. Indeed, a number of theorists and politicians have suggested that neoliberal policies of economic globalization encourage a democratization of the state (cf. Beetham, 1997).

However, these purported connections between globalization and democratization need to be qualified on at least four important counts. First, globalization has by no means constituted the sole force behind the 'third wave' of democratization. Each transition to multiparty regimes with 'free and fair' elections has drawn vital strength from locally based movements for change. Thus, for instance, local human rights activists played an instrumental role in Argentina's transition to democracy. Likewise, student activists and local NGOs have made indispensable contributions to democratization in Indonesia and Thailand. In contrast, transborder democracy support has accomplished little in countries like Kazakstan where local mobilization for liberal democracy has been weak. In short, global forces have normally only furthered a democratization of the state to the extent that these inputs have fallen on fertile ground in the country concerned.

A second objection to the thesis that globalization has advanced democracy through the state is that many if not most of the newly installed liberal mechanisms have run only skin-deep. In many cases multiparty elections have not led to wider democratic consolidation. Some new constitutions have become paper instruments. Numerous 'independent' political parties and media outlets have become tools of narrow personal ambition and élite privilege. In many of the new 'democracies' civic education has been limited and civil society frail.

Against this backdrop Fareed Zakaria has spoken of widespread 'illiberal democracy' in contemporary politics (Zakaria, 1997). Thomas Carothers has similarly distinguished a large category of 'semi-authoritarian' governments with shaky democratic credentials (Carothers, 1999). William Robinson has described new democracies in the South as 'polyarchies' where a small group dominates the state through tightly controlled electoral processes (Robinson, 1996b).

Indeed, to take up a third point of dissent, some critics have argued that liberal constructions of democracy are inherently deficient. From this perspective globalization would need to promote different kinds of collective self-determination in order to be truly democratizing. Democracy, according to this view, requires more than a multiplicity of political parties, periodic elections to representative state institutions, respect of civil rights, nonpartisan civil and military services, and the rule of law through a scrupulous judiciary. At best, these sceptics say, liberal arrangements can achieve a 'low-intensity democracy' that does little to mobilize the majority and to empower marginalized circles (Gills *et al.*, 1993). Chronic low voter turnouts and widespread cynicism about parties and politicians would seem to reflect these limitations of liberal democracy (IDEA, 1997). Indeed, a survey conducted for the European Commission in 1993 found that a record 55 per cent of voters questioned were unhappy about the workings of democracy in their country (Harvey, 1995: 256). For some social commentators, then, supplementary or alternative means are required to move from a democracy of form to a democracy of substance. On its own, liberal democracy cannot generate levels and types of participation, consultation, transparency and public accountability that constitute a veritable democracy.

Finally, a fourth major qualification to claims that globalization has democratized the state highlights the previously made observation that the state, being territorially grounded, is not sufficient by itself as an agent of democracy in a world where many social relations are substantially supraterritorial. A territorialist framework of democracy cannot adequately cover transborder flows. With globalization, McGrew has rightly noted:

> the ideal of the liberal democratic state as a self-governing, autonomous, 'national community of fate', in which government is conducted in general accordance with popular sovereignty, seems somewhat removed from 'really existing' historical conditions.
>
> (1997a: 13)

If globalization is to spur democratization, then 'rule by the people' has to extend beyond the relationship between the state and its national population.

For one thing, traditional liberal mechanisms have not adequately democratized the state's relations with global agents. As emphasized in Chapter 6, the contemporary state has served not only constituents within its territorial jurisdiction, but also supraterritorial parties such as global companies, global financial markets and global civic associations. National democratic mechanisms pursued through each state in isolation are often not sufficient to bring transborder actors and flows under the popular control of those affected. For example, the States-General in The Hague cannot exercise full democratic governance over Netherlands-based transborder corporations like Philips and Royal Dutch/Shell. Likewise, the globally circulating Japanese yen is not subject to adequate democratic supervision through the Diet in Tokyo alone. Residents of Mexico cannot obtain much democratic regulation of the Internet by voting for members of their national congress.

In addition, the territorial state is not a suitable vehicle – certainly by itself – to provide democracy for the many nonterritorial communities that have grown with globalization. As indicated in Chapter 7, we can no longer assume that the 'demos' in democracy is always a state-nation. Indeed, insofar as democracy through the state is focused in the first place on participation by, consultation of, transparency for, and public account-ability to the nation, other communities may be shortchanged. If states give precedence to a national community, can they always – or even often – provide an adequate framework of self-determination for transborder peoples like homosexuals, nomads or women?

As noted in Chapter 6, contemporary globalization has already begun to produce post-sovereign politics in which local, regional and transworld laws and institutions do not fall wholly under state control. For this reason, too, a democratization process that concentrates only on the state is today inadequate. Multiparty contests to national representative institu-tions are not enough to secure democracy in agencies such as the EU, MERCOSUR, the IMF and the UN. A few states have held national referenda on issues related to suprastate governance, but such practices have been rare. States have in most cases joined regional arrangements without directly consulting their populace, and Switzerland is the only state that has put the question of joining global governance agencies to a popular vote. (In 1992 the Swiss electorate approved membership of the Bretton Woods institutions but rejected membership of the United Nations.) In another striking departure from prevailing practice, the government of Nigeria in 1985 invited a national debate about a proposed structural adjustment programme; however, President Babangida effect-ively ignored the resulting opposition by adopting the IMF/World Bank-sponsored package (Herbst and Olukoshi, 1994: 472–7).

In sum, then, although liberal-democratic practices have proliferated in states across the world in contemporary history, democracy has not become that much stronger for it. Not only does liberal democracy have some inherent limitations, and not only have the advances of liberal democracy been tempered in many countries. In addition, the territorialist, state-centric nature of traditional liberal democracy is inadequate in a world where numerous and significant social relations are supraterritorial. Global democracy needs more than a democratic state.

Democracy in multilayered governance

As elaborated in Chapter 6, regulation occurs in contemporary world politics not only through national governments, but also through local, regional and transworld agencies. In many cases the state remains the most significant arena of governance as we enter the twenty-first century. However, this general rule does not hold equally for all states, in all issue-areas, or on all occasions. Often local, regional and transworld governance mechanisms have acquired a significant degree of autonomy from states. In such situations democratic deficits may arise that cannot be corrected through the state alone. Additional modes of participation, consultation, transparency and accountability are then needed.

In principle the growth of multilayered governance and the accompanying demise of sovereignty could be a hopeful development for democracy. After all, sovereignty entails supreme, unqualified, comprehensive and exclusive power, whereas democracy generally emphasizes decentralization, checks on power, pluralism and participation. By this logic, the retreat of sovereign statehood could encourage an advance of democracy. In practice, however, this promise has been far from realized. Experience to date has taught that decentralized, multilayered governance induced by globalization is not inherently more democratic than national self-development through a sovereign state. Indeed, in many circumstances post-sovereign governance has proved to be decidedly less democratic.

Substate democracy

Devolution of policy competences to substate authorities – encouraged by globalization as described in Chapter 6 – in principle could substantially enhance democracy. Although much of the world's population has in recent decades become involved in all sorts of global networks, that involvement has usually been strongly mediated through the locality where people live. Moreover, the growth of electronic mass media notwithstanding, at present face-to-face activities within local spaces still offer most people in most parts of the world their greatest opportunity for direct involvement in policymaking. Most citizens find local government more accessible, given the smaller scale of the operations and the closer proximity of the offices. Popularly controlled provincial and municipal institutions can normally assess local interests (including in respect of globalization) better than more remote agencies at state and suprastate levels. In this light the current worldwide trend of decentralization from national to provincial and district authorities is welcome.

Yet these benefits do not flow automatically. As Anthony Giddens has emphasized, devolution has to be made democratic (1998: 78). Local officials can be as inaccessible, unsympathetic, secretive, arbitrary and unaccountable as national authorities. A local mafia can hijack a municipal or provincial government as much as a self-serving élite can capture a national state. Devolution has brought greater popular control through the regions in Spain, but it has also brought oppression through many provinces in the Russian Federation. In short, as on so many other points, we must not romanticize the local.

Suprastate democracy: regional regimes

Regional institutions are another layer of governance in our globalizing world where democracy has proved to be problematic. As seen in Chapter 6, scores of regional regulatory schemes have emerged since the middle of the twentieth century, often because it is hoped that these suprastate frameworks can manage global flows more effectively than national governments. Yet regional regimes have usually been approached as technocratic arrangements, with little if any consideration of their democratic credentials. Apart from the Central American Common Market (CACM) and the EU, no regional institutions have had an elected popular assembly. Likewise, MERCOSUR has been exceptional in having a Socioeconomic Advisory Forum through which trade unions and other civic organizations can make representations. Most regional regimes have been utterly opaque to the vast majority of their (notional) citizens. At best, regional agencies have had crude and untested mechanisms of public accountability.

Since the 1990s the undemocratic character of existing regional governance has become an especially prominent issue in relation to the furthest developed regional apparatus, the EU (Raworth, 1994). In response to these growing concerns, the 1992 Treaty on European Union (otherwise known as the Maastricht Treaty) prescribed *inter alia* that:

(a) the European Commission should expand its policy consultations and improve citizen access to information;
(b) the Council of Ministers should open some of its sessions to the public;
(c) the popularly elected European Parliament should have increased competences; and

(d) a Committee of the Regions should be established to give local representatives direct access to the Brussels-based EU administration.

On the other hand, only a few member states of the EU put the Maastricht Treaty itself to a national vote. Meanwhile the European Central Bank and the European Court of Justice have exercised coercive powers with only the slimmest links to elected representatives, let alone to citizens at the grassroots. The decision-taking Council of Ministers has been responsible to no one: not to the Commission; nor to the Parliament; nor (as a collective body) to a multicountry electorate. The European Parliament is still unable to initiate legislation or to block the rule-making directives of the (appointed) Commission. Perhaps not surprisingly, in view of these limited powers, voter turnouts in elections to the European Parliament have been small and declining. Several distinctly European political parties have emerged in recent years, including the European People's Party and the Party of European Socialists. However, these organizations have been run through centralized professional offices, with no direct input from, or accountability to, individual party members and constituency branches.

In short, although democracy has become an openly acknowledged problem in the EU, it has been far from fully addressed. Meanwhile few other regional governance arrangements have put democracy on their agenda at all. If – as some commentators predict and/or advocate – regionalism is the road for effective governance in a global world, then – on current performance – the prospects for democracy look bleak.

Suprastate democracy: transworld regimes

In the event, governance under globalization has involved major transworld regimes alongside regional regulation. Yet, if anything, democratic deficits in global governance agencies have been even larger than those that have afflicted regional institutions. For example, 'democracy' in the UN system has generally meant little more than the crude and dubious principle of a formal equality of states. On this basis China and Vanuatu have enjoyed equal votes in the General Assembly, even though the former has a population more than 6,000 times larger than the latter. In addition, the veto power of the permanent members of the UN Security Council has no democratic justification whatsoever. At the Bretton Woods institutions, quota-based weightings have given one-quarter of the member-states control of three-quarters of the votes. As noted in Chapter 6, states can only overturn rulings of the WTO by unanimity. Meanwhile the vast majority of states have been excluded from the G7 and the OECD, even though decisions taken in these forums have worldwide effects.

It is in any case questionable whether global governance institutions can achieve an adequate level of democracy by operating with states alone. Many states have had at best shaky democratic credentials, even by liberal standards. Nor have transworld regulatory agencies related only with states. They have also dealt directly with regional institutions, substate authorities, firms, civic groups and private individuals – in some situations even more so than with states. If transworld bodies like the UNHCR or the World Bank have acquired some degree of autonomy from their state clients, then supplementary nongovernmental checks on global governance are needed to ensure democracy.

Nonstate actors have indeed begun to participate more in global policymaking. Large civil society forums have accompanied the G7 Summits, special UN gatherings, the IMF/World Bank Annual Meetings and the WTO Ministerial Conferences. Agencies like UNICEF, UNDP and the multilateral development banks have increasingly interacted with nongovernmental stakeholders about the preparation, execution and evaluation of projects and programmes. The IMF has developed considerable links with business groups, think tanks and (to a lesser degree) trade unions in the formulation and monitoring of the macroeconomic policy packages that it sponsors (Scholte, 2000c). In 1998 grassroots opposition played a notable part in blocking progress towards a Multilateral Agreement on Investment through the OECD (Kobrin, 1998; Smith and Smythe, 2000). Having had its fingers badly burnt on this occasion, the OECD has subsequently expanded its outreach activities to civil society.

However, the degree of popular participation and consultation in transworld governance must not be exaggerated. The overall level of involvement (let alone influence) of nonstate actors in suprastate policymaking has remained low. The UN Charter's slogan of 'we the people of the world' still only thinly disguises a reality of 'we the bureaucrats of the world'. Moreover – as is elaborated later in this chapter – the democratic credentials of nonstate actors like companies and civil society bodies have often been weak.

Meanwhile the alternative of directly elected representative bodies for transworld institutions seems quite unworkable for the time being. The planetary electorate is even less developed than its regional counterparts. Indeed, hundreds of millions of people have never even heard of transworld organizations like the IMF and the OECD, let alone understand their mandates and *modus operandi*. In addition, global political parties like the Liberal and Socialist Internationals are not equipped to pursue intercontinental electoral campaigns. On the technical side, too, we lack the means effectively to conduct planetary ballots. Nor is an agreed formula available for representation on a world scale. Political cultures are highly diverse across the continents, and in present circumstances most people would not accept the principle of one person, one vote in respect of world parliaments attached to institutions such as the UN and the WTO.

To their credit, many transworld governance agencies have become more transparent to the public in recent years. The operations of UN agencies and various multilateral trade and financial institutions are now considerably more visible and comprehensible to citizens than they were before the 1990s. Most of the organizations have constructed elaborate websites and have greatly expanded their production of user-friendly public relations materials like press releases, newsletters, reports, pamphlets and audio-visual productions. Transworld agencies have also made many more official documents publicly available, thereby helping citizens to make informed contributions to policy debates. For instance, the World Bank opened a Public Information Centre in 1993, and the WTO has made some of its archives directly accessible via the Internet. In contrast to the decades before 1990, most transworld governance bodies now publish at least a partial staff list, including contact details.

This is not to say that transworld regulation has become fully transparent. For example, as of the mid-1990s advance appointments were required before a common citizen could reach the 'public' information centre of the United Nations Office at Vienna. Only limited details have been publicly disclosed about the proceedings of the IMF and World Bank Boards, the UN Security Council, the G7, the BIS Board of Directors and the OECD Council. Many of the official documents released by these agencies are opaque for the uninitiated. Moreover, the institutions have often disclosed the material only *after* the related decisions have been taken, thereby limiting opportunities for citizens to influence the policy process. Even when substantial information has been available, the mainstream news media have usually provided scant coverage of the work of transworld regulatory institutions. Meanwhile few school curricula anywhere in the world have incorporated even elementary coverage of global governance, thereby leaving new generations of citizens ill-equipped to exercise democratic control over these suprastate regimes.

Transworld governance agencies have indeed largely escaped public accountability. True, some measure of indirect popular control has been available insofar as states (assuming that their governments are democratic) can withhold funds from the operating budgets of global institutions. However, such a stick is a crude instrument. More is needed in the way of open, outside, independent, published assessments of the policy performance of global governance bodies. Early steps in this direction include the work of the Operations Evaluation Department and the Inspection Panel at the World Bank, both formed in the early 1990s.

Similarly, the IMF has since 1997 arranged several external reviews of its activities. However, the scale of these accountability exercises has remained modest, and the resultant recommendations have been relatively tame. Meanwhile programmes of the various United Nations organs have rarely been subjected to systematic public scrutiny (Falk and Mogami, 1993).

In short, although transworld agencies have readily preached democracy to others, they have inadequately applied the strictures to themselves. Global institutions have tended to present themselves as objective and apolitical technocracies where 'experts' may reign without public interventions. At the UN a former Secretary-General discussed 'democracy as good governance' at some length in 1995, but devoted only five short lines of platitudes to the application of democratic principles to his own organization (Boutros-Ghali, 1995a: 48). All too often discussions of democratic reform of the UN have become mired in stale debates about revising the membership of the Security Council. Far more imaginative ideas are available, like Erskine Childers' proposal to create a UN Council on Culture, Representation and Governance, which would give debates about democracy a specific and institutionalized place within the organization (Childers, 1994: 16). However, such visions have tended to flow into file cabinets rather than public discussions.

Taking the above considerations in sum, the democratic record of suprastate regulatory agencies has been decidedly poor. On the whole regional and transworld regimes have proved to be little more accessible, representative and accountable than colonial empires in a previous era of (territorialist) world politics. To date the 'global demos' has shown comparatively little resistance to this disenfranchisement. However, various social movements have already expressed discontent with this situation, as in the so-called 'Battle of Seattle' against the WTO in late 1999. Such opposition seems likely to grow sooner than subside.

Democracy through the global marketplace?

Thus far this chapter has discussed democratic mechanisms in the public sector, across substate, state and suprastate levels. Yet rule by the people may, in principle, also be achieved (either partly or wholly) through nonofficial channels. Indeed, a number of commentators have championed markets, private communications networks and/or civil society as nongovernmental instruments of supraterritorial democracy. These notions that the popular will can be realized outside public governance have some merits; however, they also require substantial qualification.

In one variant of these arguments, some neoliberals have celebrated a contemporary spread of market democracy through globalization (as liberalization). In this conception, rule by the people is advanced through customer choice in free markets. Consumers and shareholders (rather than citizens) vote with their pocketbooks and savings (rather than their ballots) for producers (rather than governments) that provide the highest returns (rather than the greatest human betterment) in a global market (rather than a territorial state). In this reconstruction of democracy, sovereignty is purportedly relocated from the state to the market player. As the cliché would have it, 'the customer is king'. While state-centric democracy focuses on citizen rights and responsibilities, market-based democracy concentrates on product quality and rates of return to maximize collective human happiness. Even the state is 'sold' to the public as an entertainment commodity through lotteries, game-show elections, war performances, and other televised spectacles.

Admittedly the preceding remarks caricature the neoliberal position, which can be treated more seriously. Consumer power is arguably one way to express a democratic will. Indeed, carefully considered collective market choices have sometimes furthered human security and social equity in striking ways. For example, customers have sustained a number of 'fair trade' schemes for small-scale producers in the South. Public boycotts of commerical dealings with South Africa put pressure for reform on the *apartheid* regime. Consumer movements have likewise encouraged several global companies like Mattel and Nike to improve the conditions of their workers in the South. Some private investors have insisted that their capital only be placed with 'ethical' and 'socially responsible' firms.

Nevertheless, 'consumer choice' presents some insurmountable difficulties as a foundation for democracy. After all, people need assets in order to make choices and demand accountability through the marketplace. Yet the distribution of resources in markets has always been highly uneven, both within and between countries. Most of the world's population has thereby gained only limited possibilities to participate as consumers in global markets. Indeed, poverty has disenfranchised hundreds of millions of people altogether in this would-be democratic arena.

The notion of global shareholder democracy is, if anything, even more problematic. To begin with, wealth hurdles have excluded even more people from securities markets than from consumer capitalism. Shareholders have usually represented private and privileged interests rather than the demos at large; nor have investors been in any way formally and directly accountable to popular constituencies. Shareholders are not the same as stakeholders. The latter category also includes customers, employees, suppliers and the local communities around corporate facilities.

Furthermore, private individuals have exerted little influence in contemporary corporate governance. The only shareholders with any clout have been large investment trusts, pension funds and insurance companies who usually have little contact with the everyday lives of the general population. Moreover, in practice managers have often had more say than investors in running markets. Most investors cannot fathom the limited and readily distorted information that management provides them. Annual general meetings of shareholders have tended only to rubberstamp the recommendations of the boardroom. Company directors have generally been anonymous to the average citizen, self-selecting, and largely unresponsive to outside criticism.

Given this limited participation, visibility and accountability in corporate governance, the growing concentration of capital described in Chapter 5 has presented a major problem for democracy. To be sure, transborder companies have been to some extent constrained by public-sector regulation: mainly through local and national governments; and occasionally also through certain regional and transworld measures. In addition, some large corporations have undergone significant decentralization, adopting 'federal' structures in which lower levels of management have acquired greater autonomy from the executive board (Handy, 1992). However, it is questionable whether such internal and external constraints on corporate power have been sufficiently strong to ensure that global firms respect the general will, particularly in those parts of the world where states and civil societies are weak.

Meanwhile global financial markets have often acted as police, judge and jury in the world economy. A former head of Citicorp has enthused that currency traders in front of 200,000 monitors across the planet daily conduct 'a kind of global plebiscite' on the monetary and fiscal policies of governments (Brecher and Costello, 1994: 30). Yet such a 'vote' has been anything but democratic. Contemporary governance of global finance has shown highly restricted participation, no noteworthy public consultation, major shortfalls in transparency, and extremely limited public accountability mechanisms. Only the thinnest of supraterritorial democratic frameworks have been available when global finance wreaked havoc in the 1980s debt crisis, the 1992–3 devaluations in the European exchange-rate mechanism (ERM), the 1994–5 peso crisis and attendant tequila effect in Latin America, the Asia crisis of 1997–8, and so on. The afflicted poor in Zambia, workers in Britain, farmers in Mexico and women in Thailand have found little voice or redress through existent regulators like the IMF, bond-rating agencies and the London Club of bankers.

At best, therefore, global market mechanisms have only offered a supplementary input to democratic governance. More often, highly skewed distributions of world resources and tightly controlled access to corporate policymaking have marginalized most of the global demos. In the main, global markets have seen power concentrated in what Robert Cox has evocatively called the *nébuleuse*, a process of élite networking that governs largely behind the scenes and free of public accountability (Cox, 1992). No conspiracy theory is necessary to find weak democratic credentials in corporate conclaves like the WEF and private sector regulatory bodies like the ISMA.

But then markets have historically never operated democratically on their own. Market activities have not involved deliberate *collective* decisions arrived at with *equal* opportunities for all to participate in *open* deliberations. Instead, market relations have only begun to fulfil democratic criteria when a public sector and/or a civil society have promoted a level playing field and demanded accountability of the market to all stakeholders. There is no reason why global markets would be different in this regard.

Democracy through global communications?

Whereas champions of global market democracy have resided chiefly in neoliberal circles, a number of reformists and radicals have joined neoliberals in celebrating the growth of global communications as a purported boon for democracy (Rheingold, 1993; Waterman, 1998). According to these arguments, radio and television (especially interactive programmes) and the Internet provide a valuable supplement to public-sector democracy mechanisms. Indeed, some proponents have gone further to suggest that private electronic networks could partly or even wholly replace official institutions as the means to democratic governance. However, this enthusiasm for electronic democracy needs to be tempered on several grounds.

Global communications have certainly served democratic projects on many occasions. For example, in the wired world of 1989, media images of Tienanmen Square, the triumph of Solidarity in Poland, and the breached Berlin Wall spread to spark mutually reinforcing mass uprisings throughout Central and Eastern Europe and beyond (Boden, 1990; A. Jones, 1994). These and other popular movements have also used the Internet to gain unprecedented levels of information, new channels for discussion, and opportunities to reach many more potential supporters. Electronic bulletin boards, video teleconferences and interactive television have shown important possibilities of enhancing communication among citizens. Supraterritorial networks have often offered the general population closer access to policymaking than was available in the days of print communications.

Some technological utopians (including several cited in Chapter 1) have extrapolated from these recent trends to forecast a future electronic democracy that will fulfil potentials that territorial democracy could never realize. On these accounts 'netizens' in a 'virtual polis' would enjoy far higher degrees of participation, consultation, transparency and public accountability than old-style citizens could obtain *vis-à-vis* the state. Indeed, in a 'push-button democracy' of electronic referenda, people could in principle have an instant input to any policy deliberation.

Yet the politics of global communications are not as benign as that. To begin with we have the dogged problem of access. Basic radio and television sets have spread to hundreds of millions of people across the world, but hundreds of millions more still fall outside these networks. Even by the most optimistic projections it will be at least several generations before most of the world's population can access digital interactive television. Meanwhile only a minority of people – for the most part socially privileged – have fax machines or Internet connections. A computer costs the average Bangladeshi eight years' wages, whereas the average American can purchase the equipment with one month's income (UNDP, 1999: 6). In short, the demos in global communications networks has been – and for the time being will remain – small and unrepresentative.

Even if universal access to global communications were to be achieved, we could still query the democratic credentials of the resultant electronic governance. After all, television is prone to demagogic manipulation, and CD-ROMs can serve a police state as well as its opposition. Computers and electronic mass media can paralyse citizens with information overload (Schenk, 1997). Or they can anaesthetize people with a surfeit of self-indulgent entertainment. Television in particular can oversimplify issues and replace debate with performance. What depth of participation would be achieved when couch potatoes vote in push-button referenda? As Benjamin Barber has noted, 'Home voting via interactive television could further privatize politics and replace deliberative debate in public with the unconsidered instant expressions of private prejudices' (1996: 270). With broadly similar concerns, Jean-Marie Guéhenno has described the 'networked world' as one with 'freedoms and no democracy', where we have liberty without purpose and lack the aspiration to form a body politic (1995: 122–4). Indeed, global communications technologies have often tended to atomize individuals rather than deepen social bonds. What kind of collective self-determination takes place on an aeroplane where each passenger watches a private video screen and ignores even the persons seated to either side?

Finally, celebrations of electronic democracy warrant a guarded reception so long as the networks in question lie largely in private hands – and highly concentrated ownership at that. Global communications have not grown in the first instance as a democratic project, but as a lucrative form of supraterritorial capitalism. So long as telecommunications and the mass media are organized as a 'free market', it is likely that democracy will take second place to accumulation. Global communications are thus subject to the same limits on democracy that affect any 'open' global market.

Democracy through global civil society?

Having found major democratic deficits in public agencies and the market, perhaps we can find a solution for collective, equal, open governance of our globalizing world in civil society. Many advocates of progressive social change have indeed championed the 'third sector' as an arena of virtue that overcomes domination in government and exploitation in the market (Korten, 1990; Falk, 1995). Again, however, we must treat every easy formula for global democracy with caution.

First we need to define terms. The phrase 'civil society' has meant many different things over time and, like 'globalization', has often been used loosely and inconsistently in contemporary political analysis (Scholte, 2000b). For present purposes we can take 'civil society' to refer to activities by voluntary associations to shape policies, norms and/or deeper social structures. Civil society is therefore distinct from both official and commercial circles, though the lines can sometimes become blurred (for example, in a government-organized NGO or in a business lobby on social issues). Other civil society groups include academic institutes, community-based organisations, consumer protection bodies, criminal syndicates, development cooperation groups, environmental campaigns, ethnic lobbies, charitable foundations, farmers' groups, human rights advocates, labour unions, relief organisations, peace activists, professional bodies, religious institutions, women's networks, youth campaigns and more. Much of civil society is formally constituted and officially registered, but many other civic activities (especially at the grassroots) are ad hoc and informal.

Talk of *global* civil society began to spread in the 1990s (Falk, 1992b; Lipschutz, 1992; Drainville, 1998). Commentators have spoken in related veins of 'international non-governmental organisations', 'transnational advocacy networks', 'global social movements', a 'new multilateralism', and so on (Ghils, 1992; Smith *et al.*, 1997; Keck and Sikkink, 1998; Schechter, 1999b). Broadly we can consider civil society to be global when it manifests one or more of the following four features. First, global civil society may address supraterritorial issues like transworld ecological change or transborder capitalism. Second, global civic networks may use supraterritorial communications like e-mail and fax. Third, global civic activity may have a transborder organization, with coordinated branches spread across the planet. Fourth, global civil society may operate on a premise of supraterritorial solidarity, for example, between women or workers. Often these four attributes have gone hand in hand, but not in all cases. For example, some local human rights groups have been part of a global civic movement on the first and fourth criteria, even though they have not been tightly networked through supraterritorial communications and organization.

Many people have indeed found significant empowerment through global civil society (Edwards and Gaventa, forthcoming). For example, supraterritorial associations have often allowed youth, disabled persons, lesbians and gay men, and indigenous peoples to gain voice in ways and extents that have often been unavailable to them in territorial politics. In addition, some global civic activities (for example, many women's associations) have provided encouraging examples of non-hierarchical, non-authoritarian, non-violent, highly participatory politics. Environmental movements, consumer groups and human rights advocates have often contributed valuable civic education about their issues of concern. NGOs have repeatedly called official agencies to account when development projects have harmed local communities (Fox and Brown, 1998). Several foundations with global operations (e.g. Ford, MacArthur, Soros) have provided resources to support grassroots democracy in dozens of countries.

Civil society activities have also frequently enhanced democracy in globalization by stimulating debate. Democratic governance rests *inter alia* on vigorous, uninhibited discussion of diverse perspectives. Many (though by no means all) transborder civic groups have challenged established agendas, methodologies, explanations and prescriptions regarding globalization. Such pressures can help to keep official thinking rigorous and dynamic – which in turn tends to make policies more effective. Indeed, critiques from a number of civil society circles have played an important part in highlighting the shortcomings of neoliberal policies toward globalization.

More generally, civil society activities can contribute to a democratic legitimation of the governance of globalization. Authority is legitimate when stakeholders feel that governors have a right to govern over them and that they, as citizens, have a duty to submit to the established rules. There has been limited legitimacy in the governance of globalization to date. Most people have accepted most policies toward global relations with passivity, ignorance and resignation. Yet if civil society offers stakeholders civic education, opportunities to speak, and chances to debate options, then people can begin to feel that they 'own' global politics and positively endorse its outputs. Such legitimacy not only renders governance more democratic; it also tends to make policies more viable. Thus, for example, a global trade regime that is legitimated through civil society would have better chances of achieving its aims than a regime that is produced solely by technocrats.

However, the legitimating potentials of global civil society have generally remained underdeveloped to date. For one thing, substantial parts of the world (like the Middle East and countries of the former Soviet Union) have had little inputs to policies on globalization from voluntary associations. Even where global civic activism has grown on a greater scale, it has in many cases generated only modest contributions to civic education, stakeholder representation and policy debate. Much of the promise of global civil society is therefore as yet unproven.

Moreover, global civic associations have no grounds to be complacent about their own democratic credentials. On the contrary, in practice these groups have all too often given insufficient attention to questions concerning the depth of participation that they allow their constituents. In addition, civil society organizations have frequently lacked adequate consultation mechanisms, transparency and public accountability. A civic movement can be run with top-down managerial authoritarianism just as well as a government department or a firm. Indeed, groups in 'uncivil society' such as transborder mafia and neofascist associations have deliberately opposed democratic practices. Even some civic organizations that have pressed hardest for a democratization of global relations have shown substantial democratic failings in their own practices.

Only a small proportion of the world's population has thus far become actively involved in global civil society. Most people have had little participation in the policymaking processes of transborder business associations, NGOs, professional networks, religious agencies and trade unions. Even where individuals have had membership in such a group, they have often made no input to its activities beyond the payment of an annual subscription. Larger publics have tended to mobilize behind a civic campaign only on a short-term and ad hoc basis, for example, in response to calls for humanitarian relief. For the rest, global civil society has mostly been the preserve of relatively small numbers of full-time activists.

Although these civil society professionals have generally held good intentions in respect of democracy, they have not on the whole been particularly representative of the world demos. Global civic activity has occurred disproportionately among white, Northern, university-educated, computer-literate, propertied persons. Fewer than 15 per cent of the NGOs accredited to engage with the United Nations (as of the mid-1990s) were based in the South (Carlsson *et al.*, 1995: 153). Moreover, many purportedly 'grassroots' civic associations in poorer regions of the world have been branches of North-based organizations and/or have drawn their memberships chiefly from local élites in the South. To cite one illustrative example, as of July 1995 the Office of the General Secretary of the Unrepresented Nations and Peoples Organization included only one person from the indigenous groups that the agency purportedly represents. On the whole the world's underclasses have lacked the funds, language fluency (or translation facilities), and organizational capacities required for effective participation in global civil society.

Professionalized global civic associations have also tended to undertake limited consultation of their purported constituents. Many civic lobbyists who claim to speak for the grassroots have rarely ventured into the field. In 1995 the International Planned Parenthood Federation, in preparation for the Fourth World Conference of Women, required each of its more than 140 member associations to ask 180 women from all walks of life what change would most improve their lives. Yet such large-scale and carefully designed consultation exercises have been rare in supraterritorial civil society.

Global civic associations have developed other democratic deficits in respect of transparency. Transborder criminal syndicates are far from the only elements of global civil society that have obscured their operations from public view. Many legal business associations, community groups, labour movements, NGOs, religious bodies and think tanks have not made clear who they are, what objectives they pursue, where their funds originate, how they reach their policy positions, etc. Many civic groups have not issued annual reports of their activities, or have not made them readily available to the public.

Likewise, global civic associations can have a poor record of public accountability. Many have not registered with the state in the countries where they operate. (That said, in the case of some governments official recognition would tend to detract from a civic association's democratic credentials.) Most global civic groups have not held regular, independently monitored elections of their officers. Nor have these associations usually conducted and published external evaluations of their activities. All too often the staff of transborder civic organizations have been responsible only to a largely self-selected board of trustees, to private funders (some of them anonymous) and/or to official donors who have little contact with clients.

Fortunately, some civic organizers have become aware of and disturbed by the democratic shortcomings of much global civil society (Edwards, 1999). Critical voices within civic movements have demanded more social responsibility from business associations, an end to cronyism in trade unions, more 'dialogue' and 'partnership' between South-based and North-based NGOs, and greater voice in all civil society sectors for marginalized social groups. However, it is too early to say whether this promising rhetoric will bring substantial long-term democratic change in global civil society.

Conclusion

As summarized in the Box below, democracy has faced difficult times with the rise of supraterritoriality. Not only have most states had shaky democratic credentials, but in addition contemporary large-scale globalization has rendered old formulas of state-centric democracy inadequate.

To be sure, the emergence of post-sovereign governance along the lines described in Chapter 6 has encouraged some welcome innovations in democratic practice. Several political theorists have begun to explore alternative concepts of democracy (Connolly, 1991; Falk, 1995; Held, 1995a; Gill, 1997; Gilbert, 1999). In addition, innovative politicians and

---

Globalization and (un)democracy in summary

State
- transborder civic campaigns, global mass media and suprastate governance agencies have promoted democratization in some states

but
- state relations with global actors and flows have often escaped sufficient democratic controls
- statist constructions of democracy are inadequate for post-sovereign politics

Multilayered governance
- the diffusion of regulatory activity, as encouraged by globalization, can enhance democracy by decentralizing power

but
- devolution to substate authorities is not automatically democratizing
- suprastate regimes have so far shown weak democratic credentials

Unofficial channels
- globalization has opened greater space for democratic activity outside public governance institutions

but
- 'consumer democracy' through global markets has in practice allocated voice in proportion to assets
- 'shareholder democracy' through global companies has in practice concentrated voice in boardrooms and large investment funds
- 'network democracy' through global communications has in practice excluded most of the world's people
- 'civic democracy' through global civil society has in practice shown many shortfalls in participation, consultation, transparency and public accountability

---

social activists have experimented with different approaches, including devolution, the development of global communications for democratic purposes, and the expansion of global civil society.

However, the gains to democracy from these activities have remained relatively modest. We are still far from having clear and specific notions of how post-territorialist democracy could operate. On the whole the growth of global governance, global markets, global communications and global civil society have sooner detracted from than furthered popular collective self-determination in contemporary history.

This unhappy balance sheet is not predetermined and unchangeable, of course. Claude Ake and others have had reason to link globalization as it has unfolded so far with 'a politics of disempowerment' (1999: 182). However, global spaces are not inherently undemocratic. Many of the initiatives mentioned in this chapter indicate that globalization and democratization can be complementary. The future requires not a reversal of globalization, but a concerted search for new concepts and practices that can make democracy work in post-territorialist, post-sovereign politics.

Chapter 12

Humane Global Futures

Main points of this chapter
General policy strategy
Enhancing human security
Enhancing social justice
Enhancing democracy
Challenges of implementation
Conclusion

Main points of this chapter

- a strategy of ambitious reform offers the most promising way forward in respect of contemporary globalization
- various specific initiatives (especially from global public policy) can improve the outcomes of globalization in regard to human security, social equity and democracy
- implementation of these measures faces substantial but surmountable political hurdles

---

In compiling a normative assessment of contemporary globalization, the preceding chapters have consistently advanced a twofold general argument. First, globalization has to date had mixed consequences for human security, social justice and democracy – including some significant negative repercussions. Second, the downsides have resulted not from supraterritoriality as such, but from the policy orientations (mainly neoliberal) that have prevailed in respect of growing global relations during the late twentieth century. By implication, then, changes in policy approaches (in particular away from neoliberalism) could produce greater security, equity and democracy. (Other authors who have developed such arguments include Brecher and Costello, 1994; Amin, 1997: ch 1; Falk, 1999; Mittelman, 2000; Nederveen Pieterse, 2000.)

Yet what, more specifically, should that different policy course be? How can we best, as James Mittelman has put it, 'rewrite the script of globalization' (1999: 15)? It is one thing to diagnose ills and quite another to prescribe suitable treatments. Moreover, it is one thing to advance attractive proposals and another thing to get them implemented. These policy concerns are the subject of this final chapter.

In elaborating a strategy for more humane globalization, the chapter in its first section discusses several possible general policy courses that could be taken and then identifies and justifies the broad approach adopted here. This strategy, characterized as 'ambitious' or 'thick' reformism, is contrasted with neoliberal, mildly reformist, and radical perspectives. Subsequent sections of the chapter then describe various specific measures that can be taken within a general framework of ambitious reformism to enhance human security, social equity and democracy in globalization. The final section of the chapter considers the political challenges that face the implementation of an ambitious reform agenda with respect to globalization.

General policy strategy

In considering the future of globalization we do well first to formulate a general policy position. There is otherwise a danger that we pursue any number and type of specific policy initiatives, without a vision of overall and long-term objectives. The following paragraphs first survey a spectrum of possible general policy orientations toward globalization. Ambitious reformism is then identified and justified as a preferred strategy. The scene is thereby set for the discussion in later sections of particular policy measures.

Broad options

As noted in Chapter 1, three broad policy approaches toward globalization can be distinguished, namely, neoliberalism, reformism and radicalism. To be sure, this threefold distinction is overly neat. Each of the categories encompasses a range of versions from the mild to the uncompromising, and the dividing lines between the three can blur in practice. The simplified schema is employed here for analytical purposes rather than to provide precise pigeonholes into which each policy and commentator on globalization can be smoothly slotted. The broad distinction between neoliberalism, reformism and radicalism is useful as a way to stress: (a) that a wide range of policy courses can be pursued *vis-à-vis* globalization; and (b) that we face a key political choice between supporting the prevailing orthodoxy, or pursuing a programme of incremental change, or adopting a strategy of transformative change.

Neoliberal approaches to globalization have (as indicated in Chapter 1) prescribed three general policies: liberalization of cross-border transactions; deregulation of market dynamics; and privatization of both asset ownership and the provision of social services. In contrast to social democrats, neoliberals have advocated a reduced role for public policy in shaping the course of globalization. In a neoliberal strategy, official authorities create an enabling environment for markets and then let the private sector supply the social good with (according to theory) maximum efficiency.

Reformist programmes reject neoliberalism's market-centred orientation to globalization. Instead, these approaches seek to generate greater security, equity and democracy by means of proactive public policies. Such regulatory measures are pursued not only (as in past social-democratic politics) through state and substate laws and institutions. In addition, reformism when applied to globalization puts major store in suprastate policy mechanisms.

Reformist policies can involve far-reaching redirections of and limitations on markets; however, these strategies do not challenge the existing deeper social order. Thus, in terms of the primary structures highlighted in this book, reformist approaches work *within* the bounds of capitalist production, bureaucratic governance, communitarian community and rationalist knowledge. In this sense reformism pursues moderate change rather than full-scale social transformation.

In contrast to reformism, radical perspectives on globalization reject not only neoliberal policies, but also the underlying social structures that have shaped transworld relations to date. For radicals, even the best of reformist programmes cannot allow supraterritorial relations to deliver adequate security, equity and democracy, since the ills of globalization have deeper roots in primary social structures. Having made this diagnosis, radical strategies prescribe a transformation of the overall social order. Some radicals are reactive (seeking to undo globalization), while others are proactive (seeking to take globalization further on a different structural basis).

As already suggested, the threefold distinction just made between neoliberalism, reformism and radicalism must not be reified. Actual politics toward globalization have been considerably more complex, often involving a mix of several tendencies. Thus some political orientations (for instance, that of the Clinton Administration in the USA) have shown a blend of neoliberal and reformist elements. Meanwhile a number of trade unions and NGOs have straddled reformism and radicalism in their approach to globalization. Indeed, steps that have reformist implications in the short term may contribute to transformative processes in the long run.

Ambitious reformism

Likewise, the broad policy approach to globalization developed in this chapter also exhibits some mixed tendencies. The primary thrust is reformist, with an emphasis on proactive public-sector steering of globalization. However, the strategy promoted here also includes some secondary radical traits, for example, in urging fundamentally new forms of identity politics. In addition, the approach manifests traces of neoliberalism, for instance, in supporting a role for the business sector and voluntary associations in the provision of social guarantees.

Four attributes give the policy approach advocated here a reformist, social-democratic core. First, it rejects neoliberalism as a general orientation to globalization. Second, it looks to public policies – including global public policies in particular – as the principal means to assure positive outcomes of globalization. Third, it accepts and positively supports a further expansion of supraterritorial relations. Fourth, the perspective taken does not on the whole significantly challenge existing primary social structures like capitalist production or rationalist knowledge.

On three additional grounds the approach promoted here can suitably be characterized as *ambitiously* or *thickly* reformist. First, many of the public policies advanced involve major manipulations of and restrictions on market dynamics. In other words, the motivating vision is one of veritable global social democracy and not merely one of neoliberal globalization with the addition of social safety nets. Second, the strategy elaborated here pushes a number of reforms of globalization (for example, the abolition of offshore finance centres) that lie at the outer margins of what is politically practicable in current circumstances. Third, the policy course promoted here is meant to increase opportunities for the development of alternatives to established social structures. In other words, the sorts of reforms advanced below could have transformative effects in the long run.

Against neoliberalism

Why is ambitious reformism preferable to neoliberalism as a way to construct humane global futures? As preceding chapters have indicated, neoliberal policies have encouraged some important productivity gains and some spread of state-level representative democracy. However, it is by no means clear that *laissez-faire* is the only, or the most effective, way to provide for human security and democracy. Moreover, neoliberal strategies minimize deliberate measures to reduce inequities that result from arbitrary social hierarchies.

Indeed, as earlier chapters have extensively shown, neoliberal approaches to globalization can do considerable harm. 'Free markets' in supraterritorial spaces have often perpetuated or deepened ecological degradation, poverty, labour abuses, xenophobia, class and country hierarchies, democratic deficits, and other violences. Thus governance arrangements need not only to enable global capitalism, but also to harness it to serve the vulnerable as well as the advantaged.

True, neoliberalism promises prosperity for all in the long run. Wealth will 'trickle down', neoliberals assure us, after a period of painful adjustment to new global realities. However, it is disconcerting that neoliberalism's delivery date for the poor and the weak seems always to lie in the future. Thus far neoliberal policies have often exacerbated rather than alleviated subordination and pain.

In these circumstances, neoliberal discourse has sometimes appeared to be an ideology of the powerful that obscures – and in this way helps to sustain – the sufferings of the vulnerable. Indeed, is it accidental that neoliberal accounts of globalization have mainly emanated from dominant social circles and countries? This observation is not meant to suggest that proponents of neoliberalism have held a conscious objective of harming large parts of humanity. On the contrary, many committed neoliberals have in all sincerity believed that their prescriptions advance the construction of a good society. Yet, however laudable the intentions of individual neoliberals might be, this approach to globalization has in practice mostly served the interests of the privileged and all too often undermined the position of the weak.

A redirection of globalization away from neoliberal policies is therefore desirable. It is also possible. We have not, as Francis Fukuyama claimed at the dawn of the post-Cold War world, reached 'the end of history', where no alternatives to neoliberal orthodoxy are viable (Fukuyama, 1992). On the contrary, substantial possibilities exist to develop both policy tools and political constituencies to pursue different courses of globalization.

Against radicalism

However, such tools and constituencies are not available on an adequate scale in respect of fully-fledged radical strategies toward globalization. As indicated in Chapter 1, these orientations encompass both reactive and proactive positions. On the reactive side, traditionalist strains of radicalism reject globalization altogether and advocate a return to territorialist conditions. Among the proactive perspectives, global socialism aims to construct post-capitalist conditions of production in and through supraterritorial relations. Another stream of proactive radicalism, global postmodernism, seeks to use the new geography to create post-communitarian solidarities between people and post-rationalist structures of knowledge. In addition, proactive radicals could pursue an anarchistic vision where globalization would continue on a basis of non-bureaucratic governance. However, none of these strategies of wholesale social transformation is practicable in today's circumstances.

For example, traditionalist approaches to globalization are neither desirable nor viable. To be sure, critiques of contemporary globalization by economic nationalists, religious revivalists and many radical environmentalists have rightly stressed various destructive effects of contemporary globalization. Moreover, these reactions against the new geography have reflected understandable anxieties that most people feel in some measure when they are confronted with difference and change.

However, proponents of traditionalist policies tend to forget the many benefits of globalization that would be lost if the trend were reversed. As earlier chapters have indicated, the rise of supraterritoriality has encouraged many positive developments in regard to material welfare. Moreover, contrary to many traditionalist claims, and as indicated in Chapter 7, globalization has sometimes helped to reinvigorate rather than undermine cultural heritages. In addition, against another main traditionalist argument, globalization has often promoted increased rather than decreased ecological sensitivity, albeit in a context of greater environmental degradation.

At the same time as excessively demonizing globalization, traditionalists have tended to romanticize the pre-global past. After all, territorialist times also knew much – and in some cases more – poverty, arbitrary social hierarchies, authoritarian governance, warfare, disrespect of nature, and cultural destruction. Also contrary to traditionalist assumptions, and as already noted at several earlier junctures in this book, the local has not in practice always offered a cozy alternative to purportedly faceless globality.

Hence, it is not clear that de-globalization to a status quo ante would be desirable; nor is it realistic to imagine that all supraterritorial domains could be erased from contemporary social life. No social group or country can cocoon itself from global communications, global finance, global governance and the like. This is not to suggest that globalization has been inevitable or will be forever irreversible. Nevertheless, the social forces described in Chapter 4 currently hold such magnitude that a reversal of globalization looks decidedly impracticable in the short or medium term.

Likewise, proactive radical strategies toward globalization seem non-starters for the time being. As indicated in Chapter 1, global socialism and global postmodernism at present only find favour at the fringes of civil society, and these perspectives are almost completely absent from official and commercial circles. As seen in Part II, contemporary globalization has to date sooner deepened than reduced the force of capitalism (the socialists' prime target) and rationalism (the postmodernists' chief target).

Moreover, proactive radical critiques of contemporary globalization have so far generally only offered fairly vague and insufficiently convincing visions of alternative futures. For their part, global socialists have not delineated specific contours of a post-capitalist mode of production nor indicated exactly how this structure would be more equitable and democratic. Likewise, global postmodernists have not offered a precise account of post-rationalist knowledge and the ways that such modes of understanding would provide increased cultural security, deeper wisdom and greater democracy. In short, these radical approaches have provided much more detail about what they oppose in present globalization than about what they support in an alternative future.

Nor have proponents of all-out change so far developed adequate politics for implementation of their visions of transformative globalization. Publications, conferences and/or street demonstrations have helped to alert a wider public to radical critiques of globalization-as-it-is. However, these steps are no more than preliminary, and it is unclear what tactics would take the protests further. Indeed, if poorly grounded, experiments in post-capitalist and post-rationalist social practices could unleash new violences, possibly producing even greater harms than those that currently prevail.

To be sure, forward-looking radical critiques of contemporary society have some compelling logic. For example, capitalism at some level comes into conflict with social justice. This mode of production generally sustains arbitrary social divisions, since these hierarchies allow privileged circles to increase their surplus accumulation. Meanwhile bureaucratism at some level clashes with democracy. Formal, centralized, professionalized, hierarchical governance at some point invariably limits popular participation and transparency. For its part communitarianism tends by its logic to yield only shallow solidarity. After all, the communitarian emphasis of oppositional differences and exclusion encourages violence between groups and generates negatively based cohesion within groups. The logic of rationalist knowledge – with its underlying drive for human control of nature and society – readily slips into profound tension with ecological integrity and democracy. Given these fundamental contradictions, it is understandable that radicals look for a wholesale social transformation.

Yet such a transformation is not in prospect for the moment. True, as seen in Chapters 5–8, contemporary globalization has, while shifting the organization of social space away from territorialism, also promoted shifts within the prevailing modes of production, governance, community and knowledge. However, a wholesale transcendence of capital, bureaucracy, communitarian identity politics and/or modern rationality is not at hand.

For reformism

If neoliberal strategies of globalization are not desirable, and radical programmes are not viable, then we must look to reformist alternatives. To build more humane globalization at the start of the twenty-first century we do best to concentrate on well-designed public policies that alleviate sufferings and increase opportunities. Reformist approaches of this kind are both attractive and practicable.

Reform of the present general course of globalization is attractive because it promises higher human security, greater social equity and more democracy than have resulted from neoliberal policies. To be sure, the reform measures described in the next sections would not – even if completely and collectively implemented – yield immediate or total security, justice and democracy. However, these steps offer the prospect of substantial improvements in the results of globalization within a generation.

In addition, reform of globalization is attainable. Indeed, as previously noted in Chapter 1, considerable momentum has already developed in the course of the 1990s behind reform agendas. Calls now abound to humanize global capitalism, to defend global public goods, to attain global sustainable development, to promote global democracy, and so on.

Reformism has even taken hold in quarters where unquestioned neoliberalism once held sway. For example, the directors of the WEF have cautioned that 'the globalized economy must not become synonymous with "free market on the rampage"' (Schwab and Smadja, 1996). In a similar spirit, the International Federation of Stock Exchanges argued in its 1994 *Annual Report* that 'the impoverishment of a growing proportion of the population in both the developed and the emerging countries calls for . . . new policies of income redistribution' (FIBV, 1994: 15). Unadulterated neoliberalism persists in some quarters, but widespread support has grown for the view – here expressed by the head of UNDP – that 'globalization is too important to be left as unmanaged as it is at present' (UNDP, 1999: v).

Indeed, reformism has by now infiltrated enough governance agencies, market actors and civil society associations to have become almost mainstream. Many authors and reports are now again stressing the potentials of state policy as a means of steering globalization to positive outcomes (Boyer and Drache, 1996; Hirst and Thompson, 1996b). Important attention is today also being given to developing global public policies and reforming the so-called 'architecture' of global governance (Group of Lisbon, 1994; Carlsson *et al.*, 1995; Deacon, 1997; Reinicke, 1998; Kaul *et al.*, 1999).

Perhaps this rise of reformism signals a recurrence of what the social theorist Karl Polanyi with reference to the nineteenth century called a 'double movement'. In this world-systemic rhythm, a phase of *laissez-faire* gives way to a phase of increased regulation, as citizens and their governments react against the undesirable outcomes of untrammelled market capitalism (Mendell and Salée, 1991: xv–xvii; Cox, 1993a: 4–5). Polanyi, writing in the 1940s, described a double movement in relation to national, territorial capitalism. Today the pendulum may be swinging toward something of a supraterritorial Keynesianism.

To be sure, reform comes in different degrees and with different emphases, and it is not yet clear how far current impulses toward reform may go. On the 'thin' end of the spectrum, reforms take the hard edges off of neoliberalism, but leave 'free markets' at the heart of policy. In these circumstances globalization continues to be coupled with liberalization, deregulation and privatization, and the presumption persists that market forces provide the key to maximizing human security, social equity and democracy. With 'thin' reformism, proactive public regulation only enters the picture to prevent or clean up major market harms. Mild reform might in this light be characterized as 'neoliberalism with knobs on'.

In contrast, 'thick' versions of reform reject the neoliberal emphasis on market-led globalization and shift the initiative to public management. In this case state, substate and suprastate laws and institutions take firm hold of the steering wheel and harness the forces of globalization to explicit and democratically determined public policies. This approach to reform follows the lines of global social democracy.

This distinction – and choice – of reform strategies is important. Thus, for example, 'thin' reform adds welfare safety nets to structural adjustment programmes that retain a neoliberal core, whereas 'thick' reform makes poverty eradication the primary and immediate policy objective. Similarly, while 'thin' reform of global finance looks to achieve greater market stability with prudential regulation, 'thick' reform develops the possibilities in global finance (like concessional lending and the Tobin tax described below) to effect a progressive redistribution of world wealth.

As already indicated, the reformist strategy advocated here falls toward the 'thick' end of the spectrum. Ambitious reformism goes beyond band-aids for the injuries of neoliberalism and establishes a different health-care programme. To be sure, implementation of this alternative vision faces major political hurdles: some of them in terms of opposition from vested interests; others in terms of as-yet underdeveloped capacities to execute far-reaching reforms. Powerful minds have to be changed, and major resources must be committed. These difficulties – which can be overcome – are given further attention at the end of the chapter.

Enhancing human security

Before considering challenges of implementation we should establish what we might wish to implement. The next sections therefore turn from general policy visions to more specific policy measures. These pages review various steps of reformist globalization that could be pursued more or less immediately. Indeed, as seen in preceding chapters, some elements of reform are already being at least partly undertaken.

The first set of reforms addresses concerns about human security. The ten points below aim to reduce the harms identified in Chapter 9 in respect of military violence, ecological degradation, poverty, financial instability, unemployment, labour exploitation, cultural damage and social fragmentation.

1 Global regimes for arms control

As seen in Chapter 9, the growth of suprastate governance in the context of globalization has included some development of regional and transworld regimes for arms control. However, suprastate regulation to restrict the militarization of global spaces could be considerably widened beyond the NPT and the OPCW. For example, a suprastate regime to ban anti-ballistic missiles (ABMs) could be developed. This would prevent the spread of supraterritorial counter-weapons of the sort pursued by the US Government in its Strategic Defense Initiative of the 1980s and anti-missile tests of recent years. Suprastate monitoring and eventual control of the development of computer war technologies could likewise put a check on that destructive trend. Suprastate regulation of cross-border arms transfers could place far more effective controls on trade in weapons than the state-level (usually unilateral) measures that have prevailed to date. In time these different mechanisms could be linked under an umbrella global arms control authority.

2 Suprastate mechanisms for conflict management

Other suprastate mechanisms could increase protection against armed violence when it immediately looms or has already begun. For example, United Nations peacekeeping operations could be enhanced with full-scale early-warning mechanisms that linked governments and civil society watchdogs to a conflict prevention division of the Secretariat. UN contingents could then intervene in troubles sooner and with better intelligence about the local situation. In addition, suprastate peacekeeping efforts could be bolstered with the creation of permanent and specifically trained UN military units.

3 Global environmental codes

To improve environmental security, suprastate mechanisms to reduce ecological degradation could go well beyond the existing measures described in Chapters 6 and 9. For instance, the polluter-pays principle could be applied not only to greenhouse gases under the Climate Convention, but also to sulphur dioxide emissions, tropical wood consumption, pesticide use, etc. Various financial incentives, some of them administered through global programmes, could encourage the development and use of renewable energy sources. To monitor and coordinate these various efforts, UNEP could be upgraded as a World Environment Organization that worked on a par – and in collaboration – with other global bodies, especially those covering trade and finance.

In the private sector, meanwhile, companies could go beyond hijacking a slogan and make 'sustainable development' a veritable core of their business practice (Heerings and Zeldenrust, 1995; Welford, 1997). Indeed, codes of conduct for global corporations could include specific and enforceable environmental clauses.

At a personal level, various shifts in behaviour could lessen ecological degradation. These steps might encompass recycling, limiting numbers of offspring, reducing reliance on private motor cars, and making other 'green' consumer choices.

4 Socially sustainable global economic restructuring

The restructuring of capitalism with the growth of supraterritorial production, finance and trade requires adjustments in policies; however, the new governance framework need not impose the heavy social costs that have often accompanied neoliberal programmes. Approaches to global economic restructuring could be reoriented so that issues like the adequate provision of education, employment, health and shelter gain greater priority.

To this end the recent rise of social concerns at the IMF and the multilateral development banks could be taken much further than the current preoccupation with 'safety nets' for vulnerable circles. For instance, the formulation and execution of policies of macroeconomic restructuring could fully integrate relevant expertise from socially geared UN bodies like UNDP and UNICEF with that of the Bretton Woods institutions. At the same time, suprastate bodies dealing with structural adjustment could work more closely with social departments of national and local governments, as well as with trade unions and socially oriented NGOs.

Indeed, socially sustainable adjustment must rest on grassroots ownership. Policies on education, health, etc. tend not to create full or lasting benefits when the initiative and control lies in official bureaucracies. The targeted people themselves should be comprehensively integrated – and take a substantial lead – in the design and execution of social programmes.

To cite one already widely practiced example, micro-credit schemes for low-income circles can obtain their resources from transborder concessionary finance but leave programme organization largely to self-management on the part of the beneficiaries (Holcombe, 1995; Johnson and Rogaly, 1997).

5 Debt relief for poor countries

More could be done, building on the initiatives described in Chapter 9, to combat the social harms that have arisen from unsustainable transborder debts to poor countries. Relief could cover more debts, on more generous terms, and at a faster rate than has been witnessed to date under the Naples framework and the HIPC initiative. Moreover, the monies released through debt relief could be earmarked for increased social spending. This principle has already governed the HIPC programme and several cancellations of bilateral debts. Care also needs to be taken that debt relief is handled in ways that do not discourage future new transborder credits.

6 Suprastate financial regulation

More ambitious measures to reform the so-called 'global financial architecture' could be pursued than the modest tinkering that authorities have undertaken to date. It is important to stress in this regard that public-sector regulation can harness supraterritorial financial markets considerably more than globalists have tended to presume. Just as 'rocket scientists' in the commercial sector have developed ever more sophisticated financial instruments, so 'high-flier' regulators can devise ever more sophisticated supervisory mechanisms.

For one thing, a more nuanced approach could be pursued *vis-à-vis* capital controls. Even many mainstream economists now agree that liberalization of cross-border capital flows should be timed and sequenced more carefully (Griffith-Jones, 1998). Indeed, in some cases bars on capital transfers between countries (especially short-term credits) could serve positive purposes for economic and social development. More selective regulatory measures, too, could protect vulnerable markets from transborder speculative runs. For example, governments could impose a special exchange rate on equity investments from abroad or prohibit domestic borrowing by nonresidents (Williamson, 1999).

More generally, global monetary and financial regulation could be consolidated in a transworld financial authority. Such a body could be created either by upgrading the IMF or by forming a new institution that superseded the IMF and the BIS (Gunter, 1996). Whereas current IMF resources amount to only a fraction of the annual value of trade between countries, a global central bank would have sufficient means at its disposal to provide emergency support in any transborder financial crisis.

This transworld institution could also administer a distinct global currency that filled the roles now covered by transworld national denominations like the US dollar and the Japanese yen. Possibly the SDR could be upgraded into the sort of money that John Maynard Keynes envisioned in the early 1940s under the name of the 'bancor'. Alternatively, some other supraterritorial currency could be devised, for example, with reference to the value of a basket of the most traded commodities in global markets (Lietaer, 1996). In any case a single transworld denomination of this kind could remove many of the instabilities currently generated through the foreign exchange markets.

7 Public policies for job creation

As indicated in Chapter 9, global capitalism has posed major challenges to employment prospects. Job support initiatives from public-sector agencies can help to address this problem. For example, education and training programmes can be reoriented in order better to equip workers with the sorts of perspectives and skills (such as global thinking and computer literacy) that are required in supraterritorial capitalism. In addition, fiscal incentives could be set that encourage employers to retain and retrain staff as companies restructure in the face of globalization. More ambitiously, multilateral agencies could embark on job-creating global public works projects, for example, to supply underprivileged parts of the world with full telecommunications services or to undertake programmes of environmental restoration.

8 Suprastate governance of labour standards

Other reforms of globalization could improve the security of people in work. For example, the ILO could acquire greater capacities to monitor and enforce compliance with its core conventions. These legal instruments provide for freedom of association, the right of collective bargaining, the abolition of forced labour, the prevention of discrimination in employment, and a minimum age for employment. Moves could also be started toward the establishment of a global regime of minimum wages, whose levels might for the time being be weighted in relation to the per capita income of a country.

Further protection of labour conditions could be pursued outside the ILO. For example, chapters on workers' rights could be included in the WTO and all regional trade accords. In addition, security in the workplace could be a prominent feature of an independently monitored and fully enforced code of conduct for global companies. Such a regime of rigorous social auditing could perhaps be created by upgrading the OECD Guidelines for Multinational Enterprises, first adopted in 1976 and already reviewed three times since then.

Meanwhile workers themselves could improve their terms and conditions in global capitalism by nurturing transborder unionism. As Charles Tilly has argued, 'chauvinistic and protectionist responses will not defend labor's effective rights . . . workers have to invent new strategies at the scale of international capital' (1995: 20–1). A promising recent turn in this regard has seen the conclusion of several collective bargaining agreements between a global company and a global trade secretariat (rather than a national union). The first such accord was reached in 1988 between MNE Danone and the International Union of Food, Agricultural, Hotel, Restaurant, Catering, Tobacco and Allied Workers' Associations (IUF). Others followed in 1995 and 1998 involving the hotel chain ACCOR, the energy concern Statoil, and the furniture makers IKEA together with, respectively, the IUF, the International Chemical, Energy and Mining Workers, and the International Federation of Building and Wood Workers (Justice, 1999: 7).

9 Protection of cultural diversity

Cultural security – that is, safety and confidence in one's frameworks of meaning – cannot in general be legislated with specific technical regulations of the sort that might be devised for environmental protection, debt relief or workers' rights. However, various legal and institutional reforms could encourage more constructive encounters in global spaces between diverse identities and knowledges. For example, school curricula can be framed to expose young people to multiple histories and civilizations. States can accord formal recognition to minority cultures, much as the post-*apartheid* government of South Africa has declared eleven languages to be official.

In suprastate governance, regional and transworld institutions could develop more sites like the EU Committee of the Regions where substate nationalities have a voice. To take a line from the Commission on Global Governance, we should 'make global organization conform to the reality of global diversity' (Carlsson *et al.*, 1995: xvii). In particular, suprastate economic governance could be reformed in the direction of greater cultural sensitivity. The World Bank's Comprehensive Development Framework (CDF), emergent since 1998, has been a welcome turn in this regard. The CDF aspires to integrate anthropological with economic concerns and to draw information and wisdom from the grassroots as well as development professionals (World Bank, 1999).

More generally, institutions as well as individuals could nurture cultural security in globalization by developing an alternative approach to identity politics. Such a perspective might be called 'interculturalism'. Adopting this stance, different communities would encounter each other in global relations with mutual recognition, respect, responsibility and (when tensions rise) restraint. Intercultural reciprocity contrasts fundamentally with the 'us–them' framework of communitarianism, an approach that has tended to denigrate, exclude and suppress 'otherness'. In intercultural cosmopolitanism no civilization would aspire to become the universal model. (See further Scholte, 1996b: 595–600; 1999c: 66–9, 80–3.) On these lines 6,500 people from different faiths met in a Parliament of the World's Religions at Chicago in 1993 to affirm a common global ethic without erasing each other's identity (Küng and Kuschel, 1993). Such initiatives demonstrate that it is possible to have human solidarity through cultural difference.

10 Social cohesion through trilateral partnerships

Reforms of globalization that promote peace, ecological integrity, poverty eradication, financial stability, employment security and cultural security can all have concurrent effects of enhancing social integration. In addition, other initiatives could be targeted at giving more substance to programmes of 'socially responsible' global business of the kind mentioned in Chapter 9. Likewise, many transborder humanitarian NGOs could do more to develop deliberate links between their relief work and wider concerns of social cohesion. Most importantly, perhaps, companies, NGOs and public authorities could better coordinate their efforts in trilateral partnerships on social development.

In sum, each of the ten sets of reforms described above can in one measure or another enhance human security in the context of contemporary globalization. Radical critics may – in some cases quite compellingly – question the adequacy of measures such as arms control, global environmental law, debt relief, prudential oversight of global finance, corporate codes of conduct, and NGO provision of social welfare. However, to note that reformist measures might not go far enough in the long run is no reason to reject them altogether, all the more so when full-scale social transformation is not at hand.

Enhancing social justice

Reformist changes to the course of globalization can also go some way to reduce social injustices of the kind described in Chapter 10. Indeed, a number of the reforms to enhance human security discussed above can simultaneously work to alleviate the inequities that result from arbitrary social hierarchies. In regard to class, for example, measures to reduce poverty, to improve employment conditions and to increase social cohesion can at the same time lessen inequalities in life chances between various socioeconomic groups. As for the stratification of countries, steps to create socially sustainable structural adjustment, to remove excessive debt burdens and to stabilize financial markets can simultaneously narrow gaps between the North and the South. Likewise, some of the measures mentioned above could have positive implications for gender justice. For instance, many micro-credit schemes with transborder support have had especially enabling effects for women.

In addition, a number of other reforms of globalization could specifically target problems of social justice. Seven sets of measures of this kind are identified below. Again, problems confronting the implementation of these reforms are assessed toward the end of this chapter.

1 Suprastate anti-monopoly mechanisms

Measures to counter monopoly tendencies in global capitalism (identified in Chapter 5) could work against various injustices connected with social stratification. After all, market concentration has allowed investors and managers – who generally already hold considerable wealth and power advantages over other classes – to accumulate undue levels of additional surplus. Winners of the global monopoly game have also been disproportionately white, male, urban and based in the North.

Several anti-monopoly mechanisms could be developed in respect of supraterritorial capital. In regional governance, for instance, other institutions could follow the example of the EU in establishing a regime of competition rules. A rigorous global anti-monopoly framework could also be developed, building on existing modest initiatives such as the UN Restrictive Practices Code and the OECD Committee on Competition Law and Policy. These efforts could bring the creation of a Global Competition Office linked to the WTO (Fortin, 1992: 86–8) or a self-standing Global Anti-Monopoly Authority.

2 Global taxation

A second set of reforms that could enhance equity in globalization relate to transworld taxes. A host of schemes for global taxes have circulated since the 1970s (Carlsson *et al.*, 1995: 217–21; Wachtel, 2000). Much as progressive taxation by states has worked against class and other arbitrary hierarchies within countries, so supraterritorial taxation could reduce inequities between classes and countries as they are generated through global capitalism. In addition, the revenues gained could help to fund a number of programmes to enhance human security, as covered in the preceding section. All of the taxes described below are progressive: that is, they would apply mainly to those sections of the world's population that are most able to pay them.

One especially appealing proposal, the so-called 'Tobin tax', would impose a fractional charge on foreign-exchange transactions. (The levy is named after the economist James Tobin who first formulated the idea in 1971.) Given the huge volume of foreign-exchange business, even a very low rate of Tobin tax would yield considerable revenues. At the same time, the tax could also reduce volatility in foreign-exchange markets, since the charge would eliminate many of the marginal profits that attract currency speculators. (For more on the Tobin tax, see Felix, 1994; Haq *et al.*, 1996, ATTAC, 1999.)

Supraterritorial corporate taxation would be another measure to achieve a more equitable distribution of the gains of globalization. The absence of a transworld tax regime has allowed transborder companies to manipulate state tax frameworks to their advantage, for example, through transfer pricing and offshore arrangements. A global tax on corporate profits could close such loopholes, discourage tax competition between states, and ensure that transborder companies contribute their due share to public funds.

Other possible global taxes include a 'bit tax' on data sent through the Internet. Such a charge could generate more revenue than total world ODA (UNDP, 1999: 66). Meanwhile a levy of $100 on each patent registered with WIPO could have raised $350 million in 1998 (UNDP, 1999: 74). Several transworld taxes could apply to use of the so-called 'global commons', such as the deep seabed, the electromagnetic spectrum, flight paths, sea lanes and ocean fishing areas. Further global taxes have been suggested in respect of cross-border arms sales and transboundary pollution.

3 Abolition of offshore finance

A third reform to increase justice in globalization would abolish offshore finance centres. These tax havens have allowed people with means – often very considerable means – to be free riders in a world replete with need and inequality. True, offshore tax arrangements have generated some revenue for the host governments, including in some poor countries; however, these public funds have in most cases done little to eliminate underprivilege among the local population. As for employment, although offshore finance centres have created some work, these jobs could also exist if the same deposits were in onshore accounts. In short, offshore finance centres have no social justification. They should and could be eliminated through global taxation rules.

4 North–South redistribution through global economic regimes

A number of other reforms could reduce the hierarchies between countries that have been reflected in, and substantially sustained by, global economic regimes. To begin with, several steps could be taken to improve the North–South balance in global economic decision taking. For example, votes in the Bretton Woods institutions could be redistributed away from the currently prevailing quota formula that has so heavily favoured major states (Gerster, 1993). In addition, the BIS and the OECD could expand their membership to encompass governments of poor as well as rich countries. Meanwhile the central organs of the UN (where the South has greater representation and voting strength) could upgrade their involvement in global economic governance with the creation of an Economic Security Council in place of the existing rather limp Economic and Social Council (Carlsson *et al.*, 1995: 153–62).

Other reforms of globalization could aim to reduce North–South hierarchies in particular sectors of the economy. In the area of global communications, for example, many of the recommendations of the UNESCO-sponsored MacBride Commission, published in 1980, remain relevant for the twenty-first century (UNESCO, 1980; Golding and Harris, 1997). To highlight one specific proposal, more resources could be dedicated to the development of organizations like the Caribbean News Agency and the Inter Press Service that advance Southern perspectives in global journalism (Musa, 1997).

In respect of global money, the IMF could distribute substantial new allocations of SDRs largely if not exclusively to the South. This so-called 'SDR-aid link' could provide poor countries with more foreign exchange reserves and (if the cumulative SDR allocations were sufficiently large) could decrease the dominance in the world economy of North-based currencies. In another step to bolster the position of the South in global monetary affairs, poor states could be accorded greater resources to build up their central banks, making them less dependent in monetary and financial policy on suprastate agencies like the Bretton Woods institutions.

In the area of global credit, since commercial markets largely lock out poor countries, multilateral development banks could provide increased loans to the South on concessionary terms. In particular, more long-term low-interest credits of the kind supplied through the International Development Association (an arm of the World Bank) could be made available to the poorest countries. In addition, expanded micro-credit schemes of the sort described earlier could channel more transborder finance to the grassroots poor in the South.

Various other reforms could improve North–South equity in respect of global trade. For instance, suprastate initiatives could accomplish much more than the previously mentioned GSP and Lomé Conventions have done to reduce trade barriers for the South to markets of the North. Scope also exists for a large expansion of alternative trade schemes of the kind described in Chapter 10. Meanwhile the WTO could develop commodity regimes that would guarantee and enhance export earnings for poor countries of key primary products. Also through the WTO, the TRIPS regime could be amended to create protection from exploitation for people in the South who hold commercially valuable but unpatented ideas, tools, techniques, etc. The broader intellectual property regime, too, could be revised to facilitate the access of South-based producers to new technologies.

5 Gender-sensitive governance of globalization

Greater equity between men and women could be developed by making all governance of globalization explicitly gender sensitive. For instance, offices and procedures to examine the gender impacts of policy could be introduced in transworld agencies like the BIS and the WTO that have hitherto lacked such mechanisms. In addition, the development activities of multilateral agencies could extend recent steps specifically to target female poverty. Structural adjustment packages sponsored by suprastate bodies could be constructed with greater regard to the often gendered impacts of these programmes. Global labour standards could give more direct and systematic attention to promoting equal opportunities for the sexes in the workplace. Other labour protection measures with special relevance to women could also be developed, for example, in relation to the global sex trade and imported domestic workers. At the same time greater resources could be dedicated to the promotion of women's human rights through CEDAW and other suprastate mechanisms. Collectively, such steps could bring gender equity concerns to the heart of global public policy.

6 Women in global leadership

Gender justice could be further addressed in globalization with the appointment of more women to executive positions in suprastate governance, transborder business and global civil society. On the whole women tend to have greater awareness of and sympathy toward gender equity issues. Even where certain women lack these sensitivities, they can still by their example demonstrate the possibilities and accomplishments of female leadership.

7 Attention to race, urban/rural and age hierarchies in globalization

Along with reforms that address class, country and gender inequities, further measures could be taken to counter subordinations in globalization of people of colour, rural populations, children and the elderly. Several existing initiatives in these areas by UN agencies and various civic associations were mentioned in Chapter 10. However, just as problems of race, urban/rural divides and age have been less studied in relation to globalization than those of class, North/South divides and gender, so too fewer specific proposals for corrective action have emerged. More attention could be given to assessing and, as necessary, redressing these generally less highlighted forms of stratification in supraterritorial spaces.

Taking the above seven broad suggestions together, it is clear that global public policies and other reformist measures could make substantial inroads into the injustices that have developed in globalization to date. True, many socialists have concluded that the tensions between capitalism and justice run so deep that only a full-scale transformation of the mode of production can remove arbitrary hierarchies from social relations. Yet, even if we accept this argument, it remains possible and desirable to pursue reforms that lessen social injustices within capitalism, especially if acceptable and feasible post-capitalist alternatives are not immediately in sight.

Enhancing democracy

In keeping with the threefold conception of normative politics pursued in Part III of this book, reform of globalization needs to address questions of democracy together with those of human security and social justice. Indeed, some of the measures mentioned above under the headings of security and justice could also promote greater democracy in global relations. For example, steps to improve social equity can have an accompanying effect of advancing democracy, insofar as the reduction of arbitrary hierarchies increases opportunities for all people to participate in politics. Likewise, with respect to human security, policies to eradicate poverty, improve employment conditions and deepen social cohesion also create circumstances in which people are better able actively to involve themselves in collective self-determination.

The present section considers further measures that directly address the democratic deficits in contemporary globalization identified in Chapter 11. What practicable institutional and procedural reforms are available to make governance of global spaces more participatory, consultative, transparent and publicly accountable? The following paragraphs identify seven broad possibilities.

1 Maximum devolution to local government

Popular participation in the governance of global flows could be considerably enhanced with further decentralization from state and suprastate agencies to provincial and district authorities. Wherever possible, at least part of the formulation and implementation of policies relating to supraterritorial concerns should involve local government. Following the principle of subsidiarity, regulatory competences in respect of global flows could always be allocated to the 'lowest' possible tier of public authority. To be sure, national, regional and transworld agencies need to play major roles in the governance of global relations (for example, with regard to policy coordination and enforcement). However, local bodies could be much more involved than they have generally been to date.

Of course, to reiterate a caution emphasized in Chapter 11, local politics are not 'naturally' democratic. The local is not inherently more genuine and generous than other arenas. Decentralization is not a magic formula for democratic globalization. Democracy requires constant vigilance, whether the politics are played out in a local setting, a national government or a suprastate regime.

2 Popular consultations on global policies

The democratization of globalization could also be increased through more direct consultations of the general public on matters of global policy. At a local level, authorities could on suitable occasions use public hearings or referenda to consult constituents on matters concerning global relations as they affect that locality. For example, in the South and the East such public input could help to set priorities for the use of transborder development support. In this vein local communities in Thailand have convened Civic Forums to deliberate the use of a Social Investment Fund financed by the World Bank.

At the state level, more could be done to make general elections in part a popular consultation on national policies toward globalization. Political parties could give global issues more prominence in their manifestos and campaigns. Voters could thereby become more aware of these questions, and elections to representative bodies could – far more than at present – test popular views on, for instance, the way that a state responds to global ecological problems.

Other kinds of state-level consultations regarding the governance of global spaces could also take place. For instance, building on the Swiss tradition, national referenda could be used more often to gain explicit popular endorsements for a state's accession to key transworld institutions and agreements. Alternatively, governments could call ad hoc national assemblies of stakeholders to deliberate an important decision involving a country's approach to globalization. For example, the Government of Uganda has since the mid-1990s sponsored an annual national economic forum (involving academics, business leaders and trade unions as well as politicians) that *inter alia* discusses the country's approach to structural adjustment (in this case one that has closely followed IMF and World Bank prescriptions).

In regard to suprastate bodies, greater popular consultation could be achieved in some cases through the creation of directly elected representative organs like the parliaments of the CACM and the EU. As noted in Chapter 11, universal suffrage seems at present unworkable in relation to transworld agencies. However, elected assemblies could be introduced in regional arrangements like ASEAN, MERCOSUR and SADC as they reach a substantial level of institutional development.

In addition, suprastate institutions could expand ad hoc consultations with grassroots constituents. The country offices of the EU, the ILO, the IMF, UNDP, UNICEF and the multilateral development banks are well placed to meet on a regular basis with local citizens as well as the host government. In addition, visiting officials from suprastate agencies could as standard procedure directly consult citizens who have a stake in the multilateral institution's work. Some policy discussions of this kind already take place: for example, by the World Bank in regard to many of its development projects. However, these exchanges could be substantially multiplied and taken more seriously in policy formulation, implementation and review.

3 Representation of nonterritorial constituencies

Democracy could also be enhanced in our globalizing world with steps to institutionalize a voice for nonterritorial groups in policymaking. As elaborated in Chapter 7, people have in the context of globalization increasingly acquired social bonds that are not based on territorial location and state-centred nationality. Yet few current governance frameworks include a formal recognition of nonterritorial interests.

This democratic deficit could be partly met with the creation of mechanisms to represent nonterritorial constituencies in legislative and consultative assemblies. Chambers on the various tiers of post-sovereign governance could include seats related to gender, profession, religion, etc.

This principle has already operated in the national congress of Indonesia, for example. At a global level, the UN could acquire a permanent Civic Assembly (including representatives of employers, labour, women, youth, etc.) to stand alongside the General Assembly of state delegates. Similarly, the World Bank NGO Liaison Committee could be broadened to include representatives of all sectors of civil society and upgraded to provide more weighty policy inputs in that global financial institution. Other multilateral organizations could follow suit with consultative bodies made up of representatives of transborder stakeholders. Such chambers could provide a valuable alternative channel for the expression of a wide spectrum of views on global policies.

4 Scrutiny of suprastate governance by state and substate councils

Popularly elected bodies at state and substate levels could also do more to place suprastate governance under democratic surveillance. It is striking, for instance, that hardly any state legislatures, anywhere in the world, scrutinized the Uruguay Round agreements. National congresses could likewise undertake careful examinations of the macroeconomic programmes that their governments conclude with the Bretton Woods institutions. Such scrutiny would place a democratic check on the unelected technocrats who have held most of the initiative in suprastate governance.

Representative bodies at substate levels could also more thoroughly deliberate the local impacts of suprastate policies. A positive development in this direction has seen many municipal assemblies monitor the local application of Agenda 21, the manifesto that resulted from the Earth Summit of 1992. In addition, district and provincial representative assemblies could exercise greater democratic control over, for example, arrangements made by substate governments in regard to FDI or transborder credits.

5 Transparency of suprastate governance

Further democratization of suprastate governance could be achieved by extending the positive 1990s trend of increased transparency. Regional and transworld governance agencies could produce more publications, issue more press releases, maintain more extensive websites and so on. In addition, suprastate bodies could make greater efforts to publish materials in ways that are more accessible to the lay citizen (for example, with non-technical language and user-friendly websites). Fuller information of this kind could make it easier for interested citizens to determine what decisions suprastate bodies have taken, from among what options, and on what grounds. The public could then be better equipped to judge whether a given multilateral organization was acting competently and in their interest.

6 Evaluation of suprastate policies

For the rest, the democratic credentials of suprastate institutions could be enhanced with an expanded programme of independent policy evaluations. More regional and transworld organizations could undergo such account-ability exercises, which could also cover more policy areas. To encourage their autonomy, the policy auditors should be appointed by, and responsible to, an outside body and not (as sometimes currently happens) the institution whose policy is being reviewed. The assessors should take evidence from the full range of stakeholders – and not merely from technocratic 'experts'. Evaluation results should be published (with an invitation for public reactions), and the agency concerned should follow up each report with a published and carefully monitored action plan to address any criticisms and recommendations. The recent IMF reviews of ESAF programmes and surveillance activities have already followed some (though not all) of these procedures.

7 Greater role for global civil society

Several of the previous recommendations – especially those concerning greater popular consultation and increased representation of nonterritorial constituencies – could be considerably furthered through global civic associations. As noted in Chapter 11, transborder civil society has significant potentials to enhance democracy in global relations; however, much of the promise remains to be realized.

To advance in this regard, tax incentives and other policies could be adopted worldwide that encourage substantially greater resources to flow to civil society development. In addition, global civic associations could coordinate their efforts more carefully and share information more generously with each other. In some cases competition between organiza-tions for funds, members and the moral high ground has undermined civil society capacities to influence policy. Finally, civic groups could take greater care – for instance, with self-critical democracy audits – to nurture participation, consultation, transparency and accountability in their own practices. Global civil society needs to undertake internal democratization at the same time that it pursues a democratization of the rest of globalization.

In sum, ambitious reforms of existing governance frameworks could greatly increase democracy in policies toward globalization. True, even if all of the above suggestions were to be fully implemented, radical critics could still find significant shortfalls in popular control of global relations. However, we can do much to reduce democratic deficits in globalization even if we do not eliminate them.

Challenges of implementation

It is relatively easy to compile wish lists. It is something else to get wishes fulfilled. This book is not the place to develop detailed plans to guide political campaigns for reform of globalization. However, the present discussion would be incomplete – and facilely utopian – if we did not consider obstacles as well as inspirations to change.

The agenda for reform laid out above is 'ambitious' in good part because of the challenges that confront its implementation. Five main difficulties can be highlighted: the problem of overcoming strong forces that support neoliberal policies; the problem of transcending sovereignty-based policy thinking; the problem of expanding institutional capacities to handle global public policies; the problem of building broad public constituencies for ambitious reform; and the problem of negotiating cultural diversity while pursuing politics of global change. Each of these points is briefly elaborated below.

The power of neoliberalism

The programme of ambitious reformism outlined here presents an alternative to the neoliberal orthodoxy that has prevailed *vis-à-vis* contemporary globalization, especially since the late 1970s. Neoliberalism has enjoyed very powerful backing: from commercial circles, including big capital in particular; from official circles, including economic and financial policymakers in particular; and from academic circles, including main-stream social scientists in particular. Any successful campaign to reform globalization would need to overcome opposition from many powerful quarters.

The scale of this challenge must not be underestimated. Support for *laissez-faire*, market-led globalization has deep material and ideological roots. Materially, neoliberal approaches to globalization have created some very wealthy, privileged and powerful winners. Ideologically, many proponents of neoliberalism have supported this policy orientation with thorough conviction and in some cases evangelical fervour. These vested interests cannot be easily moved. To date few leading beneficiaries of neoliberal globalization have followed the example of George Soros in turning to critique (Soros, 1998).

Hence one major struggle in the politics of policy change lies in persuading supporters of neoliberalism – who include many of the world's rich and powerful – that turns toward global social democracy would serve both their interests and those of the wider public. After all, if neoliberal globalization generates major threats to human security, then these harms are likely at some point also to touch even the most advantaged people. Already the 'winners' of neoliberal globalization have felt some discomforts of ecological insecurity, financial instability and ambiguous identities. Moreover, if mounting concerns about equity and democracy in globalization are not addressed with substantial reform, then increasingly vocal and perhaps also violent opposition could develop.

Sovereignty

A second major challenge to the implementation of ambitious reformism relates to the continuing power in contemporary political thought of the sovereignty principle. Global social democracy on the lines described above involves considerably increased authority for both substate and suprastate agencies. Moves toward multilayered, diffuse governance have already progressed considerably, as indicated in Chapter 6. However, a large expansion of global public policy on the lines described above would extend the trend much further.

The persistence of sovereignty-based thinking can hinder large and rapid extensions of this kind. True, contemporary globalization has made sovereign governance impracticable, but myths of sovereignty continue to have widespread currency. Many people still insist that unilateral, supreme, comprehensive and absolute authority (usually as placed in the state) does, or can, or should prevail. Millions of politicians, civil servants and armed forces around the world who work within centralized state apparatuses have vested interests in sustaining the notion that full and final authority lies with national government (read, with them). State personnel therefore often have strong inclinations to oppose transfers of competences to other tiers of governance. In addition, hundreds of millions of citizens across the continents continue to rely heavily on notions of national-state sovereignty for their sense of identity, community and self-determination. When urging an abandonment of the sovereignty principle, we are in fact asking people fundamentally to reconceptualize their notions of self and society.

Thus campaigns for global social democracy must put major efforts into overcoming sovereignty myths. Large numbers of high-quality professionals need to be convinced that their abilities can be best used, and their ambitions best realized, as public servants in substate or suprastate governance as well as in states. At the same time citizens need to be persuaded that sovereignty – whether that power is vested in the state or elsewhere – is obsolete. People need to be convinced that, contrary to their hopes, continued invocation of the sovereignty principle actually reduces rather than enhances the possibilities of collective self-determination. The discourse of sovereignty deludes citizens into thinking that statist models of democracy can deliver, when in fact a narrow focus of democratic politics on the state leaves major sites of power in our globalizing world beyond popular control.

Institutional capacity

Policy cannot be implemented in the absence of sufficient institutional capacity. In the case of many of the reforms of globalization suggested above, current institutional capacities are not adequate to effect the desired changes. A turn to global social democracy therefore requires that governance bodies obtain considerably increased means. In some cases the agencies need a larger bulk of resources: more staff, more funds, more equipment, more offices, more data and so on. In other cases the organizations need to deploy existing resources differently to acquire new capacities.

Suprastate institutions in particular lack enough means at present to execute a programme of ambitious reform of globalization. For one thing, several new suprastate bodies are probably required, including a global arms control agency, a global environment organization, a global financial authority, a global competition authority and a global tax office. In addition, a number of existent transworld and regional governance agencies would need substantially greater capacities in order to execute a broader and/or stronger mandate. For example, tighter public regulation of global finance would require extra investment in technology and expert staff. Meanwhile all suprastate organizations would need further resources to implement mechanisms for greater democracy, like representative chambers and grassroots policy consultations. Likewise, all suprastate bodies would need to commit resources (for example, through training courses) in order for staff to acquire greater sensitivity to issues of gender and race.

So large increases in resource allocations to suprastate institutions are necessary; but proposals to this end are likely to face considerable resistance. Even the IMF, while promoting a neoliberal agenda, has endured a succession of long and hard struggles since the late 1970s to obtain increased quotas, especially from the US Congress. Meanwhile the UN, with a more reformist approach to globalization, has experienced enormous difficulties to collect even its present very modest dues from member states. Major opposition would also face attempts to establish direct funding for transworld agencies through global taxes (much as part of VAT in EU member countries has flowed directly to Brussels). Indeed, much of this resistance is justified so long as suprastate agencies are not subjected to adequate democratic controls.

Moreover, increased resources to suprastate organizations could not maximize returns unless the various institutions improved their capacities of coordination with each other. Some bureaucratic competition between official agencies – for instance, between ministries at state level – can encourage greater policy innovation and effectiveness. However, to date relations between many transworld bodies have known more turf battles than cooperation. Debilitating rivalries have surfaced between different parts of the UN system, between UN organs and the Bretton Woods institutions, between the IMF and the World Bank, between the ILO and the WTO, and so on. Many of the reforms urged earlier depend for their successful implementation on close collaboration among these and other suprastate bodies. A major shift is therefore needed with respect to the culture of inter-institutional relations in global governance.

Meanwhile, state and substate tiers of governance must have sufficient means to coordinate policy successfully with suprastate bodies. To recall an earlier example, central banks in the South need to have highly trained staff and advanced information technology in order to participate effectively in the governance of global finance. State and local authorities – especially in poor countries – also have to develop a much larger cadre with expertise relating to issues such as global environmental change, the workings of suprastate governance, macroeconomic policy, transborder investment and intercultural relations. If public policies toward globalization are to be made appropriate to the particular conditions of different countries and localities, then state and substate agencies need to be equipped to achieve that fit.

Likewise, representative organs at state and local levels must acquire the capacity to exercise informed democratic checks of the sort recommended earlier on regional and transworld authorities. We cannot expect members of state legislatures and local assemblies to be experts on the full range of global issues. In order effectively to scrutinize global policy, democratic representatives must be able to rely on adequately resourced research and advisory support. Such backing is currently lacking in most of the world.

In short, the struggle to reform globalization is in good part a struggle to supply the means to effect change. The insecurities, inequities and democratic deficits that have resulted from recent decades of globalization cannot be corrected on the cheap. If we want greater security, justice and democracy in a globalizing world, then we have to commit the resources to achieve those ends.

Popular constituencies

Resources for a more progressive road of globalization could be more readily obtained if there were large-scale public support for such allocations. Indeed, democracy requires that global reformism – like any other policy course – has a large popular base. In any case, policy is harder to implement when people are ignorant or indifferent about the issues at hand.

Various scenarios in the politics of globalization have shown how important public support for reform can be. For instance, grassroots action through the Jubilee 2000 Coalition across more than 60 countries has helped in recent years to generate increased debt relief for the South (Jubilee, 2000). Likewise, citizen mobilization against the MAI was instrumental in halting that neoliberal project in late 1998. Other examples include popular campaigns to protect endangered species and to ban dangerous advertising for infant milk formula to poor mothers who cannot afford to buy it in sufficient quantities.

However, effective public pressure for global reform has to date been the exception rather than the rule. Thus, for example, a transworld anti-monopoly mechanism will remain less attainable so long as public mobilization for such a scheme through consumer associations, trade unions and the like is lacking. Likewise, major reform of global finance will be harder so long as its operations remain a mystery to the general public. Citizens will also need to be thoroughly convinced of a good cause before they assent to global taxes.

Clearly major efforts of civic education regarding globalization are required to build widespread and sustained public support for ambitious reform. We cannot expect people to press effectively for progressive change if they are not richly supplied with relevant ideas and information. To this end, as suggested earlier, political parties need to encourage more, and more sophisticated, public debate of globalization. In addition, school curricula should be adapted in order better to prepare young people to deliberate supraterritorial issues. The mass media, too, could do much more to inform citizens about globalization and different ways to address the problems that it brings. Suprastate agencies must also considerably expand their public information activities, so that bodies like UNHCR and the WTO begin to have recognition levels that are comparable with those of states.

Once greater public awareness of globalization has been generated, proponents of reform will still have a job to nurture large popular movements in support of the sorts of measures outlined earlier. Academics, journalists and other social commentators need to articulate convincing and appealing cases for major policy changes. More – and more effectively organized – pressure groups need to ensure that public support for reform is translated into actions, in terms of votes in referenda, consumer choices, street rallies, financial contributions, and so on.

In sum, a major challenge facing reform of globalization is to acquire large-scale public support for an alternative policy course. Global social democracy cannot be imposed from above. Neoliberals have usually pursued their agenda with top-down politics, an approach that has generally proved untenable. Reformers must not repeat this mistake.

Cultural diversity

Finally, implementation of ambitious reforms *vis-à-vis* globalization faces the challenge of sustaining and indeed enhancing respect for cultural diversity. Reformers must take great care to build new politics of intercultural negotiation into the very process of changing the course of globalization. Otherwise, good intentions notwithstanding, global social democracy could easily become yet another form of imperialism. To avoid this repetition, the pursuit of global social democracy needs to conform to the kind of alternative cosmopolitanism described earlier. Intercultural dialogue might in fact produce significant shifts of emphasis in reformist agendas in respect of globalization.

Conclusion

In a word, the message of this chapter is: reform – including ambitious reform – is possible, albeit also difficult. The currently experienced harms of globalization are not integral to supraterritorial space as such. The problem is not globality per se, but the way that we govern it. As summarized in the Box below, many initiatives could steer globalization toward greater human security, social equity and democracy.

Admittedly this chapter has provided only a sketch of more progressive politics of globalization. Further research (some of it already undertaken by others) is needed to work out the details of the various reforms, to assess more precisely the technicalities of implementation, and to calculate more exactly the likely impacts of the measures. In addition, further political calculation (some of it already ongoing) is needed to determine the most effective ways of overcoming resistance against and building momentum for a programme of ambitous reform of globalization.

Reforming globalization in summary

Enhancing human security
- improve global regimes for arms control
- upgrade suprastate mechanisms of conflict management
- enhance global environmental codes, laws and institutions
- emphasize the social dimension of global economic restructuring
- increase debt relief for poor countries, linked to greater social expenditure
- expand suprastate regulation of global financial markets
- increase public policies for job creation
- intensify suprastate promotion of labour standards
- pursue deliberate protection of cultural diversity
- enhance social cohesion through trilateral partnerships of public, market and civil society agencies

Enhancing social equity
- counter monopoly tendencies in global capitalism with suprastate mechanisms
- introduce progressive global taxes
- abolish offshore finance arrangements
- pursue North–South redistribution through global economic regimes
- integrate gender equity concerns into all governance of globalization
- appoint more women to global leadership positions
- increase attention to assessing and redressing race, urban/rural and age discriminations in globalization

Enhancing democracy
- increase local government involvement in global policies
- intensify popular consultations in regard to global policies
- establish mechanisms for the representation of nonterritorial constituencies
- increase scrutiny of suprastate governance by elected state and substate bodies
- improve transparency of suprastate governance
- undertake comprehensive and systematic independent evaluation of global policies
- raise the democratic credentials of civil society

Overcoming challenges
- counter the substantial forces that support neoliberal globalization
- transcend the sovereignty mindset
- upgrade institutional capacities to formulate and implement global public policies
- build popular constituencies for ambitious global reformism
- maintain respect for cultural diversity

However, these detailed investigations go beyond the scope of the present book. This chapter has sought to lay the ground for such work by establishing the key point that major reform of globalization is available and desirable. Our concern should not be that we are powerless to correct the ills of neoliberal globalization. Rather, our disquiet should be that we have not done more to exploit the substantial potentials of reform.

Conclusion

To recapitulate 12 chapters in half a dozen sentences, this critical introduction to globalization has advanced the following replies to the six core questions that were set out in its opening paragraph:

1. In terms of definition, globality (when understood as supraterritoriality) designates something distinctive and important that other vocabulary of social analysis does not capture.
2. In terms of chronology, globalization has mainly unfolded since the third quarter of the twentieth century.
3. In terms of causation, globalization has resulted from structuration processes in which forces of rationalism, capitalism, technological innovation and regulatory facilitation have figured centrally.
4. In terms of social change, globalization has thus far brought notable shifts within – albeit not full-scale transformations of – primary structures of production, governance, community and knowledge.
5. In terms of impacts, contemporary globalization has, next to some important benefits, also in various ways undermined human security, social equity and democracy.
6. In terms of policy responses, a programme of ambitious reform can counter many potential harms and increase many potential gains of globalization.

These general conclusions have major implications for social thought and practice. In regard to social analysis, contemporary globalization has rendered methodological territorialism obsolete. We can no longer comprehend world geography in terms of territorial spaces alone, and a reorientation in this matter also changes the way that we understand other dimensions of social relations like culture, ecology, economics, politics and psychology. Thus globalization requires us substantially to rethink social theory.

In regard to social practice, contemporary globalization has significantly altered the dynamics of production, governance, community and knowledge. With the rise of supraterritoriality, capitalism has acquired different patterns of commodification and different forms of institutional organization. Expanding globality has also prompted the state to adopt different features and increasingly to share regulatory functions with substate, suprastate and nonstate entities. Proliferating transworld relations have

315

given the state-nation greater competition from ethno-nations and region-nations as well as various nonterritorial solidarities, cosmopolitan sentiments and hybrid identities. At the same time, globalization has encouraged some challenges to rationalism as the predominant framework of knowledge and brought various adjustments to ontology, methodology and aesthetics.

Yet these developments – important as they are – have not entailed a deeper transformation of the primary structures of social life. Production in the contemporary globalizing world has remained chiefly capitalist, and indeed has on the whole become *more* geared to surplus accumulation. Governance has remained predominantly bureaucratic, even if regulatory activities have become dispersed across multiple agencies in addition to the state. Community in world politics has retained a mainly communitarian character, even if some people have begun to explore alternative dynamics of intercultural relations. Knowledge has remained principally rationalist in orientation, even if many people now regard techno-scientific-instrumental reason more critically.

In short, globalization has brought *shifts within* rather than *replacements of* underlying social structures. Moreover, there is little sign that expanding supraterritoriality is in the foreseeable future taking us toward a post-capitalist, post-bureaucratic, post-communitarian, post-rationalist social order.

Of course shallower social changes can still have important impacts on everyday life. As seen in Part III, the shifts brought by globalization in respect of production, governance, community and knowledge have had some major repercussions for human security, social justice and democracy. The degree to which these consequences are positive or negative depends largely on the policies that we adopt in regard to globalization. To stress the central point again: our choices play a key role in shaping global futures.

As noted at the end of Chapter 1 and elaborated in Chapter 12, in determining those choices we face three broad options. One possibility, neoliberalism, has unacceptable social and environmental costs. A second possibility, radicalism, is currently not viable. Hence for the moment the way forward lies in reformist strategies.

Our next choice concerns the type and degree of reform that we pursue. To use previously introduced shorthand labels, will it be neoliberalism with knobs on or global social democracy? As argued in Chapter 12, the latter course of ambitious reformism holds greater promise for enhancing security, justice and democracy in a more global world. The implementation of this strategy faces substantial hurdles, but sustained and carefully executed political campaigns can move these obstacles.

On that optimistic note this critical introduction to globalization has finished. However, other work on globalization still has far to go. In terms of additional research, for example, we need further to develop the notion of globality-as-supraterritoriality. How has this new dimension of social space taken form more specifically in different realms of activity and in different cultural contexts? Major research efforts are also needed to assemble global social data. On many issues available statistics are mainly calculated on territorialist premises, that is, in relation to country units or local spaces. Other further research is needed to determine how the causes and consequences of globalization have unfolded in particular localities or in relation to particular issues.

Such research should also serve further political action. As indicated at the close of Chapter 12, effective pursuit of far-reaching reform of globalization requires: (a) sober recognition that substantial policy change faces powerful opposition; (b) major increases in the capacities of public governance agencies, especially suprastate institutions; and (c) large-scale efforts to build active support for reform among veritable 'global' citizens. I hope that this book will, while clarifying globalization intellectually, also be part of that process of building constituencies for more humane globalization.

Bibliography

Abegglen, J. C. (1994) *Sea Change: Pacific Asia as the New World Industrial Center*. New York: Free Press.

Abramson, J. B. *et al.* (1988) *The Electronic Commonwealth: the Impact of New Media Technologies on Democratic Politics*. New York: Basic Books.

Abu-Lughod, L. (1989) 'Bedouins, Cassettes and Technologies of Public Culture', *Middle East Report*, no. 159 (July–August), pp. 7–11.

Adam, B. D. (1987) *The Rise of a Gay and Lesbian Movement*. Boston, MA: Twayne.

Adams, F. *et al.* (eds) (1999) *Globalization and the Dilemmas of the State in the South*. Basingstoke: Macmillan.

Ahvenainen, J. (1981) *The Far Eastern Telegraphs: the History of Telegraphic Communications between the Far East, Europe and America before the First World War*. Helsinki: Suomalainen Tiedeakatemia.

Ake, C. (1999) 'Globalization, Multilateralism and the Shrinking Democratic Space', in M. G. Schechter (ed.), *Future Multilateralism: the Political and Social Framework*. Tokyo: United Nations University Press, pp. 179–95.

Albrow, M. (1996) *The Global Age: State and Society beyond Modernity*. Cambridge: Polity Press.

Alexander, T. (1996) *Unravelling Global Apartheid: an Overview of World Politics*. Cambridge: Polity Press.

Amin, A. (ed.) (1994) *Post-Fordism: a Reader*. Oxford: Blackwell.

Amin, S. (1996) 'The challenge of globalization', *Review of International Political Economy*, vol. 3, no. 2 (Summer), pp. 216–59.

Amin, S. (1997) *Capitalism in the Age of Globalization: the Management of Contemporary Society*. London: Zed.

Anderson, B. (1991) *Imagined Communities: Reflections on the Origin and Spread of Nationalism*, rev. edn. London: Verso.

Anderson, B. (1992) *Long-Distance Nationalism: World Capitalism and the Rise of Identity Politics*. Amsterdam: Centre for Asian Studies Amsterdam.

Anderson, W. T. (1990) *Reality Isn't What It Used To Be: Theatrical Politics, Ready-to Wear Religion, Global Myths, Primitive Chic, and Other Wonders of the Postmodern World*. San Francisco: Harper & Row.

AP (1999a) 'Indonesians Living in Poverty Reach 130 Million', Associated Press newswire, 15 January.

AP (1999b) 'World Bank Estimates 200 Million "Newly Poor"', Associated Press newswire, 3 June.

Appadurai, A. (1990) 'Disjuncture and Difference in the Global Cultural Economy', *Public Culture*, vol. 2, no. 3 (Spring), pp. 1–24.

Araghi, F. A. (1995) 'Global Depeasantization, 1945–1990', *The Sociological Quarterly*, vol. 36, no. 2 (Spring), pp. 337–68.

Archer, M. (1990) 'Foreword', in M. Albrow and E. King (eds), *Globalization, Knowledge and Society: Readings from International Sociology*. London: Sage, pp. 1–2.

Archibugi, D. (1995) 'From the United Nations to Cosmopolitan Democracy', in Archibugi and D. Held (eds), *Cosmopolitan Democracy: an Agenda for a New World Order*. Cambridge: Polity Press, pp. 121–62.

Archibugi, D. *et al.* (eds) (1998) *Re-imagining Political Community: Studies in Cosmopolitan Democracy*. Cambridge: Polity Press.

Armijo, L. E. (ed.) (1999) *Financial Globalization and Democracy in Emerging Markets*. Basingstoke: Macmillan.

Aronowitz, S. and W. DiFazio (1994) *The Jobless Future: Sci-Tech and the Dogma of Work*. Minneapolis: University of Minnesota Press.

Aslanbeigui, N. *et al.* (eds) (1994) *Women in the Age of Economic Transformation: Gender Impact of Reforms in Post-Socialist and Developing Countries*. London: Routledge.

ATTAC (1999) Website of the *Association pour une Taxation des Transactions financières pour l'Aide aux Citoyens*, http://www.attac.org.

Axford, B. (1995) *The Global System: Economics, Politics and Culture*. Cambridge: Polity Press.

Bacchetta, M. *et al.* (1998) *Electronic Commerce and the Role of the WTO*. Geneva: World Trade Organization.

Baer, J. B. and O. G. Saxon (1949) *Commodity Exchanges and Futures Trading*. New York: Harper & Brothers.

Baker, J. (1999) Information provided to the author by James Baker of the International Confederation of Free Trade Unions.

Balleroni, E. (1995) 'Women To Be Given Priority', *Politiken Summit*, 8 March, p. 7.

Bandow, D. and I. Vásquez (eds) (1994) *Perpetuating Poverty: the World Bank, the IMF, and the Developing World*. Washington, DC: Cato Institute.

Barber, B. R. (1996) *Jihad vs. McWorld*. New York: Ballantine.

Barker, D. and J. Mander (n.d.) *Invisible Government – the World Trade Organization: Global Government for the New Millennium?* San Francisco: International Forum on Globalization.

Barnet, R. J. and J. Cavanagh (1994) *Global Dreams: Imperial Corporations and the New World Order*. New York: Simon and Schuster.

Bartlett, C. A. and S. Ghoshal (1998) *Managing Across Borders: the Transnational Solution*, 2nd edn. London: Random House Business Books.

Bauman, Z. (1998) *Globalization: the Human Consequences*. Cambridge: Polity Press.

Beck, U. (1986) *Risk Society: Towards a New Modernity*. London: Sage, 1992.

Beck, U. (1988) *Ecological Politics in an Age of Risk*. Cambridge: Polity Press, 1995.

Beck, U. (1994) 'The Reinvention of Politics: Towards a Theory of Reflexive Modernization', in U. Beck *et al.*, *Reflexive Modernization: Politics, Tradition and Aesthetics in the Modern Social Order*. Cambridge: Polity Press, pp. 1–55.

Beck, U. (1997) *The Reinvention of Politics: Rethinking Modernity in the Global Social Order*. Cambridge: Polity Press.

Beck, U. (1999) *World Risk Society*. Cambridge: Polity Press.

Beetham, D. (1997) 'Market Economy and Democratic Polity', *Democratization*, vol. 4, no. 1 (Spring), pp. 76–93.

Bell, D. (1973) *The Coming of Post-Industrial Society*. London: Heinemann.

Bellamy Foster, J. (1994) 'Waste Away', *Dollars & Sense*, no. 195 (September–October), p. 7.

Bello, W. *et al.* (1994) *Dark Victory: the United States, Structural Adjustment, and Global Poverty*. London: Pluto.

Beneria, L. and S. Feldman (eds) (1992) *Unequal Burden: Economic Crises, Persistent Poverty, and Women's Work*. Boulder, CO: Westview.

Berger, J. *et al.* (1998–9) 'The Threat of Globalism', *Race & Class*, vol. 40, nos 2/3 (October–March).

Bergsten, C. F. (1996) 'Globalizing Free Trade', *Foreign Affairs*, vol. 75, no. 3 (May/June), pp. 105–20.

Beyer, P. (1994) *Religion and Globalization*. London: Sage.

Bhagwati, J. N. (ed.) (1977) *The New International Economic Order: the North–South Debate*. Cambridge, MA: MIT Press.

BIS (1996) *International Banking and Financial Market Developments*. Basle: Bank for International Settlements.

BIS (1997) *Core Principles for Effective Banking Supervision*. Basle: Bank for International Settlements.

BIS (1998a) 'The Global OTC Derivatives Market at End-June 1998'. Bank for International Settlements Press Release, 23 December.

BIS (1998b) *68th Annual Report*. Basle: Bank for International Settlements.

Blaney, D. and N. Inayatullah (1994) 'Prelude to a Conversation of Cultures in International Society? Todorov and Nandy on the Possibility of Dialogue', *Alternatives*, vol. 19, no. 1, pp. 23–51.

Bleeke, J. and D. Ernst (eds) (1993) *Collaborating to Compete: Using Strategic Alliances and Acquisitions in the Global Marketplace*. New York: John Wiley.

Boden, D. (1990) 'Reinventing the Global Village: Communication and the Revolutions of 1989', in A. Giddens (ed.), *Human Societies: an Introductory Reader in Sociology*. Cambridge: Polity Press, 1992, pp. 327–31.

Boele, R. (1995) *Ogoni: Report of the UNPO Mission to Investigate the Situation of the Ogoni of Nigeria February 17–26, 1995*. The Hague: Unrepresented Nations and Peoples Organization, 1 May.

Bolnick, J. *et al.* (1999) 'Sharing Experiences and Changing Lives'. Paper presented at the Third International NGO Conference, University of Birmingham, 10–13 January.

Booth, K. (ed.) (1991) *New Thinking about Strategy and International Security*. London: HarperCollins.

Boutros-Ghali, B. (1995a) *An Agenda for Development 1995*. New York: United Nations Department of Public Information.

Boutros-Ghali, B. (1995b) Remarks to the World Summit for Social Development, Copenhagen, 5–12 March.

Bowles, P. and B. Wagman (1997) 'Globalization and the Welfare State: Four Hypotheses and Some Empirical Evidence', *Eastern Economic Journal*, vol. 23, no. 3, pp. 317–36.

Boyer, R. and D. Drache (eds) (1996) *States against Markets: the Limits of Globalization*. London: Routledge.

Bratton, W. W. *et al.* (eds) (1996) *International Regulatory Competition and Coordination: Perspectives on Economic Regulation in Europe and the United States*. Oxford: Clarendon.

Brecher, J. and T. Costello (1994) *Global Village or Global Pillage: Economic Reconstruction from the Bottom Up*. Boston, MA: South End Press.

Brock, L. (1993) 'Im Umbruch der Weltpolitik', *Leviathan*, vol. 21, no. 2, pp. 163–73.

Brown, N. (1990) *New Strategy through Space*. Leicester: Leicester University Press.

Brown, R. (1995) 'Globalization and the End of the National Project', in J. MacMillan and A. Linklater (eds), *Boundaries in Question: New Directions in International Relations*. London: Pinter, pp. 54–68.

Brown, T. (1999) 'World Financial Crisis Not Over – UNICEF's Bellamy', Reuter's despatch of 29 April, at http://biz.yahoo.com/rf/990429/bvd.html.

Bryan, L. and D. Farrell (1996) *Market Unbound: Unleashing Global Capitalism*. New York: John Wiley.

Bryant, R. C. (1999) 'Standards and Prudential Oversight for an Integrating World Financial System'. Paper for a meeting of the Tokyo Club Foundation for Global Studies and the Royal Institute of International Affairs.

Bryant, R. C. (2000) *Turbulent Waters: Cross-Border Finance in the 21st Century*. Washington, DC: Brookings Institution.

Bryson, J. R. and P. W. Daniels (eds) (1998) *Service Industries in the Global Economy*, 2 vols. Cheltenham: Elgar.

Brzezinski, Z. (1993) *Out of Control: Global Turmoil on the Eve of the Twenty-First Century*. New York: Charles Scribner's Sons.

BT (2000) *Variety and Values: a Sustainable Response to Globalisation?* London: British Telecommunications Corporate Reputation & Social Policy Unit.

Budge, I. (1996) *The New Challenge of Direct Democracy*. Cambridge: Polity Press.

Budhoo, D. L. (1990) *Enough Is Enough*. New York: Apex.

Buell, F. (1994) *National Culture and the New Global System*. Baltimore: Johns Hopkins University Press.

Bull, H. (1977) *The Anarchical Society: a Study of Order in World Politics*. London: Macmillan.

Bunch, C. and N. Reilly (1994) *Demanding Accountability: the Global Campaign and Vienna Tribunal for Women's Human Rights*. New York: Center for Women's Global Leadership and the United Nations Development Fund for Women.

Burbach, R. *et al*. (1997) *Globalization and Its Discontents: the Rise of Postmodern Socialisms*. London: Pluto.

Burtless, G. *et al*. (1998) *Globaphobia: Confronting Fears about Open Trade*. Washington, DC: Brookings Institution.

Cable, V. (1994) *The World's New Fissures: Identities in Crisis*. London: Demos.

Cable, V. (1995) 'The Diminished Nation-State: A Study in the Loss of Economic Power', *Daedalus*, vol. 124, no. 2 (Spring), pp. 23–54.

Cairncross, F. (1997) *The Death of Distance: How the Communications Revolution Will Change Our Lives*. London: Orion Business.

Cameron, R. and V. I. Bovykin (eds) (1991) *International Banking 1870–1914*. New York: Oxford University Press.

Camilleri, J. A. and J. Falk (1992) *The End of Sovereignty? The Politics of a Shrinking and Fragmenting World*. Aldershot: Elgar.

Camilleri, J. A. *et al*. (eds) (1995) *The State in Transition: Reimagining Political Space*. Boulder, CO: Rienner.

Campbell, D. and M. Dillon (eds) (1993) *The Political Subject of Violence*. Manchester: Manchester University Press.

Campbell, T. (1987) *The Earliest Printed Maps 1472–1500*. London: British Library.

Cardoso, F.H. (1996) 'La globalización y el nuevo orden mundial', *Boletín editorial de el Colegio de Mexico*, No. 68.

Carlsson, I. *et al.* (1995) *Our Global Neighbourhood*. Oxford: Oxford University Press [Commission on Global Governance].

Carnoy, M. *et al.* (1993) *The New Global Economy in the Information Age*. University Park, PA: Pennsylvania State University Press.

Carothers, T. (1999) 'Struggling with Semi-Authoritarians'. Paper for the conference on Globalising Democracy, University of Warwick, 9–10 September.

Castells, M. (1989) *The Informational City: Information Technology, Economic Restructuring, and the Urban-Regional Process*. Oxford: Blackwell.

Castells, M. (1996–7) *The Information Age: Economy, Society and Culture*, 2 vols. Oxford: Blackwell.

Castles, S. and A. Davidson (2000) *Globalisation and Citizenship*. Basingstoke: Macmillan.

Cavanagh, J. (1997) 'Rethinking Corporate Accountability', in J.M. Griesgraber and B.G. Gunter (eds), *World Trade: Toward Fair and Free Trade in the Twenty-First Century*. London: Pluto, pp. 91–107.

Cerny, P.G. (1990) *The Changing Architecture of Politics: Structure, Agency and the Future of the State*. London: Sage.

Cerny, P.G. (1996) 'Globalization and Other Stories: the Search for a New Paradigm for International Relations', *International Journal*, vol. 51, no. 4 (Autumn), pp. 617–37.

Cerny, P.G. (1997) 'Paradoxes of the Competition State: the Dynamics of Political Globalization', *Government and Opposition*, vol. 32, no. 2 (Spring), pp. 251–74.

Chandler, A.D. (1986) 'The Evolution of Modern Global Competition', in M.E. Porter (ed.), *Competition in Global Industries*. Boston, MA: Harvard Business School Press, pp. 405–48.

Chase-Dunn, C.K. (1989) *Global Formation: Structures of the World Economy*. Oxford: Blackwell.

Chesnaid, F. (1994) *La mondialisation du capital*. Paris: Syros.

Childers, E. (1994) 'United Nations Reform: Relevance of the Southern Perspective'. Geneva: International NGO Network on Global Governance and Democratization of International Relations, Topical Papers 3.

CHIPS (2000) Website of the Clearing House Interbank Payment System, http://www.chips.org/.

Chopra, J. and T.G. Weiss (1992) 'Sovereignty Is No Longer Sacrosanct: Codifying Humanitarian Intervention', *Ethics and International Affairs*, vol. 6, pp. 95–117.

Chossudovsky, M. (1997) *The Globalisation of Poverty: Impacts of IMF and World Bank Reforms*. London: Zed.

CICC (1999) Website of the NGO Coalition for an International Criminal Court, http://www.igc.apc.org/icc.

Clairemonte, F. and J. Cavanagh (1988) *Merchants of Drink: Transnational Control of World Beverages*. Penang: Third World Network.

Clark, I. (1997) *Globalization and Fragmentation: International Relations in the Twentieth Century*. Oxford: Oxford University Press.

Clark, I. (1999) *Globalization and International Relations Theory*. Oxford: Oxford University Press.

Clark, J.D. (1999) 'Ethical Globalization: the Dilemmas and Challenges of Internationalizing Civil Society'. Paper presented at the Third International NGO Conference, University of Birmingham, 10–13 January.

Cohen, S. and J. Zysman (1987) *Manufacturing Matters: the Myth of the Post-Industrial Economy*. New York: Basic Books.

Commoner, B. (1971) *The Closing Circle: Confronting the Environmental Crisis*. London: Cape, 1972.

Connolly, W. E. (1991) 'Democracy and Territoriality', *Millennium*, vol. 20, no. 3 (December), pp. 463–84.

Connor, W. (1994) *Ethnonationalism: the Quest for Understanding*. Princeton: Princeton University Press.

Cooperrider, D. and J. E. Dutton (eds) (1999) *Organizational Dimensions of Global Change: No Limits to Cooperation*. London: Sage.

Coote, B. (1996) *The Trade Trap: Poverty and the Global Commodity Markets*, 2nd edn. Oxford: Oxfam.

Cornia, G. A. *et al.* (1987–8) *Adjustment with a Human Face*, 2 vols. Oxford: Clarendon.

Cox, K. R. (ed.) (1997) *Spaces of Globalization: Reasserting the Power of the Local*. New York: Guilford.

Cox, R. W. (1987) *Production, Power, and World Order: Social Forces in the Making of History*. New York: Columbia University Press.

Cox, R. W. (1992) 'Global *Perestroika*', in R. Miliband and L. Panitch (eds), *Socialist Register 1992*. London: Merlin, pp. 26–43.

Cox, R. W. (1993a) 'Programme on Multilateralism and the United Nations System, 1990–1995: Second Interim Report', The United Nations University, September.

Cox, R. W. (1993b) 'Structural Issues of Global Governance', in S. Gill (ed.), *Gramsci, Historical Materialism, and International Relations*. Cambridge: Cambridge University Press, pp. 259–89.

Cox, R. W. (1997) 'An Alternative Approach to Multilateralism for the Twenty-First Century', *Global Governance*, vol. 3, no. 1 (January–April), pp. 103–16.

Cruickshank, M. (1992) *The Gay and Lesbian Liberation Movement*. London: Routledge.

Cunniah, D. (1995) 'How To Use the ILO's Supervisory System', *Free Labour World* (January), p. 8.

Cutler, A. C. *et al.* (eds) (1999) *Private Authority in International Affairs*. Albany: State University of New York Press.

Czempiel, E.-O. and J. N. Rosenau (eds) (1989) *Global Changes and Theoretical Challenges*. Lexington, MA: Lexington Books.

Dawson, M. C. (1999) 'Globalization, the Racial Divide, and a New Citizenship', in R. D. Torres *et al.* (eds), *Race, Identity, and Citizenship: a Reader*. Oxford: Blackwell, pp. 373–85.

Deacon, B. (1997) *Global Social Policy: International Organizations and the Future of Welfare*. London: Sage.

Demac, D. A. (ed.) (1986) *Tracing New Orbits: Cooperation and Competition in Global Satellite Development*. New York: Columbia University Press.

Denters, E. (1996) *Law and Policy of IMF Conditionality*. Dordrecht: Kluwer.

Devall, B. and G. Sessions (1985) *Deep Ecology: Living as if Nature Mattered*. Salt Lake City: Smith.

Devine, J. (1996) *NGOs: Changing Fashion or Fashioning Change?* Bath: Centre for Development Studies, University of Bath.

DFID (1997) *Eliminating World Poverty: a Challenge for the 21st Century. White Paper on International Development*. London: The Stationery Office/Cm 3789.

Dhonte, P. and I. Kapur (1997) *Toward a Market Economy: Structures of Governance*. Washington, DC: IMF Working Paper 97/11.

Diamond, L. and M. F. Plattner (eds) (1996) *The Global Resurgence of Democracy*, 2nd edn. Baltimore: Johns Hopkins University Press.

Doggart, C. (1993) *Tax Havens and Their Uses*. London: Economist Intelligence Unit.

Doremus, P. N. *et al.* (1998) *The Myth of the Global Corporation*. Princeton: Princeton University Press.

Douglas, I. R. (1996) 'The *Myth* of Globali[z]ation: A Poststructural Reading of Speed and Reflexivity in the Governance of Late Modernity'. Paper presented to the 38th Annual Convention of the International Studies Association, San Diego, 16–20 April.

Dowmunt, T. (ed.) (1993) *Channels of Resistance: Global Television and Local Empowerment*. London: BFI/Channel 4.

DPC (1995) *A Framework for Voluntary Oversight of the OTC Derivatives Activities of Securities Firm Activities to Promote Confidence and Stability in Financial Markets*. Washington, DC: Derivatives Policy Group.

Drainville, A. C. (1998) 'The Fetishism of Global Civil Society: Global Governance, Transnational Urbanism and Sustainable Capitalism in the World Economy', in M. P. Smith and L. E. Guarnizo (eds), *Transnationalism from Below*. New Brunswick, NJ: Transaction, pp. 35–63.

Drucker, P. F. (1989) *The New Realities*. London: Butterworth.

Drucker, P. F. (1993) *Post-Capitalist Society*. Oxford: Butterworth-Heinemann.

Dubey, M. (1996) *An Unequal Treaty: World Trading Order after GATT*. New Delhi: New Age International.

Duchacek, I. D. *et al.* (eds) (1988) *Perforated Sovereignties and International Relations: Trans-Sovereign Contacts of Subnational Governments*. Westport, CT: Greenwood.

Dunn, J. (ed.) (1995) *Contemporary Crisis of the Nation State?* Oxford: Blackwell.

Dunning, J. H. (1993) *The Globalization of Business: the Challenge of the 1990s*. London, Routledge.

Eatwell, J. (1995) 'The International Origins of Unemployment', in J. Michie and J. Grieve (eds), *Managing the Global Economy*. Oxford: Oxford University Press, pp. 271–87.

Eckersley, R. (1992) *Environmentalism and Political Theory: Toward an Ecocentric Approach*. London: University College London Press.

Economist, The (1995) 'Regionalism and Trade: the Right Direction?' *The Economist*, vol. 336, no. 7932 (16 September), pp. 27–8, 33.

Edwards, M. (1999) *Future Positive: International Co-operation in the 21st Century*. London: Earthscan.

Edwards, M. and D. Hulme (eds) (1995) *Non-Governmental Organisations – Performance and Accountability: Beyond the Magic Bullet*. London: Earthscan.

Edwards, M. and J. Gaventa (eds) (forthcoming) *Global Citizen Action: Perspectives and Challenges*. Boulder, CO: Rienner.

Eichengreen, B. (1999) *Toward a New International Financial Architecture: a Practical Post-Asia Agenda*. Washington, DC: Institute for International Economics.

Einhorn, B. (1993) *Cinderella Goes to Market: Citizenship, Gender and Women's Movements in East Central Europe*. London: Verso.

EIU (1957) *A History of the London Metal Exchange*. London: Economist Intelligence Unit.

Emerson, R. (1960) *From Empire to Nation: the Rise to Self-Assertion of Asian and African Peoples*. Cambridge, MA: Harvard University Press, 1962.

Escorcia, G. (1999) Anecdote related to the author by the Director of Global Thinkers, Mexico City, 8 June.

Esping-Andersen, G. (1990) *The Three Worlds of Welfare Capitalism*. Cambridge: Polity Press.

Esping-Andersen, G. (1994) *After the Golden Age: the Future of the Welfare State in the New Global Order*. Geneva: UNRISD Occasional Paper 7, World Summit for Social Development.

Esping-Andersen, G. (ed.) (1996) *Welfare States in Transition: National Adaptations in Global Economies*. London: Sage.

Esposito, J. (ed.) (1990) *The Iranian Revolution: Its Global Impact*. Miami: Florida International University Press.

EST (1997) 'The Economist Survey of Telecommunications', *The Economist*, vol. 344, no. 8034 (13 September).

Euroclear (2000) '1999: Another Record Year as Euroclear Market Share Shows Marked Increase'. Euroclear Press Release, 16 February.

Evans, P. (1997) 'The Eclipse of the State? Reflections on Stateness in an Era of Globalization', *World Politics*, vol. 50, no. 1 (October), pp. 62–87.

Falk, R. A. (1992a) *Explorations at the Edge of Time: the Prospects for World Order*. Philadelphia: Temple University Press.

Falk, R. A. (1992b) 'The Infancy of Global Civil Society', in G. Lundestad and O. A. Westad (eds), *Beyond the Cold War: New Directions in International Relations*. Oslo: Scandinavian University Press, pp. 219–39.

Falk, R. A. (1993) 'Global Apartheid', *Third World Resurgence*, no. 37 (November), pp. 15–16.

Falk, R. A. (1995) *On Humane Governance: Toward a New Global Politics*. Cambridge: Polity Press.

Falk, R. A. (1999) *Predatory Globalization: a Critique*. Cambridge: Polity Press.

Falk, R. A. and T. Mogami (1993) 'Towards a More Democratic and Humane Multilateralism: a Few Observations on the Reform of the United Nations'. Geneva: International NGO Network on Global Governance and Democratisation of International Relations, Topical Papers 1.

FAO (1998) *The State of Food and Agriculture 1998*. Rome: Food and Agriculture Organisation.

Featherstone, M. (ed.) (1990) *Global Culture: Nationalism, Globalization and Modernity*. London: Sage.

Featherstone, M. (1991) *Consumer Culture and Postmodernism*. London: Sage.

Featherstone, M. *et al.* (eds) (1995) *Global Modernities*. London: Sage.

FIBV (1994) *Annual Report and Statistics*. Paris: Federation Internationale des Bourses de Valeur.

Findlay, T. (1995) 'Armed Conflict Prevention, Management and Resolution', in *SIPRI Yearbook 1995*. Oxford: Oxford University Press, pp. 37–82.

Flora, C. B. (1990) 'Rural Peoples in a Global Economy', *Rural Sociology*, vol. 55, no. 2 (Spring), pp. 157–77.

Ford (1999) Website of the Ford Foundation, http://www.fordfound.org/.

Fortin, C. (1992) 'The United Nations and Development in the 1990s', in P. Streeten *et al.*, *International Governance*. Brighton: University of Sussex, pp. 69–95.

Fortune (1995) 'The Merger Mania Continues', *Fortune*, vol. 132 (25 December), pp. 33–40.

Foster, R. J. (1991) 'Making National Cultures in the Global Ecumene', *Annual Review of Anthropology*, vol. 20, pp. 235–60.

Fowler, A. (1994) 'Capacity Building and NGOs: a Case of Strengthening Ladles for the Global Soup Kitchen? *Institutional Development*, 1, 1, pp. 18–25.

Fox, J. A. and L. D. Brown (eds) (1998) *The Struggle for Accountability: the World Bank, NGOs, and Grassroots Movements*. Cambridge, MA: MIT Press.

Frederick, H. (1993) 'Computer Networks and the Emergence of Global Civil Society', in L. Harasim (ed.), *Global Networks: Computers and International Communication*. Cambridge, MA: MIT Press, pp. 283–95.

Frei, E. (1995) Address of the President of Chile to the World Summit for Social Development, Copenhagen, March.

Friedman, J. (1994) *Cultural Identity and Global Process*. London: Sage.

Friedman, T. L. (1999) *The Lexus and the Olive Tree*. New York: HarperCollins.

Fry, E. H. (1995) 'The Vincibility of Modern Nation-States: Challenges from the International and Subnational Arenas'. Paper presented to the 36th Annual Convention of the International Studies Association, Chicago, 21–25 February.

FSF (1999) Website of the Financial Stability Forum, http://www.fsforum.org.

FT500 (1996) 'The FT500 Survey', *Financial Times Supplement*, 25 January.

FT500 (1997) 'The FT500 Survey', *Financial Times Supplement*, 24 January.

Fuentes, A. and B. Ehrenreich (1983) *Women in the Global Factory*. Boston, MA: South End.

Fukuyama, F. (1992) *The End of History and the Last Man*. London: Hamish Hamilton.

Funk, N. and M. Mueller (eds) (1993) *Gender Politics and Post-Communism: Reflections from Eastern Europe and the Former Soviet Union*. New York: Routledge.

G30 (1993) *Derivatives: Practices and Principles*. Washington, DC: Group of Thirty.

GACGC (1995) *World in Transition: the Threat to Soils. 1994 Annual Report*. Bonn: Economica [German Advisory Council on Global Change].

Galizia, M. (1993) Personal communication to the author from Michele Galizia of the University of Berne, July.

Gamble, A. (1994) *The Free Economy and the Strong State: the Politics of Thatcherism*. Basingstoke: Macmillan.

Gamble, C. (1994) *Timewalkers: the Prehistory of Global Colonization*. Cambridge, MA: Harvard University Press.

Gates, B. (1995) *The Road Ahead*. London: Viking.

Gaventa, J. (1999) 'Learning across Boundaries: Strengthening Participation in North and South'. Paper presented at the Third International NGO Conference, University of Birmingham, 10–13 January.

Gelber, H. G. (1997) *Sovereignty through Interdependence*. London: Kluwer Law International.

Gelernter, D. H. (1995) *1939: the Lost World of the Fair*. New York: Free Press.

George, S. and F. Sabelli (1994) *Faith and Credit: the World Bank's Secular Empire*. Boulder, CO: Westview.

Germain, R. (ed.) (1999) *Globalization and Its Critics: Perspectives from Political Economy*. Basingstoke: Macmillan.

Gerster, R. (1993) 'Proposals for Voting Reform within the International Monetary Fund', *Journal of World Trade*, vol. 27, no. 3 (June), pp. 121–36.

Geyer, R. *et al.* (eds) (1999) *Globalization, Europeanization and the End of Scandinavian Social Democracy?* Basingstoke: Macmillan.

Ghai, D. (ed.) (1991) *The IMF and the South: the Social Impact of Adjustrment*. London: Zed.

Ghai, D. (1994) 'Structural Adjustment, Global Integration and Social Democracy', in R. Prendergast and F. Stewart (eds), *Market Forces and World Development*. New York: St. Martin's, pp. 15–44.

Ghils, P. (1992) 'International Civil Society: International Non-Governmental Organizations in the International System', *International Social Science Journal*, no. 133 (August), pp. 417–31.

Giddens, A. (1990) *The Consequences of Modernity*. Cambridge: Polity Press.

Giddens, A. (1991) *Modernity and Self-Identity: Self and Society in the Late Modern Age*. Cambridge: Polity Press.

Giddens, A. (1994) 'Living in a Post-Traditional Society', in U. Beck *et al.*, *Reflexive Modernization: Politics, Tradition and Aesthetics in the Modern Social Order*. Cambridge: Polity Press, pp. 56–109.

Giddens, A. (1998) *The Third Way: the Renewal of Social Democracy*. Cambridge: Polity Press.

Gilbert, A. (1999) *Must Global Politics Constrain Democracy? Great-Power Realism, Democratic Peace, and Democratic Internationalism*. Princeton: Princeton University Press.

Gill, S. (1995) 'Globalisation, Market Civilisation, and Disciplinary Neoliberalism', *Millennium*, vol. 24, no. 3 (Winter), pp. 399–423.

Gill, S. (1996) 'Globalization, Democratization, and the Politics of Indifference', in J. H. Mittelman (ed.) *Globalization: Critical Reflections* Boulder: Rienner, pp. 205–28.

Gill, S. (ed.) (1997) *Globalization, Democratization and Multilateralism*. London: Macmillan/United Nations University Press.

Gills, B. *et al.* (eds) (1993) *Low Intensity Democracy: Political Power in the New World Order*. London: Pluto.

Gills, B. (ed.) (1997) 'Special Issue: Globalisation and the Politics of Resistance', *New Political Economy*, vol. 2, no. 1 (March).

Gilroy, B. M. (1993) *Networking in Multinational Enterprises: the Importance of Strategic Alliances*. Columbia: University of South Carolina Press.

Goldin, I. *et al.* (1993) *Trade Liberalisation: Global Economic Implications*. Paris: OECD/World Bank.

Golding, P. and P. Harris (eds) (1997) *Beyond Cultural Imperialism: Globalization, Communication and the New International Order*. London: Sage.

Goodman, D. S. G. and G. Segal (eds) (1994) *China Deconstructs: Politics, Trade and Regionalism*. London: Routledge.

Gorz, A. (1988) *Critique of Economic Reason*. London: Verso, 1989.

Gray, J. (1998) *False Dawn: the Delusions of Global Capitalism*. London: Granta.

Gregory, D. and J. Urry (eds) (1985) *Social Relations and Spatial Structures*. Basingstoke: Macmillan.

Greider, W. (1997) *One World, Ready or Not: the Manic Logic of Global Capitalism*. London: Allen Lane.

Griffith-Jones, S. (1998) *Global Capital Flows: Should They Be Regulated?* New York: St Martin's.

Group of Lisbon (1994) *Limits to Competition*. Cambridge, MA: MIT Press, 1995.

Grunberg, I. (1998) 'Double Jeopardy: Globalization, Liberalization and the Fiscal Squeeze', *World Development*, vol. 26, no. 4 (April), pp. 591–605.

Guéhenno, J.-M. (1995) *The End of the Nation-State*. Minneapolis: University of Minnesota Press.

Gunter, B. G. (1996) 'Reforming the International Monetary System towards a World Central Bank: A Summary of Proposals and Fallacies', in J. M. Griesgraber and B. G. Gunter (eds), *The World's Monetary System: Toward Stability and Sustainability in the Twenty-First Century.* London: Pluto, pp. 115–35.

Gurr, T. R. (1994) 'Peoples against States: Ethnopolitical Conflict and the Changing World System', *International Studies Quarterly*, vol. 38, no. 3 (September), pp. 347–77.

Haas, P. M. (1992) 'Introduction: Epistemic Communities and International Policy Coordination', *International Organization*, vol. 46, no. 1 (Winter), pp. 1–35.

Haas, P. M. *et al.* (eds) (1993) *Institutions for the Earth: Sources of Effective International Environmental Protection.* Cambridge, MA: MIT Press.

Halperin, M. H. and D. J. Scheffer (1992) *Self-Determination in the New World Order.* Washington, DC: Carnegie Endowment for International Peace.

Hamelink, C. J. (1983) *Cultural Autonomy in Global Communications.* New York: Longmans.

Hampton, M. P. (ed.) (1999) *Offshore Finance Centres and Tax Havens: the Rise of Global Capital.* Basingstoke: Macmillan.

Hancock, D. (1995) *Citizens of the World: London Merchants and the Integration of the British Atlantic Community, 1735–1785.* Cambridge: Cambridge University Press.

Handy, C. (1992) 'Balancing Corporate Power: a New Federalist Paper', *Harvard Business Review*, vol. 70, no. 6 (November–December), pp. 59–72.

Hannerz, U. (1987) 'The World in Creolisation', *Africa*, vol. 57, pp. 546–59.

Hannerz, U. (1992) *Cultural Complexity: Studies in the Social Organization of Meaning.* New York: Columbia University Press.

Hannerz, U. (1996) *Transnational Connections: Culture, People, Places.* London: Routledge.

Haq, M. ul *et al.* (eds) (1996) *The Tobin Tax: Coping with Financial Volatility.* New York: Oxford University Press.

Harcourt, W. (ed.) (1999) *Women @ Internet: Creating New Cultures in Cyberspace.* London: Zed.

Harman, W. and J. Hormann (1990) *Creative Work: the Constructive Role of Business in a Transforming Society.* Indianapolis: Knowledge Systems, Inc.

Harris, J. (1998–9) 'Globalisation and the Transformation of Capitalism', *Race & Class*, vol. 40, no. 2/3 (October–March), pp. 21–35.

Harrison, B. (1994) *Lean and Mean: the Changing Landscape of Corporate Power in the Age of Flexibility.* New York: Basic Books.

Harrod, J. (1992) *Labour and Third World Debt.* Brussels: International Federation of Chemical, Energy and General Workers' Unions.

Harvey, D. (1989) *The Condition of Postmodernity: an Enquiry into the Conditions of Cultural Change.* Oxford: Blackwell.

Harvey, D. (1993) 'From Space to Place and Back Again: Reflections on the Condition of Postmodernity', in J. Bird *et al.* (eds), *Mapping the Futures: Local Cultures, Global Change.* London: Routledge, pp. 3–29.

Harvey, R. (1995) *The Return of the Strong: the Drift to Global Disorder.* London: Macmillan.

Hawthorne, N. (1851) *The House of the Seven Gables: a Romance.* Edinburgh: Paterson, 1883.

Heerings, H. and I. Zeldenrust (1995) *Elusive Saviours: Transnational Corporations and Sustainable Development.* Utrecht: International Books.

Heidegger, M. (1950) 'The Thing', in *Poetry, Language, Thought.* New York: Harper & Row, 1971, pp. 165–82.

Held, D. (1995a) *Democracy and the Global Order: from the Modern State to Cosmopolitan Governance.* Cambridge: Polity Press.

Held, D. (1995b) 'Democracy and the New International Order', in D. Archibugi and D. Held (eds), *Cosmopolitan Democracy: an Agenda for a New World Order.* Cambridge: Polity Press, pp. 96–120.

Held, D. and A. McGrew (1993) 'Globalization and the Liberal Democratic State', *Government and Opposition,* vol. 28, no. 2 (Spring), pp. 261–85.

Held, D. *et al.* (1999) *Global Transformations: Politics, Economics and Culture.* Cambridge: Polity Press.

Helleiner, E. (1994) *States and the Reemergence of Global Finance: from Bretton Woods to the 1990s.* Ithaca, NY: Cornell University Press.

Helleiner, E. (1998) 'Electronic Money: a Challenge to the Sovereign State?' *Journal of International Affairs,* vol. 51, no. 2 (Spring), pp. 387–410.

Helleiner, E. (1999) 'Sovereignty, Territoriality, and the Globalization of Finance', in D. A. Smith *et al.* (eds), *States and Sovereignty in the Global Economy.* London: Routledge, pp. 138–57.

Helliwell, J. F. (1998) *How Much Do National Borders Matter?* Washington, DC: Brookings Institution.

Herbst, J. and A. Olukoshi (1994) 'Nigeria: Economic and Political Reforms at Cross Purposes', in S. Haggard and S. B. Webb (eds), *Voting for Reform: Democracy, Political Liberalization, and Economic Adjustment.* New York: Oxford University Press, pp. 453–502.

Herman, E. S. and R. W. McChesney (1997) *The Global Media: the New Missionaries of Corporate Capitalism.* London: Cassell.

Herod, A. *et al.* (eds) (1998) *An Unruly World? Globalization, Governance and Geography.* London: Routledge.

Hettne, B. (1994) 'The Regional Factor in the Formation of a New World Order', in Y. Sakamoto (ed.), *Global Transformation: Challenges to the State System.* Tokyo: United Nations University, pp. 134–66.

Hettne, B. *et al.* (eds) (1999) *Globalism and the New Regionalism.* Basingstoke: Macmillan.

Hewison, K. (1999) *Localism in Thailand: a Study of Globalisation and Its Discontents.* Coventry: ESRC/University of Warwick Centre for the Study of Globalisation and Regionalisation Working Paper Series No. 39/99.

Higgott, R. A. *et al.* (eds) (2000) *Non-State Actors and Authority in the Global System.* London: Routledge.

Hill, K. A. and J. E. Hughes (1998) *Cyberpolitics: Citizen Activism in the Age of the Internet.* Lanham, MD: Rowman & Littlefield

Hinsley, F. H. (1963) *Power and the Pursuit of Peace: Theory and Practice in the History of Relations between States.* Cambridge: Cambridge University Press.

Hirst, P. and G. Thompson (1996a) 'Globalisation: Ten Frequently Asked Questions and Some Surprising Answers', *Soundings,* vol. 4 (Autumn), pp. 47–66.

Hirst, P. and G. Thompson (1996b) *Globalization in Question: the International Economy and the Possibilities of Governance.* Cambridge: Polity Press.

Hocking, B. (1993) *Localizing Foreign Policy: Non-Central Governments and Multilayered Diplomacy.* Basingstoke: Macmillan.

Hoekman, B. M. and M. M. Kostecki (1995) *The Political Economy of the World Trading System: from GATT to WTO.* Oxford: Oxford University Press.

Hoggart, R. (1996) 'UNESCO and NGOs: a Memoir', in P. Willetts (ed.), *'Conscience of the World': the Influence of Non-Governmental Organisations in the UN System*. Washington, DC: Brookings Institution, pp. 98–115.

Holcombe, S. H. (1995) *Managing to Empower: the Grameen Bank's Experience of Poverty Alleviation*. London: Zed.

Holden, B. (ed.) (2000) *Global Democracy: Key Debates*. London: Routledge.

Holm, H. H. and G. Sørensen (1995) 'International Relations Theory in a World of Variation', in *Whose World Order? Uneven Globalization and the End of the Cold War*. Boulder, CO: Westview, pp. 187–206.

Holstein, W. J. *et al.* (1990) 'The Stateless Corporation', *Business Week*, 14 May, pp. 52–9.

Holthoon, F. van and M. van der Linden (eds) (1988) *Internationalism in the Labour Movement 1830–1940*. Leiden: Brill.

HomeNet (1999) 'Using the ILO Convention on Home Work'. Leeds: HomeNet International (homenet@gn.apc.org).

Honeygold, D. (1989) *International Financial Markets*. Cambridge: Woodhead-Faulkner.

Hoogvelt, A. (1997) *Globalisation and the Postcolonial World: the New Political Economy of Development*. Basingstoke: Macmillan.

Horsman, M. and A. Marshall (1994) *After the Nation-State: Citizens, Tribalism and the New World Disorder*. London: HarperCollins.

Hume, D. (1741–2) *Essays: Moral, Political and Literary*. London: Grant Richards, 1903.

Huntington, S. P. (1991) *The Third Wave: Democratization in the Late Twentieth Century*. Norman: University of Oklahoma Press.

Huntington, S. P. (1993) 'The Clash of Civilizations?' *Foreign Affairs*, vol. 72, no. 3 (Summer), pp. 22–49.

Huntington, S. P. (1996) *The Clash of Civilizations and the Remaking of World Order*. New York: Simon & Schuster.

Hurrell, A. and N. Woods (eds) (1999) *Inequality, Globalization, and World Politics*. Oxford: Oxford University Press.

Huth, A. (1937) *La radiodiffusion. Puissance mondiale*. Paris: Gallimard.

Hutton, W. (1996) *The State We're In*, rev. edn.. London: Vintage.

ICAO (1998) *Annual Civil Aviation Report 1997*. Montreal: International Civil Aviation Organisation – at website http://www.icao.org/.

ICFTU (1998) 'Globalisation on Trial'. Statement of the International Confederation of Free Trade Unions to the Annual Meetings of the IMF and World Bank.

ICLEI (1999) Website of the International Council for Local Environmental Initiatives, http://www.iclei.org.

IDEA (1997) *Voter Turnout from 1945 to 1997: a Global Report*. Stockholm: Institute for Democracy and Electoral Assistance.

IFAT (1999) Website of the International Federation of Alternative Trade, http://www.ifat.org/.

IFC (1996) *Emerging Stock Markets Factbook 1996*. Washington, DC: International Finance Corporation.

IIF (1999) Website of the Institute of International Finance, http://www.iif.com.

ILO (1995) *World Employment 1995*. Geneva: International Labour Organization.

Imber, M. F. (1989) *The USA, ILO, UNESCO and IAEA: Politicization and Withdrawal in the Specialized Agencies*. London: Macmillan.

IMF (1993) *International Financial Statistics Yearbook*. Washington, DC: International Monetary Fund.

IMF (1996) *Annual Report 1996*. Washington, DC: IMF.

IMF (1998) *Annual Report 1998*. Washington, DC: IMF.

IMF (1999) *Annual Report 1999*. Washington, DC: IMF.

INTELSAT (1999) *Annual Report 1998*. Washington, DC: International Tele-communications Satellite Organization.

IPCC (1995) *IPCC Second Assessment. Climate Change 1995*. Geneva: World Meteorological Organization/United Nations Environment Programme.

ISC (1999) Website of the Internet Software Consortium, http://www.isc.org/.

ISMA (1995) *Annual Report 1994*. Zürich: International Securities Market Association.

Jackson, J. H. (1998) *The World Trade Organisation*. London: Cassell.

James, H. (1996) *International Monetary Cooperation since Bretton Woods*. New York: Oxford University Press.

Jameson, F. (1991) *Postmodernism, Or, The Cultural Logic of Late Capitalism*. London: Verso.

Jameson, F. and M. Miyoshi (eds) (1998) *The Cultures of Globalization*. Durham, NC: Duke University Press.

Jarvis, A. P. and A. J. Paolini (1995) 'Locating the State', in J. A. Camilleri *et al.* (eds), *The State in Transition: Reimagining Political Space*. Boulder, CO: Rienner, pp. 3–19.

Jepsen, U. (1995) 'What Happened to Those Good Intentions', *Politiken Summit* (8 March), p. 6.

Jessop, B. (1993) 'Towards a Schumpeterian Workfare State? Preliminary Remarks on Post-Fordist Political Economy', *Studies in Political Economy*, vol. 40 (Spring), pp. 7–39

Jessop, B. (1994) 'Changing Forms and Functions of the State in an Era of Globalization and Regionalization', in R. Delorme and K. Dopfer (eds), *The Political Economy of Diversity: Evolutionary Perspectives on Economic Order and Disorder*. Aldershot: Elgar, pp. 102–25.

Joekes, S. and A. Weston (1994) *Women and the New Trade Agenda*. New York: UNIFEM.

John, J. and A. Chenoy (eds) (1996) *Labour, Environment and Globalisation: Social Clause in Multilateral Trade Agreements: a Southern Response*. New Delhi: Centre for Education and Communication.

Johnson, S. (1998) *Black Globalism: the International Politics of a Non-State Nation*. Aldershot: Ashgate.

Johnson, S. and B. Rogaly (1997) *Microfinance and Poverty Reduction*. Oxford: Oxfam/ACTIONAID.

Jolly, R. (1995) Remarks by the Acting Director of UNICEF at the World Summit for Social Development, Copenhagen, 5–12 March.

Jones, A. (1994) 'Wired World: Communications Technology, Governance and the Democratic Uprising', in E. A. Comor (ed.), *The Global Political Economy of Communication: Hegemony, Telecommunication and the Information Econo-my*. Basingstoke: Macmillan, pp. 145–64.

Jones, G. (1993) 'Multinational Banking Strategies', in H. Cox *et al.* (eds), *The Growth of Global Business*. London: Routledge, pp. 38–61.

Jones, G. (1996) 'Transnational Corporations – A Historical Perspective', in UNCTAD, *Transnational Corporations and World Development*. London: International Thomson Business Press, pp. 3–26.

Jones, S. G. (ed.) (1994) *CyberSociety: Computer-Mediated Communication and Community*. London: Sage.

Jordan, B. (1995) 'Globalizing Trade Unions', *Multinational Monitor*, vol. 16 (June), pp. 26–8.

Jubilee (2000) Website of the Jubilee 2000 Coalition, http://www.jubilee2000.org.

Juergensmeyer, M. (1993) *The New Cold War? Religious Nationalism Confronts the Secular State*. Berkeley: University of California Press.

Justice, D. W. (1999) 'The New Codes of Conduct and the Social Partners'. Geneva: International Labour Organization.

Kamel, R. (1990) *The Global Factory: Analysis and Action for a New Economic Era*. Philadelphia: American Friends Service Committee.

Kanter, R. M. (1995) *World Class: Thriving Locally in the Global Economy*. New York: Simon & Schuster.

Kaplan, R. D. (1994) 'The Coming Anarchy', *Atlantic Monthly*, vol. 273, no. 2 (February), pp. 44–76.

Kapstein, E. B. (1991–2) ' "We Are Us": the Myth of the Multinational', *The National Interest*, vol. 26 (Winter), pp. 55–62.

Kapstein, E. B. (1994) *Governing the Global Economy: International Finance and the State*. Cambridge, MA: Harvard University Press.

Kapstein, E. B. (1996) 'Workers and the World Economy', *Foreign Affairs*, vol. 75, no. 3 (May–June), pp. 16–37.

Karatnycky, A. (1999) 'The 1998 Freedom House Survey: the Decline of Illiberal Democracy', *Journal of Democracy*, vol. 10, no. 1 (January), pp. 112–25.

Katz, P. L. (1988) *The Information Society: an International Perspective*. New York: Praeger.

Kaul, I. *et al.* (eds) (1999) *Global Public Goods: International Cooperation in the 21st Century*. New York: Oxford University Press.

Kautsky, K. (1914) 'Ultra-Imperialism', *New Left Review*, No. 59 (January–February 1970), pp. 41–6.

Keck, M. and K. Sikkink (1998) *Activists beyond Borders: Transnational Advocacy Networks in International Politics*. Ithaca, NY: Cornell University Press.

Kempadoo, K. and J. Doezema (eds) (1998) *Global Sex Workers: Rights, Resistance, and Redefinition*. London: Routledge.

Kepel, G. (1991) *The Revenge of God: the Resurgence of Islam, Christianity and Judaism in the Modern World*. Cambridge: Polity Press, 1994.

Kerr, I. M. (1984) *A History of the Eurobond Market: the First 21 Years*. London: Euromoney.

Khan, L. A. (1996) *The Extinction of Nation-States: a World without Borders*. The Hague: Kluwer Law International.

Khor, M. (1995) Address to the International Forum on Globalization, New York City, November.

Khor, M. (1996) 'Globalisation: Implications for Development Policy', *Third World Resurgence*, no. 74 (October), pp. 15–21.

Kidder, T. and M. McGinn (1995) 'In the Wake of NAFTA: Transnational Workers' Networks', *Social Policy*, vol. 25, no. 4 (Summer), pp. 14–21.

Kidron, M. and R. Segal (1995) *The State of the World Atlas*, 5th edn. London: Penguin.

Kilminster, R. (1997) 'Globalization as an Emergent Concept', in A. Scott (ed.), *The Limits of Globalization: Cases and Arguments*. London: Routledge, pp. 257–83.

Kim, S. S. (1994) 'Chinese Perspectives on World Order', in D. Jacobsen (ed.), *Old Nations, New World: Conceptions of World Order*. Boulder, CO: Westview, pp. 37–74.

King, A. and B. Schneider (1991) *The First Global Revolution: a Report by the Council of the Club of Rome*. New York: Pantheon.

King, A. D. (ed.) (1991) *Culture, Globalization and the World-System: Contemporary Conditions for the Representation of Identity*. Basingstoke: Macmillan.

Knowles, T. (1994) *Hospitality Management: an Introduction*. London: Pitman.

Kobrin, S. J. (1998) 'The MAI and the Clash of Globalizations', *Foreign Policy*, no. 112 (Autumn), pp. 97–109.

Korten, D. C. (1990) *Getting to the 21st Century: Voluntary Action and the Global Agenda*. West Hartford, CT: Kumarian Press.

Korten, D. C. (1995) *When Corporations Rule the World*. West Hartford, CT: Kumarian Press.

Kotkin, J. (1992) *Tribes: How Race, Religion, and Identity Determine Success in the New Global Economy*. New York: Random House.

Krasner, S. D. (1993) 'Economic Interdependence and Independent Statehood', in R. H. Jackson and A. James (eds), *States in a Changing World: a Contemporary Analysis*. Oxford: Clarendon, pp. 301–21.

Krasner, S. D. (1994) 'International Political Economy: Abiding Discord', *Review of International Poltical Economy*, vol. 1, no. 1 (Spring), pp. 13–19.

Krause, J. (1996) 'Gender Inequalities and Feminist Politics in a Global Perspective', in E. Kofman and G. Youngs (eds), *Globalization: Theory and Practice*. London: Pinter, pp. 225–37.

Krause, K. and M. C. Williams (eds) (1997) *Critical Security Studies: Concepts and Cases*. London: UCL Press.

Kuhn, S. E. (1995) 'Winning Strategies for the Next Ten Years', *Fortune*, vol. 132, no. 25 (25 December), pp. 44–50.

Küng, H. (1990) *Global Responsibility: In Search of a New World Ethic*. London: SCM, 1991.

Küng, H. and K.-J. Kuschel (eds) (1993) *A Global Ethic: the Declaration of the Parliament of the World's Religions*. London: SCM.

Lacarrieu, M. and L. Raggio (1997) 'Citizenship within the Globalization Context: an Analysis of Trends within Mercosur', *The Mankind Quarterly*, vol. 37, no. 3 (Spring), pp. 263–81.

Lake, H. (1994) 'Wipeout in Cyberspace', *Amnesty: Campaign Journal for Amnesty International British Section*, no. 70 (November/December), pp. 10–11.

Lang, T. and C. Hines (1993) *The New Protectionism: Protecting the Future against Free Trade*. London: Earthscan.

Lapidoth, R. (1992) 'Sovereignty in Transition', *Journal of International Affairs*, vol. 45, no. 2 (Winter), pp. 325–46.

Lash, S. (1990) *Sociology of Postmodernism*. London: Routledge.

Lash, S. and J. Urry (1994) *Economies of Signs and Space*. London: Sage.

Leanne, S. (1994) 'African–American Initiatives against Minority Rule in South Africa: a Politicized Diaspora in World Politics'. Doctoral dissertation, University of Oxford.

Lee, E. (1997) *The Labour Movement and the Internet: the New Internationalism*. London: Pluto.

Lefebvre, H. (1974) *The Production of Space*. Oxford: Blackwell, 1991.

LeHeron, R. (1993) *Globalized Agriculture: Political Choice*. Oxford: Pergamon.

Lekhi, R. (2000) 'The Politics of African America On-Line', *Democratization*, vol. 7, no. 1 (Spring), pp. 76–101.

Levitt, T. (1983) 'The Globalization of Markets', *Harvard Business Review*, vol. 61, no. 3 (May–June), pp. 92–102.

Lietaer, B. (1996) 'Global Currency Proposals', in J. M. Griesgraber and B. G. Gunter (eds), *The World's Monetary System: Toward Stability and Sustainability in the Twenty-First Century*. London: Pluto, pp. 94–114.

Lim, L. (1990) 'Women's Work in Export Factories: the Politics of Cause', in I. Tinker (ed.), *Persistent Inequalities: Women and World Development*. Oxford: Oxford University Press, pp. 101–19.

Ling, L. H. M. (2000) 'Globalization and the Spectre of Fu Manchu: White Man's Burden as Dark Irony', in J.-S. Fritz and M. Lensu (eds), *Value Pluralism, Normative Theory and International Relations*. London: Macmillan, pp. 132–59.

Linklater, A. (1998) *The Transformation of Political Community: Ethical Foundations of the Post-Westphalian Era*. Cambridge: Polity Press.

Lipschutz, R. D. (1992) 'Reconstructing World Politics: the Emergence of Global Civil Society', *Millennium*, vol. 21, no. 3 (Winter), pp. 389–420.

Llambi, L. (1994) 'Comparative Advantages and Disadvantages in Latin American Nontraditional Fruit and Vegetable Exports, in P. McMichael (ed.), *The Global Restructuring of Agro-Food Systems*. Ithaca, NY: Cornell University Press, pp. 190–213.

Loader, B .D. (ed.) (1998) *Cyberspace Divide: Equality, Agency and Policy in the Information Society*. London: Routledge.

LoC (1999) Website of the Library of Congress, http://lcweb.loc.gov/catalog/, visited on 6 December.

Lorwin, L. L. (1953) *The International Labor Movement: History, Policies, Outlook*. New York: Harper and Brothers.

Lovelock, J. E. (1979) *Gaia: a New Look at Life on Earth*. Oxford: Oxford University Press.

Low, M. (1997) 'Representation Unbound: Globalization and Democracy', in K. R. Cox (ed.), *Spaces of Globalization: Reasserting the Power of the Local*. New York: Guilford, pp. 240–80.

Luke, T. W. (1995) 'New World Order or Neo-World Orders: Power, Politics and Ideology in Informationalizing Glocalities', in M. Featherstone *et al.*, *Global Modernities*. London: Sage, pp. 91–107.

Maclean, J. (1999) 'Philosophical Roots of Globalization: Philosophical Routes to Globalization', in R. Germain (ed.), *Globalization and Its Critics: Perspectives from Political Economy*. Basingstoke: Macmillan, pp. 3–66.

Madden, P. (1992) *Raw Deal: Trade and the World's Poor*. London: Christian Aid.

Magdoff, H. (1992) 'Globalization – to What End?', in R. Miliband and L. Panitch (eds), *Socialist Register 1992*. London: Merlin, pp. 44–75.

Main, J. (1989) 'How To Go Global – and Why', *Fortune*, vol. 120, no. 5 (28 August), pp. 54–8.

Manalansan, M. (1997) 'In the Shadows of Stonewall: Examining Gay Transnational Politics and the Diasporic Dilemma', in L. Lowe and D. Lloyd (eds), *The Politics of Culture in the Shadow of Capital*. Durham, NC: Duke University Press, pp. 485–505.

Mander, J. and E. Goldsmith (eds) (1996) *The Case against the Global Economy and the Turn to the Local*. San Francisco: Sierra Club Books.

Mann, M. (1997) 'Has Globalization Ended the Rise and Rise of the Nation-State?' *Review of International Political Economy*, vol. 4, no. 3 (Autumn), pp. 472–96.

Marceau, J. (1992) 'Conclusion. Reworking the World: Lessons from Everywhere', in Marceau (ed.), *Reworking the World: Organisations, Technologies, and Cultures in Comparative Perspective*. Berlin: De Gruyter, pp. 461–73.

Marchand, M. H. and A. S. Runyan (eds) (2000) *Gender and Global Restructuring: Sightings, Sites and Resistances*. London: Routledge.

Marglin, S. A. (1988) *Lessons of the Golden Age of Capitalism*. Helsinki: World Institute for Development Economics Research.

Marshall, D. D. (1996) 'Understanding Late-Twentieth-Century Capitalism: Reassessing the Globalization Theme', *Government and Opposition*, vol. 31, no. 2 (Spring), pp. 193–215.

Martin, H.-P. and H. Schumann (1996) *The Global Trap: Globalization and the Assault on Prosperity and Democracy*. London: Zed, 1997.

Martin, R. (1994) 'Stateless Monies, Global Financial Integration and National Economic Autonomy: the End of Geography?' in S. Corbridge *et al.* (eds), *Money, Power and Space*. Oxford: Blackwell, pp. 253–78.

Marty, M. E. and R. S. Appleby (eds) (1991) *Fundamentalisms Observed*. Chicago: University of Chicago Press.

Marx, K. (1857–8) *Grundrisse: Foundations of the Critique of Political Economy*. Harmondsworth: Penguin, 1973.

Marx, K. (1867) *Capital, Volume I*. London: Lawrence and Wishart, 1970.

Massey, D. (1994) *Space, Place and Gender*. Cambridge: Polity Press.

Mattelart, A. (1989) *Advertising International: the Privatisation of Public Space*. London: Routledge, 1991.

Mawle, A. (1997) 'Women, Environment and the United Nations', in F. Dodds (ed.), *The Way Forward: Beyond Agenda 21*. London: Earthscan, pp. 146–57.

Mazrui, A. A. (1994) 'Global Apartheid: Structural and Overt', *Alternatives*, vol. 19, no. 2, pp. 185–7.

McChesney, R. W. *et al.* (eds) (1998) *Capitalism and the Information Age: the Political Economy of the Global Communication Revolution*. New York: Monthly Review Press.

McCormick, J. (1989) *Reclaiming Paradise: the Global Environmental Movement*. Bloomington: Indiana University Press.

McDowell, L. and G. Court (1994) 'Gender Divisions of Labour in the Post-Fordist Economy: the Maintenance of Occupational Sex Segregation in the Financial Services Sector', *Environment and Planning A*, vol. 26, no. 9 (September), pp. 1397–1418.

McGrew, A. (1997a) 'Globalization and Territorial Democracy: an Introduction', in McGrew (ed.), *The Transformation of Democracy? Globalization and Territorial Democracy*. Cambridge: Polity Press, pp. 1–24.

McGrew, A. (ed.) (1997b) *The Transformation of Democracy? Globalization and Territorial Democracy*. Cambridge: Polity Press.

McMichael, P. (1993) 'World Food System Restructuring under a GATT Regime', *Political Geography*, vol. 12, no. 3 (May), pp. 198–214.

McMichael, P. (1996a) *Development and Social Change: a Global Perspective*. Thousand Oaks, CA: Pine Forge Press.

McMichael, P. (1996b) 'Globalization: Myths and Realities', *Rural Sociology*, vol. 61, no. 1 (Spring), pp. 25–55.

McMichael, P. (ed.) (1994) *The Global Restructuring of Agro-Food Systems*. Ithaca, NY: Cornell University Press.

Meadows, D. H. *et al.* (1992) *Beyond the Limits: a Global Collapse or a Sustainable Future*. London: Earthscan.

Mendell, M. and D. Salée (eds) (1991) *The Legacy of Karl Polanyi: Market, State and Society at the End of the Twentieth Century*. Basingstoke: Macmillan.

Meyer, B. and P. Geschiere (eds) (1998) 'Globalisation and Identity: Dialectics of Flows and Closures', *Development and Change*, vol. 29, no. 4 (October), pp. 601–928.

Miller, M. (1991) *Debt and the Environment: Converging Crises*. New York: United Nations.

Minear, L. and T. G. Weiss (1995) *Mercy under Fire: War and the Global Humanitarian Community*. Boulder, CO: Westview.

MIT (1999) Website of the Unwiring the World Project, coordinated between the Massachusetts Institute of Technology Media Lab and the Costa Rican Foundation for Sustainable Development, http://www.media.mit.edu/unwired/assumptions.html.

Mittelman, J. H. (1999) *The Future of Globalization*. Bangi: Penerbit Universiti Kebangsaan Malaysia.

Mittelman, J. H. (2000) *The Globalization Syndrome: Transformation and Resistance*. Princeton: Princeton University Press.

Mittelman, J. H. and R. Johnston (1999) 'The Globalization of Organized Crime, the Courtesan State, and the Corruption of Civil Society', *Global Governance*, vol. 5, no. 1 (January–March), pp. 103–26.

Mlinar, Z. (ed.) (1992) *Globalization and Territorial Identities*. Aldershot: Avebury.

Moghadam, V. M. (ed.) (1993) *Democratic Reform and the Position of Women in Transitional Economies*. Oxford: Clarendon.

Moon, G. (1995) *Free Trade: What's in It for Women?* Fitzroy (Australia): Community Aid Abroad.

Mosco, V. (1988) 'Introduction: Information in the Pay-Per Society' in Mosco and J. Wasko (eds), *The Political Economy of Information*. Madison: University of Wisconsin Press, pp. 3–26.

Mowlana, H. (1997) *Global Information and World Communication: New Frontiers in International Relations*, 2nd edn. London: Sage.

Munck, R. and P. Waterman (eds) (1999) *Labour Worldwide in the Era of Globalization: Alternative Union Models in the New World Order*. Basingstoke: Macmillan.

Murphy, C. N. (1994) *International Organization and Industrial Change: Global Governance since 1850*. Cambridge: Polity Press.

Musa, M. (1997) 'From Optimism to Reality: an Overview of Third World News Agencies', in P. Golding and P. Harris (eds), *Beyond Cultural Imperialism: Globalization, Communication and the New International Order*. London: Sage, pp. 117–46.

Muzaffar, C. (1993) *Human Rights and the New World Order*. Penang: Just World Trust.

My Vuong, T. (1999) 'World Wide Net: Vietnamese Using High Tech to Stay in Touch with Culture', *San Jose Mercury News*, 20 February.

Myers, N. (ed.) (1985) *The Gaia Atlas of Planet Management*. London: Pan.

Myers, N. (1993) *Ultimate Security: the Environmental Basis of Political Stability*. New York: Norton.

Myers, N. (1996) 'Problems of the Next Century'. Paper for UNED-UK seminar, Green College, Oxford, 24 June.

Myhre, D. (1994) 'The Politics of Globalization in Rural Mexico: Campesino Initiatives to Restructure the Agricultural Credit System', in P. McMichael (ed.),

The Global Restructuring of Agro-Food Systems. Ithaca, NY: Cornell University Press, pp. 145–69.

NAB (1999) Website of the New Academy of Business, http://www.new-academy.ac.uk/.

Naess, A. (1976) *Ecology, Community and Lifestyle.* Cambridge: Cambridge University Press, 1989.

Naisbitt, J. (1994) *Global Paradox: the Bigger the World Economy, the More Powerful Its Smallest Players.* London: Brealey.

Neal, L. (1985) 'Integration of International Capital Markets: Quantitative Evidence from the Eighteenth to Twentieth Centuries', *Journal of Economic History*, vol. 45, no. 2 (June), pp. 219–26.

Nederveen Pieterse, J. (1995) 'Globalization as Hybridization', in M. Featherstone *et al.* (eds), *Global Modernities.* London: Sage, pp. 45–68.

Nederveen Pieterse, J. (ed.) (2000) *Global Futures: Shaping Globalization.* London: Sage.

Nelson, P. J. (1995) *The World Bank and Non-Governmental Organizations: the Limits of Apolitical Development.* London: Macmillan.

Newell, P. and J. Whalley (1999) 'Towards a World Environment Organisation?' *IDS Bulletin*, vol. 30, no. 3 (July), pp. 16–24.

Nicholson, M. (1999) 'How Novel Is Globalisation?' in M. Shaw (ed.), *Politics and Globalisation: Knowledge, Ethics and Agency.* London: Routledge, pp. 23–34.

Niebuhr, R. (1932) *Moral Man and Immoral Society: a Study in Ethics and Politics.* New York: Scribner.

Nyerere, J. *et al.* (1990) *The Challenge to the South.* New York: Oxford University Press [South Commission].

Ó Tuathail, G. (1996) *Critical Geopolitics: the Politics of Writing Global Space.* London: Routledge.

O'Brien, R. (1992) *Global Financial Integration: the End of Geography.* London: Pinter.

O'Brien, R. J. *et al.* (2000) *Contesting Global Governance: Multilateral Economic Institutions and Global Social Movements.* Cambridge: Cambridge University Press.

OECD (1995) *A Global Marketplace for Consumers.* Paris: Organisation for Economic Cooperation and Development.

OECD (1996a) *Financial Market Trends 63.* Paris: Organisation for Economic Cooperation and Development, February.

OECD (1996b) *International Capital Market Statistics 1950–1995.* Paris: Organisation for Economic Cooperation and Development.

OED (1989) *The Oxford English Dictionary*, 2nd edn. Oxford: Clarendon.

Ohmae, K. (1990) *The Borderless World: Power and Strategy in the Interlinked Economy.* London: Fontana.

Ohmae, K. (1995) *The End of the Nation State: the Rise of Regional Economies.* New York: Free Press.

OPCW (1999) Website of the Organization for the Prohibition of Chemical Weapons, http://www.opcw.nl/.

Ortega y Gasset, J. (1930) *The Revolt of the Masses.* London: Allen & Unwin, 1961.

Ougaard, M. (1999) 'The OECD in the Global Polity'. Paper for a workshop of the Danish Social Science Research Council, Florence, 1–3 October.

Panitch, L. (1996) 'Rethinking the Role of the State', in J. H. Mittelman (ed.), *Globalization: Critical Reflections.* Boulder, CO: Rienner, pp. 83–113.

Pauly, L. W. (1997) *Who Elected the Bankers? Surveillance and Control in the World Economy*. Ithaca, NY: Cornell University Press.

Peccei, A. (1969) *The Chasm Ahead*. London: Macmillan.

Pendergrast, M. (1993) *For God, Country and Coca-Cola: the Unauthorized History of the Great American Soft Drink and the Company that Makes It*. London: Weidenfeld and Nicolson.

Pennycook, A. (1994) *The Cultural Politics of English as an International Language*. Harlow: Longman.

PEOPLink (1999) Website of the PEOPLink nonprofit marketplace, http://www.peoplink.org/.

Peters, R. (1979) *Islam and Colonialism: the Doctrine of Jihad in Modern History*. The Hague: Mouton.

Peterson, V. S. (1992) 'Transgressing Boundaries: Theories of Knowledge, Gender, and International Relations', *Millennium*, vol. 21, no. 2 (Summer), pp. 183–206.

Peterson, V. S. and A. S. Runyan (1999) *Global Gender Issues*, 2nd edn. Boulder, CO: Westview.

Petras, J. (1993) 'Cultural Imperialism in the Late 20th Century', *Journal of Contemporary Asia*, vol. 23, no. 2, pp. 139–48.

Pettman, J. J. (1996) 'An International Political Economy of Sex?' in E. Kofman and G. Youngs (eds), *Globalization: Theory and Practice*. London: Pinter, pp. 191–208.

Pettman, J. J. (1997) 'Body Politics: International Sex Tourism', *Third World Quarterly*, vol. 18, no. 1, pp. 93–108.

Pietilä, H. and J. Vickers (1994) *Making Women Matter: the Role of the United Nations*, rev. edn.. London: Zed.

Pijl, K. van der (1989) 'The International Level', in T. B. Bottomore (ed.), *The Capitalist Class: an International Study*. New York: Harvester Wheatsheaf, pp. 237–66.

Ploman, E. W. (1984) *Space, Earth and Communication*. Westport, CT: Quorum.

Poewe, K. (ed.) (1994) *Charismatic Christianity as a Global Culture*. Columbia, SC: University of South Carolina Press.

Porat, M. U. (1977) *The Information Economy*. Washington, DC: Government Printing Office [Department of Commerce, Office of Telecommunications].

Porter, G. and J. W. Brown (1996) *Global Environmental Politics*, 2nd edn. Boulder, CO: Westview.

Porter, M. E. (ed.) (1986) *Competition in Global Industries*. Boston, MA: Harvard Business School Press.

Porter, M. E. (1990) *The Competitive Advantage of Nations*. London: Macmillan.

Porter, T. (1993) *States, Markets and Regimes in Global Finance*. Basingstoke: Macmillan.

Poster, M. (1990) *The Mode of Information: Poststructuralism and Social Context*. Cambridge: Polity Press.

Price, R. (1998) 'Reversing the Gun Sights: Transnational Civil Society Targets Land Mines', *International Organization*, vol. 52, no. 3 (Summer), pp. 613–44.

Pucik, V. *et al.* (eds) (1992) *Globalizing Management: Creating and Leading the Competitive Organization*. New York: John Wiley.

Purdy, D. (1997) 'Social Policy', in M. J. Arts and N. Lee (eds), *The Economics of the European Union*, 2nd edn. Oxford: Oxford University Press, pp. 267–91.

Raghavan, C. *et al.* (1996) 'Globalisation or Development', *Third World Resurgence*, no. 74 (October), pp. 11–34.

Rajput, P. and H. L. Swarup (eds) (1994) *Women and Globalisation: Reflections, Options and Strategies*. New Delhi: Ashish.

Raworth, P. (1994) 'A Timid Step Forwards: Maastricht and the Democratisation of the European Community', *European Law Review*, vol. 19, no. 1 (February), pp. 16–33.

Ray, M. and A. Rinzler (eds) (1993) *The New Paradigm in Business: Emerging Strategies for Leadership and Organizational Change*. New York: Tarcher/Perigee.

Reed, D. (ed.) (1996) *Structural Adjustment, the Environment and Sustainable Development*. London: Earthscan.

Reinicke, W. H. (1998) *Global Public Policy: Governing without Government?* Washington, DC: Brookings Institution.

Reiser, O. L. and B. Davies (1944) *Planetary Democracy: an Introduction to Scientific Humanism and Applied Semantics*. New York: Creative Age Press.

Rheingold, H. (1993) *The Virtual Community: Homesteading on the Electronic Frontier*. Reading, MA: Addison-Wesley.

Rich, B. (1994) *Mortgaging the Earth: the World Bank, Environmental Impoverishment and the Crisis of Development*. London: Earthscan.

Rifkin, J. (1995) *The End of Work: the Decline of the Global Labor Force and the Dawn of the Post-Market Era*. New York: Putnam.

Rivera, M. *et al.* (1995) *DAWN's Perspectives on Social Development*. Santo Domingo: Center for Feminist Research and Action.

Roberts, S. M. (1995) 'Small Place, Big Money: The Cayman Islands and the International Financial System', *Economic Geography*, vol. 71, no. 3, pp. 237–56.

Robertson, R. (1992) *Globalization: Social Theory and Global Culture*. London: Sage.

Robertson, R. (1995) 'Glocalization: Time-Space and Homogeneity-Heterogeneity', in M. Featherstone *et al.* (eds), *Global Modernities*. London: Sage, pp. 25–44.

Robertson, R. and J. Chirico (1985) 'Humanity, Globalization, and Worldwide Religious Resurgence: a Theoretical Exploration', *Sociological Analysis*, vol. 46, no. 3, pp. 219–42.

Robertson, R. and W. R. Garrett (eds) (1991) *Religion and Global Order*. New York: Paragon House.

Robins, K. and F. Webster (1988) 'Cybernetic Capitalism, Technology, Everyday Life', in V. Mosco and J. Wasko (eds), *The Political Economy of Information*. Madison: University of Wisconsin Press, pp. 44–75.

Robinson, W. I. (1996a) 'Globalisation: Nine Theses on Our Epoch', *Race & Class*, vol. 38, no. 2 (October–December), pp. 13–31.

Robinson, W. I. (1996b) *Promoting Polyarchy: Globalization, US Intervention and Hegemony*. Cambridge: Cambridge University Press.

Rodrik, D. (1997) *Has Globalization Gone Too Far?* Washington, DC: Institute for International Economics.

Rohwer, J. (1992) 'China: the Titan Stirs', *The Economist*, vol. 325, no. 7787 (28 November), Supplement.

Ronit, K. and V. Schneider (eds) (1999) *Private Organisations, Governance and Global Politics*. London: Routledge.

Rosenau, J. N. (1990) *Turbulence in World Politics: a Theory of Change and Continuity*. Princeton: Princeton University Press.

Rosenau, J. N. (1997) *Along the Domestic–Foreign Frontier: Exploring Governance in a Turbulent World*. Cambridge: Cambridge University Press.

Rosenau, J. N. and E.-O. Czempiel (eds) (1992) *Governance without Government: Order and Change in World Politics*. Cambridge: Cambridge University Press.

Rubenstein, C. (1991) 'The Flying Silver Message Stick: Update 1985–86 on Long Songs Collected 1971–74', *Sarawak Museum Journal*, vol. 42, No. 63 (new series), pp. 61–157.

Ruggie, J. G. (1993) 'Territoriality and Beyond: Problematizing Modernity in International Relations', *International Organization*, vol. 47, no. 1 (Winter), pp. 139–74.

Rugman, A. M. and A. Verbeke (1990) *Global Corporate Strategy and Trade Policy*. London: Routledge.

Ruigrok, W. and R. van Tulder (1995) *The Logic of International Restructuring: the Management of Dependencies in Rival Industrial Complexes*. London: Routledge.

Runyan, A. S. (1996) 'The Places of Women in Trading Places: Gendered Global/Regional Regimes and Inter-nationalized Feminist Resistance', in E. Kofman and G. Youngs (eds), *Globalization: Theory and Practice*. London: Pinter, pp. 238–52.

Salamon, L. M. (1993) 'The Marketization of Welfare: Changing Nonprofit and For-Profit Roles in the American Welfare-State', *Social Service Review*, vol. 67, no. 1 (March), pp. 16–39.

Salamon, L. M. (1994) 'The Rise of the Nonprofit Sector', *Foreign Affairs*, vol. 73, no. 4 (July–August), pp. 109–22.

Sander, H. (1996) 'Multilateralism, Regionalism and Globalisation: The Challenges to the World Trading System', in H. Sander and A. Inotai (eds), *World Trade after the Uruguay Round: Prospects and Policy Options for the Twenty-First Century*. London: Routledge, pp. 17–36.

Santamäki-Vuori, T. (1995) 'Fighting Unemployment and Polarization: Investments in Adaptive Capacity through Broad Upgrading in Skills', in M. Simai (ed.), *Global Employment: an International Investigation into the Future of Work. Volume 1*. London: Zed, pp. 41–54.

SAPRI (1999) Website of the Structural Adjustment Policy Review Initiative, http://www.worldbank.org/htm1/prddr/sapri/saprihp.htm.

Sassen, S. (1997) *Losing Control? Sovereignty in an Age of Globalization*. New York: Columbia University Press.

Saunders, J. (1989) *Across Frontiers: International Support for the Miners' Strike of 1984–85*. London: Canary.

Sauvant, K. P. and H. Hasenpflug (eds) (1977) *The New International Economic Order: Confrontation or Cooperation between North and South?* Boulder, CO: Westview.

Schechter, M. G. (ed.) (1999a) *Future Multilateralism: the Political and Social Framework*. Tokyo: United Nations University Press.

Schechter, M. G. (ed.) (1999b) *Innovation in Multilateralism*. Tokyo: United Nations University Press.

Schenk, D. (1997) *Data Smog: Surviving the Information Glut*. New York: HarperCollins.

Schiller, H. I. (1991) 'Not Yet the Post-Imperialist Era', *Critical Studies in Mass Communication*, vol. 8, no. 1 (March), pp. 13–28.

Schiller, H. I. and A. R. Schiller (1988) 'Libraries, Public Access to Information, and Commerce', in V. Mosco and J. Wasko (eds), *The Political Economy of Information*. Madison: University of Wisconsin Press, pp. 146–66.

Schmidt, V. A. (1995) 'The New World Order, Incorporated: the Rise of Business and the Decline of the Nation-State', *Daedalus*, vol. 124, no. 2 (Spring), pp. 75–106.

Scholte, J. A. (1993a) 'From Power Politics to Social Change: an Alternative Focus for International Studies', *Review of International Studies*, vol. 19, no. 1 (January), pp. 3–21.

Scholte, J. A. (1993b) *International Relations of Social Change.* Buckingham: Open University Press.

Scholte, J. A. (1996a) 'Beyond the Buzzword: Towards a Critical Theory of Globalization', in E. Kofman and G. Youngs (eds), *Globalization: Theory and Practice.* London: Pinter, pp. 43–57.

Scholte, J. A. (1996b) 'The Geography of Collective Identities in a Globalizing World', *Review of International Political Economy*, vol. 3, no. 4 (Winter), pp. 565–607.

Scholte, J. A. (1997a) 'Global Capitalism and the State', *International Affairs*, vol. 73, no. 3 (July), pp. 427–52.

Scholte, J. A. (1997b) 'The Globalization of World Politics', in J. Baylis and S. Smith (eds), *The Globalization of World Politics: an Introduction to International Relations.* Oxford: Oxford University Press, pp. 13–30.

Scholte, J. A. (1999a) 'Globalisation and Governance', in P. Hanafin and M.S. Williams (eds), *Identity, Rights and Constitutional Transformation.* Aldershot: Ashgate, pp. 132–53.

Scholte, J. A. (1999b) 'Globalisation: Prospects for a Paradigm Shift', in M. Shaw (ed.), *Politics and Globalisation: Knowledge, Ethics and Agency.* London: Routledge, pp. 9–22.

Scholte, J. A. (1999c) 'Security and Community in a Globalizing World: African Experiences', in C. Thomas and P. Wilkin (eds), *Globalization, Human Security, and the African Experience.* Boulder, CO: Rienner, pp. 59–84.

Scholte, J. A. (2000a) 'Can Globality Bring a Good Society?' in P. S. Aulakh and M. G. Schechter (eds), *Rethinking Globalizations: From Corporate Transnationalism to Local Interventions.* New York: St. Martin's, pp. 13–31.

Scholte, J. A. (2000b) 'Global Civil Society', in N. Woods (ed.), *The Political Economy of Globalization.* London: Macmillan, ch 7.

Scholte, J. A. (2000c) '"In the Foothills": Relations between the IMF and Civil Society', in R. A. Higgott *et al.* (eds), *Non-State Actors and Authority in the Global System.* London: Routledge, pp. 256–73.

Schrijver, N. (1997) *Sovereignty over Natural Resources: Balancing Rights and Duties.* Cambridge: Cambridge University Press.

Schwab, K. and C. Smadja (1996) 'Start Taking the Backlash against Globalization Seriously', *International Herald Tribune*, 2 February.

Scott, A. (ed.) (1997) *The Limits of Globalization: Cases and Arguments.* London: Routledge.

Segal, G. (1994) *China Changes Shape: Regionalism and Foreign Policy.* London: International Institute of Strategic Studies.

Shakespeare, W. (1595–6) *A Midsummer Night's Dream* (ed. H. F. Brooks). London: Methuen, 1979.

Shapiro, M. J. (1994) 'Moral Geographies and the Ethics of Post-Sovereignty', *Public Culture*, vol. 6, no. 3 (Spring), pp. 479–502.

Shapiro, M. J. and H. R. Alker (eds) (1996) *Challenging Boundaries: Global Flows, Territorial Identities.* Minneapolis: University of Minnesota Press.

Shaw, M. (1994) *Global Society and International Relations: Sociological Concepts and Political Perspectives*. Cambridge: Polity Press.

Shaw, M. (1997) 'The State of Globalization: Toward a Theory of State Transformation', *Review of International Political Economy*, vol. 4, no. 3 (Autumn), pp. 497–513.

Shaw, M. (ed.) (1999) *Politics and Globalisation: Knowledge, Ethics and Agency*. London: Routledge.

Shelley, L. I. (1995) 'Transnational Organized Crime: an Imminent Threat to the Nation-State?', *Journal of International Affairs*, vol. 48, no. 2 (Winter), pp. 463–89.

Shin, D. C. (1994) 'On the Third Wave of Democratization: a Synthesis and Evaluation of Recent Research and Theory', *World Politics*, vol. 47, no. 1 (October), pp. 135–70.

Shiva, V. (1997) *Biopiracy: the Plunder of Nature and Knowledge*. Boston, MA: South End Press.

Simai, M. (1995) 'The Politics and Economics of Global Employment' in Simai (ed.), *Global Employment: an International Investigation into the Future of Work, Volume 1*. London: Zed, pp. 3–29.

Simpson, J. (1988) *Behind Iranian Lines*. London: Fontana, 1989.

Sinclair, T. J. (1994) 'Passing Judgement: Credit Rating Processes as Regulatory Mechanisms of Governance in the Emerging World Order', *Review of International Political Economy*, vol. 1, no. 1 (Spring), pp. 133–59.

Singer, H. W. (1995) 'An Historical Perspective', in M. ul Haq *et al.* (eds), *The UN and the Bretton Woods Institutions: New Challenges for the Twenty-First Century*. Basingstoke: Macmillan, pp. 17–25.

6, P. and I. Vidal (eds) (1994) *Delivering Welfare: Repositioning Non-Profit and Co-operative Action in Western European Welfare States*. Barcelona: Centre d'Iniciatives de L'Economica Social.

Sklair, L. (1995) *Sociology of the Global System*. 2nd edn. Hemel Hempstead: Harvester Wheatsheaf.

Skrobanek, S. *et al.* (1997) *The Traffic in Women: Human Realities of the International Sex Trade*. London: Zed.

Smart, B. (1999) *Facing Modernity: Ambivalence, Reflexivity and Morality*. London: Sage.

Smillie, I. (1999) 'At Sea in a Sieve? Trends and Issues in the Relationship between Northern NGOs and Northern Governments', in I. Smillie and H. Helmich (eds), *Stakeholders: Government–NGO Partnerships for International Development*. London: Earthscan.

Smith, A. D. (1990a) 'The Supersession of Nationalism?' *International Journal of Comparative Sociology*, vol. 31, no. 1–2, pp. 1–32.

Smith, A. D. (1990b) 'Towards a Global Culture?' in M. Featherstone (ed.), *Global Culture: Nationalism, Globalization and Modernity*. London: Sage, pp. 171–91.

Smith, A. D. (1995) *Nations and Nationalism in a Global Era*. Cambridge: Polity Press.

Smith, J. *et al.* (eds) (1997) *Transnational Social Movements and Global Politics: Solidarity beyond the State*. Syracuse: Syracuse University Press.

Smith, P. and E. Smythe (2000) 'Globalization, Citizenship and Technology: the MAI Meets the Internet'. Paper for the 41st Annual Convention of the International Studies Association, Los Angeles, 14–18 March.

Smouts, M.-C. (1994) 'La réforme de l'ONU. Une stratégie d'évitement' ['Reform of the United Nations: A Strategy of Evasion']. Paper presented at the

International Symposium on Sources of Innovation in Multilateralism, 26–28 May, Lausanne.

Smouts, M.-C. (1999) 'Multilateralism from Below: a Prerequisite for Global Governance', in M. G. Schechter (ed.), *Future Multilateralism: the Political and Social Framework*. Tokyo: United Nations University Press, pp. 292–311.

Söderholm, P. (1997) *Global Governance of AIDS: Partnerships with Civil Society*. Lund: Lund University Press.

Soroos, M. J. (1986) *Beyond Sovereignty: the Challenge of Global Policy*. Columbia: University of South Carolina Press.

Soros, G. (1998) *The Crisis of Global Capitalism: Open Society Endangered*. London: Little, Brown.

South Centre (1997) *The TRIPS Agreement: a Guide for the South*. Geneva: South Centre.

Sparr, P. (ed.) (1994) *Mortgaging Women's Lives: Feminist Critiques of Structural Adjustment*. London: Zed.

Spero, J. E. (1990) *The Politics of International Economic Relations*, 4th edn. London: Unwin Hyman.

Speth, J. G. (1992) 'A Post-Rio Compact', *Foreign Policy*, no. 88 (Fall), pp. 145–61.

Speth, J. G. (1996) 'Global Inequality: 358 Billionaires vs. 2.3 Billion People', *New Perspectives Quarterly*, vol. 13, no. 4 (Fall), pp. 32–3.

Spruyt, H. (1994) *The Sovereign State and Its Competitors: an Analysis of Systems Change*. Princeton: Princeton University Press.

Spybey, T. (1996) *Globalization and World Society*. Cambridge: Polity Press.

Staveren, I. van (2000) 'Global Finance and Gender'. Paper for a workshop on Civil Society and Global Finance, University of Warwick, 29–31 March.

Steenbergen, B. van (ed.) (1994) *The Condition of Citizenship*. London: Sage.

Stern, P. C. *et al.* (eds) (1992) *Global Environmental Change: Understanding the Human Dimensions*. Washington, DC: National Academy Press.

Stienstra, D. (1994) *Women's Movements and International Organizations*. Basingstoke: Macmillan.

Stopford, J. M. and S. Strange (1991) *Rival States, Rival Firms: Competition for World Market Shares*. Cambridge: Cambridge University Press.

Strange, S. (1986) *Casino Capitalism*. Oxford: Blackwell.

Strange, S. (1990) 'Finance, Information and Power', *Review of International Studies*, vol. 16, no. 3 (July), pp. 259–74.

Strange, S. (1994) *States and Markets*, 2nd edn. London: Pinter.

Strange, S. (1996) *The Retreat of the State: the Diffusion of Power in the World Economy*. Cambridge: Cambridge University Press.

Strange, S. (1998) *Mad Money*. Manchester: Manchester University Press.

Strassoldo, R. (1992) 'Globalism and Localism: Theoretical Reflections and Some Evidence', in Z. Mlinar (ed.), *Globalization and Territorial Identities*. Aldershot: Avebury.

Suárez Aguilar, E. (1999) personal communication to the author, June.

Sulak Sivaraksa (1999) *Global Healing: Essays and Interviews on Structural Violence, Social Development and Spiritual Transformation*. Bangkok: Sathirakoses-Nagapradipa Foundation.

Sullivan, S. (1997) *From War to Wealth: Fifty Years of Innovation*. Paris: Organisation of Economic Cooperation and Development.

Svedberg, P. (1993) 'Trade Compression and Economic Decline in Sub-Saharan Africa', in M. Blomström and M. Lundahl, *Economic Crisis in Africa: Perspectives on Policy Responses*. London: Routledge, pp. 21–40.

Sweezy, P. and H. Magdoff (1985) 'The Strange Recovery of 1983–1984', *Monthly Review*, vol. 37, no. 5 (October), pp. 1–11.

SWIFT (2000) Website of the Society for Worldwide Interbank Financial Telecommunications, http://www.swift.com.

Tanner, S. (1997) 'Healing the Sky to Survive Globalization: a Gender Analogy', in T. Schrecker (ed.), *Surviving Globalism: the Social and Environmental Challenges*. Basingstoke: Macmillan, pp. 141–57.

Tanzi, V. (1996) 'Globalization, Tax Competition and the Future of Tax Systems', *IMF Working Paper Series*, WP/96/141.

Taylor, P. J. (1995) 'Beyond Containers: Internationality, Interstateness, Inter-territoriality', *Progress in Human Geography*, vol. 19, no. 1 (March), pp. 1–15.

Taylor, P. J. *et al.* (1996) 'On the Nation-State, the Global, and Social Science', *Environment and Planning A*, vol. 28, no. 11 (November), pp. 1917–95.

Taylor, P. J. (2000) 'Izations of the World: Americanization, Modernization and Globalization', in C. Hay and D. Marsh (eds), *Demystifying Globalization*. Basingstoke: Macmillan, pp. 49–70.

Taylor, W. C. and A. M. Weber (1996) *Going Global: Four Entrepreneurs Map the New World Marketplace*. New York: Viking.

Teeple, G. (1995) *Globalization and the Decline of Social Reform*. Atlantic Highlands, NJ: Humanities Press.

Thomas, C. and P. Wilkin (eds) (1997) *Globalization and the South*. Basingstoke: Macmillan.

Thomas, C. and P. Wilkin (eds) (1999) *Globalization, Human Security, and the African Experience*. Boulder, CO: Rienner.

Thomas, D. (1999) Presentation by David Thomas of Saatchi & Saatchi to the Global Forum on Poverty Eradication, Council of Europe, Strasbourg, 15 October.

Thomson, J. E. and S. D. Krasner (1989) 'Global Transactions and the Consolidation of Sovereignty', in E.-O. Czempiel and J.N. Rosenau (eds), *Global Changes and Theoretical Challenges*. Lexington, MA: Lexington Books, pp. 195–220.

Tilly, C. (1995) 'Globalization Threatens Labor's Rights', *International Labor and Working Class History*, no. 47 (Spring), pp. 1–23.

Tober, D. (1993) 'One World – One Vision for Business', in S. Bushrui *et al.* (eds), *Transition to a Global Society*. Oxford: Oneworld, pp. 98–107.

Toffler, A. (1980) *The Third Wave*. London: Collins.

Toffler, A. and H. Toffler (1994) *Creating a New Civilization: the Politics of the Third Wave*. Atlanta: Turner.

Tomlinson, J. (1991) *Cultural Imperialism: a Critical Introduction*. London: Pinter.

Tomlinson, J. (1995) 'Homogenisation and Globalisation', *History of European Ideas*, vol. 20, nos 4–6 (February), pp. 891–7.

Toynbee, A. (1948) *Civilisation on Trial*. Oxford: Oxford University Press.

Treadgold, A. (1993) 'Cross-Border Retailing in Europe: Present Status and Future Prospects', in H. Cox *et al.* (eds), *The Growth of Global Business*. London: Routledge, pp. 119–35.

Turgot, A. R. J. (1750) 'A Philosophical Review of the Successive Advances of the Human Mind', in R. L. Meek (ed.), *Turgot on Progress, Sociology and Economics*. Cambridge: Cambridge University Press, 1973, pp. 41–59.

TWG (1993) *Third World Guide 93/94*. Montevideo: Instituto del Tercer Mundo.

UIA (1998) *Yearbook of International Organizations 1998/99, Vol. I*. Munich: Saur/Union of International Associations.

ul Haq, M. *et al.* (eds) (1995) *The UN and the Bretton Woods Institutions: New Challenges for the Twenty-First Century*. Basingstoke: Macmillan.

UN (1990) 'Directory of Departments and Offices of the United Nations Secretariat, United Nations Programmes, Specialized Agencies and Other Intergovernmental Organizations Dealing with Non-Governmental Organizations', *Transnational Associations*, vol. 42, no. 5 (September–October), pp. 292–302.

UN (1991) *The World's Women: Trends and Statistics 1970–1990*. New York: United Nations Publications Office.

UN (1997) *World Economic and Social Survey 1997*. New York: United Nations.

UNCTAD (1994) *World Investment Report 1994*. Geneva: United Nations Conference on Trade and Development.

UNCTAD (1995) *Trade and Development Report 1995*. New York: United Nations.

UNCTAD (1997) *World Investment Report 1997*. Geneva: United Nations Conference on Trade and Development.

UNDP (1991) *Human Development Report 1991*. New York: Oxford University Press.

UNDP (1994) *Human Development Report 1994*. New York: Oxford University Press.

UNDP (1995) *Human Development Report 1995*. New York: Oxford University Press.

UNDP (1996) *Human Development Report 1996*. New York: Oxford University Press.

UNDP (1997) *Human Development Report 1997*. New York: Oxford University Press.

UNDP (1998) *National Human Development Report 1998: the Russian Federation*. Moscow: United Nations Development Programme.

UNDP (1999) *Human Development Report 1999*. New York: Oxford University Press.

UNESCO (1980) *Many Voices, One World*. Paris: International Commission for the Study of Communication Problems, UNESCO.

UNESCO (1987) *Women and Media Decision-Making: the Invisible Barriers*. Paris: United Nations Educational, Scientific and Cultural Organisation.

UNESCO (1989) *World Communication Report*. Paris: United Nations Educational, Scientific and Cultural Organisation.

UNESCO (1997) *Statistical Yearbook 1996*. Paris: United Nations Educational, Scientific and Cultural Organisation.

UNHCR (1999) *1998 Global Report*. Geneva: United Nations High Commissioner for Refugees, available at http://www.unhcr.ch.

UNICEF (1991) *The State of the World's Children 1991*. Oxford: Oxford University Press.

UNICEF (1996) *The State of the World's Children 1996*. Oxford: Oxford University Press.

UNICEF (1998) *The State of the World's Children 1998*. Oxford: Oxford University Press.

UNPO (1995) *The First Three Years 1991–1994*. The Hague: Unrepresented Nations and Peoples Organization. See also http://www.unpo.org.

Vandenberg, A. (ed.) (2000) *Citizenship and Democracy in a Global Era*. Basingstoke: Macmillan.

Velea, G. (1996) 'Foreigners in Germany (III)', *Nine O'Clock* [Bucharest], No. 1118 (8–10 March), p. 3.

Vickers, J. (1991) *Women and the World Economic Crisis*. London: Zed.

Wachtel, H. (2000) 'The Mosaic of Global Taxes', in J. Nederveen Pieterse (ed.), *Global Futures: Shaping Globalization*. London: Sage, pp. 99–114.

Wade, R. (1996) 'Globalization and Its Limits: Reports of the Death of the National Economy Are Greatly Exaggerated', in S. Berger and R. Dore (eds), *National Diversity and Global Capitalism*. Ithaca, NY: Cornell University Press, pp. 60–88.

Walker, R. B. J. (1995) 'International Relations and the Concept of the Political', in K. Booth and S. Smith (eds), *International Relations Theory*. Cambridge: Polity Press, pp. 306–27.

Wallerstein, I. (1991) *Unthinking Social Science: the Limits of Nineteenth-Century Paradigms*. Cambridge: Polity Press.

Walton, J. and D. Seddon (1994) *Free Markets & Food Riots: the Politics of Global Adjustment*. Oxford: Blackwell.

Warren, K. J. (ed.) (1996) *Ecological Feminist Philosophies*. Bloomington, IN: Indiana University Press.

Waterman, P. (1998) *Globalization, Social Movements and the New Internationalisms*. London: Mansell.

Waters, M. (1995) *Globalization*. London: Routledge.

WBA (1999) Website of the World Business Academy, http://www.worldbusiness.org.

WBCSD (1999) Website of the World Business Council for Sustainable Development, http://www.wbcsd.ch.

Weber, E. J. (1977) *Peasants into Frenchmen: the Modernization of Rural France 1870–1914*. London: Chatto and Windus.

Webster (1961) *Webster's Third New International Dictionary of the English Language Unabridged*. Springfield, MA: Merriam.

Webster, D. (1984) 'Direct Broadcast Satellites: Proximity, Sovereignty and National Identity', *Foreign Affairs*, vol. 62, no. 5 (Summer), pp. 1161–74.

WEF (1994) *Annual Report 93/94*. Geneva: World Economic Forum.

WEF (1999) Website of the World Economic Forum, http://www.weforum.org.

Weiss, L. (1998) *The Myth of the Powerless State: Governing the Economy in a Global Era*. Cambridge: Polity Press.

Weiss, T. G. (ed.) (1998) *Beyond UN Subcontracting: Task-Sharing with Regional Security Arrangements and Service-Providing NGOs*. Basingstoke: Macmillan.

Weiss, T. G. and L. Gordenker (eds) (1996) *NGOs, the UN, and Global Governance*. Boulder, CO: Rienner.

Weiss, T. G. *et al.* (1994) *The United Nations and Changing World Politics*. Boulder, CO: Westview.

Welford, R. (1997) *Hijacking Environmentalism: Corporate Responses to Sustainable Development*. London: Earthscan.

Wells, C. (1987) *The UN, UNESCO and the Politics of Knowledge*. London: Macmillan.

Wells, H. G. (1938) *World Brain*. London: Methuen.

Went, R. (1996) *Grenzen aan de globalisering?* ['Limits to Globalisation?']. Amsterdam: Het Spinhuis.

Whalley, J. (1996) 'Developing Countries and System Strengthening in the Uruguay Round', in W. Martin and L. A. Winters (eds), *The Uruguay Round and the Developing Countries*. Cambridge: Cambridge University Press, pp. 409–34.

Whatmore, S. (1994) 'Global Agro-Food Complexes and the Refashioning of Rural Europe', in A. Amin and N. Thrift (eds), *Globalization, Institutions, and Regional Development in Europe*. Oxford: Oxford University Press, pp. 46–67.

Whitfield, P. (1994) *The Image of the World: 20 Centuries of World Maps*. London: British Library.

Wiener, J. (1999) *Globalization and the Harmonization of Law*. London: Pinter.

Williams, M. (1996) 'Rethinking Sovereignty', in E. Kofman and G. Youngs (eds) *Globalization: Theory and Practice*. London: Pinter, pp. 109–22.

Williams, P. (1994) 'Transnational Criminal Organisations and International Security', *Survival*, vol. 36, no. 1 (Spring), pp. 96–113.

Williamson, J. (1990) 'What Washington Means by Policy Reform', in Williamson (ed.), *Latin American Adjustment: How Much Has Happened?* Washington, DC: Institute for International Economics.

Williamson, J. (1999) Lecture at Warwick University by John Williamson, Chief Economist, South Asia Region, the World Bank, 3 February.

Willkie, W. L. (1943) *One World*. London: Cassell.

Wilmer, F. (1993) *The Indigenous Voice in World Politics: Since Time Immemorial*. London: Sage.

Wilson, E. O. (ed.) (1988) *Biodiversity*. Washington, DC: National Academy Press.

Windsperger, G. (1997) 'NGOs and IMF: Shared Goals – Different Approaches', *IMF Staff News* (March), pp. 7–9.

Winslow, A. (ed.) (1995) *Women, Politics, and the United Nations*. Westport, CT: Greenwood.

Wood, A. (1994) *North–South Trade, Employment and Inequality: Changing Fortunes in a Skill-Driven World*. Oxford: Clarendon.

Woolf, V. (1938) *Three Guineas*. London: Hogarth.

World Bank (1994) *World Debt Tables 1994–95: External Finance for Developing Countries. Volume 1*. Washington, DC: World Bank.

World Bank (1996) *Annual Report 1996*. Washington, DC: World Bank.

World Bank (1997a) *World Development Indicators 1997*. Washington, DC: World Bank.

World Bank (1997b) *World Development Report 1997: the State in a Changing World*. New York: Oxford University Press.

World Bank (1999) Webpage of the World Bank Comprehensive Development Framework, http://www.worldbank.org/cdf/.

Wriston, W. B. (1992) *The Twilight of Sovereignty: How the Information Revolution Is Transforming Our World*. New York: Charles Scribner's Sons.

WTO (1991) *Current Travel and Tourism Indicators*. Madrid: World Tourism Organization.

WTO (1996a) *Annual Report 1996, Volume I*. Geneva: World Trade Organization.

WTO (1996b) 'Ruggiero Calls for Trading System To Be Kept in Line with Globalization Process'. WTO press release, 22 February.

WTTC (1998) Website of the World Travel & Tourism Council, http://www.wttc.org/.

Wurm, S. A. (ed.) (1996) *Atlas of the World's Languages in Danger of Disappearing*. Paris: UNESCO.

Young, O. R. *et al.* (eds) (1996) *Global Environmental Change and International Governance*. Hanover, NH: University Press of New England.

Young, P. (1991) *Person to Person: the International Impact of the Telephone*. Cambridge: Granta.

Youngs, G. (1999) *International Relations in a Global Age: a Conceptual Challenge*. Cambridge: Polity Press.

Zakaria, F. (1997) 'The Rise of Illiberal Democracy', *Foreign Affairs*, vol. 76, no. 6 (November/December), pp. 22–43.

Zevin, R. (1992) 'Are World Financial Markets More Open? If So, Why and With What Effects?' in T. Banuri and J. B. Schor (eds), *Financial Openness and National Autonomy: Opportunities and Constraints*. Oxford: Clarendon, pp. 43–83.

Zysman, J. (1996) 'The Myth of a "Global" Economy: Enduring National Foundations and Emerging Regional Realities', *New Political Economy*, vol. 1, no. 2 (June), pp. 157–84.

Index

acid rain, 27, 54, 72, 84, 150, 212, 293
advertising, 51, 52, 68, 114–15, 125,
    165, 194, 199, 212
aesthetics, 93, 184–5, 191, 200–2, 316
African National Congress, 165
age, 18, 226
    as basis for transborder
        community, 56, 90, 160, 177–8
    discrimination, 6, 234–7, 255–60,
        302, 313
    see also children, elderly, youth
agent-structure problem, 91, 197
air travel, 19, 28, 51–2, 58, 60, 67, 69,
    76–7, 86, 100, 103, 115, 128–9, 145,
    165, 168, 174, 177, 180, 196,
    199–201, 211, 240, 251, 276
AIDS, 27, 175, 212
alternative trade schemes, 247, 273, 301
American Telephone & Telegraph
    Company (AT&T), 66, 74, 129,
    221
Americanization, 16, 23, 28, 45, 49,
    227
Amnesty International, 179, 187
anarchism, 287
anti-trust policies, 36, 130, 298, 309,
    311, 313
apartheid, 25, 30–1, 152, 155, 176, 179,
    255, 258, 273, 296
Argentina, government of, 210, 264
arms control, 209, 232, 292, 309, 313
ARPANET, 75
Asia Pacific Economic Cooperation
    (APEC), 147
Association of South East Asian
    Nations (ASEAN), 147, 304
Australia, government of, 153
autarky, 37, 288
automated teller machine (ATM), 52,
    79

Baha'i, 176
Bank for International Settlements
    (BIS), 53, 71, 148–9, 187, 217–18,
    227, 242, 245, 248, 271, 294,
    300–1
banking, 52–3, 59, 65, 69, 79–80, 86,
    104, 113, 117–18, 128, 149, 155,
    180, 216–17, 221, 224, 240, 244,
    248
Barings, 65, 119, 128
Belgium, government of, 135, 167
Bhutan, government of, 102
biodiversity, 27, 54, 58, 84, 86, 136,
    150, 156, 190, 212, 227, 311
biological diversity, *see* biodiversity
biological weapons, 209
biotechnology, 27, 96, 130, 212
Bolivia, government of, 135
Bolshevik Revolution, 107, 140
bonds, 53, 70, 80–1, 86, 104, 117, 119,
    244, 248
bond-rating agencies, 155, 244, 248,
    274
Brazil, government of, 48, 141
Britain, government of, 104, 125, 140,
    165, 168, 171, 210, 246
BSE, 27, 212
Buddhism, 37–8, 64, 176, 188–9, 230
bureaucracy/bureaucratism, 3–5, 8, 94,
    110, 132–4, 157–8, 161, 187, 285,
    287, 289, 316
    definition, 133, 157, 289
business associations, 71, 151, 155–6,
    228–9, 253, 270, 277, 279–80

Cable News Network (CNN), 16,
    75–6, 128
Canada, government of, 153, 167–8
capital controls, 16, 45, 102, 104,
    247–8, 294